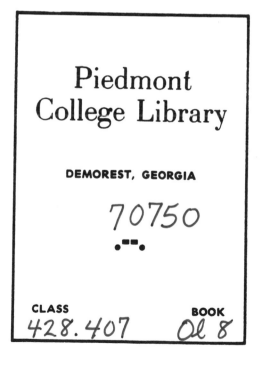

39·81

*Teaching Reading
Skills in Secondary
Schools: Readings*

Teaching Reading Skills in Secondary Schools: Readings

ARTHUR V. OLSON
Professor

WILBUR S. AMES
Associate Professor

Georgia State University

INTERNATIONAL TEXTBOOK COMPANY
An Intext *Publisher*
Scranton, Pennsylvania

The International Series in

SECONDARY EDUCATION

Consulting Editor

JOHN E. SEARLES

Pennsylvania State University

Standard Book Number 7002 □ 2255 □ 3

3/27/74 Beckers Tyler 5.50

To
AILA *and* JUDY

Preface

The materials found in this book of readings have been chosen to give prospective and in-service teachers insight into the problems, programs, and techniques of reading in the secondary school. The articles emphasize the developmental reading program with primary focus on reading in the content areas. It is the feeling of the editors that, in order for an educator to understand the reading process in the secondary school, a broad overview is necessary as well as some focus on specific subject matter areas.

Articles have been chosen from a variety of sources; monographs, yearbooks, conference proceedings, and educational periodicals. Selections vary in length. Although most are short in order to allow for greater variety, several longer articles were selected because of the excellence of the material and the contribution they make to an understanding of the process of reading.

Each selection of the book of readings is introduced with an overview to prepare the reader for the underlying concepts which tie each of the articles in the section together. In addition, each section is followed by several questions designed to stimulate thoughtful evaluation of the readings and to draw together the main ideas presented.

Arthur V. Olson
Wilbur S. Ames

Atlanta, Georgia
October 1969

Contents

I. INTRODUCTION 1

High School and College Instructors Can't Teach Reading?
Nonsense! – STANLEY E. DAVIS 3

Reading in the Secondary School: Issues and Innovations –
RICHARD W. BURNETT 11

Progress in the Teaching of Reading in High School and
College – RUTH STRANG 18

The Refinement of High School Reading Skills –
J. T. HUNT 27

II. ORGANIZATION AND ADMINISTRATION OF
SECONDARY SCHOOL READING PROGRAMS 35

Developmental Reading in Junior High School –
U. BERKLEY ELLIS 37

Reading and Study Skills Program – SALLY BERKEY and
IRWIN H. FIELDS 43

The Reading Laboratory – RALPH P. SHERLOCK 49

III. THE NATURE OF READING 53

Reading and Reading Difficulty: A Conceptual Analysis –
MORTON WIENER and WARD CROMER 55

Learning to Read – ELEANOR J. GIBSON 78

IV.   THE EVALUATION OF READING 95

The Role of Testing in Reading Instruction –
FREDERICK B. DAVIS 97

Some Pitfalls in Evaluating Progress in Reading Instruction –
ARTHUR S. MCDONALD 110

Assigning Grades to Students in Special Reading Classes –
ALBERT J. KINGSTON 116

V.   DEVELOPING VOCABULARY AND WORD
RECOGNITION SKILLS 121

Developing Vocabulary: Another Look at the Problem –
LEE C. DEIGHTON 123

Teaching Word Recognition for Better Vocabulary Development –
ARTHUR V. OLSON 131

Teaching Essential Reading Skills – Vocabulary –
EARLE E. CRAWFORD 137

VI.   DEVELOPING COMPREHENSION AND INTERPRETA-
TION SKILLS 153

*Promoting Growth in Interpreting in Grades Nine Through
Fourteen* – JAMES M. MCCALLISTER 155

The Nature and Extent of Work-Study Skills –
J. WILLIAM MCKAY 160

Comprehension Skills – OLIVE S. NILES 170

A Cluster of Skills: Especially for Junior High School –
H. ALAN ROBINSON 177

Concepts from Semantics as Avenues to Reading Improvement –
DAVID COOPER 182

Factors in Critical Reading – WILLIAM ELLER and
JUDITH GOLDMAN WOLF 191

VII.   DEVELOPING READING RATE 199

Uses and Limitations of Speed of Reading Programs in Schools –
MILES A. TINKER 201

Reading Rate is Multilevel – DON H. PARKER 211

Skimming in Reading: A Fine Art for Modern Needs –
HELEN S. GRAYUM 218

VIII. DEVELOPING READING SKILLS IN THE CONTENT
AREAS 227

Developing Reading Skills in the Content Areas –
RUTH STRANG 229

*Attitude of High School Content Area Teachers Toward the
Teaching of Reading* – ARTHUR V. OLSON 235

Reading: In and Out of the English Curriculum –
MARGARET J. EARLY 242

The Reading of Fiction – EDWARD J. GORDON 252

The Reading of Literature: Poetry as an Example –
JOHN S. SIMMONS 259

Reading – HELEN HUUS 271

Reading and the Teaching of Science –
GEORGE G. MALLINSON 290

Research on Problems in Reading Science –
J. BRYCE LOCKWOOD 296

Measuring the Readability of High School Health Texts –
AUBREY C. MCTAGGART 303

Reading in Mathematics – I. E. AARON 315

Reading and Mathematics – RUSSELL J. CALL and
NEAL A. WIGGIN 321

Reading Improvement in the Industrial Arts Class –
MALCOLM HEYMAN and RICHARD HOLLAND 335

Solving Reading Problems in Vocational Subjects –
ISIDORE N. LEVINE 340

IX. READING INTERESTS 355

Interest in Recreational Reading of Junior High School Students –
ANTHONY T. SOARES and RAY H. SIMPSON 357

*A Comparison of Reading Interests of Two Populations of
Ninth Grade Students* – ARTHUR V. OLSON and
CARL L. ROSEN 365

Developing Reading Tastes in the Secondary School –
ARTHUR W. HEILMAN 370

Fostering Interest in Reading in Grades Nine Through Fourteen –
FRANCES M. BECK 377

The Promise of Paperbacks – DAVID A. SOHN 383

Obscenity, Censorship, & Youth – FREDERIC R. HARTZ 389

X.   THE TEACHING OF READING TO SPECIAL
GROUPS 393

Our Disadvantaged Older Children – DOMINIC THOMAS 395

A Reading Program for School Dropouts – LILLIE POPE 401

*Salvaging Failures Through Improved Reading: Reading in
Vocational Classes* – ROBERT L. HARRIS 412

High School Reading for the Severely Retarded Reader –
NANCY O'NEILL VICK 417

XI.   MATERIALS AND RESOURCES 423

An Important Resource for Secondary Reading –
EDWARD G. SUMMERS 425

Programmed Reading for the Secondary School –
EDWARD T. BROWN 438

*Instructional Materials for Adult Basic Education and Literacy
Training* – EDWIN H. SMITH 444

Introduction

I

To those vitally interested in the development of reading programs at the secondary school level, progress seems at times to be dreadfully slow. There still appear to be many people who either see absolutely no need for reading instruction at the secondary level or who will accept only the idea of remedial programs at this level.

All the articles included in this introductory section are concerned with presenting a case for the inclusion of developmental reading instruction in secondary schools. In addition, the articles contain discussions of the progress that has been made and the problems that have been encountered in implementing such instruction.

In the first article, Stanley Davis specifies two reasons why elementary schools cannot be expected to have done the entire job of promoting developmental reading and therefore why secondary school teachers must assume their responsibilities. Davis goes on to present six tasks for which he feels regular classroom teachers can assume responsibility in the teaching of reading at the secondary level.

Both Richard Burnett and Ruth Strang discuss trends and issues involved in the teaching of reading at the secondary level. Burnett gives a brief historical perspective which indicates that the pleas of more than twenty-five years ago for developmental reading instruction in secondary schools are still being made today. He cites weaknesses in preservice and inservice education programs as being the main reasons for the lack of progress that has been made.

Ruth Strang presents a bit more optimistic picture. She feels that there is a growing awareness of the complexity of the reading process at the high school level, and she indicates that there is a great variety of materials and procedures being used in new developmental reading programs. Strang does emphasize that there is, at present, a lack of concrete research evidence to determine which approaches and procedures are most effective.

J. T. Hunt sees the key responsibility for secondary teachers of reading as basically that of refining skills previously introduced in the elementary grades. He presents a representative list of such reading skills and demands which should receive attention at the secondary school level. Hunt, like the previous writers in this section, feels that the secondary level reading program must be an all-school concern rather than just the job of special reading teachers.

High School and College Instructors Can't Teach Reading? Nonsense!*

STANLEY E. DAVIS

Many competent high school and college instructors recognize that they need to be concerned with helping students at all levels of competence to improve their reading skills needed in the various subject areas. But the perennial question that plagues a conscientious instructor is "How can I cover the course content assigned by the curriculum makers and at the same time teach reading?"

This article is concerned with suggesting ways that may be helpful to the instructor in high school or college who is trying to resolve the conflict between covering assigned subject matter and helping students become better readers.

The realization that learning to read is a life-long process is not new. In recent years, however, there has been a growing uneasy awareness on the part of many workers in secondary and collegiate education that they need to be doing something about helping students to improve the reading skills that are needed in high school, college, and later adult life. But it has not been clear just what should be done.

More and more high school and college instructors are realizing that something more constructive needs to be done than simply blaming the elementary schools for not doing a better job of teaching children to read. Elementary teachers and administrators, as a whole, are the first to realize that improvements in the teaching of reading need to be made, and they are doing an excellent job of making the needed improvements.

But regardless of the caliber of the work being done by the elementary schools in teaching children to read, it is now well known that the art of reading is so complex that no one, not even the brightest child in the best of all possible elementary schools, can learn all he needs to know about reading by the end of six or eight years of schooling.

Why Elementary Schools Can't Do the Whole Job

There are at least two reasons why the elementary schools cannot be

*Reprinted from *North Central Association Quarterly,* 34 (April, 1960), pp. 295-299, by permission of the author and the North Central Association.

expected to do the entire job of teaching students to read, and why high schools and colleges need to take steps to insure continued growth in the reading ability of students.

1) Reading involves interpreting printed symbols and making discriminative reactions to the ideas expressed by them. The processes of interpreting and making discriminative reactions can be taught and learned only in terms of the ideas expressed by the symbols, i.e., the content of the reading material.

The elementary school cannot prepare children to read skillfully in all the different subject areas they will meet in high school, college, and adult life. Many students are able to select from their "bag" of reading skills those that are required for reading any new bit of material, without guidance from the teacher. However, even these students would be able to select appropriate reading procedures more effectively if some guidance were provided. This is certainly not a novel idea, since our whole concept of formal education is based upon the assumption that guided learning is more efficient than unguided learning.

Most students will be more successful in reading in any subject field if they are given appropriate guidance at the appropriate time. Guidance that was given five to ten years earlier may be too remote to be adequate.

2) Individual differences in reading achievement, which have been well documented and discussed in educational and psychological literature,[1] are present at every educational level. The more effective the instruction provided at earlier levels, the greater the range of individual differences will be at the high school and college levels.

Much has been said and done about working with students who are poor readers. Many reading clinics and special reading classes have been established to provide extra help for these students. Much less thought and energy have been given to helping students who are already average or above in reading skill. In many high school and college classrooms it is the students of better-than-average competence who are "short-changed." Too frequently the assumption is made that these students can take care of themselves.

Let's consider some ways in which subject-matter instructors in high school or college can help students become better readers without taking too much of the time needed for covering course content.

How Subject-Matter Instructors Can Help Students Become Better Readers

There are two basic approaches to helping high school and college students

[1] Irving H. Anderson and Walter F. Dearborn, *The Psychology of Teaching Reading.* New York: Ronald Press, 1952, pp. 41-48.

to improve their reading skill. One of these involves setting up a special reading improvement program, with a reading specialist in charge. The other involves the provision of guidance in reading improvement by instructors in the various subject-matter classes.

Both of these approaches should be used, since each can accomplish things that the other cannot. The special reading improvement program in a high school or college should be set up to work with competent readers who can benefit from additional guided practice as well as with students who have reading difficulties. The personnel and facilities of this special program should also be available to subject-matter instructors who want to find ways to improve the reading skills of their students in their own classes.

In addition to referring some students for specialized help in reading, or even in the event that no specialized help is available, the subject-matter instructor can do certain things in his own classroom that will be helpful to even the best readers. An instructor does not need to be an expert in the teaching of reading in order to do these six things.

(1) GIVE ATTENTION TO STUDENTS' READINESS FOR READING THE ASSIGNED MATERIAL

There appear to be three primary factors that determine readiness for reading, or for learning via any other avenue, at any educational level, or in any particular subject field: (a) mental maturity; (b) background knowledge and skill; and (c) motivation for learning.[2]

An instructor can get a reasonably good indication of the mental maturity of his students in several ways: by looking at their recent intelligence or academic aptitude test scores; by looking at their records of past achievements; and by observing the daily behavior of students in the classroom and outside.

In learning about the status of the background knowledge and skill of his students, an instructor can do several things.

(1)   He can look at the scores made by students on standardized reading tests.
(2)   He can devise two or three short reading tests of his own to supplement or replace standardized reading tests. This can be done by choosing selections from the textbook(s) to be studied and composing several comprehension questions on the selections. These short tests can then be used to get an indication of students' rate of reading and comprehension accuracy on material of the kind that they will meet in his course. In making such tests the instructor will need to be careful not to select paragraphs containing technical terms that are not defined within those paragraphs, and that the student could not be expected to know

---

[2]For an excellent discussion of readiness for learning (including reading), see Lee J. Cronbach, *Educational Psychology*. New York: Harcourt-Brace, 1954, chaps. 4-8.

otherwise. Since the material for these two or three tests can be selected from the content of his course, the instructor can get objective indications of his students' reading ability at the same time that he is covering subject matter. By using two or three short tests on different days, he can be better assured of the reliability and validity of his impressions.

(3)   An instructor can devise a test on the vocabulary and concepts that students will encounter in a new assignment to determine whether the students have the background knowledge required for understanding the lesson. He can then teach any concepts and terms that may be needed, as indicated by the pretest.

If students have the mental maturity, the reading skill (and any other required skills), and the understanding of vocabulary and basic concepts required to profitably study the new material, they will be successful readers, *if they are interested.* It is well known that a strong desire to learn will compensate for many background deficiencies. In making any assignment, an instructor needs to seriously consider how he can help students to acquire the interest and drive that will help them to go ahead in spite of obstacles. The problem of motivation is, of course, an age-old one that cannot be easily solved. However, in doing the three things suggested just above, an instructor will be doing a great deal to increase the meaningfulness of reading in his subject for his students. Meaningfulness of activity is one of the major factors in motivation for that activity.

The ideas that follow also bear, at least indirectly, upon motivation.

(2) GIVE ATTENTION TO THE READABILITY OF ASSIGNED TEXTBOOKS AND SUPPLEMENTARY READING MATERIAL

Closely related to the problem of determining and increasing students' readiness for learning through reading is the question of the readability of the assigned reading matter. As early as 1923 it was recognized that much textbook material is written at an unnecessarily difficult level.[3] Since that time several "readability formulae"[4,5,6] have been devised for estimating the difficulty of reading material. Some of these formulae can be easily applied by an instructor to reading material in his courses to give him a more objective indication of the difficulty of the material than he might otherwise have.

The desirability of providing easier reading material for some students as preparation for successful handling of the normally assigned reading, and of

[3] B. A. Lively and S. L. Pressey, "A Method of Measuring 'Vocabulary Burden' of Textbooks," *Educational Administration and Supervision,* 1923, IX, 389-398.

[4] E. Dale and J. S. Chall, "A Formula for Predicting Readability," *Educational Research Bulletin,* 1948, XXVII, 11-12; 37-54.

[5] R. F. Flesch, "Marks of Readable Style," Teachers College, Columbia University, *Contributions to Education,* No. 897, 1943.

[6] Irving Lorge, "Predicting Readability," in Hunnicutt and Iverson, *Research in the Three R's.* New York: Harper and Brothers, 1958, 184-194.

providing more challenging material for others, is obvious. The argument is sometimes heard that providing reading material on different levels of difficulty, particularly easier material for the less competent students, constitutes "spoon feeding" and is not compatible with the goal of maintaining high standards in education. The necessity for maintaining high standards cannot be denied. But it would seem that a good way to help the less competent students to read better and to achieve according to the standards that we desire, is to let them read easier material on the subject as preparation for successfully handling the more difficult material that is normally assigned. Among other advantages, this would help to decrease the frustration experienced by poor readers when required to read material written in a difficult style, without adequate preparation for it.

Similarly, it seems likely that levels of achievement of the most competent students can be raised by letting them read more difficult material. This attention to readability may enable an instructor to decrease the frustration that hampers a bright student when he has to read material that is so easy as to provide no challenge for him. Even if supplementary reading material of different difficulty levels is not available, an instructor can better help students get ready to do the assigned reading if he knows something about the readability of the material.

(3) SHOW STUDENTS HOW TO PREVIEW READING MATERIAL

One of the major premises of many present-day theories of learning is that meaningful material is easier to learn and remember than is non-meaningful material. This principle is highly pertinent to learning through reading. One important way in which a reader can increase the meaningfulness of any material for himself is by previewing the material to be read before reading it in detail. This process will enable him to have some prior understanding of the content and of the major trends in the discussion. He will be less apt to let- the appearance of the trees dull his perception of the forest.

Many high school and college students, even among the brightest, have not learned to preview an article, chapter, or book before reading it in detail.[7] In helping students learn how to preview a selection, an instructor should first make clear why such a procedure is helpful. He can help students to realize that it is easier and more enjoyable to learn something when one can see how it is related to the whole. He can then show students how the preface, table of contents, section headings, summaries, footnotes, charts and graphs, topic sentences, index, appendices, glossary, etc., can be used to advantage in studying for this particular course.

The Survey Q_3R Method of reading, involving previewing as its first step, is an excellent example of a systematic approach to reading that is based upon

---

[7]D. G. Danskin and C. W. Burnett, "Study Techniques of Those Superior Students," *Personnel and Guidance Journal*, 1952, XXXI, 181-186.

experimental findings in psychological studies of learning, perception, retention, motivation, etc.[8,9,10] The few minutes required to explain and demonstrate this method of reading, using the course textbook or comparable material, will be well repaid by the increased effectiveness of students at all levels of reading skills.

(4) HELP STUDENTS REALIZE THE IMPORTANCE OF VARYING STYLE OF READING TO FIT MATERIAL AND PURPOSE

Many students, particularly the poorer ones, have the misconception that all reading should be done at the same rate and with the same thoroughness, regardless of material and purpose. An extreme example of this misconception may be seen in students who read everything with slow, careful deliberation. At the other extreme are the students who try to read everything rapidly. These students, and others between these extremes, do not realize that the rate and care with which a skillful reader reads a given bit of material depends upon the nature of the material and his purpose in reading it.

An instructor can emphasize two points with students in regard to varying rate and thoroughness of reading according to their purposes and the nature of the material.

(1) The skillful reader asks himself, before starting to read, "What do I already know about this topic? What do I want to get from this reading — all of the major ideas and their supporting details, or just the main ideas without the details, or am I looking just for some specific items of information?"

(2) The skillful reader uses a systematic approach to reading, such as the Survey Q_3R Method, varying its application according to the degree of comprehension and retention he desires.

Students who realize the importance of varying their style of reading according to their purposes and the nature of the material can achieve greater

---

[8]F. P. Robinson, *Effective Study.* New York: Harper and Brothers, 1946, Project II.

[9]S. L. Pressey, F. P. Robinson, and J. E. Horrocks, *Psychology in Education.* New York: Harper and Brothers, 1959, Chap. 17.

[10]F. P. Robinson, who originally designed the Survey Q_3R Method, gives the following explanation of it (Pressey, Robinson and Horrocks, *op. cit.,* pp. 571-572):

"Survey. The student makes a rapid survey of the headings in the assignment, to find out what major ideas are present and their sequence.

"Question. The student turns the first heading into a question in order to have a seeking attitude and to know what he is reading for.

"Read. The student reads the section under the heading, seeking the answer to his question.

"Recite. Having read the section clear through, the student writes down brief cue phrases *from memory.*(No copying is done, and complete notes are not wanted.)

"Steps 2, 3, and 4 are repeated for each succeeding section that has a heading.

"Review. Immediately after reading the whole lesson in this way, the student tries to recall the points that have been developed in it. This is a second recitation. He glances at his notes only as needed to remind him of points not immediately recalled."

mastery of subject matter in a course. They recognize that while the course textbook requires very thorough reading, supplementary readings for additional background can frequently be read less thoroughly, hence more rapidly and in greater quantity. This, of course, presupposes that students know how to find supplementary material on the subject.

(5) HELP STUDENTS TO LOCATE SUPPLEMENTARY READING MATERIAL ON THE SUBJECT

Wide reading in a subject helps a student to become better informed on the subject, and also helps him to read additional materials in that field more effectively. An instructor can help students to become more skillful readers as well as better informed students by helping them learn to locate reading material in his subject field. He should acquaint them with sources of bibliographies, with indices and abstracts, and with other appropriate guides to reference material.

(6) HELP STUDENTS IMPROVE THEIR KNOWLEDGE OF THE VOCABULARY OF THE SUBJECT

Since acquaintance with the terminology of any subject is basic to reading skillfully in that subject, a major responsibility of an instructor is to help students to acquire the desire and the necessary skills for continued vocabulary improvement in the subject.

An instructor can emphasize that extensive reading constitutes one of the best bases for vocabulary improvement. In addition, he can remind students of certain skills that are useful in deciphering the meanings of strange words. While most students probably learned these skills in the elementary school, many will profit from being reminded of the applications of these skills to the vocabulary of the particular subject being studied. Among the most important of these skills are:[11]

(a) using context clues;
(b) using phonetic clues;
(c) using structural clues — e.g., prefixes, suffixes, roots;
(d) using the dictionary.

Guidance from the instructor will help students to see how these vocabulary skills may be used in improving knowledge of vocabulary in any particular subject.

[11]G. Spache and P. Berg, *The Art of Efficient Reading.* New York: Macmillan, 1955, Chaps. IX, X, and XI.

Summary

Since learning to read is a lifetime process that cannot be completely mastered by the end of the elementary school, subject-matter instructors in high schools and colleges have a responsibility for helping students continue their growth in reading skill. This article has suggested ways in which a subject-matter instructor can help his students improve their reading skill at the same time that he is covering subject matter. An instructor does not need to be an expert in the teaching of reading in order to help students read better at the same time that he is covering course content.

Reading in the Secondary School: Issues and Innovations*

RICHARD W. BURNETT

In comparing issues and innovations in teaching reading secondary and elementary schools, we find that at the secondary level the *issues* are more obscure and far less hotly contested than at the elementary level. And the *innovations* in high school reading appear to be far fewer and not nearly so colorful or dramatic as new proposals (i/t/a/ and pre-school reading instruction, for instance) for elementary school. Furthermore, research studies in high school reading are exceeded by elementary school research studies at a ratio of about six to one.

The relative amount of controversy, innovation, and research reveals the most significant difference between the two levels. In the elementary school curriculum there is no question of whether teaching reading is and should be fundamental. On the secondary level, however, the question still persists of whether the teaching of reading is a basic part of the high school curriculum. The failure to resolve this issue clouds all others and for some time has stood in the way of important innovations for improving the reading of secondary school students. I therefore believe that this issue needs to be examined before other issues and innovations can be discussed.

Recognizing the Problem

In 1941 Bond and Bond wrote,

> The fact that in the secondary school the continued improvement in reading has been left to chance is a dark cloud on the reading horizon.
> No better results should be expected from this procedure than from leaving a vegetable garden to grow by itself without any outside care after it is once started. (4)

*Reprinted from *Journal of Reading,* 9 (April, 1966), pp. 322-328, by permission of the author and the International Reading Association.

Almost 25 years ago these authors made the first part of their book a sales talk, because a strong case had to be presented for extending reading instruction, developmental and remedial, into the secondary school. Bond and Bond stressed the need for teaching reading in every high school subject. They considered the subject matter teacher the most qualified person to teach the reading skills necessary for success in his field of specialization. They assumed, however, that every secondary teacher would be willing and able to familiarize himself with the teaching of reading, assist with appraising the reading status of his students, and be interested in improving the general reading competency of his students through teaching reading in his content area classes.

Even in 1941 it was recognized that setting up special reading classes in a junior or senior high school and hiring reading teachers to work with students with reading problems were, at best, only half-hearted attempts to deal with the responsibility the high school has in teaching reading. This, you understand, was the point of view of reading specialists about 25 years ago. What is the current picture?

In 1964, A. Sterl Artley optimistically predicted "that when the history of reading instruction is written it will show that one of the major points of emphasis of the 1960's will be the organized extension of the developmental reading program into the secondary grades." (2) However, Artely stated that, first, there is no set pattern for administrators to follow in organizing a comprehensive high school developmental reading program; second, teachers are not trained to implement such a program; and third, specialists with the proper training and experience are not available in the numbers needed to assist in setting up such programs. In fact, Artley said, "Anyone who works in this area is a pioneer." (3) This was in 1964.

Reviewing Robert Karlin's recent book on secondary reading, Oliver Andersen refers to it as a contribution to the "Great Crusade. . . namely that high school teachers must face their responsibilities as teachers of reading as well as teachers of history, literature, science, and homemaking if they are to prepare students for the demands of further education or for the experience of life." (1)

In 1964, as in 1941, we carefully attempted to distinguish between high school reading programs that are adjuncts to the whole school program and those comprehensive programs which try to involve every student and every teacher in the school. In spite of this consistent stand, Schneyer has stated that "a review of the reading research at the secondary level did not reveal a single well-designed research investigation concerned with a developmental reading program involving all members of a secondary faculty in a cooperative effort." (6) Robinson and Muskopf, however, seem to see a glimmer of light. They commented that "there does appear to be a tendency to consider reading in relation to the total curriculum rather than as an isolated segment of the school program." (5) But Umans recently maintained that "one of the most difficult tasks is to help subject-matter teachers see the necessity of teaching skills directly related to the reading of the particular subject. Somehow, the feeling persists that reading is always taught 'elsewhere' and 'at another time.' " (7)

Causes and Solutions

Why in all these years has there been so little progress in making the teaching of reading an integral part of the high school curriculum? The pre-service education of teachers is one obvious reason. Generally the junior or senior high school teacher is a product of a college or university which emphasized majoring in a content area, such as English, history, biological sciences, chemistry, or mathematics. Courses are usually textbook-centered, and teaching is likely to be mostly by lectures. Time to consider materials and methods of instruction in the content field is begrudged by content area instructors as valuable time taken from studying the subject itself. Too often, it seems, the college instructor who teaches a "methods" course is either pitied or despised by his academic colleagues — pitied if he teaches it because he must, despised if he teaches it because he wants to. The content area instructor who teaches a methods course for majors in his area is often not inclined to consider reading in his subject area; and even if he is so inclined, he probably lacks the necessary training or experience.

To advise adding a course in the teaching of reading will often ignite the content area people, usually thought to be in arts and sciences. On the other hand, to advise focusing some attention on problems prospective teachers will face in teaching reading by using time now devoted to professional education courses will invite the wrath of many of the education faculty, who feel that too much is now being presented to prospective teachers in too little time. Consequently, the orientation secondary teacher trainees receive in teaching reading is often non-existent or, at best, exceedingly general and superficial.

Secondary teacher trainees who elect a course in reading are apparently in a minority. The proportion of high school teachers who take a graduate level course in teaching reading is also small. Of those who do take a high school reading course, about 75 percent seem to be teaching or preparing to teach junior or senior high school English classes. The remainder are usually social studies teachers. The science or mathematics teacher in a reading course is a rarity.

After examining the pre-service education of teachers, we should at least acknowledge some of the problems in conducting in-service training for teachers, the domain of supervision and curriculum specialists. There are many stumbling blocks to providing effective in-service training for high school teachers to help them cope with the inevitable reading problems they will have in their classes. The first problem is penetrating the college-acquired resistance of the subject-matter specialist to any in-depth consideration of methods, materials, and techniques of teaching. This resistance to in-service training becomes hardened if he is in in-service training programs conducted by "method specialists" who are not sufficiently prepared in specific content areas to recognize the reading and instructional problems peculiar to each content area.

The catalytic agent in the imbroglio between method and content is the high school administrator, a principal or, frequently, the superintendent. As any curriculum coordinator knows from experience, an administrator who appears too directive or too "pushy," or too detached and disinterested at the other extreme, can destroy the worth of even the best-prepared and well-conducted in-service training program.

These problems in pre-service and in-service training are not insurmountable. The picture will change. Or perhaps we should believe, as Artley does, that it is changing as large numbers of secondary school people — administrators, curriculum consultants and coordinators, teachers, and reading specialists — are beginning to concede that to accept anything less than the eventual involvment of every teacher in the reading program of the high school is to fall short of meeting the needs of today's students.

Recent books such as Umans' *New Trends in Reading Instruction* and Austin, Huebner and Bush's *Reading Evaluation* (Ronald Press, 1961), and many articles in the *Journal of Reading* and *The Reading Teacher* present more detailed information than appeared in past reading literature. Included is information on how to organize a reading committee, conduct a school reading survey, select and train high school reading specialists, and provide demonstration teaching and laboratory training programs for content area teacher.

Presently many university training programs for reading specialists go beyond training a teacher to operate an instrument or use a kit of materials. More often now the attempt is being made to produce a professionally competent person who can conduct a remedial reading program for seriously disabled readers or a college-preparatory reading program for superior students in accordance with the needs of a particular school. But even beyond that, the better products of university programs have the knowledge to work with their colleagues in in-service training and can meet the challenge of mobilizing and coordinating the efforts of an entire faculty in conducting a reading program.

Other Issues

Less vital issues on setting up high school reading programs recur. These can be discussed meaningfully only in relation to the major issue just developed. One question, for example, which frequently arises is whether high schools should have special reading classes at all. The consensus in the literature and reports of current practices in junior and senior high school indicates that high schools should have special reading classes. However, their nature and structure depend upon the strengths and limitations of the total school program in meeting the students' needs for reading development.

Another issue is the place of pressure devices or reading machines in the high school. To have a good reading program, must a high school equip a special classroom with gadgets? In proper perspective this question implies that high school faculties must recognize that a beautifully equipped laboratory through which phalanxes of students march each week may not be the earmark of a good high school reading program. To convey the idea that all reading needs will mysteriously be met by using machines in a shiny laboratory is to erect another stumbling block in the path of developing a high school reading program that most reading specialists would endorse.

In spite of the stereotype many adminstrators and curriculum coordinators seem to have of a reading specialist as a machine operator, he should be the first to realize that he has defeated his own goals if he oversells machines to the point that administration and faculty let the laboratory become the total reading program. However, if the laboratory is properly used as a resource center as well as a showplace for keeping faculty and students reading conscious, it may offer benefits beyond those attributable to its use as a classroom alone.

Besides the gradual refinement of the developmental reading concept and the new emphasis on high school reading specialists, what other innovations are there in secondary reading? Several are often mentioned but seldom discussed in detail, and rarely are they the basis for published research studies in reading. Among these are television, programmed learning, teaching machines, and paperbacks.

As recognized in the literature, the major contribution of television to improving reading instruction in the high school is apparently in the value of commercial television as a motivational device and as an outside resource having much the same function as newspapers and popular magazines. In addition, more and more high schools are reportedly being equipped with closed-circuit television, which certainly ought to provide opportunities for broadening high school reading programs by teaching special reading skills, providing large group instruction followed up in smaller groups, and contributing to the in-service training of teachers. However, except for casual mention (in sources like Umans' book), detailed descriptions of programs or research specifically relating television and high school reading are difficult to find.

Programmed learning appears in a limited number of instructional materials, varying greatly in quality and utility. There are some materials to help in teaching the special reading skills needed in specific content areas such as science or social studies. Generally, though, these materials seem more acceptable for reading classes in "compromise programs" where, through default of the content area teachers themselves, English teachers or reading teachers provide some directed practice in reading in various content areas.

Now reading instruments are being regularly introduced. They are usually not the auto-instructional devices, commonly called teaching machines, which use programmed frames. Instead, a number of new tachistoscopic devices for both group and individual use have been introduced in addition to several varieties of pacers or speed-reading devices. Naturally the designers and promoters of these machines try to substantiate claims that their devices are significant innovations. But reading specialists usually are less enthusiastic. However, the layman on the school board, or the school administrator, or often the unprepared teacher drafted to be a reading teacher is frequently fascinated by these devices and expects more from them than they can realistically deliver.

The contribution of paperback books to greater flexibility of teaching in content areas is perhaps the most significant development in high school reading in several years. The Scholastic Literature Units (published by Scholastic Magazines), first available in the 1960's, are examples of how paperbacks can be used to help teachers break away from the rigidity of the one textbook approach in every class. The three-phase organization of the units – combining class reading, small group work, and individual reading – is an exciting approach to teaching literature. Improving the teaching of reading by organizing instruction around thematic units and using "transitional" literature to raise high school students' appreciation for reading seem sensible to many English teachers and reading specialists. The real breakthrough in getting reading into content areas will come when comparable programs can be supplied and are used, not only in English classes, but also in social studies, science and other areas. The key to success may lie in conceiving programs and materials which appeal first to the content orientation of teachers and only secondly to the skills orientation of the reading specialists.

In summary it must be admitted that significant changes in high school reading from 1941 to 1965 are more difficult to find than most of us would like to believe. Despite the "slower than molasses" change in actual classroom teaching practices in many high schools across the country in the last 25 years, there may still be cause for cautious optimism. Perhaps the teaching of effective reading habits will become accepted as an integral part of the high school curriculum before the elapse of another 25 years.

References

1. Andersen, Oliver. Review of *Teaching Reading in High School* by Robert Karlin, *Journal of Reading,* 8 (January, 1965), 179.
2. Artley, A. Sterl. "Implementing a Developmental Reading Program on the Secondary Level," *Reading Instruction in Secondary Schools,* Perspectives in Reading #2 (Newark, N. J.: International Reading Association, 1964), p. 1.
3. Sterl, p. 2.
4. Bond, Guy L. and Eva Bond. *Developmental Reading in High School* (New York: The Macmillan Company, 1941), p. 53.

5.   Robinson, H. Alan and Allan F. Muskopf. "High School Reading – 1963," *Journal of Reading,* 8 (November, 1964), 86.

6.   Schneyer, J. Wesley. "Significant Reading Research at the Secondary School Level," *Reading Instruction in Secondary Schools,* Perspectives in Reading #2 (Newark, N. J.: International Reading Association, 1964), p. 146.

7.   Umans, Shelley. *New Trends in Reading Instruction* (New York: Bureau of Publications, Teachers College, Columbia University, 1963), p. 7.

Progress in the Teaching of Reading in High School and College*

RUTH STRANG

Advances in the teaching of reading may take any of four forms: sounder theories, more effective programs and procedures, an increase in the number of reading specialists, and increased reading interest and efficiency on the part of students. Evidence of these kinds of progress may be obtained from articles on reading theory, surveys, descriptions of programs and procedures, experimental studies, and reports on the voluntary reading of students. However, any accurate study of trends is hampered by inadequate evaluation of many programs and procedures, and by the failure of investigators to report a survey on the same population using the same method.

Changes in Theory

In the midst of shifting emphases in reading theory, one trend seems to stand out clearly: a growing recognition of the complexity of the reading process on both the high school and the college level.

The factors that bear on the reading process are many: The physical, physiological, and neurological; mental and emotional; interpersonal and cultural (15). Forty-four separate tests failed to account for all the factors involved in the reading performance — speed and comprehension — of high school and college students (12 13). Any kind of effective reading presupposed certain vocabulary, word recognition, and literal comprehension skills. However, the mature reading that is expected of high school and college students requires additional abilities to generalize, draw inferences and conclusions, appreciate subtleties of style and content, and apply the ideas gained from reading to personal and social problems (19). This kind of reading involves a dynamic interaction between the individual and the reading situation.

*Reprinted from *Reading Teacher,* 16 (December, 1962), pp. 170-177, by permission of the author and the International Reading Association.

Progress in Reading Programs

The best thing that can be said of high school and college programs today is that they are evolving. In a sense they are experimental. Many different kinds of programs are being tried out.

There seems to be a discernable trend in high school programs. At first the focus was on small remedial groups, usually composed of retarded readers who had potential ability to improve. These students were taken out of their regular classrooms for one or more periods a week and given instruction in reading by specially trained teachers. Although only a small number of pupils in each school were aided in this way, sometimes only seventy-five to one hundred a year, the expenditure was justified, not only because it provided service to severely retarded readers, but also because it afforded the reading teacher a laboratory in which he could develop materials and methods that classroom teachers might later adopt or adapt.

In a most important advance, some school systems have moved from these small remedial groups to developmental classes in reading, for all students, which are concerned with the sequential development of the reading abilities that are appropriate to the high school and college years. These courses are usually included in the junior high school program; sometimes they are offered in the last year of senior high school to college preparatory students. The State of Pennsylvania passed a law requiring all students to take a developmental or remedial course in reading during the seventh or eighth grade (1). These classes were to be taught by elementary school teachers or by high school English teachers. An important effect of this law was to impress upon English teachers the need to know more about students' reading development during the high school years, and the ways in which they can contribute to it.

An important variation of the developmental class, combined with in-service education, was introduced by Leitha Paulsen in Bloom Township High School, Chicago Heights, Illinois. In this program all students substitute a six-week unit on reading for the same number of periods in their English class. These reading periods are devoted to group instruction and practice in study-type skills, which are analyzed in detail; vocabulary building; discovering and interpreting context clues· and critical and creative reading. To supplement the group instruction, each student has a sheet that tells him what he needs to work on each day; this device has proved effective. The in-service education feature of this program is especially significant. The English teachers, who are relieved of responsibility for teaching their classes for this six-weeks' period, have the opportunity to observe the methods and materials used by a well-trained reading consultant. If they are receptive to this opportunity, they will continue to guide the students' learning along the same lines. Later, they may conduct the reading unit themselves in their regular classes.

The final stage in the evolving high school program has been regarded as a desideratum for many years: Every teacher a teacher of reading of his subject. "The teaching of reading and study skills is an integral part of teaching any subject in which reading is a tool of learning" (5).

Some progress has been made in persuading teachers to take an interest in helping students to read their subjects more effectively. In the past, high school teachers relegated the teaching of reading to the elementary school; their responsibility, they said was to teach a subject. This attitude seems to be changing. High school teachers now realize that unless they teach students how to read their assignments they will not get the desired results. In a workshop conducted by the author seven years ago, the teachers of each department met with several of their students to analyze the reading abilities necessary for success in the subject. Then each member described procedures that he had previously used successfully, had invented in the workshop, or had found described in the literature.

Since most high school teachers have had little or no preparation for teaching reading, they need assistance. In a high school in New York City, the principal used the consultant's time to meet with teachers of various subjects during their free periods in order to discuss ways of teaching the reading of their respective content fields.

In a Philadelphia high school, the principal, who was sold on a content-field approach to the whole school reading problem, invited an experienced reading teacher to demonstrate specific methods of teaching the reading of various subjects. The reading teachers's success with classes of slow learning students and behavior problems won the acceptance and admiration of initially skeptical teachers.

In some schools remedial reading teachers have been freed to work part time with other teachers as well as with retarded readers. In certain instances, this practice led to the employment of a full-time consultant who works only with teachers. Dr. David Shepherd held such a position in the high school at Norwalk, Connecticut, some years ago. By presenting himself as a helping person, and by demonstrating that he could be of practical assistance, he gradually established his position as a valuable resource to classroom teachers.

Another step in the transition from remedial teaching to consultant service has been taken in the New York City schools. Recognizing that there were far too many retarded readers to be served in special small groups, the administration has utilized the remedial teachers from separate schools as a team to describe and demonstrate remedial methods to classroom teachers in selected junior high schools. The success of any such program of in-service education depends upon the receptivity of the subject teachers as well as on the skill with which the remedial teachers impart their instruction.

Although we have no nation-wide surveys to show the prevalence of this trend from small remedial groups to developmental reading classes for all, and finally to effective reading instruction in each of the content subjects, several recent surveys point in this direction. Whereas earlier surveys mentioned only remedial classes, the 1959 survey of 269 Illinois junior high schools (3) reported an equal number of remedial and developmental programs, mostly in the seventh and eighth grades, for which the English departments assumed major responsibility.

Various localities report varying percentages of schools that have reading programs. For example, in 1959, 65 per cent of the Illinois junior high schools were reported to be giving reading instruction (3). A survey in Florida (14) reported 54 per cent in 1958. The Claremont Reading Conference of 1961 reported that all but six of the 52 southern California schools surveyed were doing something to aid reading, at least in the ninth grade (21).

Evidence of the recent increases in high school reading programs is found in the statement made in several of these studies that the majority of the reading programs reported were established within the past four or five years.

Further testimony as to the need for high school reading programs was supplied in 1961 by the questionnaire replies of one thousand teachers in the state of Michigan (16). These replies indicated that although less than a third of the teachers felt that they were expected to assume responsibility for "reading instruction" in their classes or had been shown how to teach their students to read a chapter effectively, to solve problems through reading, or to read critically, over 90 per cent thought that prospective secondary school teachers should be taught how to help their students develop fundamental reading skills, and that a reading laboratory would be beneficial.

Furthermore, 1,029 freshmen in college stated that hardly a third of their high school teachers had helped them to improve their reading in general, to read a subject chapter effectively, to concentrate on their reading, or to read critically; of these freshmen, 83 per cent thought "a high school course in the improvement of reading would have been beneficial" (16). It is encouraging that both students and teachers recognize the need for much more reading instruction in high schools.

It seems evident that the focus on reading programs is no longer confined to the elementary school; it has widened to include all educational levels. However, the day when every teacher will be concerned and competent to foster reading improvement in his subject is still a long way off. The most discouraging circumstance is that so little has been done to implement sound ideas that were advocated and tried out years ago. For example, eighteen years ago in Rockford, Illinois, teachers in five subject areas made an analysis of the reading skills needed for achievement in their respective subjects (8). How many high schools are doing as much today?

Progress in Procedures

Many different kinds of reading procedures are to be found in high schools. At one extreme is systematic group instruction in each reading skill; at the other extreme we find reading instruction individualized by means of programmed, self-pacing, multiple-track materials as described by Noal (18). In fact, variety is more evident in these procedures than anything that seems progress.

One direction in which we should move is toward a more intensive analysis of the reading processes that are actually used by students with varying backgrounds and degrees of ability when they read different kinds of materials for different purposes. Instruction in reading has been much too general. We need to develop the student's ability to discover the author's purpose, the structure and organizing principle of a paragraph or a selection, and the process by which the author is trying to communicate his ideas to the reader. Programmed learning and machine teaching can contribute to reading instruction by analyzing the thinking-learning process that is involved in reading a given selection, and rewarding the current response at each step.

Reading Personnel

A study reported in 1956 by Dever (1) showed that positions in the field of reading were held by a wide variety of persons: some were classroom teachers with some responsibility for reading; others were reading teachers, reading consultants, and supervisors; and still others were reading specialists, employed in clinics.

A program is sometimes judged by the number of specialists it employs. This is obviously an inadequate criterion because the need for specialists depends on factors such as the prevalence of reading problems and the competency of the subject teachers to deal with them. However, it can be assumed that a reading consultant would be needed in a high school where very few of the subject teachers have taken even one course in reading. In Illinois, all teachers, high school as well as elementary, are required to take at least one course in reading.

The demand for reading consultants is shown by the fact that in one university there were requests for twenty candidates adequately trained to fill this position. Only one such person was available. Of the school in Illinois that reported reading programs in 1960, only slightly more than a third had specially trained teachers (3). This discrepancy between supply and demand often leads schools to accept ill-prepared candidates. To prevent unqualified persons from receiving appointments to reading positions, we need the safeguard of certification. Letters to Directors (17) of Certification in 46 states elicited the information that only 12 states (26 per cent) had certification requirements for specialists in reading (11). Minnesota proposed two levels: (1) reading teacher in either elementary or secondary school, and (2) reading consultant, supervisor, or coordinator. One of the recommendations of the Harvard-Carnegie Study was "that a course in basic reading instruction be required of *all* prospective secondary school teachers" (2).

Certification requirements, in turn, demand more and better university courses in the teaching of reading in secondary school and college.

Evidence of Increased Efficiency and Interest

Studies of test results over a period of years are particularly difficult to interpret on the high school and college level because of changes in the number and characteristics of students attending these institutions. It is probably true that: (1) there has been little change in average reading scores; (2) at the extremes of the distribution we will find more very poor and more very good readers; and (3) reading achievement varies greatly from school to school. For example, Conant (6) reported schools in which no one in the ninth grade was reading as low as grade six, and others in which 35 to 50 per cent of the ninth graders were reading at sixth grade level or below.

Invariably each new method is reported to produce gains in students' reading scores. However, too few investigators take the additional statistical steps needed to ascertain the significance of the differences. The characteristics of successful high school programs have been summarized by Early (9) and by Grissom (10).

Evidence of progress – or lack of progress – in reading may also be obtained from publishers and librarians, whose statistics and observations indicate whether young people are buying and borrowing – and we assume, reading – more and better books. Mersand and Maggio (17) obtained a combination of statistics and opinion from sixty-eight directors of city libraries from which they conclude that:

1. The circulation of books in general use increased.

2. Relatively more nonfiction is being read. In some localities, the circulation of biographical, religious, scientific, and historical works has doubled; in one large city, circulation of nonfiction rose from 36 per cent to 51 per cent of the total circulation in eighteen years; in another city it advanced from 25 per cent to 47 per cent from 1922 to 1958. In yet another city the increase in nonfiction books borrowed by young people was from 779 in 1954 to 4,609 in 1958 – six-fold increase. In 1938 juveniles borrowed 48,879 nonfiction books; in 1958 they borrowed 92,091.

3. A large proportion – in the New York libraries from one-quarter to one-half – of all books circulated from the adult departments are borrowed by persons thirteen through eighteen years of age. In the state of South Carolina it was reported that 2,986,380 books of high quality were read in one year by children and young people through age fourteen.

4. "The overwhelming opinion of the nation's librarians is that young people are reading more and better books now than ever before," – the classics, good modern fiction, and good nonfiction.

How much of this increased interest in reading is due to the teaching of reading in the schools we do not know. As Margaret S. Coggin pointed out, there are more teen-agers and more books than ever before, and books are more available than ever before. There are many more paperback editions of good books; adolescents as well as adults often prefer a paperback rather than bother to go to the library.

This increase in the purchase and borrowing of books may have been brought about mainly by the more able students. A question we should raise is whether we are elevating the reading interests and tastes of the middle and lowest quarters of the adolescent population. If, as one librarian reported (17), there is "a remarkable correlation between volume of reading and rates of speed, comprehension, etc.," then anything we do to improve reading efficiency should increase the amount of voluntary reading.

Reading Instruction in College

Since Shaw has recently published a comprehensive survey of college reading (20), we need do no more than make a brief summary of his chapter. Its salient points are as follows:

Reading deficiencies are prevalent among college freshmen; estimates run from 64 to 95 per cent.

By 1952 almost three-fourths of the 418 institutions studied provided some kind of reading program, either as a separate course, in combination with a language arts course, or integrated with regular instruction.

College programs have many different objectives and use various procedures; for the most part, they have not been adequately evaluated.

Increased enrollment in college reading programs was indicated by the fact that by 1959, 49 of the 233 programs reported in 1955 had doubled, and 67 showed moderate increases; 54 showed no increase.

Concluding Statement

Reading is no longer considered an elementary school subject. The need for instruction in reading in secondary school and colleges is clearly recognized (4). To meet this need, a majority of secondary schools and colleges are offering developmental programs for all students, in addition to remedial programs as needed. The tendency in these programs seems to be to move away from small remedial groups toward developmental reading for all students, and slowly toward preparing all subject teachers to take more responsibility for improving reading in their content fields. Paralleling this trend is the increasing demand for reading consultants who are well qualified to work with and through teachers.

The most effective all-school reading program provides all of the following features: recognition of the importance of reading, a stimulating curriculum, basic instruction in high-school-level reading skills, instruction and practice in the kinds of reading that each subject requires for success, and remedial and clinical service for severe reading problems.

References

1. *An Administrator's Guide to Reading.* Educational Leadership Series, No. 2. Harrisburg, Pennsylvania: Department of Public Instruction, 1958. p. 1.
2. Austin, Mary C., *et al. The Torch Lighters.* Cambridge Massachusetts. Harvard University Press, 1961. P. 147.
3. Baughman, Millard Dale. "Special Reading Instructions in Illinois Junior High Schools." *Bulletin of the National Association of Secondary School Principals,* XLIV (November 1960), 90-95.
4. Bond, Guy L., and Kegler, Stanley B. "Reading Instruction in the Senior High School," in *Development in and Through Reading.* Sixtieth Yearbook of the National Society for the Study of Education, Park I. Chicago: University of Chicago Press, 1961. P. 320-335.
5. Burton, Dwight L. "Heads Out of the Sand: Secondary Schools Face the Challenge of Reading," *Educational Forum,* XXIV (March 1960), 291.
6. Conant, James B. *Recommendations for Education in the Junior High School Years.* Princeton, N.J.: Educational Testing Service, 1960. P. 21.
7. Dever, Kathryn Imogene. *Positions in the Field of Reading.* New York: Bureau of Publications, Teachers College, Columbia University, 1956.
8. Dilley, Lois. "All Teachers Teach Reading," *School Review,* LII (December 1944), 597-604.
9. Early, Margaret J. "What Does Research Reveal About Successful Reading Programs?" in *What We Know About High School Reading,* Bulletin of the National Conference on Research in English. Champaign, Illinois: National Council of Teachers of English, 1958.
10. Grissom, Loren V. "Characteristics of Successful Reading Improvement Programs." *The English Journal,* L (October 1961), 461-464.
11. Haag, Carl H., Sayles, Daniel G., and Smith, Donald E.P. "Certificate Requirements for Reading Specialists." *Reading Teacher,* XVI (November 1960), 98-100.
12. Holmes, Jack. "Factors Underlying Major Disabilities at the College Level." *Genetic Psychology Monographs,* XLIX (1954), 3-95.
13. Holmes, Jack A. "Personality Characteristics of the Disabled Reader." *Journal of Developmental Reading,* IV (Winter 1961), 111-122.
14. Jordan, James W. "A Survey of Certain Policies and Practices in Florida Junior High Schools." *Bulletin of the National Association of Secondary School Principals,* XLII (September 1958), 71-77.
15. Langman, Muriel Potter. "The Reading Process a Descriptive, Interdisciplinary Approach." *Genetic Psychology Monographs,* LXII (July 1960), 3-10.
16. McGinnis, Dorothy J. "The Preparation and Responsibility of Secondary Teachers in the Field of Reading." *The Reading Teacher,* XV (November 1961), 92-97.
17. Mersand, Joseph, and Maggio, Joseph B. "But They Are Reading Better!" *High Points,* XLII (June 1960), 23-46.

18.   Noal, Mabel S. "Automatic Teaching of Reading Skills in High School." *Journal of Education,* XLII (February 1961), 1-71.
19.   Perry, William G., Jr., and Whitlock, Charles P. "A Critical Rationale for a Reading Film." *Harvard Educational Review,* XXIV (Winter 1954), 6-27.
20.   Shaw, Phillip. "Reading in College." *Development in and Through Reading,* Chap. XIX. Sixtieth Yearbook of the National Society for the Study of Education. Part I. Chicago: University of Chicago Press, 1961. P. 336-354.
21.   Wamba, Donald. "Reading in High School: Some Programs in Action." Claremont Reading Conference. 25th Yearbook. Claremont. California: Claremont College, 1961. P. 123-31.

The Refinement of High School Reading Skills*

J. T. HUNT

Typically and traditionally we expect most children to "learn to read" in the primary grades, if not in the first grade. Even though the teacher or parent may say that the child has learned to read, each recognizes that this is a tentative, beginning level or stage reflecting primarily some of the basic mechanical skills involved in left to right attack, in word recognition, and in understanding simple material.

If the program of a basal series is followed by his teachers, the child is exposed to a planned sequence of exercises and materials designed to increase his reading skills needed in the broadening curriculum. A well-balanced program includes both appropriate repetition of previously taught words, ideas, and skills, and also sequential introduction and training in new skills to help him gain independence in reading.

Each grade level sets new and more exacting reading requirements for the pupil. Through the grades new courses are added to the curriculum, and each new or revised textbook in the content fields, even for the same grade, appears to be more comprehensive and complex. Not only do high school courses require the refinement of reading skills previously taught but also the introduction and refinement of new skills for at least some of the students. It is probably also true that some skills, to be effectively learned, require not only continuing practice but also the additional maturity gained by high school age.

The accompanying list of needed high school reading skills is representative rather than inclusive. Almost any one of the skills could be subdivided into a number of related factors or processes; e.g., "to adjust to varied material in the content fields" could include "the condensed, symbolic language of mathematics," with its current emphasis not so much on drill and computation as on generalization and discovery. Other problems in the reading of mathematics could be pointed out in addition to those representative of the reading of social studies, science, and other areas. Most of the skills in the

*Reprinted from *High School Journal,* 49 (April, 1966), pp. 307-313, by permission of the author and the University of North Carolina Press.

following list have been taught, either directly or indirectly and with differing degrees of effectiveness, in the first six to eight grades:

Representative Reading Demands in High School

To increase vocabulary and word perception skills
    To expand both general and technical vocabulary
    To refine and sharpen meanings and differences
    To improve word analysis skills
        Structural analysis
        Phonetic analysis
    Contextual skills
    To improve dictionary skills
To improve basic comprehension skills
    To note details
    To get the general meaning or significance
    To select, understand, and organize main ideas
    To follow a sequence of ideas or events
    To follow directions
    To find the organization of what is read
    To improve reading rate
To improve work-study skills
    To locate and select needed material
        Use of book index, table of contents, chapter organization
        Use of dictionary, reference books
        Use of library card catalog
        Use of subject indexes, technical journals, abstracts and reviews, etc.
    To adjust to varied materials in the content areas
    To interpret maps, charts, and other condensed material
    To develop flexible reading rates and patterns according to purpose
    To summarize, outline, and organize material for different purposes
To read critically and evaluate what is read
    To obtain both literal and figurative meanings
    To react suitably to mood, tone, and "message" of the selection
    To draw inferences
    To anticipate outcomes
    To distinguish between statements of fact and opinion
    To adjust to the broad scope of forms of writing and of style
    To evaluate facts or ideas in terms of experience and the supporting
        evidence
    To evaluate the author's coverage of a topic and his competence in the
        field

To develop more mature reading interests and tastes
  To expand recreational reading interests
  To develop an appreciation for beauty, style, creative expression
  To develop discrimination in the evaluation of literary merit
  To obtain — and give — pleasure in oral interpretation

Even though high school students may have been exposed to an excellent reading program in the elementary grades, it is presumptuous to assume that all previously taught skills have been mastered — even by the average or bright student. In any high school marked differences are likely to exist in performance among students on any given basic reading skill and also among skills for any one student. Excellent instruction would be expected to increase the range of performance among students; poorer instruction, to reduce not only the range of individual differences but also the level of performance.

If it is true that different degrees of inter- and intra-student mastery of specific reading skills will be found, then it follows that the refinement of reading skills at the high school level is primarily an individual matter. Some students may still have difficulty utilizing rather simple contextual clues or getting the main idea of a paragraph while other students may be performing at a high level on some of the more difficult critical reading skills. On the other hand, a student may show proficiency in getting the main ideas on relatively simple or practice material but reveal a marked deficiency in the same reading task on more complex textual or reference material.

In order to determine the level of ability on a variety of reading skills such as those listed previously and thus to determine the type of reading program needed, the school will need a comprehensive testing and evaluation program which includes both survey and diagnostic tests as well as informal appraisal by the classroom teachers. Most group tests of reading not only measure a limited number of relatively simple skills (Hunt, 1954), but also yield little more than a level of average reading performance. Typically, the kinds of reading demands made by the individual teacher will probably have to be evaluated by that teacher on the types of reading material encountered in that course.

A comprehensive testing program would doubtlessly reveal many individual and group problems. Although reading level as determined by a survey test may show a range of eight grades or more in the school, the range on specific reading skills would be even greater. Some students might be generally low on almost all of the skills appraised, and some few might be generally high on almost all of these. The school or a given grade might be relatively low on certain skills but average or high on other skills.

An important decision that must be made after such testing — and of course, preferably *before* such testing — is the goal of the reading program. Should it be a remedial one limited to the bottom 10 to 25 per cent? Should reading classes be substituted for certain English classes? Should all English classes be reorganized to include a balance of attention to all the language arts, including reading? Should special reading classes or laboratories be set up on an elective basis? Should reading supervisors as well as reading teachers be added? Should a division of labor be made, with content teachers identifying specific skills to be stressed in their classes? Should a limited number of the more basic comprehension skills be singled out for special attention throughout the school? Should the good reader be helped to become an excellent one?

Obviously only a limited number of skills for a limited number of students will be refined unless the decision is made that the improvement of reading skills for the total school is not only a desirable but an essential part of the curriculum. It is interesting to note that English grammar and composition are taught and frequently required throughout high school, but that formal reading instruction in too many school systems ends as early as the sixth grade. In a questionnaire study of 371 colleges and universities by Austin (1961), the supervisors of student teachers reported a disturbing absence of instruction in reading skills at the intermediate level; further, when any formal teaching was done at all, it usually consisted of reteaching the primary grade skills. Presumably these schools had sought out the best situations for their student teachers! A proposal that English not be taught after the sixth grade except for a limited number requiring remedial English would be considered ludicrous, but yet there appears to be little evidence to suggest that the skills of reading are sharpened and refined to any greater degree without direct guidance and instruction than are those of English grammar and composition. Refinement of reading skills – just as those of other language arts skills – will be facilitated if each teacher assumes some responsibility for them in his own classes.

Most high schools are not yet geared to an all-school reading program. Some of the more important reasons for this appear to be lack of trained personnel, lack of commitment to a program stressing more than remediation, and the reluctance of individual teachers to be personally involved with giving instruction in reading. The extension of reading instruction into the seventh and eighth grades on a state-wide basis in Pennsylvania in 1959 was reported with some pride by the state superintendent (Boehm, 1961). Half of the teachers in the new program had received no preparation in the teaching of reading, however, even though a considerable number of elementary-trained teachers were participating. A follow-up study by Madeira (1961) of the Pennsylvania program revealed that a typical comment of the highly vocal minority was that not all pupils in the seventh and eighth grades needed any instruction in reading. McGinnis (1961) reported, from an analysis of 570 questionnaires from a random sampling of high school teachers in Michigan, that only about one-third were expected to assume any responsibility for the teaching of reading. The teachers revealed further that about one-third of their students could not read well enough to do the work expected. Surveys by Braam and Roehm (1964), Simmons (1963), and Thornton (1957) point out that even in those secondary schools having some type of reading program most of the reading teachers and supervisors had had little or no training in reading.

Surveys of the status of reading instruction in junior and senior high schools by Baughman (1960), Glake (1961), Grissom (1961), Jordan (1958), Smith (1956), and Thornton (1957) are in general agreement that although new reading programs of some type are increasing, only a limited beginning has been made. Many such programs are remedial rather than developmental or both. They are not aimed at refining reading skills so much as to helping the poorer student come up to a minimal level on some of the basic comprehension skills such as finding details, getting the main idea, recognizing simple contextual clues, etc.

Just as the established needs of the student should dictate the goals of the reading improvement program, so will the organization of the staff be determined by the interests and competence of the teachers and the resources of the school. Typically, however, little improvement will be made unless the program is an extensive, on-going one in which students and teachers alike are convinced that the refinement of reading skills is a continuous, active process that should not be left to chance or to others. The sometimes seemingly astonishing gains in reading level made by students in special reading classes of only five or six weeks duration may do more harm than good by deceiving the student and the teacher as to the real gains made and to the permanence and utility of the "gain," frequently a spurious artifact of testing. The teaching of certain skills by the reading teacher in classes running throughout the year still requires, for both permanence and refinement, the application of those skills to the learning of content in the various subject matter areas.

At the present time it may be a bit unrealistic, however, to expect many subject matter teachers to be efficient in the application and extension of reading skills without more training and support. Actually, many English teachers who are frequently called upon to teach reading have had no more training for this assignment than other teachers have had. One of the responsibilities of the trained reading teacher might well be to help the other teachers develop the philosophy that teaching reading is the responsibility of all teachers and then to provide help in gaining knowledge about reading appraisal and teaching techniques. A big boost to the refinement of reading skills will take place as more and more teacher training institutions require at least one course in the teaching of reading as part of the preparation of secondary school teachers.

In spite of much of the controversy over the teaching of beginning reading, learning to read initially is a reasonably easy and short process. Developing proficiency in many new, expanded, and more complex reading skills is a difficult, slow, or even laborious process which may extend over the entire academic years or beyond. Goethe was surely thinking of the *refinement* of reading skills when he said, "The dear people do not know how long it takes to learn to read. I have been at it all my life and I cannot yet say I have reached the goal."

Bibliography

Austin, Mary, and others. *The Torchlighters: Tomorrow's Teachers of Reading.* Cambridge, Massachusetts: Harvard University Press, 1961.

Baughman, M. D. "Special Reading Instruction in Illinois Junior High Schools." *Bulletin of The National Association of Secondary School Principals* 44: 90-95 November 1960.

Boehm, Charles H. "A State Superintendent Comments on Some Problems in a State Reading Program." *The Reading Teacher* 14: 319-22; May 1961.

Braam, Leonard S., and Roehm, Marilyn A. "Subject-Area Teachers' Familiarity with Reading Skills." *Journal of Developmental Reading* 7: 188-96; Spring 1964.

Glake, Robert R. "Michigan High Schools Stress Special Reading Programs." *Michigan Education Journal* 39: 262-63; November 1964.

Grissom, Loren V. "Characteristics of Successful Reading Improvement Programs." *English Journal* 50: 461-64; October 1961.

Hunt, J. T. "Selecting a High School Reading Test." *High School Journal* 38: 58-61; November 1954.

Jordan, James. "A Survey of Certain Policies and Practices in Florida Junior High Schools." *Bulletin of The National Association of Secondary School Principals* 42: 71-77; September 1958.

McGinnis, Dorothy J. "The Preparation and Responsibility of Secondary Teachers in the Field of Reading." *The Reading Teacher* 15: 92-101; November 1961.

Madeira, Sheldon. "Reading in Pennsylvania Schools." *The Reading Teacher* 14: 314-18; May 1961.

Simmons, John. "Who Is Responsible? The Need for Qualified Supervisors of Reading Programs," *English Journal* 52: 86-93; February 1963.

Smith, Donald E. P. "The Status of Reading Instruction in Michigan Public Schools." University of Michigan, *School of Education Bulletin* 27: 91-94; March 1956.

Thornton, Robert. *Developmental Reading in Texas Secondary Schools.* Texas Study of Secondary Education. Research Study No. 23. Austin: State Department of Education, 1957.

Questions for Discussion

1. To what extent are teachers in your own school system in agreement with the contention expressed in the preceding articles that all secondary level teachers do have responsibilities for promoting reading development in their subject matter area field? How would you answer the argument that the demands in covering content are such that teachers have no time to devote to the teaching of reading?

2. Do you agree with Strang's contention that young people are reading more and better books than ever before? What effect has reading instruction on the secondary level had in this regard?

3. Do you agree with Hunt's position that the basic task in reading instruction on the secondary school level is to refine skills already

introduced in the elementary grades? Are there any new reading skills that may be introduced for the first time at the secondary school level?

Organization and Administration of Secondary School Reading Programs

II

Once a school administrator or staff member has become convinced that his school must begin to assume its responsibilities in providing reading instruction for all students, then a number of important decisions must be made. One set of decisions deals with how best to convince the rest of the staff and the public of the need for a reading program, and then decisions must be made regarding where and how the program should be placed in the school curriculum.

The first two articles in this section contain rather detailed descriptions of secondary school reading programs that have been put into operation. U. Berkley Ellis describes a junior high level program where reading instruction is carried on in combination English—social studies classes. These content classes are grouped by three reading achievement levels; materials available are sequenced and designated for each level. Ellis does present some evidence as to the effectiveness of the program.

Sally Berkey and Irwin Fields describe a high school developmental reading program concentrated in ninth grade English classes. Although the major part of the instruction takes place in reading laboratories, the program does include both orientation and follow-up phases. Evaluation procedures are described and student gains on reading tests are presented. Interpretation of these gains, however, is hampered by the lack of a control group with which to compare.

In the last article in this section, Ralph Sherlock does not actually describe an ongoing program but rather presents a case for the advantages of the reading laboratory plan of organization. Sherlock places great importance on the need for careful diagnosis of students' reading needs before any instructional program can be designed and carried out in the laboratory.

Developmental Reading in Junior High School *

U. BERKLEY ELLIS

The Junior High Schools of the Delhaas Joint School District (Franklin D. Roosevelt Junior High, Rogers Road, Bristol, Pa., Benjamin Franklin Junior High, Millcreek Road, Levittown, Pa.) have been involved in a developmental reading program for the past six years. It started with the meager attempt to provide aid to remedial readers and has progressed to a very intensive program offering reading instruction to meet the needs of all students. The staffs of our junior high schools have recognized the vital importance of the reading tool to the successful performance of students in the multitude of classroom experiences. Through the diligent study, the willingness to experiment, the tireless effort and the cooperation of these teachers, the developmental reading program described below has taken form.

Our junior high school staff accepts developmental reading as a reading program which:

(1)   Involves all students of all reading levels — primer to senior high or above.

(2)   Involves all students in extending, reinforcing and mastering of the basic reading skills — word attack, word recognition, vocabulary development, comprehension.

(3)   Introduces all students to new reading skills that are suited to the reading maturity level of the student — reading with facility in all content areas, adjusting reading rate to the purpose for reading, critical interpretation, perfection of study skills.

(4)   Encourages all students to develop their individual independent reading interests for personal growth and for recreation.

Beginning

For several years teachers were available to offer aid to students with the

*Reprinted from *Journal of Developmental Reading,* 6 (Autumn, 1962), pp. 41-49, by permission of the author and the editor.

most severe reading difficulties. These boys and girls were excused from classes two or more periods per week to receive special help with basic reading skills. Our English-social studies teachers soon recognized that a more intensive program was desirable to provide the reading instruction so sorely needed by the many students they found struggling to read the grade-level textbooks.

It was suggested that the staff and administration study a plan to group students by reading ability and to provide more instruction in reading.

It was agreed to administer to each student an Individual Reading Inventory Test developed by Dr. Botel and teachers in our county. This test was composed of a sight recognition section and a word opposites section. A student was tested until he demonstrated levels. His functional reading level was determined to be the lowest level at which he was successful in eighty percent of the replies.

Students were then sectioned according to reading levels. The three main groupings were "Reading Improvement," primary to third reading level; and "On Level," junior high and senior high reading levels. There were enough sections available to limit classes to no more than two reading levels at the beginning of the year. It should be pointed out here that students of low intelligence potential, I.Q. of below eighty-five, are placed in special education classes. Trained teachers are available for these sections for their academic classes.

Materials were at first very scarce. The basic materials for the reading improvement group was the Lyons and Carnahan, *Bond Developmental Reading Series.* The "Functional" and "On Level" readers used the Scott Foresman, *Basic Reading Skills,* and their literature books. The major emphasis at this point was in helping all teachers to perfect their ability to teach basic reading skills. This was accomplished by departmental meetings, teaching demonstrations, visits to conferences and classroom visits.

Present Program

The present developmental reading program employs the grouping of students in the same three major groupings. However, within these groups students are placed in sections dependent upon the following criteria: reading level, teacher judgment, achievement test scores, and intelligence tests. After the guidance personnel complete the sectioning, the teachers of each grade level meet to study the composition of the section and to suggest student adjustments according to their personal observation of the student's past performance.

The seventh and eighth-grade students are assigned to the same teacher for English and social studies; the "Reading Improvement Groups" meet for fourteen forty-two minute periods per week; the "Functional" and "On Level" readers are assigned twelve periods of English and social studies. The ninth grade "Reading Improvement" sections meet with the English teacher for nine periods;

the "Functional" reading sections meet seven or nine periods; and the "On Level" sections meet five periods a week (see Chart I).

CHART I

SUBJECT AND PERIOD ASSIGNMENTS FOR DEVELOPMENTAL READING
INSTRUCTION FOR READING GROUPS AT EACH GRADE LEVEL

Reading Level	*Grade English, Social Studies Reading*	*Ninth Grade English, Reading*
Reading Improvement (P-3)	14 periods*	9 periods
Functional (4-6)	12 periods	7-9 periods
On Level (Junior-Senior High)	12 periods	5 periods

*Periods forty-two minutes in length.

After experimentation with the large variety of reading materials that are now available and careful evaluation of their use, Chart II was developed to supply the teacher with a sequential order for the use of this material. This was necessary to insure the orderly advance of students through each level of reading material as they progressed in reading ability. Also, it provided the psychological factor of offering new materials for students who made little progress or who needed to review and to reinforce basic skills before undertaking new materials at each grade level.

The basic materials listed on Chart II for the "Reading Improvement" groups are employed to teach basic reading skills through the use of content materials:

(1) Word Recognition Techniques
    (a) Meaning aids
    (b) Visual and structural aids
    (c) Auditory and phonetic aids
(2) Comprehension Abilities: reading to
    (a) Retain information
    (b) Organize
    (c) Evaluate
    (d) Interpret
    (e) Appreciate

(3)   Basic Study Skills
    (a)   Locating information
    (b)   Use of general reference
    (c)   Use of visual materials
    (d)   Organizing
(4)   Basic Meaning Development
    (a)   Paragraph meaning and organization
    (b)   Word meaning

The supplementary materials are employed to reinforce the basic reading skills with drills and experiences in specific skills. The advantage of such materials as *My Weekly Reader* and the *Reader's Digest Skill Builder* is that their high interest and maturity level are attractive to the junior high school student.

The "Functional" reading sections must still devote much effort to the review and to the reinforcing of basic reading skills. At this level students experience individual reading success, and are encouraged to strengthen their personal reading through use of the many high-interest, low-reading level stories found in the supplementary series listed for each grade level.

The "On Level" sections continue the reinforcing and the reviewing of basic reading skills. Time is devoted to the development of the more mature skills of critical interpretation, of adjustment of rate for the purpose of reading, and of study skills. Increased attention is given to developing comprehension and speed. The *Be A Better Reader* and *S.R.A. Reading Lab. IV* are employed for these outcomes.

Motivation for the extension of their personal reading and their appreciation of literature is promoted through class reading and discussion of novels at each grade level: seventh grade, *Tom Sawyer;* eighth grade, *Red Badge of Courage;* ninth grade, *Silar Marner.* The "On Level" reading students also use the *Scholastic Literature Units* which are composed of a class set of an anthology accompanied by a series of eighty separate titles supplementing these stories. A different set is directed to attract interest of each grade level-seventh grade, *Animals;* eighth grade, *Courage;* ninth grade, *Mirrors.* Dependent upon the ability and the ease at which the sections master these materials, teachers are free to provide experiences in other books such as *Animal Farm, Hiroshima, David Copperfield,* and many others.

At all reading levels students are taken to the library once a week for free reading periods. Here the teachers and the librarian devote the time to guiding boys and girls to selecting books of their reading level. Books for all reading levels are provided for the students.

At all reading levels a multi-level spelling program is used in English classes to improve spelling skills. An intensive vocabulary development program is also included as a phase of this training. In each of the subject areas teachers develop vocabulary and spelling lists from the content material presented. Much emphasis is placed upon vocabulary and directed reading activities with the content area textbooks. In science, history and mathematics, textbooks of fourth to sixth reading level are provided for below grade level readers; however, many more low reading level, high interest materials are needed. These subject areas need further direction and help in order to complete the goals of our developmental reading program.

To aid the below-level readers still further, several teachers have been assigned to aid the regular class teachers of the "Reading Improvement" sections and the lowers "Functional" reading sections. For two periods a week the "helping teacher" assists the class teacher with the students in the classroom. As the teachers become more aware of the individual problems of students, the class may be divided into two groups of from ten to twelve each to work in a separate classroom with each teacher.

This practice has had two-fold results. First, the students have received more individual attention and personal instruction. Secondly, this is an important phase of our in-service training program for teachers. In each case a teacher more experienced in teaching reading is paired with a less experienced teacher; thus, the teachers receive individual help and are able to share experience and knowledge with one another.

Evaluation

The staff uses many tools for evaluating the progress of students in the developmental reading program. An I.R.I. is given each spring and the results are compared with the past years' scores to view the growth of individuals and of classes. There has been a constant movement of students through the reading levels so that the "On Level" sections have increased from thirty percent in seventh grade to sixty percent of the ninth grade. Also, while we have from two or three "Reading Improvement" groups at the seventh-grade level, there is but one on the ninth-grade level. This past year the teacher of this ninth-grade section made a study of the records of the "Reading Improvement" students. In the class of twenty-eight students ten or thirty-five percent entered the school district in September of this year; fourteen, or fifty percent had entered the district in junior high school. Only one student had started first grade in our district.

Much of our evaluation of the developmental reading program is based upon the observation and experience of the teachers who have worked with it. They all report increased student interest in reading and increased desire of students to want to learn to read. Individual reading records and book reporting activities demonstrate increased student recreational reading. Also, teachers from all content fields have experienced improvement in research and reporting skills. Students are no longer satisfied to rely upon one source when they are preparing reports for class assignments.

CHART II
READING MATERIALS FOR DEVELOPMENT READING PROGRAM
FRANKLIN DELANO ROOSEVELT JUNIOR HIGH SCHOOL
DELHASS JOINT SCHOOL DISTRICT

Reading Levels	Grade Levels	Seventh	Eighth	Ninth
Reading Improvement	Basic	BOND DEVELOPMENT READING SERIES	BOND DEVELOPMENT READING SERIES	READER'S DIGEST READING SKILL BUILDER, 2-6
	Supplementary	MY WEEKLY READER Nos. 2-5	MY WEEKLY READER Nos. 2-5	S.R.A. READING LAB. (Elementary)
P. 1-3		BUILDING READING SKILLS	PHONICS SKILL TEXT A to B / DEEP SEA ADVENTURE SERIES	BUILDING READING SKILLS 1-6 levels
Functional Readers	Basic	BASIC READING SKILL	S.R.A. READING LAB. (Secondary)	BUILDING READING SKILLS Levels 1-6
P. 4-6	Supplementary	BOTEL INTERESTING READING SERIES / PARADES	DEEP SEA ADVENTURE SERIES / PHONICS SKILL TEXT A to D / PANORAMAS	TEEN AGE TALES Books A, B, I to VI
"On Level"	Basic	BE A BETTER READER–I / MORE PARADES / TOM SAWYER	BE A BETTER READER–II / MORE PANORAMAS / RED BADGE OF COURAGE	BE A BETTER READER–III / S.R.A. READING LAB. IV A / SILAS MARNER / WORLDS TO EXPLORE
Jr.-Sr.	Supplementary	READ MAGAZINE / CURRENT EVENTS / SCHOLASTIC LITERATURE UNIT ANIMALS	READ MAGAZINE / CURRENT EVENTS / SCHOLASTIC LITERATURE UNIT COURAGE	READ MAGAZINE / CURRENT EVENTS / SCHOLASTIC LITERATURE UNIT MIRRORS

Reading and Study Skills Program*

SALLY BERKEY AND IRWIN H. FIELDS

The program described in this article is the result of a concentrated effort on the part of teachers and administrators to improve the quality of reading in the four high schools of the Centinela Valley Union High School District.

Located in Southwest Los Angeles, the Centinela Valley Union High School District is made up of four high schools: Hawthorne, Lawndale, Lennox, and Leuzinger. This district began its much needed reading program in September, 1959.

For several years prior to this date, Superintendent Jefferson L. Garner, along with his administrators and teachers, became increasingly concerned with the reading problem throughout the district. Since standardized achievement tests indicated that our students were not reading up to their ability, Superintendent Garner began exploring every possibility of improving reading in the four high schools. Said Dr. Garner, "The improvement of reading should be a *continuous* process. It should *not* stop when the student gets to high school. It should continue in high school, college, and throughout life. Those students who *are not* reading up to their ability should be given special help, and those students who *are* reading up to their ability should be taught to refine and polish their reading skills and techniques. Therefore, the Reading and Study Skills Program is the answer to our problem."

The first concern of the administration in getting the program underway was to get the approval of the Board of Trustees. In June, 1959, Dr. Garner met with the Board and discussed at length the need for a reading program, outlining in detail just how such a program might be incorporated into the high school curriculum. The Board, unanimously agreeing that the program be introduced, provided a budget.

The second concern was to select competent personnel. As in all worthwhile undertakings, this selection could not be made spontaneously.

*Reprinted from *Journal of Secondary Education,* 36 (April, 1961), pp 197-202, by permission of the authors and the California Association of Secondary School Administrators.

Careful consideration was given to the matter of choosing the *right* person for the *right* job.

Dr. Garner chose for his reading coordinators two district teachers, Mrs. Sally Berkey and Mr. Irwin Fields. Both Mrs. Berkey and Mr. Fields, having had much experience in the field of reading and special training in reading instruction, were given the responsibility of planning the reading program, developing the course of study, ordering materials and equipment, setting up the labs, training new teachers, and supervising the over-all reading program in the four high schools.

Four special reading lab teachers, one for each of the high schools, were hired to work under the supervision of the two coordinators. These lab teachers were instructed to work with and help the reading teachers in their respective schools and to conduct the program according to plans.

Endeavoring to secure competent reading instructors, the district encouraged its English teachers who were to be involved in the program to take a summer course in developmental reading at the University of California, Los Angeles, with all expenses paid. Approximately twenty teachers, being fully aware that reading is one of the most important tools in the learning process, were eager to avail themselves of this opportunity. They finished the course, full of enthusiasm and confident that they were much better prepared to participate in the total reading program.

The physical layout of the Reading and Study Skills Program is a rather extensive one. In each of the four high schools there are two complete reading laboratories, which have the latest and best of equipment and materials. Set up to accommodate fifteen students at a time, each lab has four tables with sixteen chairs, ten individual reading booths, an optiglow screen, a wall clock for timed reading, a portable cabinet for projectors, magazine stands, book shelves, filing cabinets, and a teacher's desk and chair.

The reading improvement aids in each lab consist of the following: one tachistoscope, one controlled reader, one tachist-o-flasher, one S.R.A. reading accelerator, one shadowscope, and one tape recorder. Graded film and tape are available for these instruments.

There is a variety of reading materials in each lab. Carefully selected for interest as well as instructional level, these materials range from grade two through fourteen. Among the graded reading materials are the following: S.R.A. (Science Research Associates) Reading Labs, IIA, IIB, IIIA, IVA; S.R.A. Reading for Understanding Labs; *Better Reading Books,* I, II, III, by Elizabeth Simpson; *Be A Better Reader* series, I, II, III, IV, V, VI, by Nila Banton Smith; *Transfer Reading Manual,* Educational Developmental Laboratories; *Effective Reading for Adults,* by Selmer Herr; *Word Attack,* by Clyde Roberts; *Reading for Meaning,* by W. S. Guiter and J. H. Coleman; *Skill Builder* series, Reader's Digest; *How to Become a Better Reader,* by Paul Witty; and *Teen Age Tales*, by Ruth Strang and

Ralph Roberts. Included also are paperback books, dictionaries, reference books, magazines and newspers.

The warm and pleasant atmosphere of each of these fully equipped labs is conducive to reading. The attractive exhibits and the bulletin board displays of colorful book jackets serve as an incentive even to the non-reader.

Concentrated in the freshman English classes, the reading program is a *required* course. It is *mandatory* for every ninth grade student in the district to spend eight weeks of the school year in the reading lab. (During the year 1959-1960 the lab period was only six weeks.) After all of the freshmen complete their training, the program is then offered to upper classmen for a period of four weeks, college prep students being given first preference.

Generally, the Reading and Study Skills Program was planned to help the students improve their reading habits and their study skills, two of the most important areas of the high school curriculum. Specifically, the goals of the program are to increase the reading rate, to enlarge the vocabulary, to raise the level of comprehension, and to teach the students how to study in all subject fields.

Five major tasks confront each teacher in helping his students accomplish these goals. Those tasks are as follows: (1) the development and refinement of reading techniques and skills, (2) the development of vocabulary and background concepts, (3) the development of reading interests and tastes, (4) the development of independence in reading, and (5) the development of differential attack — ability to adjust reading skills at hand.

The main emphases of the program should be noted. Reading — *always* for a *purpose* — is stressed throughout the course. Flexible reading habits to *suit* the *purpose,* skimming, rapid reading, and study reading are given great emphasis. Among the specific exercises stressed are vocabulary building, rate building, reading for main idea, reading for details, reading to evaluate, reading to apply, reading for implications, newspaper and magazine reading, using the card catalogue, using the table of contents, indexes, etc., and using dictionaries, atlases, and encyclopedias.

Important also are the many study aids which our students are encouraged to use in all of their classes. Some of the most worthwhile ones are the following: The S Q 3 R Study Formula, the T Q L R Listening Formula, How to Build a Vocabulary, How to Learn to Spell, How to Take Notes, How to Outline, How to Underline, How to Take a Test, How to Use the Dictionary, and How to Use the Library. From these study aids, as well as from the many reading techniques and skills, the students have a definite carry over not only to their English classes but to all other subjects in school.

In attempting to teach those salient points outlined above, the teacher makes every effort to consider the individual needs of his students. He uses a variety of approaches and methods geared to meet those individual needs. He starts each student at his present reading level and encourages him to work up to his potential.

Before our students begin their training in the reading lab, they go through a period of motivation and orientation. During this time, the teacher constantly *talks* reading to the students and explains to them how important reading is to their success in high school and throughout life. The students visit the reading labs and become acquainted with the over-all program. They also visit the library and receive instruction in its use. Here they are encouraged to check out books and to begin building up their own home libraries.

During this period the students are also made to realize the importance of general health and its relation to reading. The school nurse gives a physical check-up to all students, carefully examining their ears and eyes for every possible defect. Immediately following the examination, the nurse sends a report to the teachers and notifies the parents if corrections should be made.

This period of motivation and orientation is of paramount importance. It is during this time that the students begin to realize that reading is basic to *all* subjects and that *all* students, regardless of their reading levels, can learn to improve their reading skills and techniques.

The testing program also serves as a part of motivation. It is pointed out to the students that tests are given for *their* benefit, in order that they may know just where their strengths and weaknesses lie. The *Nelson Silent Reading Test,* Form A, is given to the students before they begin their lab training. Form B of the same test is given at the end of the lab session to see how much progress is made during the training period. Form C of the *Nelson Test* is given at the close of the school year to determine how much carry-over there is and how much achievement is made during the entire year.

When the students are thoroughly motivated and are ready to go into the reading lab for their training, the class of thirty, which is homogeneously grouped for English I, is divided in half. The regular English teacher takes fifteen of these students into one of the two reading labs, and the special reading teacher takes fifteen in the other. For a period of eight weeks these students follow a concentrated program of reading skills, techniques and study aids, as outlined above. They keep a record of their work and chart their progress in a student syllabus *specifically* developed for use in the course. At the end of the lab session, the students receive the results of the B test, and their over-all performance is discussed with them.

The follow-up phase of the reading program is perhaps one of the most important parts of the course. The students return to their regular English classes, and for the remainder of the year they spend at least one day each week in supervised classroom reading. During this time, they put into practice the reading skills and techniques which they learned in the lab. The students also continue to develop and refine their techniques. They work on vocabulary and strive to develop reading interests and tastes, as well as independence in reading.

For this all important follow-up procedure, special materials and aids are available for the classroom teacher to use.

Working closely with the freshmen English teachers and the reading lab teachers in both the lab program and the follow-up procedure is the school librarian. In addition to instructing the students in the normal use of library materials, the librarian is always ready to guide the students in independent reading for both recreational and research purposes.

As was stated earlier in this article three forms of the *Nelson Silent Reading Test* are given to all ninth graders, Form A at the beginning of the lab session, Form B at the end, and Form C at the close of the school year. The improvement made by our students during the school year 1959-1960 indicates that the reading program has merit. Nine hundred and seven (907) freshmen went through three six-week sessions. The first session started in September, 1959; the second in November, 1959; and the third in January, 1960. The average reading level of all students at the beginning of the program was seventh grade, six months (7.6). The average reading level at the end of the lab session was eighth grade, second month (8.2). This makes a total gain of six (6) months in six weeks, or one month for each week of instruction. At the end of the school year, after the students had gone through their follow-up program, the average reading level was ninth grade, five months (9.5), a gain of thirteen months (1.3) since the lab period. These figures show that an over-all increase of one year and nine months (1.9) was made during the school year.

Significant also is the fact that the majority of our students made many gains which cannot be measured statistically. The strength of the total program was mirrored in the students themselves. Along with their appreciable improvement in reading, our students gained a feeling of self-confidence. They developed socially as well as educationally. Many students, for the first time, began checking books out of the classroom and school libraries. Almost all of our students seemed to have a more favorable attitude toward reading and toward school in general.

The Reading and Study Skills Program has a much broader aspect than that which is outlined above. It is the opinion of the writer that a reading program, to be complete, must be school-wide. During the school year 1959-1960, the reading coordinators endeavored to make the reading program a part of the total school system. In each school a central reading committee made up of the special lab teacher and the school librarian was set up. This committee met periodically throughout the year with each of the twelve departments in school. The purpose of these meetings was to discuss ways and means of improving reading in each subject field. The librarian offered assistance with reading materials, and the lab teacher helped with skills and techniques. This procedure proved to be very effective in that it made the majority of teachers in school realize that the teaching of reading is their responsibility.

Special counseling also became a part of the schoolwide program. A special reading counselor in each high school was chosen to do individual case studies where results of the reading program were unusual. This helped to point to the kinds of changes or emphases that the reading teachers, counselors, and administrators should consider.

As a result of all of these efforts on the part of the teachers and administrators, the reading atmosphere permeated the entire school district, and the Reading and Study Skills Program was coordinated with the over-all school curriculum.

During the present school year, 1960-1961, our reading program is off to a good start. Already two freshman groups have gone through the concentrated program with results comparable to those of last year. The school-wide aspect is being given even greater emphasis with the hope that *all* teachers will become teachers of reading and will feel responsible for the reading habits of their students.

Our school library is becoming more popular every day. The circulation of books is increasing and research materials are being used more extensively. Students find it enjoyable and helpful using the reading accelerators which are placed in the libraries to stimulate the over-all program. They also find a special challenge in selecting and purchasing paperback books on sale in each library. In fact, the school library is beginning to be the center of our reading program.

By no means is our reading program a perfect one. It still has much ground to cover. As the program progresses from year to year, improvements and necessary changes will have to be made. Methods and procedures will have to be adjusted; new materials and equipment will have to be added; and new teachers will have to be trained. All of these modifications, and probably many others, will be made with a sole purpose in mind — that of meeting the individual needs of our students.

The Reading Laboratory *

RALPH P. SHERLOCK

The Reading Laboratory in the secondary school of today is not an innovation. It exists in many schools. A comprehensive high school which does not contain a reading laboratory is, in all likelihood, ignoring the needs of a certain segment of its student body. It is forfeiting the opportunity to increase pupil reading proficiency and thereby decreasing the efficiency of the entire instructional program. Secondary pupils will show an average growth rate of two years in a properly functioning reading laboratory in a semester of instruction, provided they are two or more years retarded in reading.

The function of the Reading Laboratory is simple: to improve the reading comprehension and speed of the pupil in need of such instruction. The effective use of the Reading Laboratory revolves around six instructional activities: (1) identifying, (2) diagnosing, (3) motivating, (4) teaching, (5) stimulating, and (6) evaluating. Grouping for instruction may be refined to the extent possible in each school with remedial, corrective, developmental, advanced, and other levels being offered depending upon school size, resources, and interest, but the pattern of instruction will not vary appreciably.

In order to ascertain the group or groups in need of reading instruction, formal and informal procedures may be used, the latter always supplemented by the former. Where professional persons informally refer pupils for reading instruction this should be followed by a test or reference to a past test to corroborate the judgment and to place the youngster at a definite point in reading skill development. *It is necessary to know the present level of reading comprehension and speed of each pupil.* Until it is known further activity is likely to be fruitless. At this stage, a standardized test will suffice, assuming that a decision on a breaking point has been made.

Once identification is completed, pupils are scheduled to the Reading Laboratory. Testing then becomes more sophisticated. *It is necessary to ascertain the specific areas of weakness which account for retardation of each*

*Reprinted from *Journal of Secondary Education,* 38 (October, 1963), pp. 19-21, by permission of the author and the California Association of Secondary School Administrators.

pupil, or which, if eliminated, will further increase reading skill. The choice of diagnostic tests is important, of course. They should include a number of sub-test scores in order to produce a maximum of information on pupil reading-ability characteristics. Inventories, questionnaires, and check-lists should be devised to be filled out by both pupils and parents in order to provide full information to the teacher.

Diagnosis of a given group of pupils will provide the skeletal outline for the planning of the specific program. It will point toward the kinds of weaknesses that must be attacked and the best materials to use. Effort should be made to identify levels of performance in the following areas: (1) vocabulary, word knowledge (2) understanding literal meaning and following directions, (3) understanding central thought and drawing inferences, and (4) judging the purpose of the author. An indication of reading rate, or speed, should be sought.

Diagnosis, properly handled, will provide the stepping-stone to interest-building. Since so many pupils encountered in the Reading Laboratory cannot read more proficiently simply because they do not read, creating interest in any way possible is essential. *It is necessary to kindle in each pupil a desire to improve, to help him to see the social and individual importance of reading proficiency.*

This is possible in a number of ways. His interest will revolve around something he knows something about. His knowledge-area, his awareness, will have to be identified. Enlisting the pupil's participation in keeping daily records of reading attempted, and of reading accomplishments, will give him a sense of responsibility. Allowing him to work out self-study lists and to maintain these will provide desirable habit patterns.

Open discussion of reading patterns of people helps to motivate youngsters. Pointing out such poor reading habits as lipmoving, plodding, use of fingers as guides, swinging the head instead of the eyes, daydreaming, repeating words and phrases will help pupils along the path toward selfanalysis. Too, the use of current crises may send pupils in search of information. Reading aloud to the class in the initial stages of instruction will reach some pupils.

Machines are valuable motivating devices beyond the function of providing practice in eye-movement skill or phrase recognition. They grasp the attention of most pupils immediately, and, if employed judiciously, will assist in maintaining interest.

It is probably true, as it maintained, that every teacher of reading should be a "diagnostic" teacher, not inclined toward the "cookbook" method. However, a certain structure has a place in the Reading Laboratory. *It is necessary that day-by-day reference plans be available for the group with equally structured plans for sub-groups and for individuals so that pupil deficiencies may be attacked directly with suitable procedures and materials.* Teaching begins, therefore, with the accumulation of the variety of materials needed to equip a laboratory and the parallel planning of a program designed to remedy individual weaknesses and to strengthen individual interests. Once related to the deficiency of a youngster, a specific plan, containing a series of obligations for the pupil to assume, provides an individual objective as well as a group objective, and sets the course for growth.

Step-by-step guidance by the teacher will be required for many individuals. Check lists should be maintained; analytic listening by the pupil to his oral reading habits should take place; word games may be appropriate. Included in plans should be instruction in the use of the table of contents, the index, the dictionary, reading a graph and a table, and similar skills.

Materials must be provided which will allow each pupil to progress from his present level of reading ability to the level of his capability. Individual reading is a very important activity of the Reading Laboratory program, and through the provision of a wide range of books, selected with both reading level and reading interest in mind, students may be expected to read some each day and to keep a record of the amount of daily reading.

Enthusiasm on the part of the pupil, once gained, should not be allowed to decrease. *It is necessary to encourage each pupil constantly, to buttress the desire to learn and to reinforce awareness of the need for reading skills.*

Self-evaluation, to maintain pupil interest in the rate at which he is progressing will help. Pupil-teacher conferences to discuss progress, to probe changing interests, will assist in retaining enthusiasm if the teacher is enthusiastic. Flexibility in the program, for a pupil whose interest appears to be lagging, is appropriate. Throughout the course of instruction, attractively arranged bulletin boards, book displays, and chalk-board designs will make reading seem worthwhile to a pupil.

A plan to assess growth is essential in the Reading Laboratory program. Both pupil and teacher performance will be on a higher level if such a formalized plan exists. *It is necessary to ascertain amount and rate of growth and to modify future instructional patterns through elimination of least fruitful methods, techniques, and materials, and increased attention to the most fruitful ones.* Follow-up tests should include a number of sub-test scores in the same reading-ability areas tested before instruction began. Follow-up inventories, questionnaires, and check lists should be circulated to pupils and parents to ascertain changes in attitudes and habits.

Continuous evaluation throughout the period of instruction will suggest certain re-grouping arrangements to the teacher and the necessity for review and reteaching of certain skills.

A reading laboratory may be a simple classroom well-equipped with teaching aids and materials. It may be a more elaborate arrangement of booths, group centers and common class area, together with auxiliary rooms for special purposes. Whatever the physical arrangement, it will be a reading skills improvement center if staffed with a competent, enthusiastic teacher.

To recapitulate: effective use of the Reading Laboratory involves identifying the student. This means testing. It involves diagnosing the student's problem. This means more testing, accumulating coroborative evidence, and delving into both pupil and parent attitudes and home environment. It includes motivation, the provision of bulletin-board materials, attractive curiosity-creating displays, films, film-strips, and the use of machines. Its nucleus is teaching, and this means relating *specific materials to specific pupils, constant appraisal of progress, grouping and re-grouping around specific deficiency-areas, self-learning and group-learning.* The pupil must be provided the opportunity to read materials of interest to him which are within the range of his ability. It includes stimulating, establishing and empathic relationship with each pupil, constantly holding up the objective in front of the group, exhorting, cajoling, searching for new materials, praising. It concludes with evaluation. This means more testing, ascertaining attitude changes, checking on library usage, and making graphs of individual and group change over a period of time. If these steps are followed by a proficient professional person, pupil reading skills will grow.

Questions for Discussion

1.   Besides those discussed in the previous articles, what other strategies would be appropriate to use to convince a staff of the need for their school to provide reading instruction for all its students?
2.   What strengths and weaknesses do you see in the reading programs described by U. Berkley Ellis, Sally Berkey, and Irwin Fields?

The Nature of Reading

III

Much of the current controversy over which methods or approaches are most effective in the teaching of reading can be demonstrated to be, in part, a controversy over the very nature of the reading process. Alternative instructional programs are now available which exemplify quite different views of this process.

The editors of this volume feel that those interested in the teaching of reading at the secondary school level should have a clear understanding of the various points of view regarding the nature of reading. Such people should also be knowledgeable concerning current research efforts designed to increase our understanding of the reading process.

By becoming acquainted with these views, teachers can begin to formulate their own definitions of reading and will then be better able to plan an instructional program in keeping with these definitions. As has been pointed out before in the professional literature, one's view of the process should be a major factor in determining how one then teaches reading.

In the first article in this section, Wiener and Cromer present a penetrating logical analysis of various concepts of reading and reading difficulties. The writers first identify four important issues which they feel are at the heart of the confusion and ambiguity over defining the reading act. Various definitions selected from the literature are then examined in light of these four issues.

In the second half of the article, Wiener and Cromer conduct a detailed analysis of the term *reading difficulty* and its etiology. They identify four assumptions which have been used to explain the term and then they present six causative theory models.

The second article by Eleanor Gibson is included in this section to demonstrate how experimental psychologists are now attempting to help educators gain better insights into the process by which one does learn to read. Gibson presents her ideas on what stages of learning one must go through to develop skill in reading and describes experiments that have been conducted to determine more precisely what is involved in each of the stages.

Reading and Reading Difficulty: A Conceptual Analysis*

MORTON WIENER AND WARD CROMER

In trying to impose some coordinating conceptual framework upon the phenomena subsumed under reading and reading difficulty, we believe with T. L. Harris (1962) that "the real issues arise from different conceptions of the nature of the reading process itself and of the learning processes, sets and principles to be stressed" (p.5.). In the present paper we will specify and discuss a number of issues which we believe must be considered to develop a more adequate conceptual framework. The issues are derived from an analysis of the diversity of definitions of reading and the variety of explanations offered to account for reading difficulty. Once the issues are clearly defined, a coordinating framework may be possible. We will spell out what we think to be one such conceptualization of reading and reading difficulty.

An Analysis of Reading Definitions

Four interrelated issues emerge from an examination of the many definitions of reading. Discussion of these issues may help clarify some of the present ambiguity and confusion about reading.

IDENTIFICATION VERSUS COMPREHENSION

The first issue is, what behaviors define reading? Some definitions focus primarily on the identification of the stimulus configurations (letters, letter patterns, words, clauses, sentences) appearing on the printed page, while others emphasize the comprehension of the material. When identification skills are emphasized, the defining attribute of reading is the correct "saying" of the word. Comprehension, on the other hand, implies the derivation of some form of meaning and the relating of this meaning to other experiences or ideas.

*Reprinted from *Harvard Educational Review,* 37 (Fall, 1967), pp. 620-643, by permission of the authors and the editors. Copyright, (c) 1954 by President and Fellows of Harvard College.

The assessment of identification is restricted to some evaluation of what and how words are "said." (How the word is to be pronounced and the variability permitted are both based on some implicit consensus.) Comprehension, on the other hand, is assessed by such criteria as the ability of the reader to paraphrase, to abstract the contents, to answer questions about the material, or to deal critically with the contents. Comprehension can also be inferred partly from the relative quality of identifications, i.e., by the tone, inflection, and phrasing of the identifications. However, the inability to demonstrate comprehension in any of these ways may be a function of restricted language, restricted experience, limited intelligence, or combinations of these three, rather than a function of a reading difficulty. If comprehension is used as the criterial behavior of reading, then these other possible antecedents of noncomprehension must be ruled out before the problem can be called a "reading difficulty."

When both kinds of behaviors are included in definitions of reading, the question arises whether these are solely a matter of emphasis on two parts of one process, or whether different activities are implied? At first glance, it would appear that these differences are matters of emphasis only. For those holding a single process view, identification can be considered a necessary antecedent to comprehension. Closer examination of the relationships between identification and comprehension shows, however, that rather than this one relationship, several are possible.

Although both identification and comprehension require some discrimination process (i.e., to identify or comprehend the reader must be able to distinguish among words), comprehension and identification do not necessarily imply each other. One example of the occurrence of identification without comprehension is the child who may be able to read (i.e., "say") the words printed in a scientific journal with some facility without having any notion of the meaning of the words. Another example is an American or a Frenchman who, with only a limited amount of training, can pronounce most words in Italian (a language which has a high relationship between spelling and sound), without knowing the meanings of the words. Whether these instances are considered reading depends upon the definition. We recognize that there may be differences between the saying aloud of material by individuals who do not comprehend and by those who do. Comprehension can sometimes be inferred from inflections, tone, and pauses, all of which may be derived from the context of the material read rather than from the sentence construction. These differences, when present, are often both subtle and difficult to denote reliably.

The occurrence of comprehension without identification, on the other hand, is less evident and examples are somewhat more difficult to cite. The best single example is given by Geschwind (1962) in his work with aphasics. He finds that some aphasic patients are able to respond appropriately to the meaning of a written communication, but apparently are unable to identify the words, i.e., to say them. As we understand it, some aphasics may be able to follow printed instructions without being able to "say" them aloud. A more subtle example can be found in "speed reading" which appears to exemplify nonidentification in that the very speed required makes identification unlikely. To acquire speed reading the individual must learn to eliminate persisting identification patterns. We hold, first, that the behavior occurring in speed reading is similar to that of more typical fast readers and, second, that in the advanced stages of reading, the presence of certain identification activities may interfere with the speed of reading and may result in less than maximum comprehension. Once reading skills have been acquired, reading may go from the discrimination of stimuli directly to comprehension without concomitant identification. Further, in good readers identification occurs primarily for novel or difficult material where there is an attempt to achieve some auditory or other discriminations which can be the basis for comprehension[1] (e.g., by sounding out an unfamiliar word).

ACQUISITION VERSUS ACCOMPLISHED READING

A second issue emerging from comparisons of definitions of reading is, does reading refer to the behavior occurring during acquisition of skills or to the behavior manifested after these "skills" have been achieved? Investigators who define reading in terms of accomplished reading often imply that certain other skills are present without spelling them out. Those who emphasize the acquisition of reading give definitions which focus on the skills that need to be mastered, often without stating what constitutes the end-product.[2]

Definitions of reading generally associate acquisition with identification behavior on the one hand, and comprehension with accomplished reading on the other. An emphasis on problems associated with the acquisition of skills most often implies a focus on identification skills, while a focus on accomplished reading often implies a stress on comprehension activities.

The failure to distinguish between acquisition and accomplished reading in definitions partially accounts for the confusion about the *relationship* between identification and comprehension. In the acquisition of reading skills, identification may be a necessary *antecedent* to comprehension (as we will discuss in more detail below, word meanings are typically available to the child primarily in auditory form). But identification, which is essential in the

---

[1]We will attempt later to make a distinction between visual and auditory comprehension as components in the acquisition of reading.

[2]The research literature on reading difficulties reflects these same differences in emphasis. Some researchers focus on difficulties that can be considered as problems of acquisition, e.g., difficulty with word recognition or phonetics, etc. (Budoff, 1964; Elkind, 1965; Goens, 1958; Robeck, 1963; Goetzinger, 1960; Marchbanks; 1965). Others focus on difficulties that occur after acquisition is relatively complete, e.g., advancement of comprehension skills, critical reading, or enchancement of experiences (Robinson, 1965; Woestehoff, 1960; Chapman, 1965; Emans, 1965; Gray, 1960).

acquisition phase for comprehension, may be irrelevant for the skilled reader who already has meaning associated with the visual forms and who may go directly from the written forms to the meaning without identification: that is, without an intermediary "verbal-auditory" transformation. Put another way, although some form of identification (saying a word either aloud or subvocally) may be essential for comprehension during acquisition, its nonoccurrence is not a problem for an experienced reader. Thus, the final product of reading need not include components that went into its acquisition. To draw an analogy, many of the components that go into the acquisition of good driving skill disappear as the driver becomes more proficient. In early learning there is much more cognitive behavior associated with the sensory-motor behavior, while in the later phases operating a car is almost totally sensory-motor.

RELATIVE VERSUS ABSOLUTE CRITERIA

Another source of ambiguity for conceptualizing reading is the different implicit criteria used for designating "good" reading. Sometimes, reading skill (and reading difficulty) is defined in terms of absolute or ideal criteria, but more often in terms of relative criteria. Both approaches present problems. When absolute or ideal criteria are used, a good reader is typically specified as someone able to read a certain number of words at a given rate with some particular level of comprehension. Insofar as ideal criteria are arbitrary, standards can be designated which include differing proportions of the reading population. Using absolute criteria, children during the acquisition of reading skill would not be considered good readers.

A relative definition of reading skill invokes criteria which specify, either implicitly, or explicitly, some normative group. The implication of a relative criterion is that the same kind or level of skill may be called "good or bad reading" depending on who is doing what and when. For example, a second-grade child who has difficulties in phonetic skills (such as blending of sounds into words, which may be a necessary precursor of auditory comprehension) is not considered a reading problem when relative criteria are used, while a child in the sixth grade who lacks this skill is labeled as having a reading difficulty. In both instances, the same skill is missing. In this context, a sixth-grader may be defined as a poor reader, yet a third-grader behaving the same way (as far as we can determine) might be considered a good reader. It becomes evident that very little information can be communicated by statements about good or poor readers unless they are accompanied by clear specifications of the normative group's behaviors. Further, unless the relative criteria are made explicit, there can be no basis for comparing two "poor readers" since they might have been defined as such by different criteria.

The most important problem raised by a relative point of view is that very different behaviors may be given the same label. Having been given the same label, these different behaviors may later be treated as if they were the same phenomenon. The reading-research literature gives evidence that this danger is real in that poor reading is used as a generic term, apparently without the recognition that different investigators may be talking about very different forms of behaviors.

Research approaches and inferences are influenced by whether a relative or an absolute point of view is assumed. These different viewpoints implicitly specify the groups to be studied (those who are taken to be poor readers) and, more importantly, what is considered to be the appropriate control group for the study (the normative baseline against which the experimental group is to be compared). If the criteria are not made explicit, inappropriate control groups may often be established. For example, if a third-grader with an IQ of 75 is compared with other third-graders, he may be defined as a poor reader. Yet if he is compared with other children with IQ's of 75 in the third grade, he may be labeled a good reader by some relative criterion. In the former case, what is at issue may be relevant to intelligence, not to reading.

It may be more useful to specify the "ideal" case of reading and what its components or essential behaviors are. Having spelled out the ideal case, different people can be compared in terms of the presence or absence of these specifications, independent of distinctions between a person learning to read and an accomplished reader, and independent of evaluative statements as to how "good" the reading is.

READING VERSUS LANGUAGE SKILLS

Investigators vary in the extent to which they emphasize the role of already present auditory language (i.e., knowledge of word meaning and the availability of grammatical forms) either as a separate skill or as one included in reading. There may be little or no concern with previously acquired auditory language capabilities when reading is considered as identification. When reading is considered as comprehension, some investigators (Fries, 1962; Lefevre, 1964; Bloomfield, 1961) deal explicitly with the role of language in reading. The majority of research is less explicit, even though comprehension implies the utilization of meanings already available in some other (usually auditory) form. In studying reading difficulty, Milner (1951) explicitly notes the differential experience with verbal language skills in children from middle and lower socioeconomic backgrounds and its relationship to reading skill. Bereiter and Engelmann (1966) also consider this issue a major one as evidenced by their attempt to train culturally deprived children in language skills before introducing reading. A failure to be explicit about the relationship between reading and previously acquired auditory language often leads to ambiguities as to whether a particular difficulty is a reading problem, language problem, or both.

Examination of Specific Definitions

Having noted some issues, we can now examine specific definitions[3] of reading in order to demonstrate their varying degrees of emphasis on: (a) discrimination, identification, and comprehension; (b) acquisition versus the final product of accomplished reading; (c) absolute versus relative criteria for good reading; and (d) the relation of language skills to reading skills.

The first definition reveals an emphasis on the acquisition of reading skills without specification of the attributes of an accomplished reader. More particularly, it focuses on the development of identification processes with comprehension skills noted only incidentally:

> There are several ways of characterizing the behavior we call reading. It is receiving communication; it is making discriminative responses to graphic symbols; it is decoding graphic symbols to speech; and it is getting meaning from the printed page. A child in the early stages of acquiring reading skill may not be doing all these things; however, some aspects of reading must be mastered before others and have an essential function in a sequence of development of the final skill. The average child, when he begins learning to read, has already mastered to a marvelous extent the art of communication. He can speak and understand his own language in a fairly complex way, employing units of language organized in a hierarchy and with a grammatical structure. Since a writing system must correspond to the spoken one, and since speech is prior to writing, the framework and unit structure of speech will determine more or less the structure of the writing system, though the rules of correspondence vary for different languages and writing systems. . . .
>
> Once a child begins his progression from spoken language to written language, there are, I think, three phases of learning to be considered. They present three different kinds of learning tasks, and they are roughly sequential, though there must be considerable overlapping. These three phases are: learning to differentiate graphic symbols; learning to decode letters to sounds ("map" the letters into sounds); and using progressively higher-order units of structure. (Gibson, 1965, pp. 1-2)

In that the above definition focuses on acquisition, we can infer that a relative scale would be used for designating individuals who are not progressing adequately. What is most noteworthy is that there is also some ambiguity in this definition as to whether the development of language skills is part of reading or prior to and/or independent of reading.

In contrast to Gibson, Geschwind (1962, p. 116) working with aphasics,

---

[3] The particular definitions offered here are not meant to be exhaustive but were chosen primarily because they appear to exemplify the different emphases with which we are concerned.

offers a definition which focuses only on the accomplished reader and comprehension and which makes no reference to identification behaviors or processes in acquisition of reading:

> The word *read* is used in the narrow sense of "ability to comprehend language presented visually" and not at all in the sense of "ability to read aloud."

By this definition, any reading without comprehension would be designated either as non-reading or as a reading problem, though it does not require "saying" for "reading" to occur. The definition makes no reference to the role of discrimination of the printed stimuli, which we assume must occur in order for comprehension to take place. Further, no explicit statement is made about either the relative or the absolute amount of comprehension which must be present for an individual to be designated a good or poor reader.

The following definition is ambiguous about the relationship of identification to comprehension:

> ... reading involves... the recognition of printed or written symbols which serve as stimuli for the recall of meanings built up through the reader's part experience. New meanings are derived through manipulation of concepts already in his possession. The organization of these meanings is governed by the clearly defined purposes of the reader. In short, the reading process involves both the acquisition of the meanings intended by the writer and the reader's own contributions in the form of interpretation, evaluation, and reflection about these meanings. (Bond & Tinker, 1957, p. 19)

The word "recognition," as used here can be taken to mean either discrimination or identification; both usages are incidental to the role of comprehension. Further, this definition refers almost exclusively to the activities of the accomplished reader without apparent concern for the activities necessary for acquiring reading skills (other than the acquisition of meaning). By this definition, most children could be designated as having reading difficulties in that they have not yet acquired the "recognitions" nor the "meanings intended by the writer." This definition also makes little distinction between reading and language skills, thereby making it possible to confuse a language deficiency with a reading difficulty.

In contrast, the next definition makes an explicit distinction between language usage and reading.

> The first stage in learning the reading process is the "transfer" stage. It is the period during which the child is learning to transfer from the auditory signs for language signals, which he has already learned, to a set

of visual signs for the same signals. This process of transfer is not the learning of the language code or a new language code; it is not the learning of a new or different set of language signals. It is not the learning of a new "word," or of new grammatical structures, or of new meanings. These are all matters of the language signals which he has on the whole already learned so well that he is not conscious of their use. This first stage is complete when within his narrow linguistic experience the child can respond rapidly and accurately to the visual patterns that represent the language signals in this limited field, as he does to the auditory patterns that they replace.

The second stage covers the period during which the responses to the visual patterns become habits so automatic that the graphic shapes themselves sink below the threshold of attention, and the cumulative comprehension of the meanings signalled enables the reader to supply those portions of the signals which are not in graphic representation themselves.

The third stage begins when the reading process itself is so automatic that the reading is used equally with or even more than live language in the acquiring and developing of experience – when reading stimulates the vivid imaginative realization of vicarious experience. (Fries, 1962, p. 132)

This definition is also more explicit than most in distinguishing between acquisition and the accomplished reader, the relation of identification to comprehension, and the difference between language skills and reading skills. It does not, however, specify the forms of behaviors which would constitute reading difficulty, except those skills necessary for adequate "transfer" to occur.

The next definition focuses on the sequential development of reading from identification to comprehension. It does not make explicit the role identification plays in the skills which develop later. It also exemplifies the relativity of definitions of reading when it states that what constitutes reading skill depends upon the level of the learner as he progresses from acquisition to accomplished reading.

We may define reading as the act of responding appropriately to printed symbols. For the beginner, reading is largely concerned with learning to recognize the symbols which represent spoken words. As proficiency in reading increases, the individual learns to adapt and vary his method of reading in accordance with his purpose for reading and the restrictions imposed by the nature of the material. As the learner achieves skill in the recognition side of reading, the reasoning side of reading becomes increasingly important. The nature of the reading task, therefore, changes as the learner progresses from less mature to more mature levels; reading is not one skill, but a large number of interrelated skills which develop gradually over a period of many years. (Harris, A. J., 1948, p. 9)

These examples should make evident the diversity of emphases, the ambiguity and confusion in definitions of reading. Further, this discussion has shown that investigators, with few exceptions (e.g., Fries), have not made distinctions between reading activities and language activities, or if so, they have been ambiguous as to the independence or interdependence of language and reading. All definitions that focus on meaning or comprehension imply language as an antecedent, but do not necessarily offer a basis for identifying poor reading as a reading difficulty rather than as a language difficulty.

An Analysis of Reading Difficulty

The issues raised thus far have been related to different usages of the term "reading." Other issues emerge when the term "reading difficulty" is examined. An analysis of the usages of the terms "reading difficulty" indicates that four different assumptions are used to account for reading difficulty and its etiology. Each of the four models implies particular kinds of remediation.

THE ASSUMPTION OF DEFECT

Investigators who hold that reading difficulty is attributable to some malfunction, i.e., something is not operating appropriately in the person so that he *cannot* benefit from his experiences, exemplify what we call a defect model. This approach generally implies that this impairment is considered to be relatively permanent. Defect explanations typically involve sensory-physiological factors. For example, Reitan (1964) discusses "reading impairment... and its relationship to damage of the left cerebral hemisphere" (p. 104). Some investigators appear to assume a defect whenever there is a reading difficulty. We hold that while an assumption of defect may be appropriate for some instances (e.g., cases of visual, hearing or other sensory impairment) there is no evidence that an assumption of defect accounts for all reading difficulties. Further, investigators holding a defect view often do not distinguish between the implications of a defect during acquisition of reading skill and after acquisition has taken place (e.g., blindness, brain damage). This type of explanation also implies that for "normal" reading to occur in individuals with a defect, change must occur (e.g., brain surgery) relatively independent of reading, or a different sequence in the acquisition must be utilized (e.g., teaching a blind person to read through the use of the tactual modality).

THE ASSUMPTION OF DEFICIENCY

Other investigators have argued that reading difficulty is attributable to the *absence* of some function, i.e., a particular factor or process is absent and must be *added* before adequate reading can occur. Most attempts at remedial reading instruction are based on this interpretation of reading difficulties. The child must learn something he has not yet learned (e.g., phonetic skills, language skills, etc.) in order to make up his deficiency. In contrast to the defect explanation of reading difficulty, reversibility is almost always assumed.

THE ASSUMPTION OF DISRUPTION

A third type of model used to account for reading difficulty assumes that the difficulty is attributable to something which is *present* but is *interfering* with reading and must be *removed* before reading will occur. For example, if a child is "anxious," "hyperemotional," or has "interpsychic conflicts," he may be unable to learn to read (cf, Koff, 1961). An assumption of disruption is implicit in investigations of so-called neurotic learning disabilities. It is also implicit in any approach which maintains that using the wrong methods to teach reading will disrupt and interfere with the learning that takes place when the correct teaching method is used. Occasionally the assumption of disruption operates jointly with the deficiency assumption, the notion being that first the interference must be removed and then the missing components must be added.

THE ASSUMPTION OF DIFFERENCE

Lastly, various researchers assume that reading difficulty is attributable to *differences* or mismatches between the typical mode of responding and that which is more appropriate, and thus has the best payoff in a particular situation. This model assumes that the individual would read adequately if the material were consistent with his behavior patterns; thus, a *change* in either the material or in his patterns of verbalization is a prerequisite for better reading.

Cromer and Wiener (1966) posit that poor readers have evolved different response patterns; i.e., they elaborate "cues" in a manner different from that of good readers. Within their framework, both good and poor readers "scan" and derive partial information from the printed stimuli; the specific difference between the good and poor readers is that poor readers generally elaborate these cues by responding more idiosyncratically than do good readers, either because they have not learned consensual response patterns or because they have learned idiosyncratic patterns too well. In this framework, reading difficulty is expected to occur when there is a mismatch between the material being read and the response patterns of the reader.

An example of a mismatch is when auditorally-and visually-presented languages are discrepant, as might be the case for a lower-class child who speaks a neighborhood "slang." The child may not be able to elaborate the cues in "formal language patterns." He does not read well because he does not draw from the same language experiences as does the middle-class child for whom a typical reading test is written; there is a mismatch between the reading material and his typical pattern of responding. If, however, the material were presented in the same form as his spoken language, we posit that he would then be able to read more adequately. This child would not be considered a reading problem but rather a language problem in that he does not draw from the same language experiences as the middle-class child for whom a typical reading text is written.

Still another example of a mismatch involves the reading of highly technical material. An individual may have difficulty because he (in contrast to an expert in the same area) has sequences which are less likely to match the reading input. A psychologist reading a physics book or a physicist reading a psychology book would be slowed down, would show more errors in his reading, and would have less comprehension than when each reads in his own field. In this instance, there are differences in reading abilities, depending on the material being read. It does not seem meaningful, however, to consider these differences in skill as reading problems. Thus no pathology is posited for a "reading difficulty" stemming from a mismatch.

Associated with each of the assumption models are implicit differences in the kinds of factors-sensory-perceptual (physiological), experiential-learning and personality-emotional (psychological)-assumed to account for reading difficulty. Pointing to physiological factors generally implies a defect; i.e., the individual has not learned a particular skill or has learned a different one. On the other hand, explanations that focus on psychological factors imply a disruption and/or a deficiency. In sum, not only are there different assumptions to account for reading difficulty but in addition, each assumption model implies a particular set of operative factors and a particular form of intervention or remediation.

Models for Conceptualizing Reading Difficulty: Antecedent-Consequent Relationships

Another source of confusion in the literature is the form of explanation offered to account for "reading problems." Some investigators refer to single "causes" of reading difficulty while others state that multiple "causes" need to be invoked. Applying a formal or logical analysis to these kinds of explanatory statements reveals additional conceptual problems. This task can be facilitated by reformulating and extending a model developed by Handlon (1960) to spell out possible forms for explaining schizophrenia.[4] We have substituted the term "reading difficulty" where in Handlon's original application the term schizophrenia appears. We will try to "explain" reading difficulties by relating the variables associated with reading (antecedents) to the variables associated with reading difficulties (consequents).

---

[4]Handlon, in his model called. Single-Multiple Causal Factors uses the terms "cause" and "effect"; with our philosophical bias we prefer the terms "antecedent" and "consequent." These terms will be used here in a conditional ("If, then") rather than a causal form. The conditional statement is not meant to imply either a spatial or temporal relationship, but a relationship in a formal-logical sense. We thank Dr. Roger Bibace who brought this article to our attention.

1. *Model One* (in Handlon's form of explanation) states that reading difficulty "is a class with a single member, this member having a single radical cause." In our conditional form, Model One is "If A, then X," where A is a single specific antecedent and X is a class ("reading difficulty") in which each instance of a reading difficutly is considered equivalent.

An example of Model One is Carrigan's (1959) synaptic transmission (chemical) theory of reading disability. She maintains that disabled readers are part of a population of slow learners characterized by a typical production of two chemicals, ACh (acetycholine) and ChE (cholinesterase). Although the balance and concentration level of these chemicals is affected by environmental (anxiety producing) factors, it is the chemical factor itself which is seen to underly reading disability, that is, reading disability is presented also as if it were a single member class. Another example of Model One, Delacato's (1959) theory of "central neurological organization," attributes reading difficulty to a lack of cerebral cortical dominance.

Although logically possible, Model One does not seem very promising. Most investigators reject both the notion that a single antecedent accounts for all reading difficulties, and the notion that reading difficulty is in fact a class with only a single member.

2. *Model Two* states that reading difficulty is "a class with a single member, that member having multiple factors constituting the radical cause."[5] In our conditional form, Model Two is "If A or B or C . . . , then X, "where A, B, etc. are particular and independent[6] antecedents, and, as in Model One, X is a class with a single member called "reading difficulty."

Rabinovitch (1959) appears to use a Model Two form of explanation. He defines reading retardation as reading achievement two or more years below the mental age obtained on performance tests and then goes on to list three subclasses of antecedents of reading difficulty (exogenous, i.e., cultural and emotional factors; congenital brain damage; and endogenous, i.e., biological or neurological disturbances). Similarly, Roswell and Natchez (1964) in their treatment of reading disability argue for a multi-causal model and describe a series of antecedents that can "cause" reading difficulty (e.g., intellectual, physical, emotional, environmental, educational, and growth factors). Investigators using this model might *consider* reading difficulty as different for the different "causes," but they do not *specify* nor delineate these differences;

---

[5] We will consider this statement only in the form "If A or B or C, then X" rather than the form "If A and B and C, then X," since the latter is logically reducible to "If A, then X," where A stands for a conjunctive category.

[6] By using the symbols A,B,C,. . .and X_1, X_2, X_3, etc., there is a possible implication that these symbols may be treated as an ordinal series, with the later implying the earlier. In each model except for Model Six (see below), these symbols are used only in the sense of a nominal scale (Stevens, 1951) and could be written in the form "If alpha, then X_{alpha}; if aleph, then X_{aleph}; etc."

that is, they seem to treat reading difficulty as if it were a single member class.

Although this form of explanation may also be logically tenable, we are convinced that the assumption that reading difficulty is a class with a single member is unacceptable. Our belief is that reading difficulty is a multiple-member class and that Model Two forms of statements might better be changed to "If A, then X_1; "If B, then X_2"; "If C, then X_3" where X_1, X_2, X_3 are particular and independent manifestations within the class reading difficulty (Model Five, See below). We maintain that if an investigator looks carefully enough, he will find different members within the class X which might better meet the criteria of a class with a single member associated with a particular antecedent, and that it is incumbent on investigators to explore their "single consequent" in a multiple-antecedent/single-consequent model to determine whether the consequent is in fact a class with only a single member.

3. *Model Three* states that reading difficulty "is a class with several members, all members having the same single. . . cause." This statement can be represented in the following form: "If A, then X_1 or X_2 or X_3 . . . " where A is a particular antecedent and X_1, X_2, etc. are particular members of the class called "reading difficulty." To the extent that investigators have not labeled the specific forms of reading difficulty (that is, different members of the class reading difficulty), then they would be unlikely to apply a model using a single antecedent and multiple consequents. In fact, no appropriate examples of Model Three were located in the literature. Those that appeared at first to be examples of Model Three were found to be more appropriately assigned to Model One, which treats the consequent as a single-member class.

4. *Model Four* states that reading difficulty "is a class with several members, each having single or multiple causes that are not necessarily unique to that member." In other words, there are many antecedent variables and many manifestations of reading difficulty (consequents) and the relationships between these antecedents and consequents are unspecified or unspecifiable. This model can be represented in the form: "If A and/or B and/or C. . . , then X_1, or X_2, or X_3 . . . "

This form of explanation appears to be most popular in the current literature; for examples one can turn to almost any comprehensive book on the "diagnostic teaching of reading." (e.g., Strang, 1964; Bond and Tinker, 1957; Bryant, 1963). These textbook approaches list all the possible "causes" of reading difficulty and then discuss techniques for remedial instruction. The relationships between the many antecedents and the many consequents are never clearly specified. The problems inherent in this approach are exemplified most clearly in a study reported by Goltz (1966). Working with "individual remedial reading for boys in trouble," he advocates the simultaneous use of five basic approaches to the teaching of reading (sight word, phonics, combination, linguistic, experiential) in the hope that one will work (he draws the analogy of shotgun pellets). The results of this approach were "some astounding successes and remarkable failures." The need for a theoretical rationale for relating possible difficulties and specific types of intervention is obvious. Again, we argue that it is incumbent on investigators to attempt to locate the particular antecedent and its relationship to a particular consequent.

5. *Model Five* appears to be the most acceptable form for explaining the phenomenon called reading difficulty. It states that reading difficulty is "a class with several members, each member having a single, unique cause." This statement can be represented in the form: "If A, then X_1; or if B, then X_2; or if C, then X_3..." where the X's represent different particular patterns of less-than-ideal reading. This model says that there are many antecedent variables and many manifestations under a general rubric "reading difficulty"; and the relationships between the antecedents and the consequents are, at least in theory, specifiable. Both Model Five and Model Four have multiple antecedents and multiple consequents. Model Five, however, associates a different antecedent with a specific consequent. For example, de Hirsch (1963) attempts to distinguish between two groups of adolescents with language disorders by suggesting that the etiology of each is different. Kinsbourne and Warrington (1963) note that two syndromes of developmental cerebral deficit seem to be associated with different forms of reading difficulty.

6. Model Five assumes that each of the manifestations of reading difficulty (i.e., the X's) is a member of the general class called reading difficulty and that each of these forms is independent. It may be, however, more meaningful to conceptualize the manifestations within the class, reading difficulty, in a model which includes a notion of sequence. This kind of model is not considered by Handlon; we will elaborate it as *Model Six*. This model can be represented in the following form: "If A, then X_1" and "If X_1, then B" and "If B, then X_2" and "If X_2, then C" and "If C, then $X_3 \ldots X_n$." If, for example, C does not occur nor does X_3, then X_n, the particular form of behavior defined as reading, would not be expected to develop (X_n being defined as a class with a single member, a particular form of reading which is the end-product of the sequence and can be considered as an indicator on an absolute scale). Model Six explicitly includes the notion of an ordinal series and implies that if any member of the sequence were missing, further evolution of the sequence would not be expected, or at least not in the acquisition phase of learning to read. If the sequence has already evolved and there is a disruption, then depending on the point in the sequence where disruption occurs, later forms of reading may be present, even though some or all earlier forms are absent. This kind of formulation can account for differences in the kinds of reading difficulties noted when a disruption is present during acquisition or occurs in an accomplished reader (e.g., the reading of brain-damaged adults who were previously good readers versus the reading of brain-damaged children during the acquisition phase). Another implication is that the arbitrarily designated end point of a

sequence specifies the antecedents and prior sequences to be included.

A Conceptualization of Reading
and Reading Difficulty

We pointed out earlier that some investigators treat reading as identification while others treat it as comprehension and that this difference has implications for what was defined as reading difficulty. In an effort to integrate these seemingly disparate approaches, reading will be conceptualized and discussed as a two-step process involving first identification and then comprehension. During the discussion, the antecedents for identification will be considered first and then comprehension will be considered.

Identification

Identification will be used to mean "word-naming," in the context of a transformation of stimuli.[7] In the discussion that follows, our formulation comes from an analysis of visual-to-auditory transformation; similar analyses could be derived for other transformations. We assume a physiological substrate which is adequate for "normal" functioning to occur.

"Discrimination" constitutes one set of antecedents to identification. Prior to discrimination, however, a child must attend to the stimulus to make sensory input possible. Given sensory input, the child must then be able to make form discriminations. By discrimination, we mean the ability to make proper focal adjustments; to distinguish figure-ground, brightness, lines, curves, and angles; and to respond to differences in the amount of white space surrounding the forms (this latter discrimination is involved in the delineation of word units). These forms of discrimination are antecedents of identification.

Given the ability to discriminate, the child can begin to identify by

[7]Identification presupposes a discrimination of one graphic symbol from others, discrimination of auditory symbols from others, and a transformation of these symbols from one form (usually visual) to a second form (usually auditory). The original visual forms and the transformed auditory forms are considered to be equivalent, differing only in that the referents are represented in different modalities. The two symbol forms are considered equivalent in that they contain the same information for members of a communication group. Essentially, then, the major critical antecedents of identification are the discriminations among the original symbols, the discriminations among the transformed symbols, and a "knowledge" of the principles of transformation from one form to the other. Implicit in this conceptualization is that the transformed symbols (i.e., words as said aloud) can become an input for another individual. Implied also is that there is some consensual basis to assess the adequacy of the identification, with consensus meaning only that there is agreement within the group using the particular language or dialect.

distinguishing on the basis of angles and curves ("man" from "dog") or word length ("dog" from "good"), by responding to variations in relations among letter sequences ("on" vs. "no"), and by responding to spatial orientations of visual stimuli (left/right and up/down). These antecedents not only make possible new identifications but also make earlier forms of identification easier because the reader can respond to more of the available and co-occurring cues. For example, "dog" and "good" can be discriminated on the basis of word length, and the orientation of the first and last letters.

Using discriminations among sequences and general configurations, the child can now learn to identify a relatively large number of words solely by discriminating the first and last letters in an otherwise similar configuration (e.g., length, round vs. angled, internal letters, etc.). Although this discrimination may be adequate in the early stages of reading acquisition, the child must later learn to discriminate other components in the word such as internal letters ("bat" vs. "but" vs. "bet" vs. "bit"), sequence of letters ("there" vs. "three"), additions of letters ("smile" vs. "simile"), etc. In these cases, to increase speed, it would appear that the child has to learn to respond to the variety of available cues and the order of their importance as the basis of discrimination of words within his language.

Antecedents for the identification of words in isolation are not sufficient for reading words in a sequence such as a phrase or a sentence; the individual must learn to say the words in the order given, although he does not necessarily have to "look" at them in that order. A knowledge of language and language sequences will facilitate the discrimination of words in a sequence insofar as the co-occurrences of words can become an additional basis for discrimination, e.g., "the horse's mane" vs. "the horse's mine."

The antecedents discussed thus far are associated with learning to read using the "look-say" approach, which is essentially how one learns to read an ideographic language. Both this approach and languages requiring its use present special difficulties in that the reader must maintain a great many specific forms in his memory. Although he can discriminate new from old words and even among new words, he has no readily available way of identifying ("saying") the new words. If it were possible for a child to have a source of identifying words the first time he encountered them (e.g., via another person reading it or a speaking typewriter), and if he had the ability to store and recover the words as presented and as said, then the "look-say" method would be sufficient for reading. However, if new or novel words occur and there is no external source for initial identification, then a skill for identifying by oneself is required.

There are at least three different ways in which identification of new words occurs. They can be ordered by degree of explicitness for relating visual to sound forms. First, the individual may respond to some similarities among graphic forms, and he may also respond to some of the patterns of similarity among associated auditory forms. For example, the word "mat" looks like "man" and "hat," such that one approximation of the sound of "mat" could be the combination of the first part of "man" and the last part of "hat." The first sound approximated might not have exactly the same form as if it were emitted in the presence of the object. It could be corrected, however, by the reader's recognizing that the word as said sounds like some other word he had said at some other time.

The second way is like the first in that the reader uses similarities among graphic forms to aid his identification. In the first case, however, this response to similarity is incidental; in the second, it is systematic. An example of a systematic approach is the use of what linguists (such as Fries, 1962) call "spelling patterns." The individual is taught to look for similarities among visual and auditory forms by systematic exposure to various types of possible patterns, their variations, and their associated sounds. For example, if the individual learns to identify the words "man," "ban," "hat," and "fat," he will be able to identify the word "mat." Other examples of spelling patterns are mane/bane/hate/fate; and mean/bean/heat/feat. Thus, the possible similarities among visual forms, among auditory forms, and between visual and auditory forms are made somewhat more explicit by example.

In contrast to these two ways where similarity among graphic configurations is the basis for identifying new configurations, the third way requires the reader to know more explicit rules for transforming specific visual configurations into specific sounds, i.e., phonetics, to use Fries' terminology. For example, there is a "rule" that says when there is only one vowel in a word and it comes at the beginning or middle of a word, it is usually short ("hat," "and," "bed," "end"). These rules also include the notion that various locations and combinations of letters are associated with different sounds. One example is the "rule" that a vowel when followed by an "r" is neither long nor short, but is controlled by the "r"; e.g., "fur," "bird," "term."[8] One major difference between the phonetics approach and the other two is that identification of new words does not require previous experience with similar old words. However, the use of phonetics requires one additional ability, that of ordering letters from the beginning through to the end of a word. This skill, called "scanning," involves systematic eye movements from left to right and an organization of the input in that order.

Knowledge of co-occurrence of letters and words within a language will increase the rate of reading. Because not every word can come at a particular point in a sequence, the individual can identify words or groups of words rapidly even from very brief scanning of the material. Thus, "knowledge" of language of word sequences independent of visual input will reduce the amount of

[8] In this context, ITA (cf., Downing, 1964; Downing 1965) is seen as a procedure for simplifying acquisition; that is, for decreasing the number of "rules" the child must learn during acquisition of reading.

information required from scanning for identification to occur. At later stages, the reader may even be able to skip some of the words in a particular sequence, yet respond adequately with this decreased information. We propose that the ability to respond to this partial information, that is, the "elaboration" of these cues, can be based on learned patterns of sequential occurrences or what has been called "previously learned co-occurrence probabilities" (Kempler and Wiener, 1963). Differences among readers in their ability to identify a sequence correctly may be explained by differences in response availabilities rather than by differences in visual inputs. Since response patterns may be differentially available among individuals, given specific reading materials, a reader may "respond" to the same material with differing degrees of adequacy depending upon the availability of appropriate response patterns, even assuming the "same" input.

Comprehension

If comprehension[9] is now included in the definition of reading, additional antecedents must be considered. In our usage, comprehension refers to the addition of some form of meaning associated with the identifications or discriminations, i.e., the words elicit shared associations, or consensual indicator responses to or about the referent, or a synonymous response. At least during acquisition, comprehension can occur and be examined at any point at which identification can occur; once the visual forms are transformed to auditory forms, there is a possibility of comprehension, given the presence of appropriate language skills. These language skills can be learned either before or along with the acquisition of identification skills. Language can include not only meaning but also those subjects typically dealt with by linguists (patterns, grammar, sequences, meaningful units, and so on). To the extent that these structural components are critical for meaning, these forms must also have been mastered or, alternatively, they must be learned during the acquisition phase.

It has been implied that meaning is available primarily through language as it occurs in the auditory form. We also have assumed implicitly that once there is a transformation from the visual to the auditory form, comprehension would follow. If the reader's auditory transformation (identification) corresponds to his already available auditory language forms, then meaning can be associated with the visual forms. For example, if a child in his identification says the word "ball" in the same way as he has heard it or as he says it in the presence of the referent object, then meaning can be transferred to the visual form. The assumed

---

[9] A concern with the definition of comprehension and meaning would take us too far afield, even if we were competent to deal with this complex problem.

sequence has been: discriminations among input forms and output forms; transformation; identification; comprehension — all of these being required.

In all of the discussion thus far, individual differences have not been considered. Yet recognition of individual differences may be highly relevant in accounting for differences in forms of discrimination, identification, or comprehension. For example, individuals with low intelligence or with restricted language skills or restricted experiences might better be considered as having "problems" in these particular areas rather than in reading *per se*. Similarly, there are other instances of non-reading which might better be attributed to the conditions under which reading occurs, the content of the material being read, or the "motivation" of the individual reader and his interest in the material. In these instances, a reading problem cannot be assessed until learning has been tried under more "ideal" conditions with materials of more significance to the reader.

We can now note some instances: (a) where auditory transformations may not lead to comprehension although the reader ostensibly uses the same language as is used in the printed material; and (b) where comprehension facilitates or even makes possible identification which would not otherwise occur.

A first instance of an identification without comprehension is when the reader has had either insufficient or no previous experience with the referent so that it is not part of his meaning-vocabulary. For example, a story about children playing with a kite may elicit no referent (and no meaning) in an individual in a subculture where no one plays with kites. A second instance of identification without comprehension can occur in individuals who have had experience with the referent, but in circumstances where these referents are typically communicated in nonverbal forms such as gesture or tone. This problem is likely to occur in individuals who use what is sometimes called "expressive language" or nonverbal rather than verbal language. For example, a child could point and say "ball" in a particular tone as a substitute for saying, "I want this ball!" or "May I please have the ball?" or "Give me the ball" (cf. Bereiter and Engelmann, 1966; Bernstein, 1965; Deutsch, 1962). For comprehension to occur in these instances, the individual must be taught to use verbal language or at least to recognize that the "message" he communicates gesturally can also be communicated through words. A third way identification can occur without comprehension is when the sounds of the words as read are different from the sounds of the words as they occur in the reader's vocabulary. For some rural Southern children "y' all" may be the commonly heard and said form of "you." If a reader identifies (says) the word "you," he may not transfer the sound "you" to the meaning of "y' all." Another example is a child from a lower-class background who may not "say" the words in the same way or in the same sequence as his middle-class teacher; and therefore, if he makes his transformations into the teacher's language, comprehension may not occur. A fourth instance of identification without appropriate comprehension is when there is a lack of correspondence between the reader's auditory language and that of the material being read. For example, note how difficult it is to read and comprehend the following passage, which is a description of Harlem.

> On school: "Everyone shouting and screaming and nobody care about what they is going on. But at least it somewhere to stay away from when they make you go." And on the purpose of fighting gangs: "In this bizness you got have a place of your own and a chain of command and all that. Everything go by the book. Then you get a name. And when you get the name maybe you can stay live a while. Thas why most men get in gangs. To stay live. Thas why the gangs form in the first place." (Time Magazine, February 24, 1967, p. 96)

In the third and fourth examples, there is a discrepancy between the language of the material being read and the reader's own language. This discrepancy can be resolved either by "correcting" the reader's language so that it matches the written form or by modifying the written material to correspond to his language patterns. As Labov (1967) notes, however, if the teacher is to locate the source of the difficulty and take appropriate remedial steps, he should "know" the child's nonstandard language. Labov spells out in some detail the possible discrepancies between the disadvantaged students and their teachers in their pronunciations and uses of grammar. He also discusses some of the implications of such discrepancies in the teaching of children who speak a nonstandard dialect.

One further way in which identification can occur without comprehension is when the particular meaning of the graphic material is different from the meaning typically elicited in the individual (e.g., slang, idiomatic expressions, and poetry), all of which depend on less consensual meanings. An example is a foreigner trying to read a popular detective story which uses slang and colloquialisms. Another example would be an accomplished reader reading James Joyce, where the words have highly personalized referents.

On the other hand, comprehension can facilitate identification if the reader has highly advanced language skills available, e.g., vocabulary, sequences, appropriate generating grammar (in Chomsky's, 1957, sense). To the extent that each of these skills facilitates identification by decreasing the range of possibilites of what is likely to occur in the written material, less information is necessary from the visual input to to elicit the whole sequence. Thus, there are a number of ways in which knowledge of language in terms of both meaning and structure may aid identification and even make possible specific identifications which otherwise would not occur. First, the context and meaning of the material already read may generate and/or limit new forms of identification via the individual's understanding and elaboration of the material being read. For example, all other factors being constant, two scientists will differ in the rate and understanding of specific scientific material if they have a different familarity with the subject matter. A second way in which language aids identification is through the structure of the language which limits the possible types of words or sequences which can occur at any given point. Further, comprehension may make possible identifications which otherwise might not occur. A beginning reader who has not learned phonics but who has a good vocabulary and uses language as it typically occurs in written form may be able to "guess" a word he has not previously identified. He can identify the word on the basis of his comprehension of the context, or familiarity with the structure of the language, or both. To exemplify how the structure and context contribute to identification, all one needs to do is to remove words randomly from a story (Cloze technique, Taylor, 1953) and note the limited number and types of word insertions which occur. Third, extensive language experience facilitates speed of reading. Having learned (and being familiar with) possible elaborations, the reader requires fewer cues for a particular response to occur; the assumption here is that the requirement of fewer cues is associated with more rapid scanning, e.g., speed reading of familiar material. Fourth, comprehension facilitates the recognition of errors in reading when there is a mismatch between any of the three possible sources of information mentioned above and the identification as "said." For example, when the word elaborated from the cues is not congruent with later elaborations — it does not fit the content, context, or sequences as previously experienced — the reader will experience the possibility of an error and "check" the input for more cues.

Once reading is defined as comprehension (which we hold can occur only after basic identification and language skills have been mastered), then identification becomes secondary and may eventually be eliminated except for identifying new words. As noted earlier, an individual with good language (meaning and structure) skills can, in the case of speed reading, go directly from the discrimination to the meaning without the intermediate step of (auditory) identification. Typically, readers use identification in "reading" (here "reading" is being defined in terms of comprehension) in the following ways: first, to make the words auditorally overt (i.e., saying the words aloud so they can be understood); second, to make the words covertly auditory (i.e., lip moving); then, implicit identification (i.e., the reader experiences the words as if they were said aloud but there is no evidence of overt saying); and, finally, identification is eliminated when the reader goes directly from the visual configuration — without experiencing the words as auditory forms — to their associated meaning, e.g., speed reading. Theoretically, at least, identification (in contrast to discrimination) is not necessary and, in fact, may not occur in the accomplished reader. It is even possible that a method could be devised for teaching reading (i.e., comprehension) without the intermediate step of auditory identification. If, for example, we could evolve principles for understanding how a child learns his original language — which includes the transformation of the experience of objects into words in auditory form — we might begin to understand how a child might learn to go from an original visual form directly to meaning without an immediate auditory "naming."

We hope this attempt to impose some order on the diversity of phenomena included under reading or reading difficulty will be of heuristic value to other investigators. Recognizing that we have only touched on the complexities of reading behavior, we hope others will bring to bear other coordinating principles to this area of investigation.

References

Bereiter, C. & Engelmann, S. *Teaching Disadvantaged Children in The Preschool.* New York: Prentice-Hall, 1966.

Bernstein, B. A socio-linguistic approach to social learning. In J. Gould (Ed.), *Social Science Survey.* New York: Pelican, 1965.

Bloomfield, L. & Barnhart, C. L. *Let's Read.* Detroit: Wayne State Univer. Press, 1961.

Bond, G. & Tinker, M. *Reading Difficulties: Their Diagnosis and Correction.* New York: Appleton-Century-Crofts, 1957.

Bryant, N. D. Learning disabilities in reading. Mimeo.

Budoff, M & Quinlan, D. readiness as related to efficiency of visual and aural learning in the primary grades. *J. Educ. Psychol.,* 1964, 55 (5), 247-252.

Corrigan, Patricia. Broader implication of a chemical theory of reading disability. Paper presented at Amer. Psychol. Assn. Meeting, 1959.

Chapman, Carita. Meeting current reading needs in adult literacy programs. In H. A. Robinson (Ed.), *Recent Developments In Reading.* Supplementary educ. Monogr., Univer. of Chicago Press, 1965, No. 95.

Chomsky, N. *Syntactic Structures.* The Hague: Mouton & Company, 1957.

Cromer, W. & Wiener, M. Idiosyncratic response patterns among good and poor readers. *J. Consult. Psychol.,* 1966, 30 (1), 1-10.

De Hirsch, Katrina. Two categories of learning difficulties in adolescents. *Amer. J. Orthopsychiat.,* 1963, 33, 87-91.

Delacato, C. H. *The Treatment and Prevention of Reading Problems.* Springfield: Charles C. Thomas, 1959.

Deutsch, M. The disadvantaged child and the learning process: some social, psychological and developmental considerations. Paper prepared for the Ford Foundation "Work Conference on Curriculum and Teaching in Depressed Urban Areas." New York: Columbia Univer., 1962.

Downing, J. A. *The Initial Teaching Alphabet.* New York: Macmillan, 1964.

Downing, J. A. *The i.t.a. Reading Experiment.* Chicago: Scott, Foresman, 1965.

Elkind, D., Larson, Margaret, & Van Doorninck, W. Perceptual decentration learning and performance in slow and average readers. *J. Educ. Psychol.,* 1965, 56 (1).

Emans, R. Meeting current reading needs in grades four through eight. In H. A. Robinson (Ed.), *Recent Developments in Reading.* Suppl. educ. Monogr., Univer. of Chicago Press, 1965, No. 95.

Fries, C. C. *Linguistics and Reading.* New York: Holt, Rinehart, and Winston, 1962.

Geschwind, N. The anatomy of acquired disorders of reading disability. In J. Money (Ed.), *Progress and Research Needs in Dyslexia.* Baltimore: John Hopkins Press, 1962.

Gibson, E. J. Learning to read. *Science,* 1965, *148,* 1066-1072.

Goens, Jean T. *Visual Perceptual Abilities and Early Reading Progress.* Suppl. educ. Monogr., Univer. of Chicago Press, 1958, No. 87.

Goetzinger, C. P., Dirks, D. D., & Baer, C. J. Auditory discrimination and visual perception in good and poor readers. *Annals of Otology, Rhinology, and Laryngology,* March 1960, 121-136.

Goltz, C. Individual remedial reading for boys in trouble. *Reading Teacher, 19* (5).

Gray, W. S. The major aspects of reading. In H. A. Robinson (Ed.), *Recent Developments in Reading.* Suppl. Educ. Monogr, Univer. of Chicago Press, 1965, No. 95.

Handlon, J. A. metatheoretical view of assumptions regarding the etiology of schizophrenia, *AMA Archives of Gen. Psychiat.,* January 1960, 43-60.

Harris, A. J. *How to Increase Reading Ability.* London: Longmans, Green, 1948.

Harris, T. L. Some issues in beginning reading instruction. *J. Educ. Res.,* 1962, 56(1).

Kempler, B. & Wiener, M. Personality and Perception in the recognition threshold paradigm. *Psychol. Rev.,* 1964 70, 349-356.

Kinsbourne, M. & Warrington, E. K. Developmental factors in reading and writing backwardness. *Brit. J. Psychol.,* 1963, 54, 145-156.

Koff, R. H. Panel on: Learning difficulties in childhood. Reported by E. A. Anthony, *J. Amer. Psychiatric Assn.* 1961, 9.

Labov, W. Some sources of reading problems for Negro speakers of nonstandard English. In A. Frazier (Ed.), *New Directions in Elementary English,* Nat. Council of English, 1967.

Lefevre, C. A. *Linguistics and the Teaching of Reading.* New York: McGraw-Hill, 1964

Marchbanks, Gabrielle & Levin, H. Cues by which children recognize words. *J. Educ. Psychol.,* 1965, 56 (2), 57-61.

Milner, Esther. A study of the relationship between reading readiness in grade-one school children and patterns of parent-child interaction. *Child Devel.,* 1951, 22 (2), 95-112.

Rabinovitch, R. D. Reading and Learning Disabilities. In S. Arieti (Ed.), *American Handbook of Psychiatry.* New York: Basic Books, 1959.

Reitan, R. Relationships between neurological and psychological variables and their implications for reading instruction. In H. A. Robinson (Ed.), *Meeting Individual Differences in Reading.* Suppl. educ. Monogr., Univer. of Chicago Press, 1964, No. 94.

Robeck, Mildred. Readers who lacked word analysis skills: a group diagnosis. *J. Educ. Res.,* 1963, 56, 432-434.

Robinson, Helen M. Looking ahead in reading. In H. A. Robinson (Ed.), *Recent Developments in Reading.* Suppl. educ. Monogr. Univer. of Chicago Press, 1965, No. 95.

Roswell, Florence & Natchez, Gladys. *Reading Disability: Diagnosis and Treatment.* New York: Basic Books, 1964.

Strang, Ruth. *Diagnostic Teaching of Reading.* New York: McGraw-Hill, 1964

Stevens, S. S. (Ed.) *Handbook of Experimental Psychology.* New York: John Wiley and Sons, 1951.

Taylor, W. "Cloze procedure": a new tool for measuring readability. *Journ. Quart.,* 1953, 30, 415-433.

Woestehoff, E. Methods and materials for teaching comprehension – in corrective and remedial classes. In Helen Robinson (Ed.), *Sequential Development of Reading Abilities.* Suppl. educ. Monogr., Univer. of Chicago Press, 1960, No. 9.

Learning to Read *

ELEANOR J. GIBSON

Educators and the public have exhibited a keen interest in the teaching of reading ever since free public education became a fact (1).† Either because of or despite their interest, this most important subject has been remarkably susceptible to the influence of fads and fashions and curiously unaffected by disciplined experimental and theoretical psychology. The psychologists have traditionally pursued the study of verbal learning by means of experiments with nonsense syllables and the like – that is, materials carefully divested of useful information. And the educators, who found little in this work that seemed relevant to the classroom, have stayed with the classroom; when they performed experiments, the method was apt to be a gross comparison of classes privileged and unprivileged with respect to the latest fad. The result has been two cultures: the pure scientists in the laboratory, and the practical teachers ignorant of the progress that has been made in the theory of human learning and in methods of studying it.

That this split was unfortunate is clear enough. True, most children do learn to read. But some learn to read badly, so that school systems must provide remedial clinics; and a small proportion (but still a large number of future citizens) remain functional illiterates. The fashions which have led to classroom experiments, such as the "whole word" method, emphasis on context and pictures for "meaning," the "flash" method, "speed reading," revised alphabets, the "return" to "phonics," and so on, have done little to change the situation.

Yet a systematic approach to the understanding of reading skill is possible. The psychologist has only to treat reading as a learning problem, to apply ingenuity in theory construction and experimental design to this fundamental activity on which the rest of man's education depends. A beginning has recently been made in this direction, and it can be expected that a number of theoretical and experimental studies of reading will be forthcoming (2).

*Reprinted from *Science,* 148 (May, 1965), pp. 1066-1072, by permission of the author and the American Association for the Advancement of Science.
†Numbers in parentheses refer to references at end of article.

Analysis of the Reading Process

A prerequisite to good research on reading is a psychological analysis of the reading process. What is it that a skilled reader has learned? Knowing this (or having a pretty good idea of it), one may consider how the skill is learned, and next how it could best be taught. Hypotheses designed to answer all three of these questions can then be tested by experiment.

There are several ways of characterizing the behavior we call reading. It is receiving communication; it is making discriminative responses to graphic symbols; it is decoding graphic symbols to speech; and it is getting meaning from the printed page. A child in the early stages of acquiring reading skill may not be doing all these things, however. Some aspects of reading must be mastered before others and have an essential function in a sequence of development of the final skill. The average child, when he begins learning to read, has already mastered to a marvelous extent the art of communication. He can speak and understand his own language in a fairly complex way, employing units of language organized in a hierarchy and with a grammatical structure. Since a writing system must correspond to the spoken one, and since speech is prior to writing, the framework and unit structure of speech will determine more or less the structure of the writing system, though the rules of correspondence vary for different languages and writing systems. Some alphabetic writing systems have nearly perfect single-letter-to-sound correspondences, but some, like English, have far more complex correspondence between spelling patterns and speech patterns. Whatever the nature of the correspondences, it is vital to a proper analysis of the reading task that they be understood. And it is vital to remember, as well, that the first stage in the child's mastery of reading is learning to communicate by means of spoken language.

Once a child begins his progression from spoken language to written language, there are, I think, three phases of learning to be considered. They present three different kinds of learning tasks, and they are roughly sequential, though there must be considerable overlapping. These three phases are: learning to differentiate graphic symbols; learning to decode letters to sounds ("map" the letter into sounds); and using progressively higher-order units of structure. I shall consider these three stages in order and in some detail and describe experiments exploring each stage.

Differentiation of Written Symbols

Making a discriminative response to printed characters is considered by some a kind of reading. A very young child, or even a monkey, can be taught to point to a patch of yellow color, rather than a patch of blue, when the printed characters YELLOW are presented. Various people, in recent popular publications, have seriously suggested teaching infants to respond discriminatively in this way to letter patterns, implying that this is teaching them to "read." Such responses are not reading, however; reading entails decoding to speech. Letters are, essentially, an instruction to produce a given speech sound.

Nevertheless, differentiation of written character from one another is a logically preliminary stage to decoding them to speech. The learning problem is one of discriminating and recognizing a set of line figures, all very similar in a number of ways (for example, all are tracings on paper) and each differing from all the others in one or more features (as straight versus curved). The differentiating features must remain invariant under certain transformations (size, brightness, and perspective transformations and less easily described ones produced by different type faces and hand-writing). They must therefore be relational, so that these transformations will not destroy them.

It might be questioned whether learning is necessary for these figures to be discriminated from one another. This question has been investigated by Gibson, Gibson, Pick and Osser (3). In order to trace the development of letter differentiation as it is related to those features of letters which are critical for the task, we designed specified transformations for each of the groups of standard, artificial letter-like forms comparable to printed Roman capitals. Variants were constructed from each standard figure to yield the following 12 transformations for each one: three degrees of transformation from line to curve; five transformations of rotation or reversal; two perspective transformations; and two topological transformations (see Fig. 1 for examples).

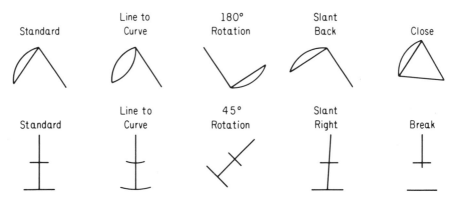

Fig. 1. Examples of letter-like figures illustrating different types of transformation.

All of these except the perspective transformations we considered critical for discriminating letters. For example, contrast V and U; and U; O and C.

The discrimination task required the subject to match a standard figure against all of its transformations and some copies of it and to select only identical copies. An error score (the number of times an item that was not an identical copy was selected) was obtained for each child, and the errors were classified according to the type of transformation. The subjects were children aged 4 through 8 years. As would be expected, the visual discrimination of these letter-like forms improved from age 4 to 8, but the slopes of the error curves were different, depending on the transformation to be discriminated (Fig. 2). In other words, some transformations are harder to discriminate than others, and improvement occurs at different rates for different transformations. Even the youngest subjects made relatively few errors involving changes of break or close, and among the 8-year-olds these errors dropped to zero. Errors for perspective transformations were very numerous among 4 year-olds and still numerous among 8-year-olds. Errors for rotations and reversals started high but dropped to nearly zero by 8 years. Errors for changes from line to curve were relatively numerous (depending on the number of changes) among the youngest children and showed a rapid drop among the older — almost to zero for the 8-year-olds.

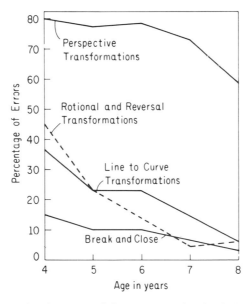

Fig. 2. Error Curves showing rate of improvement in discriminating four types of transformation.

The experiment was replicated with the same transformations of real letters on the 5-year-old group. The correlation between confusions of the same transformations for real letters and for the letter-like forms was very high (r = + .87), so the effect of a given transformation has generality (is not specific to a given form).

What happens, in the years from 4 to 8, to produce or hamper improvement in discrimination? Our results suggest that the children have learned the features or dimensions of difference which are critical for differentiating letters. Some differences are critical, such as break versus close, line versus curve, and rotations and reversals; but some, such as the perspective transformations, are not, and must in fact be tolerated. The child of 4 does not start "cold" upon this task, because some of this previous experience with distinctive features of objects and pictures will transfer to letter differentiation. But the set of letters has a unique feature pattern for each of its members, so learning of the distinctive features goes on during the period we investigated.

TABLE 1

NUMBER OF ERRORS MADE IN TRANSFER STAGE BY
GROUPS WITH THREE TYPES OF TRAINING

	Types of Training		
Group	Standards	Transfor- mations	Errors
E1	Same	Different	69
E2	Different	Same	39
C	Different	Different	101

If this interpretation is correct, it would be useful to know just what the distinctive features of letters are. What dimensions of difference must a child learn to detect in order to perceive each letter as unique? Gibson, Osser, Schiff, and Smith (4) investigated this question. Our method was to draw up a chart of the features of a given set of letters (5), test to see which of these letters were most frequently confused by prereading children, and compare the errors in the resulting "confusion matrix" with those predicted by the feature chart.

A set of distinctive features for letters must be relational in the sense that each feature presents a contrast which is invariant under certain transformations, and it must yield a unique pattern for each letter. The set must also be reasonably economical. Two feature lists which satisfy these requirements for a specified type face were tried out against the results of a confusion matrix obtained with the same type (simplified Roman Capitals available on a sign-typewriter).

Each of the features in the list in Fig. 3 is or is not a characteristic of each of the 26 letters. Regarding each letter one asks, for example, "Is there a curved segment?" and gets a yes or no answer. A filled-in feature chart gives a unique pattern for each letter. However, the number of potential features for letter-shapes is very large, and would vary from one alphabet and type font to another. Whether or not we have the right set can be tested with a confusion matrix. Children should confuse with greatest frequency the letters having the smallest number of feature differences, if the features have been chosen correctly.

We obtained our confusion matrix from 4-year-old children, who made matching judgments of letters, programmed so that every letter had an equal opportunity to be mistaken for any other, without bias from order effects. The "percent feature difference" for any two letters was determined by dividing the total number of features possessed by either letter, but not both, by the total number possessed by both, whether shared or not. Correlations were then calculated between percent feature difference and number of confusions, one for each letter. The feature list of Fig. 3 yielded 12 out of 26 positive significant correlations. Prediction from this feature list is fairly good, in view of the fact that features were not weighted. A multi-dimensional analysis of the matrix corroborated the choice of the curve-straight and obliqueness variables, suggesting that these features may have priority in the discrimination process and perhaps developmentally. Refinement of the feature list will take these facts into account, and other methods of validation will be tried.

Features	A	B	C	E	K	L	N	U	X	Z
Straight segment										
Horizontal	X			X	X					X
Vertical		X		X	X	X	X			
Oblique	X			X					X	X
Oblique	X			X		X		X		
Curve										
Closed		X								
Open vertically								X		
Open horizontally			X							
Intersection	X	X		X	X				X	
Redundancy										
Cyclic change		X		X						
Symmetry	X	X	X	X	X			X	X	
Discontinuity										
Vertical	X				X				X	
Horizontal			X			X	X			X

Fig. 3. Example of a "feature chart." Whether the features chosen are actually effective for discriminating letter must be determined by experiment.

Detecting Distinctive Features

If we are correct in thinking that the child comes to discriminate graphemes by detecting their distinctive features, what is the learning process like? That it is perceptual learning and need not be verbalized is probable (though teachers do often call attention to contrasts between letter shapes.) An experiment by Anne D. Pick (6) was designed to compare two hypotheses about how this type of discrimination develops. One might be called a "schema" or "prototype" hypothesis, and is based on the supposition that the child builds up a kind of model or memory image of each letter by repeated experience of visual presentations of the letter; perceptual theories which propose that discrimination occurs by matching sensory experience to a previously stored concept or categorical model are of this kind. In the other hypothesis it is assumed that the child learns by discovering how the forms differ, and then easily transfers this knowledge to new letter-like figures.

Pick employed a transfer design in which subjects were presented in step 1 with initially confusable stimuli (letter-like forms) and trained to discriminate between them. For step 2 (the transfer stage) the subjects were divided into three groups. One experimental group was given sets of stimuli to discriminate which varied in new dimensions from the *same standards* discriminated in stage 1. A second experimental group was given sets of stimuli which deviated from *new standards,* but in the same dimensions of difference discriminated in stage 1. A control group was given both new standards and new dimensions of difference to discriminate in stage 2. Better performance by the first experimental groups would suggest that discrimination learning proceeded by construction of a model or memory image of the standards against which the variants could be matched. Conversely, better performance by the second experimental group would suggest that dimensions of difference had been detected.

The subjects were kindergarten children. The stimuli were letter-like forms of the type described earlier. There were six standard forms and six transformations of each of them. The transformations consisted of two changes of line to curve, a right-left reversal, a 45-degree rotation, a perspective transformation, and a size transformation. Table 1 gives the errors of discrimination for all three groups in stage 2. Both experimental groups performed significantly better than the group given new transformations of old standards.

We infer from these results that, while children probably do learn prototypes of letter shapes, the prototypes themselves are not the original basis for differentiation. The most relevant kind of training for discrimination is practice which provides experience with the characteristic differences that distinguish the set of items. Features which are actually distinctive for letters could be emphasized by presenting letters in contrast pairs.

Decoding Letters to Sounds

When the graphemes are reasonably discriminable from one another, the decoding process becomes possible. This process, common sense and many psychologists would tell us, is simply a matter of associating a graphic stimulus with the appropriate spoken response – that is to say, it is the traditional stimulus-response paradigm, a kind of paired-associate learning.

Obvious as this description seems, problems arise when one takes a closer look. Here are just a few. The graphic code is related to the speech code by rules of correspondence. If these rules are known, decoding of new items is predictable. Do we want to build up, one by one, automatically cued responses, or do we want to teach with transfer in mind? If we want to teach for transfer, how do we do it? Should the child be aware that this is a code game with rules? Or will induction of the rules be automatic? What units of both codes should we start with? Should we start with single letters, in the hope that knowledge of single-letter-to-sound relationships will yield the most transfer? Or should we start with whole words, in the hope that component relationships will be induced?

Carol Bishop (7) investigated the question of the significance of knowledge of component letter-sound relationships in reading new words. In her experiment, the child's process of learning to read was simulated by teaching adult subjects to read some Arabic words. The purpose was to determine the transfer value of training with individual letters as opposed to whole words, and to investigate the role of component letter-sound associations in transfer to learning new words.

A three-stage transfer design was employed. The letters were 12 Arabic characters, each with a one-to-one letter-sound correspondence. There were eight consonants and four vowels, which were combined to form two sets of eight Arabic words. The 12 letters appeared at least once in both sets of words. A native speaker of the language recorded on tape the 12 letter-sounds and the two sets of words. The graphic form of each letter or word was printed on a card.

The subjects were divided into three groups – the letter training group (L), the whole-word training group (W), and a control group (C). Stage 1 of the experiment was identical for all groups. The subjects learned to pronounce the set of words (transfer set) which would appear in stage 3 by listening to the recording and repeating the words. Stage 2 varied. Group L listened to and repeated the 12 letter-sounds and then learned to associate the individual graphic shapes with their correct sounds. Group W followed the same procedure, except that eight words were given them to learn, rather than letters. Learning time was equal for the two groups. Group C spent the same time-interval on an unrelated task. Stage 3 was the same for the three groups. All subjects learned to read the set of words they had heard in stage 1, responding to the presentation of a word on a card by pronouncing it. This was the transfer stage on which the three groups were compared.

At the close of stage 3, all subjects were tested on their ability to give the correct letter-sound following the presentation of each printed letter. They were asked afterward to explain how they tried to learn the transfer words.

Figure 4 shows that learning took place in fewest trials for the letter group and next fewest for the word group. That is, letter training had more transfer value than word training, but word training did produce some transfer. The subjects of group L also knew, on the average, a greater number of component letter-sound correspondences, but some subjects in group W had learned all 12. Most of the subjects in group L reported that they had tried to learn by using knowledge of component correspondences. But so did 12 of the 20 subjects in group W, and the scores of these 12 subjects on the transfer task were similar to those of the letter-trained groups. The subjects who had learned by whole words and had not used individual correspondences performed no better on the task than the control subjects.

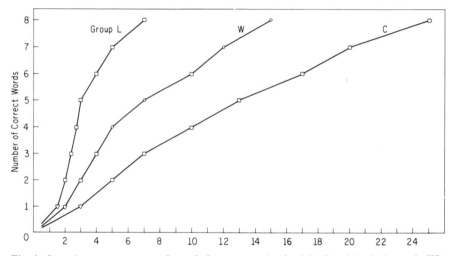

Fig. 4. Learning curves on transfer task for group trained originally with whole words (W), group trained with single letters (L), and control group (C).

It is possible, then, to learn to read words without learning the component letter-sound correspondences. But transfer to new words depends on use of them, whatever the method of original training. Word training was as good as letter training if the subject had analyzed for himself the component relationships.

Learning Variable and Constant
Component Correspondences

In Bishop's experiment, the component letter-sound relationships were regular and consistent. It has often been pointed out, especially by advocates of spelling reform and revised alphabets (8), that in English this is not the case. Bloomfield (9) suggested that the beginning reader should, therefore, be presented with material carefully programmed for teaching those orthographic-phonic regularities which exist in English, and should be introduced later and only gradually to the complexities of English spelling and to the fact that single-letter-to-sound relationships are often variable. But actually, there has been no hard evidence to suggest that transfer, later, to reading spelling-patterns with more variable component correspondence will be facilitated by beginning with only constant ones. Although variable ones may be harder to learn in the beginning, the original difficulty may be compensated for by facilitating later learning.

A series of experiments directed by Harry Levin (10) dealt with the effect of learning variable as opposed to constant letter-sound relationships, on transfer to learning new letter-sound relationships. In one experiment, the learning material was short lists of paired-associates, with a word written in artificial characters as stimulus and a triphoneme familiar English word as response. Subjects (third-grade children) in one group were given a list which contained constant graph-to-sound relationships (one-to-one component correspondence) followed by a list in which this correspondence was variable with respect to the medial vowel sound. Another group started with a similarly constructed variable list and followed it with a second one. The group that learned lists with a variable component in both stages was superior to the other group in the second stage. The results suggest that initiating the task with a variable list created an expectation of learning set for variability of correspondence which was transferred to the second list and facilitated learning it.

In a second experiment, the constant or variable graph-sound relation occurred on the first letter. Again, the group with original variable training performed better on the second, variable list. In a third experiment adult native speakers of English and Spanish were compared. The artificial graphs were paired with nonsense words. Again there was more transfer from a variable first list to a variable second list than from a constant to a variable one. Variable lists were more difficult, on the whole, for the Spanish speakers, perhaps because their native language contains highly regular letter-sound relationships.

A "set for diversity" may, therefore, facilitate transfer to learning of new letter-sound correspondences which contain variable relationships. But many questions about how the code is learned remain to be solved, because the true units of the graphic code are not necessarily single letters. While single-letter-sound relations in English are indeed variable, at other levels of structure regularity may be discovered.

Lower- and Higher-Order Units

For many years, linguists have been concerned with the question of units in language. That language has a hierarchical structure, with units of different kinds and levels, is generally accepted, though the definition of the units is not easily reached. One criterion of a unit is recodability — consistent mapping or translation to another code. If such a criterion be granted, graphic units must parallel linguistic units. The units of the writing system should be defined, in other words, by mapping rules which link them to the speech code, at all levels of structure.

What then are the true graphic units? What levels of units are there? Exactly how are they mapped to linguistic units? In what "chunks" are they perceived? We must first try to answer these questions by a logical analysis of properties of the writing and speech systems and the correspondences between them. Then we can look at the behavior of skilled readers and see how units are processed during reading. If the logical analysis of the correspondence rules is correct, we should be able to predict what kinds of units are actually processed and to check our predictions experimentally.

Common sense suggests that the unit for reading is the single grapheme, and that the reader proceeds sequentially from left to right, letter by letter, across the page. But we can assert at once and unequivocally that this picture is false. For the English language, the single graphemes map consistently into speech only as morphemes — that is, the names of the letters of the alphabet. It is possible, of course, to name letters sequentially across a line of print ("spell out" a word), but that is not the goal of a skilled reader, nor is it what he does. Dodge (11) showed, nearly 60 years ago, that perception occurs in reading only during fixations, and not at all during the saccadic jumps from one fixation to the next. With a fast tachistoscopic exposure, a skilled reader can perceive four unconnected letters, a very long word, and four or more words if they form a sentence (12). Even first graders can read three-letter words exposed for only 40 milliseconds, too short a time for sequential eye-movements to occur.

Broadbent (13) has pointed out that speech, although it consists of a temporal sequence of stimuli, is responded to at the end of a sequence. That is, it is normal for a whole sequence to be delivered before a response is made. For instance, the sentence "Would you give me your   ?" might end with any of a large number of words, such as "name" or "wallet" or "wife." The response depends on the total message. The fact that the component stimuli for speech and reading are spread over time does not mean that the phonemes or letters or words are processed one at a time, with each stimulus decoded to a separate response. In fact that o is pronounced differently in BOAT and BOMB is not a hideous peculiarity of English which must consequently be reformed. The o is read only in context and is never responded to in isolation. It is part of a sequence which contains constraints of two kinds, one morphological and the other the spelling patterns which are characteristic of English.

If any doubt remains as to the unlikelihood of sequential processing letter by letter, there is recent evidence of Newman (14) and of Kolers (15) on sequential exposure of letters. When letters forming a familiar word are exposed sequentially in the same place, it is almost impossible to read the word. With an exposure of 100 milliseconds per letter, words of six letters are read with only 20 percent probability of accuracy; and with an exposure of 375 milliseconds per letter, the probability is still well under 100 percent. But that is more than 2 seconds to perceive a short, well-known word! We can conclude that, however graphemes are processed perceptually in reading, it is not a letter-by-letter sequence of acts.

If the single grapheme does not map consistently to a phoneme, and furthermore, if perception normally takes in bigger "chunks" of graphic stimuli in a single fixation what are the smallest graphic units consistently coded into phonemic patterns? Must they be whole words? Are there different levels of units? Are they achieved at different stages of development?

Spelling Patterns

It is my belief that the smallest component units in written English are spelling patterns (16). By a spelling pattern, I mean a cluster of graphemes in a given environment which has an invariant pronunciation according to the rules of English. These rules are the regularities which appear when, for instance, any vowel or consonant or cluster is shown to correspond with a given pronunciation in an initial, medial, or final position in the spelling of a word. This kind of regularity is not merely "frequency" (bigram frequency, trigram frequency, and so on), for it implies that frequency counts are relevant for establishing rules only if the right units and the right relationships are counted. The relevant graphic unit is a functional unit of one or more letters, in a given position within the word, which is in correspondence with a specified pronunciation (17).

If potential regularities exist within words — the spelling patterns that occur in regular correspondence with speech patterns — one may hypothesize that these correspondences have been assimilated by the skilled reader of English (whether or not he can verbalize the rules) and have the effect of organizing units for perception. It follows that strings of letters which are generated by the rules will be perceived more easily than ones which are not, even when they are unfamiliar words or not words at all.

Several experiments testing this prediction were performed by Gibson, Pick, Osser, and Hammond (18). The basic design was to compare the perceptibility (with a very short tachistoscopic exposure) of two sets of letterstrings, all nonsense or pseudo words, which differed in their spelling-to-sound correlation. One list, called the "pronounceable" list, contained words with a high spelling-to-sound correlation. Each of them had an initial consonant-spelling with a single, regular pronunciation; a final consonant-spelling having a single regular pronunciation; and a vowel-spelling, placed between them, having a single regular pronunciation when it follows and is followed by the given initial and final consonant spellings, respectively—for example, GL/UR/CK. The words in the second list, called the "unpronounceable" list, had a low spelling-to-sound correlation. They were constructed from the words in the first list by reversing the initial and final consonant spellings. The medial vowel spelling was not changed. For example, GLURCH became CKURGL. There were 26 such pseudo words in each list, varying in length from four to eight letters. The pronunciability of the resulting lists was validated in two ways, first by ratings, and second by obtaining the number of variations when the pseudo words were actually pronounced.

The words were projected on a screen in random order, in five successive presentations with an exposure time beginning at 50 milliseconds and progressing up to 250 milliseconds. The subjects (college students) were instructed to write each word as it was projected. The mean percentage of pronounceable words correctly perceived was consistently and significantly greater at all exposure times.

The experiment was later repeated with the same material but a different judgment. After the pseudo word was exposed, it was followed by a multiple-choice list of four items, one of the correct one and the other three the most common errors produced in the previous experiment. The subject chose the word he thought he had seen from the choice list and recorded a number (its order in the list). Again the mean of pronounceable pseudo words correctly perceived significantly exceeded that of their unpronounceable counterparts. We conclude from these experiments that skilled readers more easily perceive as a unit pseudo words which follow the rules of English spelling-to-sound correspondence; that spelling patterns which have invariant relations to sound patterns function as a unit, thus facilitating the decoding process.

In another experiment, Gibson, Osser, and Pick (19) studied the development of perception of grapheme-phoneme correspondences. We wanted to know how early, in learning to read, children begin to respond to spelling patterns as units. The experiment was designed to compare children at the end of the first grade and at the end of the third grade in ability to recognize familiar three-letter words, pronounceable trigrams, and unpronounceable trigrams. The three-letter words were taken from the first-grade reading list; each word chosen could be rearranged into a meaningless but pronounceable trigram and a meaningless and unpronounceable one (for example, RAN, NAR, RNA). Some longer pseudo words (four and five letters) taken from the previous experiments were included as well. The words and pseudo words were exposed tachistoscopically to individual children who were required to spell them orally. The first-graders read (spelled out) most accurately the familiar three-letter words, but read the pronounceable trigrams significantly better than the unpronounceable ones. The longer pseudo words were seldom read accurately and were not differentiated by pronunciability. The third-grade girls read all three-letter combinations with high and about equal accuracy, but differentiated the longer pseudo words; that is, the pronounceable four-and-five-letter pseudo words were more often perceived correctly than their unpronounceable counterparts.

These results suggest that a child in the first stages of reading skill typically reads in short units, but has already generalized certain regularities of spelling-to-sound correspondence, so that three-letter pseudo words which fit the rules are more easily read as units. As skill develops, span increases, and a similar difference can be observed for longer items. The longer items involve more complex conditional rules and longer clusters, so that the generalizations must increase in complexity. The fact that a child can begin very early to perceive regularities of correspondence between the printed and spoken patterns, and transfer them to the reading of unfamiliar items as units, suggests that the opportunities for discovering the correspondences between patterns might well be enhanced in programming reading materials.

I have referred several times to *levels* of units. The last experiment showed that the size and complexity of the spelling patterns which can be perceived as units increase with development of reading skill. That other levels of structure, both syntactic and semantic, contain units as large as and larger than the word, and that perception of skilled readers will be found, in suitable experiments, to be a function of these factors is almost axiomatic. As yet we have little direct evidence better than Cattell's original discovery (12) that when words are structured into a sentence, more letters can be accurately perceived "at a glance." Developmental studies of perceptual "chunking" in relation to structural complexity may be very instructive.

Where does meaning come in? Within the immediate span of visual perception, meaning is less effective in structuring written material than good spelling-to-sound correspondence, as Gibson, Bishop, Schiff, and Smith (20) have shown. Real words which are both meaningful and, as strings of letters, structured in accordance with English spelling patterns are more easily perceived than nonword pronounceable strings of letters; but the latter are more easily perceived than meaningful but unpronounceable letter-strings (for example, BIM is perceived accurately, with tachistoscopic exposure, faster than IBM). The role of meaning in the visual perception of words (more than one) are dealt with. A sentence has two kinds of constraint, semantic and syntactic, which make it intelligible (easily heard) and memorable (21). It is important that the child develop reading habits which utilize all the types of constraint present in the stimulus, since they constitute structure and are, therefore, unit-formers. The skills which the child should acquire in reading are habits of utilizing the constraints in letter strings (the spelling and morphemic patterns) and in word strings (the syntactic and semantic patterns). We could go on to consider still superordinate ones, perhaps, but the problem of the unit, of levels of units, and mapping rules from writing to speech has just begun to be explored with experimental techniques. Further research on the definition and processing of units should lead to new insights about the nature of reading skill and its attainment.

Summary

Reading begins with the child's acquisition of spoken language. Later he learns to differentiate the graphic symbols from one another and to decode these to familiar speech sounds. As he learns the code, he must progressively utilize the structural constraints which are built into it in order to attain the skilled performance which is characterized by processing of higher-order units – the spelling and morphological patterns of the language.

Because of my firm conviction that good pedagogy is based on a deep understanding of the discipline to be taught and the nature of the learning process involved, I have tried to show that the psychology of reading can benefit from a program of theoretical analysis and experiment. An analysis of the reading task—its discriminatory and decoding aspects as well as the semantic and syntactical aspects – tells us *what* must be learned. An analysis of the learning process tells us *how*. The consideration of formal instruction comes only after these steps, and its precepts should follow from them.

References and Notes

1. See C. C. Fries, *Linquistics and Reading* (Holt, Rinehart, and Winston, New York, 1963), for an excellent chapter on past practice and theory in the teaching of reading.
2. In 1959, Cornell University was awarded a grant for a Basic Research Project on Reading by the Cooperative Research Program of the Office of Education, U.S. Department of Health, Education, and Welfare. Most of the work reported in this article was supported by this grant. The Office of Education has recently organized "Project Literacy," which will promote research on reading in a number of laboratories, as well as encourage mutual understanding between experimentalists and teachers of reading.
3. E. J. Gibson, J. J. Gibson, A. D. Pick, H. Osser, *J. Comp. Physiol. Psychol.* 55, 897 (1962).
4. E. J. Gibson, H. Osser, W. Schiff, J. Smith, in *A Basic Research Program on Reading*, Final Report on Cooperative Research Project No. 639 to the Office of Education, Department of Health, Education, and Welfare.
5. The method was greatly influenced by the analysis of distinctive features of phonemes by Jakobsen and M. Halle, presented in *Fundamentals of Language* (Mouton, the Hague, 1956). A table of 12 features, each in binary opposition, yields a unique pattern for all phonemes, so that any one is distinguishable from any other by its pattern of attributes. A pair of phonemes may differ by any number of features, the minimal distinction being one feature opposition. The features must be invariant under certain transformations and essentially relational, so as to remain distinctive over a wide range of speakers, intonations, and so on.

6. A. D. Pick, *J. Exp. Psychol.*, in press.
7. C. H. Bishop. J. *Verbal Learning Verbal Behav.* 3, 215 (1964).
8. Current advocates of a revised alphabet who emphasize the low letter-sound correspondence in English are Sir James Pitman and John A. Downing. Pitman's revised alphabet, called the Initial Teaching Alphabet, consists of 43 characters, some traditional and some new. It is designed for instruction of the beginning reader, who later transfers to traditional English spelling. See I. J. Pitman. *J. Roy. Soc. Arts* 109, 149 (1961); J. A. Downing, *Brit. J. Educ. Psychol.* 32, 166 (1962);——, "Experiments with Pitman's initial teaching alphabet in British schools," paper presented at the Eighth Annual Conference of International Reading Association, Miami, Fla., May 1963.
9. L. Bloomfield, *Elem. Engl. Rev.* 19, 125, 183 (1942).
10. See research reports of H. Levin and J. Watson, and H. Levin, E. Baum, and S. Bostwick, in *A Basic Research Program on Reading* (see 4).
11. R. Dodge, *Psychol. Bull.* 2, 193 (1905).
12. J. McK. *Cattell. Phil. Studies* 2, 635 (1885).
13. D. E. Broadbent, *Perception and Communication* (Pergamon, New York, 1958).
14. E. Newman, *Am. J. Psychol.*, in press.
15. P. A. Kolers and M. T. Katzman, paper presented before the Psychonomic Society, Aug. 1963, Bryn Mawr, Pa.
16. Spelling patterns in English have been discussed by C. C. Fries in *Linguistics and Reading* (Holt, Rinehart, and Winston, New York, 1963), p. 169 ff. C. F. Hockett, in *A Basic Research Program on Reading* (see 4), has made an analysis of English graphic monosyllables which presents regularities of spelling patterns in relation to pronunciation. This study was continued by R. Venezky (thesis, Cornell University, 1962), who wrote a computer program for obtaining the regularities of English spelling-to-sound correspondence. The data obtained by means of the computer permit one to look up any vowel or consonant cluster of up to five letters and find its pronunciation in initial, medial, and final positions in a word. Letter environments as well have now been included in the analysis. See also R. H. Weir, *Formulation of Grapheme-Phoneme Correspondence Rules to Aid in the Teaching of Reading,* Report on Cooperative Research Project No. 5-039 to the Office of Education, Department of Health, Education and Welfare.
17. For example, the cluster GH may lawfully be pronounced as an F at the end of a word, but never at the beginning. The vowel cluster EIGH, pronounced /A/ (/ej/), may occur in initial, medial, and final positions, and does so with nearly equal distribution. These cases account for all but two occurences of the cluster in English orthography. A good example of regularity influenced by environment is (c) in a medial position before 1 plus a vowel. It is always pronounced /S/ *social, ancient, judicious*).
18. E. J. Gibson, A. D. Pick, H. Osser, M. Hammond, *Am. J. Psychol.* 75,554 (1962).
19. E. J. Gibson, H. Osser, A. D. Pick, *J. Verbal Learning Verbal Behav.* 2, 142 (1963).
20. E. J. Gibson, C. H. Bishop, W. Schiff, J. Smith, *J. Exp. Psychol.*, 67, 173 (1964).
21. G. A. Miller and S. Isard, *J. Verbal Learning Verbal Behav.* 2, 217 (1963); also L. E. Marks and G. A. Miller, *ibid.* 3, 1 (1964).

Questions for Discussion

1. Does Wiener and Cromer's conceptualization of reading as a two-step

process seem defensible to you? How would *you* define and explain the reading process to a group of parents?

2.   Do you see any weaknesses in Gibson's conceptualization of the reading process? What similarities and differences are there between Gibson's views and those of Wiener and Cromer?

3.   If there is a remedial reading program currently being operated in your school system, which of Wiener and Cromer's four assumptions regarding reading difficulty and its treatment seems to be prevalent in the program?

The Evaluation of Reading

IV

A very important aspect of any reading program on the secondary school level is the evaluative procedures used both to diagnose students' strengths and weaknesses and to determine the extent to which a reading program has been effective. To develop a reading skills program without a thorough diagnosis of students' needs is foolhardy; equally foolhardy is the practice of implementing a secondary school reading program and then assuming without question that the program has been effective. The articles in this section have been selected to present a clear picture of the problems one faces in implementing proper evaluative procedures in reading on the secondary school level.

In the first article, Frederick Davis delineates various aspects of a testing program in reading. Of particular interest is his discussion of the problems involved in measuring rate of reading and levels of comprehension.

Davis also presents detailed procedures to follow in more accurately assessing change in reading performance over a period of time. This presentation is of particular relevance for those who are attempting to set up procedures to determine the effects of a reading program on the students involved.

Arthur McDonald also discusses problems encountered in evaluating progress of a reading program. The suggestion is often made that a control group be included in any attempt to assess the success of a reading program. McDonald warns that such comparable-group methods of evaluation are very likely to be confounded by the "Hawthorne" and "placebo" effects, and he makes suggestions as to how one can avoid such contamination of results.

In the final article of this section, Albert Kingston faces up to the difficult problem of assigning grades to students who are enrolled in special reading classes. The advantages and disadvantages of three traditional approaches to grading are presented and some new plans are proposed.

The Role of Testing in Reading Instruction*

FREDERICK B. DAVIS

In papers presented at previous reading conferences, Arthur E. Traxler discussed various aspects of the role of tests in the measurement of ability to read. In 1951, he provided a critical survey of tests for identifying difficulties in interpreting what is read.[1]

In 1958, he discussed the values and limitations of standardized reading tests.[2] His main point was one with which this writer heartily concurs; namely, that the process of reading is so complex that tests of ability to read must be carefully constructed on the basis of a thorough and systematic analysis of the process and of the outcomes desired. This point will be elaborated later, using Traxler's excellent paper as a point of departure.

Broadly speaking, testing plays three major roles in reading instruction. Tests are used to (1)† assess an individual's performance in reading at a given point in time, (2) assess changes over a period of time in the reading of individuals or groups, and (3) estimate the degree to which individual or group potential for reading has been realized.

Reading Mechanics

Although the fundamental objective of reading is comprehension, this objective cannot be attained efficiently (or even at all) unless the reader is able to convert symbols, which we may call graphemes, into meaningful concepts.

*Reprinted from *Reading: Seventy-Five Years of Progress*, Supplementary Educational Monographs, No. 96, edited by H. Alan Robinson (1966), pp. 178-189, by permission of the University of Chicago Press.

[1]Traxler, "Critical Survey of Tests for Identifying Difficulties in Interpreting What Is Read," in *Promoting Growth toward Maturity in Interpreting What Is Read,* edited by William S. Gray ("Supplementary Educational Monographs," No. 74; Chicago: University of Chicago Press, 1951), pp. 195-200.

[2]Traxler, "Values and Limitations of Standardized Reading Tests," in *Evaluation in Reading,* edited by Helen M. Robinson ("Supplementary Educational Monographs," No. 88; Chicago: University of Chicago Press, 1958), pp. 111-17.

†Numbers in parentheses refer to references at end of article.

This conversion is an associative and reasoning process that can profitably be separated into two stages: first, the mechanics of recognizing the symbols; and, second, the evocation of associations and the weaving together of these associations to recreate the ideas that the author had in mind.

Although effective silent reading should not involve vocalization or even perceptible subvocalization of phonemes (combinations of graphemes), an analysis of reading skill may often profitably require that tests of oral reading of graphemes, words, sentences, and so on, be made. If an individual can convert graphemes into phonemes and blend phonemes into words with a high degree of skill and fluency, any difficulty he has in comprehending what he is reading must lie in his lack of experiential associations or his inability to weave these together through reasoning.

The mechanics of reading involve eye movements, perceptual accuracy, the association of graphemes with the corresponding phonemes, the blending of phonemes to form words, and word recognition. A number of elaborate diagnostic tests are now available to measure various components of the mechanics of reading. The *Gates-McKillop Reading Diagnostic Tests* (Bureau of Publications, Teachers College, Columbia University, 1962), the *Durrell Analysis of Reading Difficulty* (Harcourt, Brace & World, Inc., 1955), George D. Spache's *Diagnostic Reading Scales* (California Test Bureau, 1963), and the *Diagnostic Reading Tests* (Committee on Diagnostic Reading Tests, Inc., 1963) come readily to mind.

The diagnosis of difficulty in reading is a clinical problem and should be carried on by specialists. All of the tests mentioned above should be used only by such specialists since these tests are sometimes difficult to administer and yield scores that can be unreliable and tricky to interpret, partly because differences among the scores are even less reliable than the scores taken one by one.

Rate of Covering Material

To the layman, the measurement of rate of reading sounds like a simple undertaking, requiring only that the number of words covered per minute be determined. Unfortunately, careful consideration of the problem quickly reveals that a count of the number of words covered per minute may be a meaningless figure.

It is apparent on a moment's thought that any reader's rate is greatly affected by his purpose in reading. How greatly is illustrated by some data reported by Frank Laycock.[3] The average rate of 391 applicants for admission

---

[3] Laycock, "Significant Characteristics of College Students with Varying Flexibility in Reading Rate: I. Eye-Movements in Reading Prose," *Journal of Experimental Education,* XXIII (June, 1955), 311-30.

to college when they were asked to read a passage at their normal rate was 220.4 words per minute. When they were given a similar passage and were asked to read as fast as possible without missing important points on which they would be tested, they averaged 308.1 words per minute. Another request for them to increase their speed of reading without sacrificing comprehension resulted in an immediate 40 per cent average gain in rate. Three important implications for the measurement of rate of reading may be derived from these data:

(1)   Rate of reading must be measured under conditions that unambiguously define the purpose for which the reading is to be done and that provide assurance that this purpose is being fulfilled by the reader.

(2)   Evaluation of the results of training programs for increasing speed of reading should always exclude any increase in speed that a reader could have made before the training began by simply stepping up his speed of reading without appreciable loss of comprehension.

(3)   Very different tests are required for measuring the rate at which material is covered for different purposes.

Rate of reading is also greatly influenced by the complexity or difficulty of the material that an individual is seeking to understand. Data published by John C. Flanagan provide an illustration.[4] He administered three equivalent reading scales of twenty items each to 317 twelfth-grade students in such a way that they worked at different predetermined rates on each of the three scales. The average score of the group was 10.5 in eighteen minutes of working time, 9.7 in twelve minutes of working time, and 7.0 in six minutes of working time. Thus, with a clearly defined purpose (that of responding correctly to test items of a familiar kind at predetermined rates), these students sustained a loss of comprehension when their working time was cut by one-third and then by two-thirds.

Analysis of the data showed that the percentages of loss of comprehension between the twelve-minute and six-minute working times were nearly the same for students whose scores in the eighteen-minute working time were in the highest, middle, and lowest thirds of the group. This result suggests that, with the purpose of the reader and the complexity of the material held constant, there is a fairly uniform *inverse* relationship through-out the range of ability between *rate* of reading and *level* of comprehension. It may be noted in passing that the students could refer back to the reading passages as they responded to the comprehension questions; hence, memory played no appreciable part in determining the results of this experiment.

[4]Flanagan, "A Study of the Effect of Comprehensions of Varying Speeds of Reading," in *Research on the Foundations of American Education,* Official Report of the American Educational Research Association (Washington, D. C.: American Educational Association, 1939), pp. 47-50.

The inverse relationship between *rate* of reading and *level* of comprehension under the conditions of Flanagan's experiment makes such good sense that one wonders why anyone has ever thought the relationship to be otherwise. The reason is, doubtless, that the correlation coefficient between rate of reading (indicated by the number of test items read during a time limit) and level of comprehension (indicated by the number of items answered correctly when every student has had time to consider every item) has been found to be positive. As a matter of fact, Flanagan found it to be .17 in his group of 317 students. In a classic experiment Paul Blommers and E. F. Lindquist found it to be .30 in a sample of 672 students in grades eleven and twelve.[5]

Procedures used to check comprehension in reading at the same time that rate is being measured have usually been inadequate in at least one of the following ways:

1. The tests commonly include a fairly large percentage of items that can be answered by many examinees before they have been shown the passages on which the items are based.

2. The tests are often administered with such short time limits that every examinee does not have time to try every item, and scores are not corrected for chance success. In these circumstances, an examinee who is tested at the beginning and at the end of a reading-training course may read the test material so rapidly on the second testing that his comprehension is markedly lower than on the first testing. Yet, he can obtain a higher comprehension-test score on the second testing than on the first simply by marking answers to more items – at random, if necessary. With no correction for guessing, he is likely to answer a fraction of the items correctly by chance alone. His test scores will then give the false impression that he has greatly increased his rate of reading while maintaining or even improving upon his original level of comprehension. The most effective remedy for this situation is to use the conventional correction for chance success, especially if every examinee does not have time to consider every item within the time limit. Naturally, a test designed to measure speed cannot permit chance to effect results.

3. Estimates of individual and group gains during reading-training courses have often been based on a direct comparison of scores on equivalent forms of a test properly administered before and after the course without taking into account the fact that the training received during the course may have so altered the purposes of the examinees that the initial and final scores are not equivalent. In other words, tests that measure equivalent mental functions when they are administered to randomly determined parts of a group of examinees at one sitting may not measure the same mental functions when they are administered

[5]Blommers and Lindquist, "Rate of Comprehension of Reading: Its Measurement and Its Relation to Comprehension," *Journal of Educational Psychology*, XXXV (November, 1944), 449-73.

to the same group of examinees before and after a period of training.

At the sacrifice of established norms, the mental functions measured by tests given before and after a training period can usually be made more nearly equivalent by instructing the examinees before the initial testing that they should read as rapidly as possible while still getting the information needed to answer questions about the material. This, either explicitly or implicitly, is a principal effect of most remedial or other training courses in reading.

4. Estimates of individual and group changes produced by training courses in reading have rarely taken into account possible regression to population means. Still more rarely have estimates of changes been compared with the appropriate standard errors of measurement (or standard errors) to determine whether they are statistically significant. (I shall discuss this point further in a later section of this paper.)

5. The tests are given after the material on which they are based has been removed from sight. As a consequence, they measure a combination of comprehension and memory of the facts and understandings presented in the material.

To avoid some of the problems involved in measuring rate of reading, tests of rate of comprehension have become increasingly popular. The scores from these tests measure the rate at which the examinees are able to read material and respond correctly to questions about it while the material remains in front of them for reference. The best-known tests of this type are probably the *Cooperative English Test: Reading Comprehension* (Cooperative Test Division, 1960), the *Davis Reading Tests* (Psychological Corporation, 1962), the *Nelson-Denny Reading Tests* (Houghton Mifflin Co., 1960), and parts of the *Iowa Silent Reading Tests* (Harcourt, Brace & World, Inc., 1956).

Any speed-of-comprehension score should be corrected for chance success. Of the tests mentioned that yield speed-of-comprehension scores, only the *Davis Reading Tests* (Psychological Corporation, 1962) yield scores that are so corrected. It has been suggested that, instead of correcting for guessing, all students be instructed to mark answers to all items even if they have not read some of them. This procedure introduces chance elements into the scores, and the more conscientious students find it hard to carry out.

Level of Comprehension

As Traxler and others have indicated, any test of comprehension in reading, whether also a test of speed or not, should be carefully planned and constructed to measure the most important elements or skills involved. This is particularly true of level-of-comprehension tests, which are so constructed that few, if any, examinees are not able to consider every item within the time limit.

Such tests should include passages and items that cover a wide range of difficulty, with a few items near the end so penetrating that only a few examinees can be expected to answer them correctly.

Of the tests now available, the new *Cooperative English Test: Reading Comprehension* (Cooperative Test Division, 1960) and the *Davis Reading Test* (Psychological Corporation, 1962) were designed to provide level-of-comprehension tests. The effect of this arrangement is that the score on the complete test becomes a speed-of-comprehension score and that on the first half a level-of-comprehension score, because all, or almost all, examinees have time to consider every item in the first half in the time limit. This procedure leads to efficiency in testing because the more rapid readers are kept busy providing data during the entire time limit. It also tends to make the purpose of all examinees uniform in taking the test; almost no one has time to go back and double-check his responses to the items in the first half (that yield his level-of-comprehension score). In other types of relatively unspeeded tests in comprehension, the faster readers are, in effect, given a second chance at the items yielding their level-of-comprehension score. Their greater speed provides time in which they can check their work and to some extent causes a spurious inflation of their comprehension scores.

Relatively unspeeded tests of comprehension in reading of the conventional type include the paragraph-reading sections of the *California Achievement Test* (California Test Bureau, 1957), the Survey Section of the *Diagnostic Reading Test* (Committee on Diagnostic Reading Tests, Inc., 1963), the *Iowa Tests of Basic Skills* (Houghton Mifflin, 1956), the *Iowa Tests of Educational Development* (Science Research Associates, Inc., 1963), the *Metropolitan Achievement Test* (Harcourt, Brace & World, Inc., 1962), the *Sequential Tests of Educational Progress* (Cooperative Test Division, 1963), and the *Stanford Achievement Test* (Harcourt, Brace & World, Inc., 1964).

Now let me consider which skills of comprehension in reading should be measured. When the *Cooperative English Tests: Reading Comprehension* were first designed in 1939, a search of the literature was made to find which skills had been suggested as important by authorities in the field. As soon as these were put in a single list, it was found that they overlapped very greatly. By eliminating overlap and skills that seemed impossible to measure by objective items that could be easily scored, the list was reduced to nine operational skills:

(1)   Remembering word meanings
(2)   Deducing the meaning of words from context
(3)   Following the organization of a passage, as in identifying antecedents and references
(4)   Identifying the main thought of a passage
(5)   Answering questions for which explicit or paraphrased answers are given
(6)   Weaving together the ideas in a passage

(8)   Recognizing literary devices and identifying an author's tone and mood
(9)   Drawing inferences about an author's purpose and point of view

These constituted the basic framework on which the original tests were constructed.

To determine whether each of these skills is, at least to some extent, unique in the list of nine, an analysis of their variances and covariances was made. The identities of the resulting uncorrelated factors were adduced from a knowledge of the nine skills that had determined them. These fundamental abilities in comprehension are the following:

I.   Remembering word meanings
II.   Reasoning with verbal materials
VII.   Following the organization of a passage
VIII. Recognizing literary devices and identifying the author's tone and mood
III.   Focusing on the implied meanings of a passage
IV.   Drawing inferences about an author's intent, purpose, or point of view
VI.   Finding correct answers to questions to which explicit or paraphrased answers are given
V.   Deducing word meanings from context
IX.   Identifying the main thought of a passage

You will note that the Roman numerals attached to these fundamental abilities are not in numerical order. This is because they are arranged in order of their reliability coefficients. The first ability, "Remembering word meanings," had a reliability coefficient of .94, which can be regarded as very high. This ability is basically memory of meaningful material — namely, words. The data show that, as might be expected, it is the most important ability that underlies comprehension in reading.

The second ability, "Reasoning with verbal materials," is of next greatest importance in reading comprehension. It involves weaving verbal ideas together. In one study, reasoning in verbal materials had a correlation with arithmetic reasoning of -.32 and with figure analogies (a non-verbal test) of -.12. With syllogistic reasoning (expressed in verbal form), reasoning in verbal materials correlated only to the extent of +.05. These data point to the conclusion that this fundamental ability is not a general reasoning skill; it is instead specific. If it is to be developed, the training will probably have to be done by means of practice exercises based on passages like those in typical reading tests. Longer stories may also be used. But the responses made by readers should always be discussed and correct answers to questions identified and explained. By comparison with the first two abilities, the others are much less influential in determining a reader's level of comprehension. In fact, the last three on the list (VI, V, and IX) were not firmly established by the study from which these data have been taken.[6] This may be only because they were unreliably measured in the original study. To explore this possibility, the writer is now engaged in a study of the more subtle skills in comprehension that will utilize the relatively new technique of cross-validated uniqueness analysis.

Although the abilities III-IX are not of as fundamental an importance as abilities I and II, they may be of great consequence in certain types of reading. For example, the comprehension of literature (which involves the recognition and understanding of such literary devices as allusion, metaphor, and simile) depends greatly on ability VIII. The understanding of editorials and political tracts depends heavily on ability IV. The social consequences of increasing by only a small amount the ability of American citizens to evaluate propaganda and advertising appeals are obviously of great importance in a democratic society. These may be only tiny aspects of comprehension in reading, but they may be potentially very important.

In constructing the *Davis Reading Tests* (both Series 1 for grades eleven and twelve and for college freshmen and Series 2 for grades eight through eleven), certain of the nine skills were grouped and skill 1, "Remembering word meanings," was omitted. As already mentioned, this skill is inevitably measured in the process of measuring the others because they are all expressed in words. In assembling the tests, about 25 per cent of the items were selected to measure skill 5; 25 per cent to measure skills 4 and 6 combined; 25 per cent to measure skills 2, 7, and 9 combined; 12.5 per cent to measure skill 8; and 12.5 per cent to measure skill 3. Regardless whether one agrees with this assignment of percentages, one at least knows the basis of the decision.

The use of comprehension tests in reading is increasing most rapidly for programmed instruction and for informal purposes in the classroom. In programmed instruction, testing is an integral part of the teaching-learning process to an extent rarely attained in conventional teaching procedures. After a sequence of learning exercises has been presented and covered by the pupil at a rate appropriate for him, a check test is given. This often consists of a single question. If the pupil answers correctly, he is shown the next sequence of learning exercises; if he answers incorrectly, he repeats the sequence, or some suitable remedial exercises are provided. Thus, programmed instruction is a melding of teaching, testing, reteaching, testing, and teaching. Instant diagnosis of failure to learn a step in the programmed sequence and immediate confirmation of successful learning are provided by check tests.

The danger in this procedure is the astonishing degree of unreliability tolerated in the check tests. A single question may be found to have a reliability coefficient of the order of .15 to .20. For an item of 50 per cent difficulty that is scored *one* if answered correctly and *zero* if answered incorrectly, a standard

---

[6]Frederick B. Davis, "Fundamental Factors of Comprehension in Reading," *Psychometrika*, IX (September, 1944), 185-97.

error or measurement of about .46 results. Inaccuracy of this relative magnitude would be regarded as intolerable in an ordinary reading test. In programmed instruction, it must lead to a good deal of inefficiency in learning, because pupils who fail a check item when their true score is "pass" have to repeat sequences unnecessarily; conversely, pupils who pass a check item when their true score is "fail" are moved on to subsequent learning exercises for which they may lack some foundation element.

Even more serious is the risk of low content validity in a single check item; that is, the question may measure only one (or, in general, fewer than all) of the elements in the material that has just been taught. This danger argues for the very frequent use of single check items immediately after each element of the material has been covered.

The same problems beset the use of informal teacher-made tests in reading instruction. In addition, such tests rarely have adequate norms or norms expressed in meaningful units, such as percentile ranks in defined groups at specified stages of instruction.

There is little doubt that check tests in programmed instruction and informal tests for classroom use will increase more rapidly than any other types of tests. Their shortcomings and dangers must be kept in mind if their efficiency and accuracy are to be increased.

Assessment of Change in Reading Performance

Since the primary purpose of teaching is to produce learning — that is, change — in students, the estimation of the amount of change is of paramount importance in education. Yet, surprisingly enough, until recently there has been a decided lack of information about the best techniques for accomplishing the assessment of change. Some of the most important considerations are discussed at this point.

TEST VALIDITY

The first requirement in selecting a testing instrument is to be sure that it measures the learnings that the teaching is intended to produce. It is sometimes difficult to find standardized tests that have two or more equivalent forms available that meet this requirement. In addition to test content, the directions for administering the tests and scoring them affect validity. If a student learns over a period of instruction to mark answers at random on all items he has not had time to consider carefully, his final score can differ greatly from his initial score. Yet the change will not reflect any actual improvement in his ability to read accurately with comprehension. Therefore, it is especially important that speeded tests yield scores that have been corrected for chance success.

TEST RELIABILITY

Other things being equal, the higher the reliability coefficient of a reading test the better. Because, as Traxler pointed out in 1958, a reading-comprehension item takes a great deal of examinee time (in contrast with a recognition-vocabulary item, for example), the reliability of reading tests is usually low per unit of time. Since publishers encounter resistance to long tests, most tests of a readers's level of comprehension yield scores of only moderate reliability — say, about .80. For this reason, it is often good practice to use two equivalent forms of a reading test and average the examinee's scores. It should be noted that, if this practice is followed, norms cannot be based on the administration of a single form to each examinee.

RANGE OF ABILITY MEASURED

Tests used to measure change should cover a wide enough range of ability that no examinee will get an initial score equal to that which would be yielded by chance selection of answers and no examinee will get a final score that is perfect. Otherwise, we cannot tell how much higher or lower these students might have scored, and the resulting gain or loss scores will be underestimates of true change.

UNITS OF MEASUREMENT OF SCORES

It is too much to hope that increments of ability represented by one score point will be the same at all levels of scores. Nonetheless, if scores from a reading test are expressed in score units like Flanagan's Scaled Scores, Gardner's K Scores, stanines, or some other kind of normalized standard scores, there is a tendency for the increment of ability represented by one score point to be more nearly the same throughout the range of scores than if raw scores are used.

ESTIMATES OF CHANGE

The simplest way to estimate the amount of change made by an individual pupil is to administer equivalent forms of a test at the beginning and at the end of a training period. The initial score is subtracted from the final score, and the resulting difference is used as a crude estimate of change. This estimate is shown on the first line of equations on the left-hand side of Table 1. The smallest difference worth paying serious attention to is shown on the same line to the right. The second line of equations in Table 1 shows how to make a crude estimate of the average change made by a group and how to judge whether it is large enough to warrant serious attention.

These procedures should not be used to compare changes made by students or groups with widely different initial scores; neither should they be used to estimate changes made by students or groups selected for training on the basis of the initial test scores. For such purposes, refined estimates must be

TABLE 1

THE ASSESSMENT OF CHANGE

Crude Estimate of Change	*Smallest Change Worthy of Serious Consideration*

Individual:

$$C = B - A$$

$$\frac{3}{2}\sqrt{s^2_{\text{meas } B} + s^2_{\text{meas } A}} \qquad (1)$$

Group:

$$\overline{C}s = \overline{B}s - \overline{A}s$$

$$\frac{3}{2}\sqrt{\frac{s^2_{\text{meas } B} - s^2_{\text{meas } A}}{Ns}} \qquad (2)$$

Refined Estimate of Change

Individual:

$$\hat{C} = W_B B + W_A A + K$$

$$\frac{3}{2}\sqrt{W^2_B\, s^2_{\text{meas } B} + W^2_A\, s^2_{\text{meas } A}} \qquad (3)$$

Group:

$$\hat{\overline{C}}s = W_B \overline{B} + W_A \overline{A} + K$$

$$\frac{3}{2}\sqrt{\frac{W^2_B\, s^2_{\text{meas } B} + W^2_A\, s^2_{\text{meas } A}}{Ns}} \qquad (4)$$

Key:

A = individual score on Test A (initial test)
B = individual score on Test B (final test)
C = crude estimate of individual change
$\hat{C}$ = refined estimate of individual change
$\overline{C}s$ = crude estimate of mean change in subsample s
$\hat{\overline{C}}s$ = refined estimate of mean change in subsample s
$\overline{A}$ = mean score on Test A in a single age or grade group
$\overline{B}$ = mean score on Test B in a single age or grade group
$\overline{A}s$ = mean score on Test A in subsample s
$\overline{B}s$ = mean score on Test B in subsample s
N = number of cases in a single age or grade group
Ns = number of cases in subsample s
$s_A'\ s_B'\ r_{AA}'\ r_{BB}'\ s_{\text{meas } A}'$ and $s_{\text{meas } B}$ = familiar statistics computed in a single age or grade group

$$W_A = \frac{r_{AB}\, s_B\, (1 - r_{BB}) - s_A\, (r_{AA} - r^2_{AB})}{s_A\, (1 - r^2_{AB})}$$

$$W = \frac{s_B(r_{BB} - r^2_{AB}) - r_{AB}\, s_A(1 - r_{AA})}{s_A\, (1 - r^2_{AB})}$$

$$K = \overline{B} - \overline{A} - W_B\overline{B} - W_A A$$

employed. The equations in line three of Table 1 should be used to make and evaluate refined estimates of changes for individuals, and those in line four for groups. Again, the smallest difference that is worth paying attention to is given on the right-hand side of each of these lines.

Estimating Potential for Performance in Reading

Teachers of reading at every grade level, especially teachers of remedial reading, constantly feel the need for estimating the potential performance level in reading of individuals or groups. Usually, this is done by administering individual tests of mental ability that require little or no reading or by so-called non-verbal group tests. The scores from such tests are compared with scores, such as age- or grade-equivalent scores, from reading tests in some common scale. The differences between an individual's scores on the mental-ability, non-verbal, test and the common scale are then used to decide whether he is falling short of his potential.

To be effective, this procedure demands that three basic conditions be satisfied:

1. The test used to measure performance in reading must be a valid measure of the particular skills involved.

2. The test used to estimate potential must measure an ability (or cluster of abilities) that is crucial for learning the particular skills measured by the reading test. The best information we have regarding the nature of human abilities indicates that many of them are only loosely correlated with one another. Thus, it is possible that ability in spatial visualization is not at all important in the comprehension of stories that a student is required to read in English classes. Scores on a non-verbal figure-analogies test may have little or no relevance to an estimate of a child's potential for pronouncing words. Such tests would also have little or no value for measuring the realization of potential for performance in reading.

Th measurement and statistical techniques required for testing potential have been worked out in detail by the writer presented in *Educational Measurements and Their Interpretations.* [7]

3. Any differences between the measures of potential and actual reading performance must be evaluated to determine whether they could easily be explained as a chance deviation from a true difference of zero.

The first and third conditions can usually be satisfied reasonably well if due care is exercised, but not the second condition. Unfortunately, it is always difficult and often impossible to find a test of abilities that are crucial to the

---

[7]Frederick B. Davis, *Educational Measurement and Their Interpretation* (Belmont, Calif.: Wadsworth Publishing Co., 1964), chapter xi.

performance of reading skills that does not demand the use of these skills. In short, it is usually not possible to measure potential for reading satisfactorily, and as a result, it is also not usually possible to estimate the extent to which an individual or group has realized its potential. Perhaps the best approach to an estimate can be made by a skilled clinical psychologist. But even this approach must be employed with more caution than is usually displayed. Performance in various aspects of reading is not primarily dependent on *non-verbal* abilities but on a cluster of *verbal* abilities. Yet clinicians often use differences between non-verbal test scores and reading-test scores as one basis for diagnosing disability in reading.

Some Pitfalls in Evaluating Progress in Reading Instruction*

ARTHUR S. McDONALD

In the past few years, dramatic results have been claimed for one after another "new method" of teaching reading. In the January, 1963, PHI DELTA KAPPAN, the editor warned that most of these results had not been evaluated for possible contamination by the "Hawthorne effect." In point of fact, a number of pitfalls have been overlooked by many researchers in assessing reading instruction.

From the beginning of formalized reading instruction, various kinds of appraisal have been carried on to ascertain progress of an individual and/or a group. Research studies aimed at assessing the effectiveness of different kinds of reading instructional programs have also been conducted.

My own review of published studies in the past ten years shows that the three most commonly used methods for evaluating progress in reading programs are:

(1) Determining reading gains by comparison of pre- and post-test scores on alternate test forms of both standardized and informal tests, and finding differences in test performance from that expected (e.g., "Johnny gained six months in reading test performance during a six-week reading program").

(2) Comparing test gains with the national average yearly gains made with those made in the local reading program.

(3) Comparing test-retest results of the remedial group with test-retest performance of a control group.

Of these three methods, the first one is most commonly used in classroom and reading clinic descriptive reports. The third is most usual in published reports of research studies.

*Reprinted from *Phi Delta Kappan* 45 (April, 1964), pp. 336-338, by permission of the author and Phi Delta Kappa.

Sources of Error

In recent years, several writers have pointed out the dangers inherent in these methods. Among pitfalls are these:

(1)   Failure to correct for regression to the mean. (Most remedial students are selected on the basis of low initial reading test scores. On a second testing, persons so selected are likely to make higher test scores whether or not they have *actually* improved in reading ability.)

(2)   Treating reading grade scores as empirically obtained indications of month-by-month progress. In reality, reading grade scores are extrapolated from one grade level to another. (Spache has pointed out that experiments using repeated testing indicate that reading growth is not evenly distributed throughout the year but occurs in an initial spurt during the first few weeks or months of the year.[1])

(3)   Interpretation of test scores on the assumption that the tests used provide reliable and valid measures of the most important aspects of reading.

(4)   Spurious scores obtained from the use of a single test over wide educational (or performance) levels. (For instance, on one commonly used type of reading test a non-reader can miss all the questions and earn a reading grade score of 1.6. If another level of this test were used with the same child, his score would be approximately third reading grade level.)

(5)   Use, for checking comprehension, of test questions which can be answered by most children from their background knowledge (i.e., without even reading the selection).

(6)   Errors in interpretation because of use of inappropriate norms, failure to allow for interform differences in equivalence, etc.

(7)   Failure to select a really comparable control group.

Other Sources of Error

Even a carefully designed study, however, one carried out with comparable experimental and control groups under conditions providing for control of many important variables (including student and teacher motivation), may still be vitiated by errors. These errors may arise, in part, because too little attention is paid to reading as a *form of behavior* and, in part, because of errors *inherent in the experimental model itself.*

Thus, in the absence of special precautions, the results obtained by use of

[1] George D. Spache, *Toward Better Reading.* Champaign: Gerrard Press, 1963.

comparable-groups methods are likely to be confounded by "Hawthorne" and "placebo" effects.

Cook has defined the Hawthorne effect as ". . . a phenomenon characterized by an awareness on the part of the subjects of special treatment created by artificial experimental conditions."[2]

As partial explanation of this consequence, Orne has shown that "as far as the subject is able, he will behave in an experimental context in a manner designed to play the role of a "good subject."[3] In other words, the student in either an experimental or control group will try to validate the experiment as he understands it.

A special form of the Hawthorne effect accompanies the use of apparatus, equipment, drugs, special instructional material, ritual, "secret methods," etc. This is called "placebo response."

Following Fischer and Dlin,[4] a "placebo" may be defined as a chemical, mechanical, electronic, or psychological agent or treatment employed, with or without ritual, but always with the suggestion or implication of its powerful and helpful properties. The "placebo response" is that effect of the agent or treatment which cannot be due to the agent or treatment itself but which must be due to some other aspect of the situation.

Thus the placebo effect may be related to the attitude (enthusiasm, belief, optimism, etc.) of the administrator, to the administrator, to the atmosphere (security, insecurity, competitiveness, challenge, etc.), to the treatment situation itself, to the expectancy of *both* the subjects and the experimenter.

Often overlooked in assessment studies, in fact is the considerable research evidence available that the subject's expectations, the cues provided by the environment and the attitudes and expectations of the instructor or experimenter, may significantly alter the effectiveness of the treatment used and the consequences of the study.

As an example, college students who believed they were getting dexedrine (and who *were* receiving dexedrine) had typical energizer-like reactions in both mood and psycho-motor performance, while students who received dexedrine (but *believed* they were getting a barbiturate) showed a tendency toward barbiturate-like reactions. It should be noted that the percentage of such typical *student* responses, however, dropped markedly when the *experimenters* knew what drug was being administered.[5]

[2] Desmond L. Cook, "The Hawthorne Effect in Educational Research," *Phi Delta Kappan,* 44, 1962, p. 118.

[3] Martin T. Orne, "On the Social Psychology of the Psychological Experiment: With Particular Reference to Demand Characteristics and their Implications," *American Psychologist* 17, 1962, p. 778.

[4] J. K. Fischer and B. M. Dlin, "The Dynamics of Placebo Therapy: A Clinical Study," *American Journal of Medical Science,* 232, 504-512, 1956.

[5] Jonathan O. Cole, "The Influence of Drugs on the Individual," in Seymour M. Farber and Roger H. L. Wilson (eds.), *Control of the Mind.* New York: McGraw-Hill, 1961, 110-120.

In another experiment college students were *not* aware that decaffeinated and regular coffee were administered (to the entire group) at different times, but were told that tests were being made to check certain effects of caffeine. The same effects were reported in a similar way for *both* kinds of beverage. When the subjects were told, however, that decaffeinated coffee was being used "just to prove that it was the caffeine that produced the changes" (but *both* regular and decaffeinated coffee were administered as before to all students), *all* effects being measured returned to pretest conditions.[6] (It is interesting to note that an earlier variation of this experiment, using milk, has often been cited in popular articles as proving that caffeine does not keep one awake.)

Considerable research has shown that the *mere act* of using special treatment or instructional devices, material, drugs, etc., strongly increases their effect. Furthermore, the *intra*individual variation in response to Hawthorne and placebo effects has been shown to be as great as the *inter*individual variation of such responses. The Hawthorne and placebo effects produced depend not only on the particular agent or ritual used and the method of administration but also on the circumstances under which these are used and how the effects are measured. Thus the expectations of the subject, the experimenter, and the nature of the situation in which an agent is administered, a device used, or a course of remediation carried out are important determiners of the effects. Vague means of measuring outcomes, tests with low reliability, and heavy reliance on subjective evaluation strongly favor contamination of results with placebo and Hawthorne responses.

Thus unwanted Hawthorne and placebo contamination is particularly likely in reading programs where the instructors rely heavily on special instrumentation (and themselves believe in the unique beneficial effects of the instruments), or believe strongly in the "powerful" effects of a novel method of instruction, or have found a completely new means of instruction which they believe cannot be measured by existing assessment instruments.

The greater the stress, anxiety, or hope surrounding the circumstances of the treatment or experiment, the greater the desire of the subject to improve, the higher the enthusiastic belief of the experimenter or instructor in the agent and technique used, the greater the tendency for Hawthorne and placebo responses to appear.

Investigations have shown that completely inert substances, useless agents, or exhortations (such as "read faster, comprehend more"), when used with the understanding that they would produce certain effects, did indeed cause such effects to appear in 20 to 60 per cent of the subjects. Lehmann reported that "giving a placebo capsule in a well-controlled, double-blind experimental procedure produced test-retest differences which were larger and of greater

[6] L. D. Goodfellow, "Significant Incidental Factors in the Measurement of Auditory Sensitivity," *Journal of General Psychology,* 35, 33-41, 1946.

significance than the administration of effective doses of psychoactive drugs.

Experimenter Must Be 'Blind'

Nash has pointed out the importance of measures taken by the experimenter to increase his "blindness" concerning the subjects in the experiment and the absolute necessity of his paying close attention to his own desires regarding the outcome of the experiment so that he can erect safeguards against the operation of bias or placebo effects arising from experimenter or subject expectancy. He concludes that systematic errors due to suggestion can be reduced if the conditions affecting suggestion and expectancy are kept approximately the same for control and experimental subjects.[8]

Thus in any study of the effects of initial instruction or corrective or remedial treatment, it is absolutely necessary to assess the Hawthorne and placebo reactions. To show that a certain kind of program or type of reading instruction produces more than a nonspecific Hawthorne or placebo response, it must be shown that its effects are stronger, last longer, and are qualitatively different from those produced by placebo agents (as defined in this article) or by the Hawthorne effect, or that the program affects different kinds of subjects than do placebo and Hawthorne reactions.

In this connection, Spache has warned that by dramatic use of novel methods or impressive equipment "it is possible to produce for a brief space of time what appears to be more than normal progress by remedial techniques or methods that are completely contradictory or even irrelevant to the causes of the reading retardation."[9]

My review of relevant research published in the last ten years shows that more than 80 per cent of the studies dealing with evaluation of progress in reading programs of various types at all levels of instruction from elementary to college suffer from serious (but apparently unsuspected or unassessed) contamination due to the Hawthorne and placebo effects.

Implications

Improved evaluation of reading progress requires:

(1)   Careful delineation of objectives in *operational* terms. (What kinds of

[7]Heinze E. Lehman, "The Place and Purpose of Objective Methods in Psychopharmacology," in Leonard Uhr and James G. Miller (eds.), *Drugs and Behavior*, New York: John Wiley and Sons, 1960, pp. 107-127.

[8]Harvey Nash, "The Design and Conduct of Experiments on the Psychological Effects of Drugs" in Leonard Uhr and James G. Miller (eds.), *Drugs and Behavior*, New York: John Wiley and Sons, 1960, pp. 128-156.

[9]Spache, *op. cit.*

reading problems can we help with testable techniques and materials? What kinds of reading problems remain unaffected by our current procedures or show only Hawthorne and placebo reactions?)

(2)   Appropriate generalization from the experimental or clinical situation to the daily teaching situation *elsewhere*.

(3)   Controlling for Hawthorne and placebo contamination. (Cook cites suggestions that the placebo treatment be used to control the Hawthorne effect. For example, avoid singling out experimental and control groups. Use some form of special instrumentation, specially scheduled time and instructional material, stamped "Experimental Edition," with all students. This approach must contain safeguards against teacher expectancy.)[10]

(4)   What conditions and procedures in commonly used remedial programs are especially favorable for the occurrence of Hawthorne and placebo responses? What are the most common responses of the nature encountered?

[10]Cook, *op. cit.*

Assigning Grades to Students in Special Reading Classes *

ALBERT J. KINGSTON

Considerable attention has been devoted to methods designed to identify the child who needs special assistance in reading, to diagnose his individual needs, and to assist him in overcoming his difficulties. Similarly, numerous suggestions have been made to assist the high school reading teacher in evaluating the progress or the lack of progress made by pupils enrolled in remedial or special reading classes. Unfortunately, few readings specialists have concerned themselves with a major problem faced by nearly all high school reading teachers: What criteria should be employed in assigning grades to the reluctant reader and in reporting his progress to his parents?

Apparently most high school administrators agree with Rothney that "although teachers' marks are often unreliable and invalid indexes of growth, they are indispensible tools." (11)† As far as can be determined, most high school reading classes, whether developmental or remedial, carry some type of credit and the teacher is expected to assess the student's progress and to grade his achievements. Generally the child's progress is translated into the grading scheme employed by the school and incorporated into the reporting system used by the school system.

There appears to be evidence that both parents and students prefer traditional report systems. (7,8,12) Apparently, parents have greater faith in the reliability of grades earned by children than do educators. (10) All experienced teachers, however, realize the difficulty in reliably and validly assessing the degree to which their pupils achieve adequate progress toward the established educational objectives. The high school reading teacher not only faces the problems of evaluation common to all teachers but indeed has special problems which grow out of the unique nature of his work.

Central to the problem of assessing student progress in reading is the establishment of educational goals and objectives. Most reading specialists

*Reprinted from *Journal of Reading*, 10 (October, 1966) pp. 39-42, by permission of the author and the International Reading Association.
†Numbers in parentheses refer to references at end of article.

recognize the need for establishing goals for their pupils in terms of their needs and abilities. Goals in reading. hence, are individualized. Anderson (1) has suggested that our grading systems tend to reflect comparisons between children and that the reference point has been academic growth. Obviously, if the pupils assigned to the high school reading program have been selected because of low ability in reading, any grading system based upon a comparison of their reading achievements with those of other students inevitably means the bulk of their grades will be C's, D's, or F's, or whatever symbols are used by the school to indicate less than satisfactory progress.

The reading teacher also is on shaky grounds if he attempts to set a general level of achievement which he expects all of his pupils to achieve in a given period of instruction. Any attempt to employ a common standard, whether based upon standardized or informal tests or the completion of certain exercises or tasks also violated the philosophy of individual differences implicit in reading improvement programs. Reading authorities unanimously agree that for remedial work to be effective, the work should be highly individualized. The establishment of identical goals for all students therefore should be avoided at all costs.

On the other hand, establishing individual goals and objectives is also difficult. With standardized and informal measures the teacher often can discover what reading skills a given student lacks. It is considerably more difficult, however, to determine his capacity for learning or to develop valid and reliable criteria which can be used as a basis for prognosis. (4) Not only is reading itself complex, but reading disability also is complex. Some children have difficulties which baffle our best diagnostic and instructional procedures. Most experienced reading teachers have worked with students who far exceed or fall far short of the "levels of expectancy" which were established. Obviously there is a tendency to give a higher grade to the child who exceeds the teacher's expectations than there is to the student who fails to achieve at the anticipated level. Too often grading schemes based upon the setting of individual objectives are highly subjective and reflective of the adequacy of the diagnosis rather than of the pupil's progress.

Some reading teachers also base their grades largely upon the personal-social characteristics of their students. A student who is cooperative, appears to be hard working, causes no difficulties, and seems to be interested or motivated often is thought to be making good progress. His assigned grade is likely to indicate his teacher's satisfaction with him as a person rather than his progress in learning to read. On the other hand, a child who is highly anxious, hostile, poorly motivated toward reading or toward school is likely to receive a lower grade. A few remedial teachers apparently assume that the retarded reader can regulate his behavior at will and uncooperative children obviously are either lazy or deliberately frustrating the teacher's efforts to help him.

Obviously, all three approaches to grading leave something to be desired. Probably most high school reading teachers would be happy if they could be freed of the necessity of assigning grades to their pupils or were permitted to employ other methods of reporting the progress being made by their students. It is encouraging to note that school personnel appear to be increasingly aware that the traditional reporting systems must be supplemented with other means of contact between school and home. Phone conversations, correspondence, parent-teacher interviews, the systematic transmission of samples of the student's work have been used to advantage. (3,9) High school reading teachers probably should make greater use of these procedures in reporting pupil progress and rely less on the traditional report forms.

Although it is more commonly employed in the elementary school than in the high school, another possible approach to easing the grading and reporting problem is the utilization of a dual marking system. (5,6) A dual marking system provides two grades. One grade provides information concerning the student's achievements in comparison to the group norm. The other grade reflects his achievements in terms of his own potentialities and abilities. Austin has suggested that such procedures have merit in assessing student achievement in reading. (2) As high school reading programs continue to expand, and various types of grouping or teaching schemes become more prevalent, the problems of assigning meaningful grades to students undoubtedly will become more acute. High school reading teachers need to concern themselves more with the problem, for the published literature in reading indicates a dearth of research about this troublesome problem.

References

1.   Anderson, Robert H. "The Importance and Purposes of Reporting," *The National Elementary Principal,* 45 (May, 1966), 6-11. 18 (May, 1965), 660-663.
2.   Austin, Mary C. "Report Cards and Parents," *The Reading Teacher* 18 (May, 1965), 660-663.
3.   Boyd, Margaret. "School Standards in Promotion: Testing, Reporting, Grading," *Theory Into Practice,* 4 (June, 1965), 95-98.
4.   Cleland, Donald L. "Clinical Materials for Appraising Disabilities in Reading," *The Reading Teacher,* 17 (March, 1964), 428-434.
5.   Halliwell, Joseph W. "Parental Interpretation of and Reaction to Dual Report Cards," *Clearing House,* 36 (December, 1961), 245-247.
6.   ———. "The Relationship of Certain Factors to Marking Practices in Individualized Reporting Programs," *Journal of Educational Research,* 54 (October, 1960), 76-78.
7.   Kingston, Albert J. and James A. Wash, Jr. "Research on Reporting Systems," *The National Elementary Principal,* 45 (May, 1966), 36-40.
8.   Morris, Lucille. "Evaluating and Reporting Pupil Progress," *Elementary School Journal,* 53 (November, 1952), 144-149.
9.   Reavis, William C. "Report Cards," *School Review,* 60 (April, 1952), 199-200.
10.   Richardson, Sybil. "Reporting to Parents," *Instructor,* 69 (June, 1960), 9.
11.   Rothney, John W. M. *Evaluating and Reporting Pupil Progress,* Bulletin No. 7 (Washington, D. C., Department of Classroom Teachers and American Educational Research Association, 1955).

12. Yauch, Wilbur A. "School Marks and Their Reporting," *NEA Journal,* 5 (May, 1961), 50-58.

Questions For Discussion

1. Frederick Davis sets forth three basic conditions that should be satisified in any procedure used to estimate potential for performance in reading. What procedures are you acquainted with that have been used to determine potential for performance in reading and to what extent are these three conditions met in these procedures?

2. What definite procedures could be used in assessing reading programs to overcome possible confounding by the "Hawthorne" and "placebo" effects?

3. What do you see as the advantages and disadvantages of the dual marking system suggested by Kingston?

Developing Vocabulary and Word Recognition Skills

V

Previous sections in this text have been concerned with such matters as defining the nature of reading, justifying the need for reading programs at the secondary school level, discussing ways to organize and administer such programs, and clarifying issues involved in the evaluation of reading skill development growth. Beginning with this section, the focus turns to a consideration of those reading skills felt to be most important to develop at the secondary school level. This particular section includes articles on various vocabulary and word recognition skills.

In the first article, Lee Deighton notes that high school students in their speech and writing use relatively few of the words they see and hear. He presents four factors which he feels are reasons for this condition.

Deighton believes that a necessary prerequisite for any successful vocabulary development program is student interest in words for themselves and feels that well-developed units on the history of our language can help instill this student interest. In addition, Deighton presents five principles which he feels are of great importance in developing vocabulary units at the secondary school level.

In the second article in this section, Olson concentrates on a presentation of the phonics and structural analysis he feels should be stressed in a secondary school reading program. He recognizes the fact that these skills will have originally been taught at the elementary school level but feels they need further review and refinement because of the more complex words that students must cope with at the secondary school level.

Earle Crawford makes a number of detailed suggestions for increasing the reading vocabularies of junior and senior high school students. Of particular interest are his ideas for teaching students to recognize the importance of such qualifying words as *many, almost,* and *all* in determining sentence meaning. Crawford also puts considerable emphasis on the need for teachers to help their students understand the various forms of figurative language.

Developing Vocabulary:
Another Look at the Problem*

LEE C. DEIGHTON

Vocabulary growth begins in the first years of human life and continues until the last months of active intelligence. It occurs in school and out. It is encouraged by parents, siblings, peers, business associates, and — teachers. It is implemented by signboards, advertisements, television, radio, and even by comic books. Since the opportunity for vocabulary growth is so general, it is fair to ask why there is a problem. Why do we find such relative poverty of expression among high school students and among their parents?

In speculating about the answer to this question, we must note that the word *vocabulary* itself is somewhat ambiguous. Actually, each of us has several different vocabularies. There is a speech vocabulary, the words we use freely, readily, habitually in talking with others. There is a writing vocabulary, the words we use in writing. There is also an aural vocabulary, the words to which we respond when we hear them spoken. Finally, there is a reading vocabulary, the words to which we respond when we see them in print.

These four vocabularies overlap, but no two of them are identical. Each develops in its own way from a separate kind of experience, and each must therefore be studied and developed separately. It is for this reason that a word acquired in reading does not immediately and automatically appear in a student's writing and speech.

Usually, when we speak of vocabulary growth, we are thinking of the vocabularies of speech and writing. We can now rephrase our starting question something like this: Why is it that high school students employ in their speech and writing relatively so few of the words that they see and hear?

Without attempting a complete explanation, we can suggest several relevant factors. First, it requires much less effort to understand a spoken or written word than to use it effectively. In reading and listening, a superficial understanding is sufficient for our purposes. We need only enough understanding of an unfamiliar word to get the general sense of the passage. As we meet it, the

*Reprinted from *English Journal,* 49 (February, 1960), pp. 82-88, by permission of the author and the National Council of Teachers of English.

word occurs in a context supplied by the author, and the context may provide clues to meaning. To use this same word in our speech and writing, we must originate the context, and we must know enough about the word to make sure that it fits the context. In short, the new words acquired in a student's reading vocabulary do not immediately transfer to speech and writing because they are imperfectly understood.

Second, the situations in which we speak, students and adults alike, do not usually permit time to dredge up from memory the word that most precisely fits the occasion. The ready speaker whose conversation sparkles with apt and precisely chosen words is the exception. Under the time pressure of ordinary speech, most of us fall back upon the generalized words of our own personal Basic English.

Third, the climate of our school society is not right for experimenting with new words, not at least, in oral situations. For the student, the experimental use of new words leads often to error, and error in the use of words produces laughter. Even the precise use of an unfamiliar word leads to the raising of eyebrows. Moreover, outside the classroom, few audiences in our society place a premium upon careful and colorful speech. It is the hardy soul who is willing to defy the label of "intellectual" for the use of words beyond the limits of the few hundred with which most adults conduct their affairs.

Finally, a special limitation is placed upon the development of a writing vocabulary simply because we do not write often enough. If the student is to experiment with new words in writing, he must have judgments as to the effectiveness of his experiment. This means close reading by a teacher, with approval or correction of word choice. And this gets us into the really troubled area of high school composition. Without prejudice as to how papers are to be read, we can say that a student's writing vocabulary will expand in direct proportion to the opportunities he has for writing something that is read and evaluated, and that normally these opportunities are too few.

The diagnosis is not encouraging, but neither is it frustrating. There are no elements in the situation that cannot be mastered. There are many things we can do in the classroom to improve the situation. I should like to point out for special emphasis what seems to me the most important of them.

Building Interest in Words

It is my belief that nothing substantial can be accomplished in vocabulary development unless the student is infected with a continuing and consuming interest in words for themselves. This kind of interest is not inborn; it is learned. Or more precisely, it is instilled. It is instilled most readily by teachers who are themselves fascinated by this stubborn, illogical, knuckle-headed English language of ours.

Interest can most readily be kindled by giving attention to words, by pointing out what happens to them, by making them seem important. We may note, for example, that the original meaning of *with* was "against," and that we still give the word this meaning. During our lifetime, the word *inflammable* has disappeared from oil trucks in favor of the less ambiguous *flammable.* Herein lies a whole sermon on the variant meanings of the prefix *in-*; The word *idiot* comes from a Greek word meaning "without professional knowledge, an ignorant, common person." In short, to the doctor, lawyer, or military man, every layman is an idiot. The changing fashion in labels, the attempt by words alone to make things seem less horrifying, revolting, or disastrous is endlessly amusing. This is the kind of thing noted by Galbraith in *The Affluent Society:*

> In the last century, the term crisis was employed. With time, however, this acquired the connotation of the misfortune it described. And Marx's reference to the 'capitalist crisis' gave the word an ominous sound. The word panic, which was a partial synonym a half century ago, was no more reassuring. As a result the word depression was gradually brought into use. This had a softer tone; it implied a yielding of the fabric of business and not a crashing fall. During the Great Depression the word depression acquired from the event it described an even more unsatisfactory connotation. Therefore the word recession was substituted . . . But this term eventually acquired a foreboding quality and the recession of 1953-54 was widely characterized as a rolling readjustment. Should we have a really serious rolling readjustment this phrase would become taboo.

An interest in words will lead the student to acquisitions that he can use with comfort in any situation. But to be comfortable with a word, one must know it thoroughly. This principle suggests a way of proceeding in the classroom. Most of us know from direct experience that to assign a list of words with meanings to be memorized is both fruitless and boring. Little is known, to be sure, about how vocabularies grow, but we do know that memorized lists of words make little permanent change in student vocabularies. I would suggest as a contrasting alternative that a narrow range of words be studied in depth. For this kind of study, a dictionary is indispensable.

There must, of course, be a reason for studying a word. Its fortuitous appearance in press, radio, or television reports is reason enough. Recourse to a dictionary would show that the word has several meanings, that the etymology throws light on several of these meanings, and that the word may appear in interesting idioms. Perhaps the new word is formed by prefix and suffixes from a familiar base word. With this background, the teacher may find occasion to use the word from day to day in differing context, and the students may be put into situations where they too must use the word.

There is another approach that students and teachers alike will find challenging. In the black-or-white world of student life, persons, automobiles, books, and clothes are all favorably referred to as *cool* or *neat* and unfavorably designated as *square*. These undifferentiated mass-words have only a positive or negative valence. They tell nothing about the person or thing under observation. They merely project the speaker's own reaction.

What can be said more specifically and precisely about a person, for example? What can be said of his personality, his appearance, his manner, his intelligence, or his character? There are words to express favor, disfavor, indifference, or uncertainty in these details with precision and clarity. They are the means of clear, precise thought. To learn these words to the point of being able to use them accurately is to open up whole new worlds in which intelligence may operate. And by some innate magic, they make the person or thing described seem much more *cool, neat,* or *square* than the mass labels do. It could be very profitable indeed to take class time for the study of specific words used in evaluating things, people, and events.

Ultimately, the responsibility for vocabulary growth like any other intellectual growth rests with the student. We cannot learn words for him. We cannot with much success impose words upon him. What we can do is to create a climate favorable to vocabulary growth, and we shall find that this climate must persist from day to day. We must make words seem important and interesting all of the time.

We have thus far been considering the problems of developing the vocabularies of speech and writing and specific methods that may be useful. These devices may be used at any time. They may be used effectively, for example, during the periods devoted to literature. But there is in addition a body of information about words and meanings that must be presented sequentially and by itself in periods, days, or even weeks devoted to nothing else.

Principles of Vocabulary Study

Five principles in particular are of the greatest importance: (1) *Most words used colloquially or in literature have more than one meaning.* The more often a word is used, in general, the greater its number of meanings. In addition, many words in common use have infrequently-used meanings. Others in general use have a particular and quite special meaning in science or other branches of knowledge. It is fatal, therefore, to proceed at any time on the basis of equating a word with a single meaning. It cannot be said too often that words are not like coins of fixed value. You can put a dime into the slot of a parking meter anywhere in the country with a reasonable assurance of what will happen. You cannot drop a fixed meaning for a word into a sentence slot with any assurance whatever.

Perhaps it is appropriate at this time to say a word about synonyms. For the past forty years, textbook writers and English teachers have invested synonyms with a kind of mystic value. Properly used, of course, they can be most helpful; improperly used, they lead to irresponsible and witless expression. The English language is not a system of interchangeable parts. You cannot substitute synonyms at random. One word is synonymous with another only in respect to a particular meaning. The acquisition of synonyms wholesale can lead only to improvident and inexact expression.

(2) *Context determines which of a word's meanings fits a particular passage.* We usually think of context as consisting only of surrounding words. We should also think of it in terms of the total situation in which a word is used. Does the word occur in a physics text or in a newspaper account of court proceedings? Does it occur in the dialogue of a story or in a formal Presidential address to Congress? The situation will determine which of the meanings of a word is relevant.

(3) *We never get all of a word's meaning at any one encounter.* We must not suppose that having figured out a meaning for one context, we may use that meaning indiscriminately thereafter. Words have more meanings even than those pinned down by lexicographers. They have colorations acquired from long use in familiar context. They acquire new colorations from use in new contexts. Ours is a living language, and it is the nature of a living language that the meanings of its words are pushed, hammered, stretched, and extended to answer the needs of new experiences. It is therefore to the point to explain to students that they must not expect meanings to stay put, that they will be master of a word only after wide experience with it and only by watching it carefully from year to year.

(4) *Meaning comes from experience.* Meaning comes to an individual from reading experience, where a word is used in the presence of other words that illuminate it. Meaning also comes from direct experience with a word in the presence of the person, thing, or event it names. Here we can point and say, "That is what we mean by *carburetor.* This is an example of *self-honesty,* and so on."

The psychology of learning has established that concepts are learned gradually. They acquire layers of meaning year after year as they are encountered in varying contexts. We may regard the meanings of words as concepts. We acquire these meanings for a word as we have new experiences with it. Turning back for a moment to lists of words to be memorized, isn't it likely that the ineffectiveness of this method comes from the complete lack of real experience with the words so listed?

(5) *Finally, we get clues to the meanings of words from context, from word parts, and from phonetics.* These clues are of special importance in development of reading vocabulary. In facing an unfamiliar word, we are on an even level with our students, for all of us meet new words in our reading. What choices do we have when we come upon an unfamiliar word? We can ignore it and try to get on with our reading. Or we can get up from our comfortable chairs, cross the room to a dictionary, and find the appropriate meaning. We

may do this once or twice on a rainy evening, but when the third or fourth unfamiliar words appear, we are likely to slump down a notch, reflecting that we are not as young as we once were, and that this dictionary calisthenics is really for the very young.

We have other means at our disposal. First, as to phonetics; it is now generally agreed that the six-year-old child comes to school with an aural vocabulary in excess of 10,000 words. The reading problem is to help the child tie the printed symbol on the page to the familiar and meaningful sounds in his aural memory. It is at this point that knowing the sounds of letters and letter combinations becomes useful. It remains useful forever thereafter. Thanks to television, radio, and other influences, our aural and reading vocabularies are never identical. We always know some words by sound that we have not seen or have not seen frequently in print. A full course in phonetics for high school students may be neither practical nor necessary, but a review of the sounds of letter combinations, of silent letters, and of syllabication could prove most helpful. It would do two things: (1) It would help the student match his aural vocabulary to printed words; (2) it would encourage him to face up to new words that he otherwise passes by. Incidentally, it might also provide an answer to the perplexing question: "How do I look up a word that I don't know how to spell?"

May I digress for a moment about syllabication. It must be remembered that there is one kind of syllabication for pronunciation and another for writing. They are not the same. The syllabication acceptable in writing was devised for their own convenience by eighteenth-century printers who were neither consistent, logical, nor scientific. Their work is embalmed for the ages in the entry words of our dictionaries. There is no way to outguess it. To make sure that you have broken a word acceptably at the end of a line, you must consult a dictionary. But to break a word into pronounceable segments, you have only one rule to follow: get a vowel sound into each part. It is therefore sensible in classroom instruction to keep these two kinds of syllabication apart and not to insist on the standard printed form when we are concerned with pronunciation.

For the chair-fast reader there is a second source of aid in a knowledge of word parts and word-formation. This knowledge can be of real assistance in attacking unfamiliar words, provided that we keep basic principles in mind. Word parts will not yield the whole meaning but only clues to the meaning of a word. The whole of a word is considerably greater than the sum of its parts. We must avoid the simple-minded arithmetic which assumes that prefix plus base word plus suffix gives the meaning of a word. In the first place, it is folly to think of the meaning for most words in common usage. In the second place, prefix, suffix, and base provide only a "literal" meaning, which may be far afield from common contemporary usage.

Nonetheless, some prefixes and suffixes do add predictable meaning to many words. A very few of these affixes have a single, invariant meaning. We can use these effectively, but we must be careful not to assign a single value to the others, saying for example, that *trans* means "across" or that *pre-* means "before" or that *in-* always means "not."

We may get a great deal of help from suffixes that are used regularly in English word-building to make one part of speech from another. Thus, the suffixes *-ment, ation,* and *-ness* are used to make nouns from verbs and adjectives. The suffixes *-fy* and *-ize* are used to make verbs from nouns. The suffix *-ous* is used to make adjectives from verbs and nouns. This process of word formation in English is completely fascinating, and an understanding of it will encourage students to stand without fear in the presence of polysyllables.

It would be impossible to prove, but it does seem likely, that most of us acquire most of our word meanings through context clues. Context, you remember, always determines which meaning of a word is pertinent. Context also at times throws light upon the intended meaning. Unfortunately, context does not illuminate meaning nearly so often as we have supposed. But when it does, its aid is invaluable. It permits us to remain comfortably in our easy chairs instead of making the long trip across the room to a dictionary.

Context operates in four to five distinct ways to give meaning to a word. A relatively full analysis has been made elsewhere and is available for those who are interested. [1] Here we may say that context throws meaning upon words through outright definition, through restatement, examples, and inference. A knowledge of how context operates and of when it is operating should be of very great assistance to high school students in attacking unfamiliar words.

In composing this paper, I have been beset by the frustrating problem of presenting both a point of view and specific methods and procedures within seemly time limits. The subject is thoroughly suited to nothing less than four or five hours of discourse. To give this paper the appearance of usefulness, let me set forth a bill of particulars.

(1) The point of view is that vocabulary development must pervade the English curriculum with suitable attention every day.
(2) It is well to set aside a period of days or weeks in which to present sequentially certain basic aspects of words and meanings.
(3) We must provide a favorable climate for experimental use of new words by our students.
(4) We can encourage the replacement of mass-words by acquainting students with a range of specific terms used in expressing reactions to people, things, and events.
(5) Study of a limited number of words in depth is more productive than superficial acquaintance with lists of words.

[1] Lee C. Deighton,, *Vocabulary Development in the Classroom* (Bureau of Publications, Teachers College, Columbia University), 1959.

(6))   A knowledge of word-formation through a study of suffixes, prefixes, and base words will prove helpful.

(7)   An understanding of context clues to meaning and a knowledge of certain aspects of phonetics will help the student deal effectively with unfamiliar words.

It would be comforting now to suppose that the application of these ways and means will solve the problem. Nothing could be further from the truth. No antiseptically administered program of vocabulary development will succeed by its own momentum. What is needed is a consuming student interest in words for themselves, an interest fed by the example of the genuine excitement of teachers over the variety, the flexibility, and the unpredictable nature of our language.

Teaching Word Recognition for Better Vocabulary Development *

ARTHUR V. OLSON

In the corridors of junior and senior high schools one often hears teachers say, "He can't read the words and I'm not sure he would know the meaning if he could." To know how to correct this problem, it is important that we understand the process of unlocking words and the techniques by which we can help students to apply their skills more productively.

Words are symbols that mean nothing by themselves. They take on meaning only to the extent that we can bring meaning to them, understand their relationship to other words and make sense out of the combinations. Without this ability to translate, there can be no effective communication and thoughts cannot be expressed.

In the learning of language, there are five vocabularies that we use: non-verbal, listening, reading, speaking, and writing.

The non-verbal vocabulary is by far the largest, how large we are not sure. Many of the understandings that we have are the result, not of spoken words, but of gestures, facial expression, and body movement. These may help to convey the meaning of words and, at the same time, give more meaning than the words do by themselves. Studies of underprivileged students indicate that this type of communication is, in effect, the primary means of communication for them and takes on the aspects of a language itself. For some of the students with limited vocabulary this type of communication is a vital factor in understanding.

The listening vocabulary is the second largest and, like the non-verbal, is an extremely important means of acquiring information for the culturally deprived or the slow learner. We can often understand the meaning of what a person is saying by the emphasis, pitch, and tone of his speech. These factors, along with the non-verbal, expand our understanding to a point that far exceeds that achieved by any other vocabularies we may have.

As the student grows in his ability to work with words, builds concepts, and broadens his understandings, his ability to recognize and understand words

*Reprinted from Clearing House, 40 (May, 1966), pp. 559-562, by permission of the author and the editor.

in his reading expands rapidly. There are many words that he will read and understand in the context of the material but will never use in either speaking or writing. The reading vocabulary is limited by what experiences and concepts the reader can bring to the material. There is no oral interpretation (except his own) and he cannot rely upon gestures and facial expression to help him understand. In reading, the student is in an "isolation booth."

The speaking vocabulary is even more limited than the others previously mentioned. Students will accept the standard of the peer group and limit themselves to the accepted means of expression. Unless the student is helped to understand that there are many means of expressing ourselves verbally and that various situations demand different kinds of vocabulary, he will remain at one level only. The means of expression fit the situation and the thoughts we are trying to express. If the student is not put into various situations where he has a chance to use and develop the vocabulary, however, there is very little chance of his seeing any use for learning such things.

Educationally, we have done a very poor job of encouraging students to have a large spelling vocabulary. We have emphasized correct spelling to the point where most students do not dare put on paper a word they aren't absolutely sure of spelling correctly. Spelling is important and should be emphasized, but the most important element is the thought. After the thought has been expressed, then is the time to make corrections. If we expect the student to think with his large vocabulary and then translate this down into the lowest vocabulary of his spelling words, it is no wonder that most students play it safe.

It is axiomatic that the larger the vocabulary of the student, the more accurately he will understand what he reads. He will also be able to read more rapidly. It is also evident that the extent and depth of the vocabulary are going to have noticeable effect upon his ability to think and to exchange ideas with others.

The number of words in all of our vocabularies will increase proportionately to the opportunities we have to learn new words. The commonly used school practice of introducing 20 new words per week has very little meaning unless we multiply the chance to use each word by at least ten experiences. "New words for new words' sake" outside of a learning situation is ridiculous. Words have meaning only as they help us to express and understand ideas. They have little "show case value."

Here are some ways to assist students with vocabulary development:

(1) Write out all new important words. The words can be kept on cards or in a notebook. Each word should be defined and an example of its use given. For example: Procrastination-pro (for the benefit of) + crastination (tomorrow). "Stop all of your procrastination and do it now." Pneumatic-pneumat (air, vapor, gas) + ic (relating to). "The pneumatic gun had tremendous force."

(2) Try to get the meaning of a strange word from the context. The

student must understand, however, that the context will reveal only a single meaning of the word.

(3) Many words are formed by adding prefixes and suffixes to the root word or stem. An understanding of the meanings of the common prefixes and suffixes will help greatly in getting meaning. Overemphasis upon this type of analysis can be misleading, since the same prefix may have several meanings. The prefix "de-," for example, has four meanings.

(4) Know how to use the dictionary well enough to find the appropriate meaning for a word, correct pronunciation, spelling (preferred), part of speech, and etymology. Have the students make a list of words they have read in textbooks, newspapers, magazines, or other sources. Ask them to list only those words of which they are unsure. Put this list on the board or mimeograph it. Encourage all of the students to use the words with each other and to look for them in other sources as they read or listen.

(5) Studying the origins of words and words changes can be interesting in a book such as *Thereby Hangs a Tale,* by Charles E. Funk, published by Harper and Brothers, New York, 1950 ($3.75).

(6) Study how new vocabulary words come about and are accepted into our language. The students might even make up words and ask others to tell what they mean. For example: washeteria, Beatlorama, stealogy.

Word Recognition

Knowledge of how words are put together is basic to vocabulary development. The able reader has many techniques for attacking words which are unknown or difficult for him. Most adult readers use four basic aids in attacking new words. These aids are:

Context – the way in which the word is used.

Structure – the arrangement of the word, root, prefix, suffix, or inflectional ending.

Sound – the sounds of the letter combinations in the word.

Dictionary – the key to meaning and pronunciation if the previous three approaches fail.

The experienced reader is able to get general meaning and the pronunciation of many words that he has never seen or heard before because of his ability to use the word-attack skills. The context clues often provide enough information to enable the reader to understand a sentence even though a particular word in the sentence may be completely unknown. Many unfamiliar words, when analyzed for structure, contain elements that are familiar in other words and give a clue to pronunciation. Experience with words not only helps us to notice familiar elements, but also gives us clues as to the possible sounds that combinations of letters can make. A mature reader will try these aids in attempting to pronounce an unknown word, with the assumption that if he pronounces it correctly he may well know the general meaning from having heard the word before. If neither context, structure, nor sound clues provide satisfactory help, the dictionary becomes the final authority.

Context, structure, and sound have been presented independently, but with the experienced reader all are probably used almost simultaneously. In unlocking words, the structure and sound are so interrelated that one cannot be used profitably without the other.

The word which a student understands when he hears it aurally may be a complete mystery when it appears in print. Students first learn the skills of attacking new words phonetically in the elementary grades, but there is a clear need to review at every level in the secondary school. As the words that they use become increasingly complex, students need help in applying the principles learned with less complex words.

Pronouncing Polysyllables

Words of more than one syllable are difficult to attack, and students usually need help in noting the general structure of each word and analyzing it into the fewest number of parts. It is virtually impossible to attack a long word by sounding the separate letters. Polysyllable words are of four types:

(1)   Compound words.
       Examples: craftsman, gateway, commonwealth, overtime.
(2)   Words which contain a known stem to which prefixes or suffixes have been attached.
       Examples: independently, deoxygenize, indispensable.
(3)   Words which may be analyzed into familiar or phonetically pronounced syllables.
       Examples: conception, fervor, meager, amplify.
(4)   Words that have so many non-phonetic parts that the dictionary offers the only help.
       Examples: avoirdupois, Tchaikovsky, schism.

Examples of these four types of polysyllables can be found in any content area textbook and should be taught by every teacher using the specialized vocabulary. The teacher should present the vocabulary on the board and help the students to look for the best way to analyze the word.

In the initial presentation, the four types may be discussed and examples drawn from the book. New or difficult words should be presented as the need arises, with class discussion contributing to the lesson. Lessons of this type should probably not be any longer than five minutes except in the first presentation.

Phonics and Syllabication

Without knowledge of certain generalizations concerning phonics and syllabication, students in the secondary schools will certainly face some reading problems. A valuable resource for any teacher who is interested in knowing what to teach and how to teach it is *Phonics in Proper Perspective,* by Arthur Heilman (Charles E. Merrill Books, Inc., 1968).

Beyond the general phonic and structural skills needed by every reader, there are some generalizations that need special consideration. First, the primary goal of breaking words down into syllables and then applying our knowledge of letter combinations to produce sound is to approximate the sound of a word. If, because of our previous experiences, the approximation is close enough to the correct pronunciation of the word, we will recognize it and make an adjustment, if needed. If the approximation is not close enough, we may try to analyze more closely, ignore the word if we don't need to understand the meaning of the material, or consult a dictionary if its meaning and pronunciation are necessary.

Second, many of the generalizations learned concerning silent consonants and adjacent vowels have more exceptions in the secondary school than they do in the elementary. This is true because of the increased vocabulary and various derivations of the technical words which do not fit the generalizations. For this reason, each teacher must take the time to aid the student with the analysis of the vocabulary unique to their subject.

Third, the purpose of syllabication is to help the reader break words down into units that are easily pronounced. There are no rules about syllabication, but there are three generalizations that have wide application. The three generalizations are:

(1)   Prefixes and suffixes generally form separate syllables.
(2)   Syllables generally divide between two consonants or double consonants.
(3)   Words ending in *le* usually take the consonant immediately before it and form the final syllable.
        Example: no ble.

In the final analysis, it does not matter if the reader divides the word "melo-di-ous" or "mel-o-di-ous" or "me-lo-di-ous." What does matter is the resulting familiar sound that has meaning.

Conclusion

The primary objective in teaching vocabulary development and word recognition skill is to increase the independence of the student. If the learning is to be meaningful, the learner must be actively involved in the process or there will be no lasting change. There must be interest and a sense of accomplishment.

Teaching Essential Reading Skills— Vocabulary *

EARLE E. CRAWFORD

Improvement of Vocabulary

Two closely related fundamental skills in reading are recognition of words and symbols and an understanding of the language used. Effective instruction in vocabulary building contributes to the pupil's understanding of what is read, to growth in expressing ideas both in oral and in written form, and to an understanding of ideas presented orally.

A. BACKGROUND EXPERIENCES

Pupils frequently fail to understand what is read because the vocabulary is not within their experience. Therefore, provision for common background experiences to enable pupils to understand many words before they meet them in reading about a problem or a topic helps in overcoming vocabulary difficulties. The following suggestions apply especially to slow readers.

(1) Use these general guides for preparing pupils to read a selection:
    (a) Provide concrete background experiences.
    (b) Use visual aids, such as maps, diagrams, charts, pictures, models, and motion pictures.
    (c) Use words in conversation and explain specific terms.
(2) Provide exercises giving specific helps for developing readiness to read a particular selection:
    (a) Change the language of the text to one the pupils understand.
    (b) Write difficult words in the lesson on the board. After each word, list the page on which it is found. In an informal discussion, have pupils find each word and tell what it means. Select difficult words from the lesson. After each word, write the page on which it is

*Reprinted from *Bulletin of the National Association of Secondary-School Principals,* 34 (February, 1950), pp. 56-68, by permission of the author and the National Association of Secondary School Principals.

found. In another column write a word or phrase that has the same meaning.

B. DEVELOPMENT OF VOCABULARY

The emphasis in vocabulary building should be on meaning. In the best classroom practice, procedures for improving word recognition and pronunciation and for developing wider meaning vocabulary will be closely related. In this way, word meaning will be constantly emphasized. Specific exercises should be given for improving the mechanics of word recognition and pronunciation because " . . . comprehension cannot be raised to a high degree if the learner is struggling with the mechanics of the reading process."[1]

Although certain types of vocabulary drill are not always successful and the degree of improvement does not always justify the effort expended to produce it, the majority of research studies seems to justify well-motivated vocabulary training which grows out of the pupil's reading experience or other use of words.

The following suggestions, according to Ruth Strang, have proved to be of value:[2]

(1)   Note definitions which frequently follow the introduction of technical words. The definitions given in the text are often preferable to definitions found in a standard dictionary.

(2)   Check lightly unfamiliar words which are not defined in their context, and later look them up in a dictionary. Write each at the top of a small card. At the bottom of the card should appear a synonym, and in the middle of the card a sentence using the word, or a familiar word derived from or giving derivation to the unfamiliar one. These cards may then be used for individual practice. When the word is not immediately recognized, the "player" looks down to the "connecting link" in the middle of the card. If this does not bring about the recall of the meaning, he must resort to the synonym or definition at the bottom of the card. Junior-high-school youngsters enjoy playing games with such cards and finding the words in new contexts. Adults find such a method of keeping up their recently acquired vocabulary useful because a knowledge of the range of literal meanings of a large number of words helps the reader to grasp its meaning in context.

[1] *A Preliminary Survey of a Reading Program for the Secondary Schools,* Bulletin 202. Harrisburg, Pennsylvania: Department of Public Instruction, Commonwealth of Pennsylvania, 1939, p. 32.

[2] Ruth Strang, with the assistance of Florence C. Rose, *Problems in the Improvement of Reading in High School and College.* Lancaster, Pennsylvania: The Science Press Printing Co., 1938, p. 84.

Throughout his reading experience, an individual tends to read about things more or less familiar to him. Each new bit of reading increases his fund of ideas, gives him new understandings and wider experiences, often vicarious, all of which builds up a certain ability to infer meanings.

When new words are encountered for the first time, great dependence is placed upon context clues. In fact, familiarity with ideas being expressed gives the reader his first clues to word symbols. In normal reading development, occasional unfamiliar words present little difficulty since meanings can often be derived from the otherwise familiar context. The more remote the subject matter from the reader's background of experience, the less able is he to anticipate or infer meanings. Thus, the poor reader with inadequate skill in word perception goes down under a too heavy load of unfamiliar words encountered in his reading.

Most of the instruction which is directed toward enlargement of students' vocabularies is based upon use of the dictionary. Instruction and practice in dictionary use are often carried to such a point that pupils feel helpless without a dictionary or, as a labor-saving substitute, a teacher who will define unknown words. Since, in practice, mature readers use context clues far more frequently than they use dictionaries in arriving at word meanings, it is highly desirable to give pupils some comprehension of the process involved and some training in applying it. All pupils need some help in this area and less alert ones must have intensive practice in it. To enrich the background and to choose material not too far above the level of the pupil's reading ability are first steps in specific training to use context clues as an aid to word recognition as well as to word meaning.

The next step might well be to help pupils become aware that words and meanings may be guessed, at times. Practice on familiar expressions will serve to awaken pupils to the realization that many words may be read without having been printed in the sentence. This is easily demonstrated by completing the following phrases:

Early in the   .   .   .   .   His one .   .   .   . interest
As light as a   .   .   .   .   Flew in a straight   .   .   .   .

Other types of clues should be analyzed and taught specifically. Often an unfamiliar word is merely a synonym for a word previously used, as illustrated in the following two sentences:

Today he tells the *property man* what he wants and tomorrow he finds the items waiting on the set. The *property custodian* has become the movie director's Santa Claus.

An unfamiliar word may be an antonym for a known word, for example:

Water is *seldom* found in the desert, but springs *frequently* occur in the surrounding hills.

Organized and systematic instruction on the use of these and other types of clues should form a part of the reading program throughout elementary-and high-school grades. Awareness of context clues and skill in using them are indispensable for independent and intelligent reading. Pupils must be able to use context clues in various ways:

(a)   In associating meaning with known word forms.
(b)   In discriminating between words which are very much alike in sound and form but not in meaning.
(c)   In checking on pronunciation derived from phonetic analysis.
(d)   In determining which one of the various sounds of a certain vowel is appropriate in a given word.[3]

C. QUALIFYING WORDS

Common qualifying words are important to the meaning of a sentence, yet many pupils fail to understand the idea expressed in a sentence because they pass over the qualifying words. Common qualifying words include *many, no, more, most, less, few, only, almost, always* and *all.* Short phrases and clauses are frequently used in a qualifying manner, and pupils should be trained to notice the way in which such phrases, as well as words similar to the ones listed above, change the meaning of a sentence. The following types of exercises have been found helpful in training pupils to notice how qualifying words or phrases change the meaning of a sentence.

(1)   Write on the blackboard sentences containing qualifying words or give them orally. Discuss with pupils the way in which the words affect the meaning of the sentence.
(2)   Write a group of sentences on the blackboard with the instructions to copy these sentences and draw a line through each qualifying word.
         Example: There are *many* apples on the plate.
         (a)   After the sentences have been discussed and all pupils have drawn a line through each qualifying word, have them recite each sentence and substitute another qualifying word for the one used.
         (b)   Discuss the meaning of these rewritten sentences to show how qualifying words make distinct changes in the meaning of a sentence.
(3)   Write on the blackboard sentences containing qualifying words or phrases. Check the pupils' knowledge of how the words or phrases change the

[3]William S. Gray and Lillian Gray, *Guidebook for Streets and Roads.* Chicago: Scott, Foresman and Company, 1941, p. 29.

meaning of the sentence by making them answer yes or no to questions about the sentences.

Example: The old Indian nearly always came to the trading post in the morning.

Questions:

(1) Did the old Indian always come to the trading post in the morning?
(2) Did the old Indian usually come to the trading post in the morning?
(3) Is it true that the old Indian seldom came to the trading post in the morning?

Oral discussion is a vital factor in all preceding procedures. It should be used freely.

D. WORDS COMMONLY OVERWORKED

Some words are so badly overworked that they have almost lost their specific meanings. They are the "maids of all work" and are used principally by the language beggars. High-school pupils need to be helped to overcome the tendency to use trite phrases and overworked words. The following exercises have been useful for this purpose.

(1) Write on the blackboard from 1 to 15 sentences each containing the word "got." Have pupils substitute a verb with specific meaning for the overworked verb "got" in each sentence.
(2) Have pupils develop a list of frequently overworked words, such as asked, awful, divine, fix, grand, great, keen, lovely, neat, nice, perfect, replied, said, swell, take, terrible, thing, want, wonderful.

E. FIGURATIVE AND OTHER NONLITERAL LANGUAGE

How far the teacher can go in teaching junior or senior high-school pupils to understand the various forms of nonliteral writing depends on the same factors which limit teaching in other fields: the intelligence and cultural background of the pupils, the size of the class and the consequent ease or difficulty of conducting class discussions, the availability of good textbooks and of supplementary material, the rigidity of the course of study, and the teacher's own knowledge and love of literature. Every English teacher, however, should feel that he is remiss in his duties if he fails to open to his pupils the door to the infinite wealth of allusion, description, and suggestion which the intelligent writer and reader may enjoy.

Many teachers overlook the fact that figurative language is not confined to poetry, fairy tales and legends, and similar imaginative writing and limit their teaching of figures of speech to these rather limited areas, leaving largely untouched the much wider and more important fields of idiom, satire, irony, and the innumerable symbolically used words and phrases which appear in daily speech, in advertising, and in newspapers, books, and magazines. Pupils are left floundering in a sea of dimly or wrongly understood language. It is small wonder that they do not read more enthusiastically.

A brief consideration of sample passages from a newspaper, a textbook, and from ordinary conversation will show the necessity for teaching pupils to interpret this prosaic type of nonliteral language. The following samples may not appear to the average adult to be figurative at all because they are so familiar:

> A thousand bills were thrown into the legislative hopper.
> A chorus of protest arose throughout the land.
> I almost died laughing.
> The winning candidate swept the field.
> The United States is a melting pot.
> The enemy line crumbled.

In junior high school it is probably better to explain figures of speech as they arise in regular class work than to present them "cold" as a unit of study unrelated to the rest of the work in literature, composition, and grammar. The teacher should scan carefully all assigned reading for phrases which might offer difficulty in interpretation and should himself bring them up for class discussion if one of the pupils does not do so.

At first, most of the initiative for such discussions will have to come from the teacher. Most pupils hesitate to admit their inability to understand the real meaning of something the surface import of which is clear. Only when they realize that adults, too, need help in interpretation will they bring their problems into the open. The teacher soon finds that sheer ignorance is the cause of many of the difficulties which pupils have. Biblical, historic, legendary, and artistic references can convey no meaning to those who lack a background of knowledge. "As strong as Samson" might just as well be "As strong as George" so far as many contemporary pupils are concerned. "Mars stalked the earth" creates confused astronomical impressions in the minds of pupils who have been deprived of the Greek myths. Specific instances of this sort give the alert teacher an excellent opportunity to create in his classes an interest in reading some of the basic literature of our civilization. The classroom or school library should, of course, be ready to provide appropriate books for the pupil whose curiosity is thus aroused.

Lack of knowledge in other areas increases the difficulties of interpretation. "The log-roller lost his footing" was interpreted by a pupil as meaning that the man's foot had been amputated; the reader had no idea of the process of log-rolling. The acquisition of knowledge is, obviously, a never-completed process. The teacher can help himself to appreciate his pupil's shortcomings in this respect by thinking of the gaps in his own information.

It is an accepted principle of education that learning takes place best when the learner participates actively in the process. Thus pupils learn to understand the figurative speech of others when they use such figures themselves. At first, they may simply be asked to complete common similes. These are cliches to the adult, but not to the junior high-school pupil.

The following list[4] of incomplete similes is suggestive:

black as	quick as . . . .
straight as	light as . . . .
wise as	clear as . . . .
brown as	sharp as . . . .
white as	sober as . . . .
busy as	hungry as . . . .
cold as	sly as . . . .
hard as	happy as . . . .

If some of the pupils' responses differ from the conventional ones which the teacher expects, these can be used as a point of departure for a discussion of the value of originality and vividness in figurative speech. The next step, of course, is to have some actual writing done by the pupils. The subjects assigned should be simple and of a nature to encourage the use of simile and metaphor. Short, carefully prepared compositions are preferable to long ones. Sample passages dealing with subjects similar to those assigned may be read to furnish pupils with ideas and inspiration. The best compositions may be read to the class, and particularly happy figures of speech may be pointed out and praised. It is easily understood that no public notice should be taken of the inevitable unsuccessful excursions into writing.

Bright pupils enjoy and benefit from learning the names of the various kinds of figures of speech and differences among them. However, merely learning to recognize and name them is a sterile exercise if it does not lead to understanding and appreciation.

Figurative language often offers the inexperienced and perhaps more literal-minded pupils some difficulty in comprehension. The junior high-school pupil can understand onomatopoetic words, alliteration, and similes, but the more complex aspects of figurative language should be developed at the eleventh — and twelfth — grade levels. At the outset the pupil must learn that figurative language occurs more frequently in poetry than in prose. He must be taught some of the basic distinctions between the two forms.

[4] Adapted from list in Frieda Radke, *Living Words.* New York: The Odyssey Press, 1940, p 153.

Prose	*Poetry*
(1) No regular beat or rhythm.	Definitely measured and rhythmical
(2) No particular form.	Definitely shaped and often divided into stanzas.
(3) Often low in emotional tone.	Often concentrated and intense in tone.
(4) Usually involves facts and information.	Usually involves feelings.
(5) Often detailed and precise.	Imaginative and suggestive.

Perhaps the best way to teach the pupil to interpret figurative language is by pattern. Once an easy pattern is established, the pupil can gradually learn to recognize the same type of pattern in his reading. Alliteration and onomatopoeia are so obvious they can be understood without difficulty. The more complex forms require examples, such as the following:

(1) Simile (similarity).
    (a) Like a cloud of fire.
    (b) My love is like a red, red rose.
    (c) My heart is like a rhyme.
(2) Metaphor (identification transfer).
    (a) The moon is a ghostly galleon.
    (b) The road is a ribbon of moonlight
    (c) Sarcasm is a dangerous weapon.
(3) Personification (having the attributes of a person).
    (a) . . . the jocund day, stand tiptoe on the misty mountain top.
    (b) Now morning from her orient chambers came and her first footsteps touched a verdant hill.
(4) Apostrophe (addressing the dead as living, or the absent as present).
    (a) Phoebus, arise and paint the sable skies.
    (b) Build me straight, O Worthy Master.
    (c) Mother, come back from that echoless shore.
(5) Metonomy (associating an object that is closely connected with the idea).
    (a) The *pen* is mightier than the sword.
    (b) Polly, put the *kettle* on and we'll have tea
    (c) A man should keep a good *table*
(6) Synecdoche (using a part to represent the whole).
    (a) She gave her hand in marriage
    (b) I'll not lift a finger
    (c) Fifty sails were seen on the horizon

The pupil can increase his enjoyment of the daily newspaper by learning to recognize both simile and metaphor as used so frequently in the headlines. He can have fun noticing the clever use of cliches in various radio plays and will discover that these cliches often are similes or metaphors. By training his ear to catch such cliches as "red as a beet," "bitter as gall," and "mad as a hornet," he can immeasurably improve his own speech and writing. Constant alertness on the part of the teacher and the pupil is necessary to enable the pupil to understand the great masterpieces. Nor can this be done in one semester; it must be part of a well-planned English program through the entire secondary school.

F. RETENTION OF NEW VOCABULARY

In order that words may become a permanent part of a pupil's vocabulary, word study must be vitalized for the individual through purposeful listening and reading so that vocabularies are enriched both for oral and written expression.

Extensive Reading.   Wide and extensive reading is necessary if pupils are to develop rich vocabularies and wider interests in the world about them. Too often a pupil reads only one type of book — an adventure series, or radio magazines. Frequently, as pupils advance through junior high school, other interests take the place of reading; many pupils never read anything, even a magazine, unless required to do so by a teacher.

More extensive reading habits can be developed by the use of reading books of wider interest or more mature nature. Books or magazine stories germane to the subject matter studied in class or to popular motion pictures, radio programs, and the like may be recommended. A classroom library, attractive displays, bulletin boards, reading nook, are all helpful. The pupil should be given time to read. Sometimes, as a special treat, the teacher may read aloud a portion of a book from the library, stopping at some interesting point. Pupils will have to read the book themselves to find out the rest of the story.

The teacher himself will have to know books in order to provide a graded vocabulary load. A poor reader cannot acquire a good vocabulary and effective reading habits by being plunged into difficult reading material full of unfamiliar words. Second, the teacher must check the reading by discussion of the problem of the book, the characters, or the author and make use of the new words in conversation and in class.

> The most common way of improving one's vocabulary is through extensive and varied reading. The meaning of words is acquired through the recognition and use of words as parts of words of dynamic thought patterns. . . .
>   . . . It is advantageous, however, for teachers to increase their students' acquaintance with words by using repeatedly in their conversation during a week several important new words in their field.[5]

[5] Ruth Strang, with the assistance of Florence C. Rose, *Problems in the Improvement of Reading in High School and College.* Lancaster, Pennsylvania: The Science Press Printing Company, 1938, pp. 82-83.

Enlisting Pupils' Co-operation. Teachers should use a variety of procedures to (1) make the below-average pupils conscious of their need of knowing more words to meet everyday problems; (2) stimulate an interest in increasing vocabulary for the average pupil; and (3) help pupils to overcome their adolescent tendency to censure those pupils who use their vocabularies more effectively than others.

Functional Vocabularies. The functional vocabulary is the vocabulary which the pupil used to express himself in writing and in speech. Activities in which pupils of difficult levels of maturity may use this functional vocabulary are suggested below:

(1)   The *below-average* pupil may talk about actual experiences, such as home, school, and church activities; movies, radio programs, and community affairs. He may also write letters and fill out applications. In his writing, the pupil should strive for short paragraph development.

(2)   The *average* pupil may talk about various experiences gained through reading as well as through actual participation. His vocabulary should show increased maturity and his talks should show greater detailed observation than those of the below-average pupil. The average pupil should engage in considerable writing of an expository or narrative nature and should write letters.

(3)   The *above-average* pupil should be able to make deductions from listening and reading activities and should participate imaginatively in the experiences about which he is reading. The writing of above-average pupils should show maturity of thought and expression.

Recognition Vocabularies. The recognition vocabulary is largely a listening or reading vocabulary. The *below-average* pupil will get general meanings only. He will read the vocabulary of current events. He will learn technical words largely through listening. The *average* pupil should work for more exactness in interpretation of thought through word study. The *above-average* pupil should approximate a more "ultimate" truth: i.e. get implications. Reflection on subjects about which he reads may lead to participation in his chosen field.

Devices for Making Permanent the Pupils' Enriched Vocabulary. A variety of procedures may be used to help pupils incorporate words into their permanent vocabularies. The following suggestions are offered:

(1)   Teach pupils to discriminate between the various meanings of words and phrases. Suggestions for below-average, average, and above-average pupils are listed on the next page:

Word	Below Average	Average	Above Average
root	The root of the plant is large.	The root word comes from Latin. Take square root of four. A pig roots in the ground.	The root of all evil.
ordinary	The ordinary way of doing the home work all right.	It is a very ordinary procedure.	The ceremony was most ordinary.
pass	The pass is narrow. Pass the cake.	The hall pass is needed. He was passed to first base.	Things have come to a pretty pass!
ground	The apple fell on the ground. The meat is being ground.	This is the ground floor. This is made of ground glass.	He stood his ground. The ground swell is heavy today.
see	I see my way. I see a house.	I see what you mean. I shall come to see you.	He shall never see death.

(2) Teach pupils to learn new words from context and not alone from dictionary definitions.

(3) Have pupils listen to an auditorium program or a radio speech, listing unfamiliar words and reasoning out their meanings from the contexts.

(4) Organize a vocabulary club in the classroom, members of which will be responsible for bringing in words from all subject fields and sharing them with the class.

(5) Have pupils classify words for special study from a selected list, noting those foreign in meaning and those they may be using or may be taught to use in formal spoken and written English.[6]

(6) Study words in *phrase groupings,* not as isolated vocabulary. Pupils and teachers should use them consciously in later discussions.

(7) Increase vocabulary of meanings by learning new words through specifically purposeful meanings for written composition.

(8) Point out for special study: (a) powerful verbs, and (b) colorful adjectives with fine discrimination of meaning, as they are discovered in reading.

(9) Use the "Word to the Wise" section in *Scholastic Magazine* as a weekly check.

(10) Provide exercises on synonyms, with dictionary help.

(11) Make vocabulary matching games for drill several times a term.

(12) Have pupils deduce meanings of words from good oral reading by the teacher.

(13) Have pupils analyze words through detection of familiar stems, prefixes, and suffixes.

(14) Encourage pupils to be watchful for new words and their implications in wide and varied reading.

G. EXERCISES FOR IMPROVEMENT OF VOCABULARY

In addition to the suggested drills and exercises which have been given in connection with discussions on the various phases of improvement of vocabulary in the prededing sections, the following specific exercises for identifying and analyzing compounds, finding words within words, developing pronunciation from known parts of known words, and certain kinesthetic techniques may help to strengthen the program.

Compounds.   Knowledge of the use of compounds and attention to their form is an excellent means of extending vocabularies. Exercises such as the ones given below are effective in this field.

(1)   Choose from a current reading lesson several solid compound words (not hyphenated) and write them on the board. Ask pupils to examine them for

[6]William M. Tanner, *Correct English,* Vol. I. Boston: Ginn and Company, 1931, p. 408.

Word	Below Average	Average	Above Average
hostile	My enemy is hostile.	He is a hostile witness.	He is hostile to my interests.
leg	The boy broke his leg.	The first leg of the journey is over.	He hasn't a leg to stand on.
propaganda propagandize	Do not listen to enemy propaganda.	To propagandize is unfair.	Propaganda is often a falsification of news.
object objective	Please pick up the object.	I object to your going to the party.	What is your ultimate objective?
proof	What is your proof of that statement?	We shall make a proof of the picture.	The proof of the pudding.

any unfamiliar parts. Point out that either part of each word may be used alone.

(2)   Let each pupil choose a compound word which he will separate into parts, using each part in a sentence. He then makes a third sentence in which he uses the compound.

(3)   Have pupils make sentences containing two or more compound words, for example, John's *workshop* was full of model airplanes made from *cardboard.*

(4)   Illustrate (when pupils are ready for it) the difference between the two big families of compounds: (a) the solids, as bookworm, roadbed; and (b) the hyphenated compounds, as long-eared, old-fashioned.

Finding Words Within Words.   As an aid to discovering similarities in word forms and, sometimes, word meaning, practice on identifying short words within longer words in helpful. Seeing that *management, carpenter, attendant,* etc., contain familiar phonetic elements which are words, themselves, is often an awakening to the pupil who has had difficulty with word perception.

Practice in finding small words may be given in the following way: Pupils select from the context being read a list of long words. Small words within these words are then underlined. Caution must be used to prevent the identification of a small word which is not heard as the long word is pronounced: that is, it would be incorrect to underline *as* in *fashion.*

Developing Pronunciation From Known Parts of Known Words.   Young and relatively immature pupils in junior high school may profit from some of the elementary techniques and exercises noted below.

(1)   Brief drills on consonant digraphs will facilitate recognition of known parts of words. Sight rather than sound should influence the recognition. List five to ten initial digraphs on the board – bl, br, ch, cl, ch, fl, etc. After each one write, in parentheses, the remainder of a word – bl (ack); cl (ean). First see that pupils are familiar with the completed words, then ask them to see how quickly they can find additional words having the same beginnings, using a reading selection for the source.

(2)   Sentences including numerous digraphs offer a challenge. Give a sample sentence, as "The hunters blew *their* horns; the hounds *brayed,* and the *chase* was on! The horses *cleared* the fences, *crossed* the meadows and *sped* toward the fleeing fox." Have pupils try writing sentences having two or more of the digraphs illustrated.

(3)   Common phonograms of three or four letters, especially end-phonograms, furnish worth-while association material. Well-rhymed poetry provides good patterns. Have pupils find pairs and mark the endings that rhyme.

(4)   Write a paragraph on the board containing many familiar word endings,

something like this: "*Wake up, Jake;* you're an hour *late,* now. *Shake* yourself and *dive* into your clothes. I'll *drive* you as far as *State* Street if your pride won't be hurt by a *ride* in my old *crate.*" Ask pupils to see whether they can outdo the teacher by bringing a similar paragraph of their own the next day.

Questions for Discussion

1. What importance do you see in the distinction that Deighton makes between syllabication for pronunciation and syllabication for writing?
2. To what extent do you agree with Olson's contention that teachers have generally done a very poor job of encouraging students to have a substantial spelling vocabulary?
3. What would be the proper course of action to follow in developing students' abilities to make use of contextual aids to determine word meaning?
4. If you are a content area teacher, look at some of the reading material you assign to students. What words do you feel are of such importance that you should help students with them before assigning the material? What procedures would you use to help students with the words?

Developing Comprehension and Interpretation Skills

VI

Most writers in the field of reading agree that the successful development of vocabulary and word recognition skills is not sufficient to insure effective reading among all students. These writers believe that direct and concentrated attention must also be given to the development of various comprehension, interpretation, and study skills. The articles in this section explore various views of what these skills are and how they should be developed in a secondary school reading program.

In the first article, James McCallister presents his definition of the term *interpretation* which states that it occurs when the literal meaning of a writer has been ascertained and a reader begins to use that meaning in his own thinking. McCallister admits that research evidence is lacking concerning what the exact components of interpretation are, but he does present four sets of abilities that he feels are probably involved.

J. William McKay concentrates on the topic of developing the study skills of secondary school students. Among the study skills he includes are using book parts, using sources of information, and perceiving the organization of material.

In the third article of this section, Olive Niles develops a number of important ideas concerning reading comprehension. Niles believes that reading comprehension can best be thought of as consisting of three basic abilities; the ability to observe and use the relationships of ideas, the ability to make proper adjustments dependent upon the purpose for reading, and the ability to make use of real and vicarious experience. She suggests that careful use of teacher questions and use of the directed reading lesson plan can contribute considerably toward improving students' abilities to comprehend.

H. Alan Robinson focuses his attention on one particular cluster of comprehension skills — the "key thought" cluster. He presents detailed outlines of lessons designed to develop the concept in junior high school students that there is a relationship between the key words in a sentence and the main thought of a paragraph.

The fifth article in this section was written specifically for English teachers. David Cooper demonstrates how certain key concepts drawn from the field of semantics could be the bases for lessons designed to improve the comprehension and critical reading abilities of secondary school students.

In the final article, Eller and Wolf present a substantial review of research conducted by social psychologists and communication theorists in recent years and they relate the findings and conclusions to the teaching of critical reading. Among other implications drawn by the writers is that reading comprehension is even more complicated than methods texts have indicated.

Promoting Growth in Interpreting In Grades Nine Through Fourteen *

JAMES M. McCALLISTER

In articles dealing with high-school and college reading programs, the word *interpretation* is seldom defined. The definitions that do appear are those of mental processes ranging all the way from the ascertaining of literal meaning to the application of ideas in creative thinking. In this paper we shall consider interpretation as that aspect of reading which occurs when the reader has ascertained the literal or sense meaning of what an author is saying and begins to utilize that meaning in his own thinking. By this definition, interpretation enters into the reading act at the point the reader begins to think about or do something with what the author has said.

Although research has not identified the components of interpretation or determined the sequence in which they operate, it can at least be said that these components are called into operation when the reader exercises associative abilities. For practical purposes, these abilities may be considered in four groups: (1)† relating the reader's own experience to what the author has said, (2) selecting the meaning that conforms to the reader's purpose at the moment, (3) objectively evaluating the author's point of view, and (4) synthesizing two or more meanings to compose new ideas or opinions. These four items do not comprise a complete list of the componets of interpretation, but they suggest approaches that the teacher can make in attempting to promote interpretation as an accompaniment of reading in his classes.

Relating The Reader's Experience to Meaning

Interpretation is a thinking process. All that the printed page can do is assist the reader to weave a fabric of meaning out of his own experience. We know that the members of any high-school or college class will vary greatly in the experiential content that they can apply to any reading situation. Because of

*Reprinted from *Reading: Seventy-Five Years of Progress,* Supplementary Educational Monographs, No. 96, edited by H. Alan Robinson (1966), p. 89-93, by permission of the University of Chicago Press.
†Numbers in parentheses refer to references at end of article.

variations in experience, we cannot expect the same interpretation from all members of a class. One of the disappointing discoveries that teachers, especially inexperienced teachers, frequently make is that students do not independently arrive at the interpretations that the teacher, who is familiar with the subject, expects.

These shortcomings in experience may be minimized by providing in advance some of the necessary background before students begin independent reading. This procedure will be especially necessary in content subject if the teacher expects the students to arrive at particular interpretations. Even when a variety of interpretations is desirable, appropriate background will be essential to assist students in their thinking. The different techniques the teacher may use include questioning, laboratory experimentation, class demonstrations, discussions, and assistance in selecting appropriate materials.

As a high-school or college student advances in the study of any content field, he naturally grows in experience in the field; but unless he receives guidance from the teacher in acquiring the prerequisite understandings for interpretation, he will probably get farther and farther into material unrelated to his experience. The cumulative effect of outdistancing his experience will generally inhibit his interest and progress. In most cases, it will be desirable to delay reading assignments until the essential concepts have been developed and explained through other classroom procedures. The need for pre-reading instruction will vary with individuals, but will always be necessary to some extent. When experiential background is limited, biased, or completely missing, the level of interpretation will be limited accordingly.

Using Purpose to Guide Interpretation

Intelligent interpretation is always influenced by the purpose in reading. First of all, the reader searches for the writer's original intent. Misinterpretation is always possible if emphasis is placed on the literal meaning of the words instead of on the writer's purpose. Sometimes purpose is definitely stated by the author; at other times it must be detected by "reading between the lines."

One approach to discovering the author's purpose is to examine the organizational pattern of the material. The reader should note the introductory statements, if any, to ascertain whether the writer gives a clue to the pattern he will follow. If no pattern is indicated, the purpose must be detected as the organization unfolds during reading. Patterns vary with the character of the selection, of course.

To determine purpose, it is also especially helpful to be acquainted with the devices that writers often use to influence the reader's interpretation. Reference has already been made to the use of introductory statements. Does the introductory statement relate the new material to something studied previously? As the writer develops his discussion further, does he introduce problems or questions to guide the thinking of the reader? Does he follow a logical sequence? Does he follow a time sequence? Does he introduce concrete examples to illustrate principles or processes? Does he discuss cause and effect relations? Are factual definitions of new terms included? These questions should remind us of the many such devices commonly found in textbooks.

In literary works different devices may be used. Russell B. Thomas suggests that literature may be approached as an expression of the personality of the author, as an instrument of communication between the author and the reader, as an account of the past, as a poetic construction, or as a demonstration of knowledge about things.[1] The purpose of the author will determine the special devices and manner of writing.

Whenever a reader encounters a writer's device and recognizes it as a sign of his purpose, his thinking is changed or directed accordingly. For the mature reader, this happens more or less automatically. The teacher may aid students in developing this ability by being sure that they are prepared to recognize and respond to such devices effectively.

Often a student will need to read to discover not the exact purpose of a writer but his contribution to some topic or problem in which the student is interested. For example, in preparing a report or a paper, the student may read several references; as he discovers ideas or thoughts which are useful, he makes note of them. In this way he is disregarding the author's purpose and substituting his own purpose. As opportunities for such selective reading are provided, the reader will grow in purposeful interpretation.

Objective Evaluation an an Aspect of Interpretation

After a reader has determined his purpose for reading and has begun to extract ideas or information from a selection, he must of necessity evaluate the usefulness, authenticity, accuracy, and truthfulness of what he is reading. The first step in evaluation is naturally the reader's personal reaction. If the reader relies on personal reactions alone, however, he will not go beyond traditional attitudes, prejudices, and falso-to-fact information. The teacher has the opportunity — and the necessity — of providing objective standards or habits which will act as a corrective for the shortcomings of personal reaction. An objective approach is implied in such questions as the following. (1) Do I understand what the writer is trying to convey? (2) Do I think about what I have

---

[1] Thomas, "Relation between the Nature of the Material Read and Methods of Interpretation," in *Promoting Growth toward Maturity in What Is Read,* compiled and edited by William S. Gray ("Supplementary Educational Monographs," No 74; Chicago: University of Chicago Press, 1951), P. 62-66.

read before accepting it? (3) Should I check the accuracy of the author by reading other sources? (4) Am I aware of facts that the author may have omitted? (5) Does the author's background indicate that he is competent to write on this subject? (6) Which of several writers is the best informed and the most competent to set forth a position on this subject? (7) What proposition or position is consistent with the welfare of the greatest number of individuals? (8) Which propositions are consistent with accepted standards of value? Of course, the questions asked will vary with the purpose of the reader and the character of the selection, but it is important that the reader know what kinds of questions to ask in a given situation. By asking such questions, the reader practices the skills of weighing and considering data, detecting false inferences and unsubstantiated facts, testing the authenticity of sources, suspending judgment, and formulating valid conclusions.

The type of interpretation described in the preceding paragraph is the slowest and most difficult kind of reading. It requires active, careful reflection on the ideas expressed and a rigidly exacting analysis before arriving at conclusions. It may involve a search for the mood or tone of the author, a recognition of any devices of propaganda, and an understanding of the time and locale in which the writing occurred, among other considerations. Years of directed practice are necessary to develop the attitudes and thinking essential to this type of independent reading.

Interpretation Through Creative Synthesis

If reading is defined as a thinking process, interpretation cannot really be considered complete until the reader synthesizes or integrates the new meanings into his own experience. Of necessity, much instruction emphasizes efficiency in identifying, recording, memorizing, and repeating facts; but once students have the information, they need practice in such activities of independent thought as extracting and organizing meanings common to two or more statements, supplying or anticipating meanings not stated precisely, speculating on what happened between events, anticipating what will happen next, and reasoning from cause to effect.

The teacher's questions may be one of the most effective means of developing this kind of interpretation. A teacher who primarily asks questions requiring factual answers will get literal responses with little or no creative thinking on the part of readers. On the other hand, the teacher who asks questions which demand some form of organized thinking will be able to see the growth of abilities in synthesis and integration. Oral discussion is also a useful device to promote interpretation because associative responses are enhanced by an exchange of ideas. Through skillful questioning and directed discussion, the formulation of original ideas may be stimulated, misconceptions may be clarified, and information may be integrated with other learnings for future use.

Concluding Statement

As conceived in this discussion, interpretation is a cumulative ability which develops with a student's increasing experience. Its promotion is a function of all teachers — not just reading or English teachers. Whether intentionally or not, most teachers probably contribute to its growth, since it results from varied learning activities which bring into play different mental processes. Therefore, students in grades nine through fourteen are going to develop some power of interpretation regardless of what their teachers can do. The question is, "Can teachers enhance or accelerate growth by trying to direct it?" They undoubtedly can, and the most effective means is by purposeful guidance of reading activities.

The Nature and Extent of
Work-Study Skills*

J. WILLIAM McKAY

In these times of intensive emphasis on the grades attained by students, it is readily apparent to many teachers that secondary school pupils have the proverbial two strikes on them because only a few have been trained to employ the skills that will help them study, which in turn, produces the coveted grades – which, in turn, bring parental approval, increased job opportunity, admission to college or university, and later, financial reward.

For what has seemed to be endless decades, many teachers have assumed that high school students were acquainted with the study skills. Over the years thousands of assignments have been made, which included outlining, notetaking, summarizing, using the parts of a book, using reference sources, word study, and numerous organizational activities. These assignments were frequently made without regard for students' skill in such study tasks or even for their possession of the skill. There is hope that the demands of present-day education have emphasized this weak aspect of reading sufficiently that schools will do something about it.

So that the reader may understand what is included in the term "study skills," allow me to state that, generally, any technique students use in learning school assignments might aptly be called a study skill. Bamman (1)† proposes that study skills refer to application of reading skills to specific study tasks, organizing and scheduling one's time for study, taking good notes, and preparing for and taking examinations.

Karlin (6) uses Nila Banton Smith's classification: selection and evaluation; organization; location of information; following directions; and specialized skills such as the reading of graphs, tables, charts, and maps. Marksheffel (8) in summarizing the literature lists such skills as: following directions, reading, listening, outlining, locating materials, writing reports, organizing, remembering, reviewing, making study schedules, summarizing, and taking exams. Among more specific skills he includes picking out main ideas and

*Reprinted from Proceeding of the University of Pittsburgh's 22nd Annual Conference on Reading, 1966, p. 53-63, by permission of the author and the editor.
†Numbers in parentheses refer to references at end of article.

topic sentences; determining relationships between or among paragraphs; using tables of contents, indexes, and library card files; reading and interpreting cartoons, charts, and graphs. But he groups all the skills under three main headings; (1) following directions; (2) locating, selecting, and evaluating information; and (3) organizing information.

But whatever the classifications — whatever the inclusions and exclusions — the facts remain that relatively few students learn how to study efficiently without directed practice and guidance by a teacher and that there are certain basic study skills that students must acquire and use for successful classroom learning. Study skills must be taught!

A closer look at the skills will tell us that high school students either can perform them or should be able to perform them by the time they reach secondary school. A closer look at the classrooms in many high schools might show that teachers, generally at least, tend to take for granted that their students can do these things and accordingly offer little or no instruction along these lines. Unfortunately, for us and the victimized students, our high schools, somewhat overcome by the increased emphasis on subject matter, are still dispensing facts when in reality most students need to know how to locate facts, examine them, then use or discard them.

These things may be accomplished by either one of two means — by direct teaching in reading classes or in English classes or by timely and useful instruction in the various content areas. The latter method is preferred because the skills are taught and practiced when they are needed and in proper combination for the particular subject area, rather than in isolation. In addition, the actual materials of the course are used for the teaching and practice so that students can see the usefulness of the skills.

An alignment of skills somewhat different from those previously mentioned is to be found in the International Reading Association publication, *Perspectives in Reading, No. 4, Developing Study Skills in Secondary Schools.*[1] It gives more emphasis to organization and organizational patterns than others, especially as those patterns are to be observed by students and later produced by them.

Word Study Skills

Most teachers and many students are fully aware that there is no possible substitute for a rich vocabulary. How important words always are! How very important they are when they are used to express, explain, and discuss the major concepts of a course in school, or when they are the sole means of a student's

---

[1] The author is indebted to this source for the order of presentation of the study skills in this paper.

understanding the course because they comprise the key technical and basic vocabulary.

Instructors need to know the status of their students' vocabularies as to extent, usefulness, and word attack skills. They need also to know what kind of instruction in word study the students have been exposed to as expressed by Simmons (22). Since mass instruction is common in vocabulary, it often consists of pure drill – quite isolated, repetitious, and devoid of interest. Consequently, this type of teaching yields few dividends. The small group approach and the individualized approach produce better results but, of course, are harder to plan and implement. One thing is certain: understanding words needs more reinforcement through live, meaningful classroom experiences.

Rather than lamenting and bemoaning the fact that secondary students use the same words over and over in essay-test answers and themes and speeches, let's teach them how to augment their word stock by working with words both in and out of context. Let's explain and illustrate and practice with both connotation, a whole new world to many students, and denotation. Let's use structural analysis – prefixes, suffixes, and roots – whenever the situation permits in science, history, English, or in any content field. Teachers in all areas have the responsibility, through oral and written activities, of helping students to enrich their general vocabularies as well as the technical, specialized ones.

Let's do away with memorized word lists and tests therefrom; let's make certain that we do not prolong word exercises until the class is bored; let's use various word study approaches; let's show our students how fascinating words are by whatever means are required to do the job. Let's make analogies, synonyms, and antonyms a regular part of our instruction in each content field. Interesting material and an enthusiastic teacher can do wonders for an impoverished vocabulary. Anything in print is a potential vocabulary builder for someone. Remember: there can be little or no skill of comprehension with a poor vocabulary.

Using Book Parts

The current explosion of knowledge has produced so much information that even the person with a photographic memory cannot keep pace. Helping a student learn how to learn is one of the teachers's genuine challenges. For instance, showing him how to use his textbook and yours can help him handle this flood of facts.

So many teachers take for granted that students know the parts of a book. So few take time to explain in the early stages of a course what role the text will actually play. By thinking through some answers to the following questions, re-evaluate and refresh your knowledge of these very pertinent considerations of texts:

(1) What is the purpose of a textbook?

(2) How do you use yours?

(3) Do you use the text to best advantage?

(4) How can you improve your usage of the text?

(5) Do you teach the relationship of one part to another? For example, do you teach the preface or the table of contents as they relate to the rest of the book?

(6) Why did you or the principal or the school board choose the book?

(7) Have you some criteria for evaluating texts?

(8) Do your students have skill in using the texts?

An open-book test will often divulge answers to some of these queries. Try administering such a test and use the results to diagnose students' strengths and weaknesses and to devise future instructional plans.

As many of us are now discovering, it is impossible to develop everything that is known about a subject because so much new knowledge is continually being added. What is known today may be refuted tomorrow. In order to help students and ourselves keep pace, we need to assist them in obtaining a knowledge of sources of information and proficiency in their use. Stress must be placed on the students' independent use of these sources. Consider what this means and what is required of you in teaching it.

According to Shepherd (21), students are obliged to acquaint themselves with three basic types of sources: (1) references containing specialized information, (2) books and pamphlets pertinent to a particular content area, and (3) periodical sources pertaining to a specific area.

It is generally acknowledged that certain prior skills are necessary to the proper use of source materials. Students need to learn how to use the card catalog and the library classification system so that they know where to go for various types of information.

They must have an understanding of "key" or "entry" words, where to find an author's basic point of view of purpose, how to read and interpret pictures and get information from them, how to read charts, graphs, maps, and tables, and how to locate introductions, topical headings and summaries.

Among the comprehension skills, students should be able to select main ideas, supporting details, and sequences of data and to detect the author's pattern of organization so that they may adapt and fit the information gleaned from sources into their research topics or questions.

Being adept in the use of *Reader's Guide to Periodical Literature* is absolutely necessary. Do not assume that students know how to use it; do not simply tell them that they should use it. Show them how! Help them learn how to determine the best sources of information; teach them how to list sources in their papers, how to make up a bibliography or list of references, and how to quote and acknowledge in good taste and form.

Research assignments can and should be frequently planned by the teachers and students. Do not assign research and then turn students loose on their own. Make the whole business of research and its methods a definite part of the classroom instruction in all content areas. No one on the staff knows scientific or historical source materials better than the science teacher or the teacher of social studies. Why, then restrict research to the English class?

Perceiving Organization

Efficiency of recall depends in part upon the students' sensing some kind of order or system in material. Niles (12) suggests a method of testing that awareness and if you have the slightest doubt about the value of perceiving organization as a study skill, you should try it. The device consists principally of giving students two selections to read with different directions to follow – one set very brief and terse, the other naming the topic, advising the class to watch for cause-effect patterns and to pay attention to effects. In both sets of directions would be the statement: "You will be asked to write a summary." Give suitable time for study. The results will probably astound you because there will be great differences in the amount and quality of recall.

Now that you have discovered that organization does make a difference, give some instruction in organized patterns.

Niles (12) states, "All good writing has some kind of organization or structure even though this structure may be a deliberate lack of structure which is itself a kind of structure." She mentions that the structure and charm found in Charles Lamb and Cornelia Otis Skinner are both products of their obvious lack of direction, which implies that if students are to derive understanding, satisfaction, or enjoyment from reading what these two essayists have written the students must have ability to sense and understand organization – even though none is apparent.

A study of social studies, science, and language textbooks showed that the following major patterns abound in factual writing: (1) enumerative order, (2) time order, (3) cause-effect, (4) comparison-contrast. This list might be enlarged to include repetition, examples, details, space order, and any combination of patterns of developing a writer's ideas. It may not always be necessary to show students all these variations, but it is important to teach them to look for order in every thing they read and to know what to do with it when they find it.

English teachers usually assume the responsiblity of teaching the patterns of imaginative writing. But awareness to literary patterns is meaningful to the student only if he can relate form and meaning or sensory effect, Niles (12). For example, most important about teaching a sonnet is that it must contain fourteen lines. Such a pattern is more effective for unique ideas. Helping students see the relationship of form to idea and emotional impact is much more beneficial to students than simply knowing form in literature.

Content area teachers, by using the regular instructional materials of their courses, can do this teaching of organization well and they should be encouraged to do so rather than be ridiculed and criticized for not doing what they have never been shown how to do. A teacher can help his students perceive orderliness in printed matter in the following ways:

(1) By being aware of its values and patterns himself.
(2) By asking the kinds of questions which encourage students to observe the structure of what they have read.
(3) By surveying the next lesson with his class, calling attention to the organization they are about to study.
(4) By alerting them to headings which almost outline the material.
(5) By reading materials to his class and asking anticipatory questions with a focus on structure.
(6) By using visual aids such as colored overlays on an overhead projector.
(7) By showing students *how* to take notes and *how* to outline.

Mature readers need these skills; they must learn to discipline their thinking in the author's terms, temporarily at least, to follow his patterns, and then to create their own. High level comprehension skills are attainable only after systematic understanding and orderly recall of what the author has said, Niles.(12)

Producing Organization

Since we have discussed how to perceive organization, the next logical step is to guide students to attack study materials, written or dictated, read or heard, and to record the essential ideas for orderly study and use. Thus, their presentation of material, oral or written, contains organization and reflects their ability to perceive it.

Having sensed the type of organization a selection has — or having detected a speaker's pattern — how does a student take notes, outline, summarize, or abstract essentials for later reference or reflection? These skills should aid the student in producing an orderly pattern of his own when he reviews or when he uses his own creative ability to write or speak. Occasions for the use of such skills become more and more frequent and more and more sophisticated as school years go by.

The ability to organize oral and written material does not come naturally — at least not to many of us. Nor is it a natural outgrowth of intelligence. Rather it appears that this skill must be learned through instruction, practice, and refinement. It seems obvious too that this training should be sequential and that the genuine, top-flight command of the skill cannot be achieved by either incidental or sporadic instruction)– nor by isolated drill, Courtney (4).

In most secondary school classes students need to be able to recall both studied and oral material so that they may participate in class and take examinations with some degree of skill. We expect them to collate ideas from lecture notes, from study and reading done independently, and from their own thinking into some kind of unified impression. We expect them also to collect data from a variety of sources and combine it clearly and meaningfully into a paper or a speech. We are saying in effect that they will produce better reports, themes, and speeches because experience has taught them that unity, logic, and organization are to be found in most printed matter. But we supply the experience!

Again it becomes apparent that certain sub-skills are prerequisite to the acquisition of other, higher skills. Such necessities as intelligence and insight point up the fact that some students will never achieve much while others have unlimited potential. Other fundamentals such as the language arts skills, familiarity with vocabulary and the technical aspects of different subject disciplines, sentence and paragraph structure, devices of style, and knowledge of literary types are all skills closely akin to producing organized thought. General study conditions including interest, motivation, perseverance, and physical conditions are likewise deemed essential to competency.

Efficiency in reading and studying developed by specific study techniques such as SQ3R also tend to bring out organizational skills in students. High school and college students especially seem to derive help from it. Its five-step method may be briefly outlined as follows:

Step 1 – Survey –   Getting a general idea of the overall content by reading rapidly the headings, sub-headings, topic sentences, introduction, and summary.

Step 2 – Question –Questioning the material, using the headings to guide one's thinking.

Step 3 – Read –   Reading for understanding, guided by questions from the previous step.

Step 4 – Recite –   Testing recall information by answering questions.

Step 5 – Review –   Testing one's self by recalling main ideas.

Francis Robinson (16) creator of this study technique, states that students not only gain in their studying skills but in their personal security and confidence as well.

Unfortunately many subject teachers feel that students should already have mastered the skill, even in the teachers' own areas, by the time they reach secondary level or that the skills should be learned elsewhere. This attitude must be changed! Teachers must be convinced that the responsibility for instructing their pupils in the necessities for effective study is *theirs*! We must not assume that students have these skills — we must be certain that they do.

Motivation for These Skills

Reading teachers are convinced of and committed to the value of these skills, but their enthusiasm needs to be extended to all teachers and all students. It is almost never enough for the teacher to proclaim the value, the economy, and the persistent application of these skills to his students. As in most learning, the student must arrive at this conclusion through his own experience. He will not take notes or outline or summarize until he experiences the advantages of these activities. "Efficiency" does not move him; he does things the long, cumbersome, time-consuming way because it is comfortable and familiar. But he will come around when he enjoys the result of new behavior which comes about from using the skills.

The highly motivated secondary students may heed suggestions about improving study habits, but the majority of students need patient, supervised practice in seeing the difference between good and bad noted and the difference between outlining and not outlining.

Class participation, oral reports, written work, lab reports, vocabulary accuracy, in fact all types of school work will improve if content teachers will work at adding these organizational skills to the study repertory of their students. Let's give some additional impetus to note-taking, outlining, and summarizing by providing live, enthusiastic, practical activities for students.

Conclusion

It is highly improbable that educators can agree on which study skills to teach, but they can perhaps agree that the skills need to be taught. It is quite probable that the term "study skills" should be widened to include attitudes, interests, and motivation — and still other areas such as following directions, underlining, and skimming.

We know that some students do not use the skills. We know that many students do not know how to use them. But we also know that most students benefit from an orderly plan of learning.

All content area teachers have in common the desire to have their students demonstrate high proficiency in that area. From a rather selfish point of view, then, these teachers can expect rather astonishing results very soon after beginning study skills instruction. As occasions present themselves, try some on-the-spot help for your poor note-takers, poor outliners, poor summarizers.

Then share your success with other teachers who have not attempted it.

Do not let such threats as "You must teach reading" or "You must teach study skills" frighten you. You know much better than reading teachers know what skills you want your students to excell in and how you want them taught. I encourage you to work at it and reap the pleasures from your efforts.

References

1.   Bamman, Henry A., Ursual Hogan, Charles E. Greene. *Reading Instruction in The Secondary School.* New York: David McKay, 1961.
2.   Barbe, Walter B. "A Reading Program That Did Not Work," Journal of Developmental Reading, I (October, 1957), pp. 17-21.
3.   Catterson, Jane H. "Successful Study Skills Programs," *Developing Study Skills in Secondary Schools,* Perspectives in Reading No. 4, Newark, Delaware: International Reading Association.
4.   Courtney, Brother Leonard, "Organization Produced," *Developing Study Skills In Secondary Schools,* Perspectives in Reading No. 4, Newark, Delaware: International Reading Association, 1965, pp. 77-96
5.   Early, Margaret J. "The Meaning of Reading Instruction in Secondary Schools," *Journal of Reading,* VIII (October, 1964), p. 29.
6.   Herber, Harold L. "Teaching Secondary Students to Read History," *Reading Instruction in Secondary Schools,* Perspectives in Reading No. 2, Newark, Delaware: International Reading Association, 1964.
7.   _____ "Developing Study Skills in Secondary Schools: An Overview," *Developing Study Skills in Secondary Schools,* Perspectives in Reading No. 4, Newark, Delaware: International Reading Association, 1965, pp. 1-12.
8.   Jewett, Arno. "Using Book Parts," Developing Study Skills in Secondary Schools, Perspectives in Reading No. 4, Newark, Delaware, International Reading Association, 1965, pp. 32-41.
9.   Karlin, Robert. *Teaching Reading in High School.* Indianapolis: Bobbs-Merrill, 1964.
10.   Marksheffel, Ned D. *Better Reading In The Secondary School.* New York: Ronald Press. 1966.
11.   Niles, Olive S. "How Much Does a Content Teacher Need to Know About the Teaching of Reading?" *Improvement of Reading Through Classroom Practice,* IRA Conference Proceedings IX. Newark, Delaware: International Reading Association, 1964.
12.   _____ "Organization Perceived," *Developing Study Skills in Secondary Schools,* Perspectives in Reading No. 4, Newark, Delaware: International Reading Association, 1965, pp, 57-76
13.   _____ "Does Note-Taking Interfere with Listening Comprehension?" *Journal of Developmental Reading.* VI (Summer 1963), pp. 276-278.
14.   Pauk, Walter. *How To Study in College.* Houghton-Mifflin, 1962.
15.   Preston, R. C. Teaching Study Habits and Skills, New York: Rinehart, 1959.
16.   Robinson, Francis P. *Effective Study.* New York: Harper & Bros., 1946.
17.   Salisbury, Rachel. "Some Effects of Training in Outlining." *English Journal,* XXIV (1935), pp. 111-116.
18.   Schleich, Miriam, "Improving Reading Through the Language Arts: In Grades Nine Through Fourteen," *Reading and the Language Arts,* Reading Conference

Proceedings (H. A. Robinson, ed) Volume XXV, Chicago: University of Chicago Press, 1963, pp. 37-41

19.   Shepherd, David L. *Effective Reading in Science.* Evanson, Illinois: Harper and Row, 1960.

20.   _____ *Effective Reading In Social Studies.* Evanson, Illinois: Harper and Row, 1960.

21.   _____ "Using Sources of Information," *Developing Study Skills in Secondary Schools,* Perspectives in Reading No. 4, Newark, Delware: International Reading Association, 1965, pp. 13-31

22.   Simmons, John S. "Word Study Skills," *Developing Study Skills in Secondary Schools,* Perspectives in Reading No. 4, Newark, Delware: International Reading Association, 1965, pp.13-31;

23.   Smith, Nila Banton. "Patterns of Writing in Different Subject Areas," *Journal of Reading*, VIII (Ocotober, 1964), pp. 31-37.

24.   Strang, Ruth, Constance McCullough, and Arthur E. Traxler. *The Improvement of Reading,* Third Edition, New York: McGraw-Hill, 1961.

25.   Summers, Edward G. "Utilizing Visual Aids in Reading Materials for Effective Learning," *Developing Study Skills in Secondary Schools,* Perspectives in Reading No. 4, Newark, Delaware: International Reading Association, 1965 pp. 97-155.

Comprehension Skills*

OLIVE S. NILES

Middle-of-the-road reading teachers seem universally to agree that teaching students to read with comprehension is their major responsibility. Colleagues to the far right sometimes appear to leave the concept of comprehension out of their definition of reading. They talk as if they equated word pronunciation with reading. If this equation existed, phonics might indeed be the panacea for all ills. Colleagues on the far left, on the other hand, among them those who favor the more extreme forms of "individualized reading," often exhibit surprising faith that ability to comprehend will appear somehow with a minimum of specific teaching of comprehension skills.

Lists of comprehension skills which appear in professional books on the teaching of reading often seem formidable to teachers, who wonder how they can teach all the comprehension skills and also the word recognition and word meaning skills, the locational skills, the oral reading skills, and perhaps others. The question arises: Is it really necessary to teach all these skills separately? Are they truly basic or are they, perhaps, at least one step removed from those abilities, probably much fewer in number, which are truly fundamental to the process of comprehension?

The number of skills to be taught could probably be reduced if teachers got closer to an understanding of what is essential. Also, the time and effort expended in teaching skills would have a greater effect upon the student's power to read. In the writer's opinion, there are three abilities which clearly differentiate between the reader who comprehends well and the one who does not.

The first of these abilities is the power to find and understand thought relationships: in single sentences, in paragraphs, and in selections of varying lengths. Ideas are related to each other in many ways. Here is a simple example of the most common kind of thought relationship:

*Reprinted from *Reading Teacher,* 17 (September, 1963), p. 2-7 by permission of the author and the International Reading Association.

> During our visit to the museum, we saw the first Stars and Stripes
> ever carried in battle; after that we enjoyed a collection of old silverware,
> later wandered into the room filled with Indian relics, and finally found
> ourselves absorbed in a display of old wedding gowns.

The parts of this sentence, obviously, are related to each other chronologically.
We follow the trip through the museum in the time order in which the rooms
were visited. Now examine the same sentence parts arranged in a different way:

> During our visit to the museum, we saw a collection of old
> silverware, an absorbing display of old-fashioned wedding gowns, a room
> filled with Indian relics, and the first Stars and Stripes ever carried in
> battle.

This sentence tells less than the preceding one. We know what the visitor saw,
but we cannot follow him from room to room. The relationship present among
the parts of this second sentence is a simple listing.

Here is another sentence:

> During our visit to the museum, we enjoyed seeing the first Stars and
> Stripes ever carried in battle and the absorbing display of old-fashioned
> wedding gowns much more than we did the room filled with Indian relics
> and the collection of old silverware.

Now the ideas have a comparison-contrast relationship. The things the author
saw have fallen into two groups: two displays which he enjoyed, two others he
liked much less. An important *additional* meaning has been added because the
relationship of the parts of the sentence is different.

Once more, observe the same facts but in a fourth relationship:

> Because, on our visit to the museum, we had seen the first Stars and
> Stripes ever carried in battle, a room full of Indian relics, a display of old
> silverware, and a collection of old-fashioned wedding gowns, we were able
> to present a successful class program in which we compared relics of the
> past with their modern equivalents.

In this last sentence, we have a cause-effect relationship. The experiences of the
museum visit have produced an effect: a successful class program.

These four kinds of thought relationship — time, simple listing,
comparison — contrast, and cause-effect, plus others — occur in a great many
combinations, some of them complex. The ability to observe and to use these
relationships seems to be one of the basic comprehensions skills.

The ability to set specific purposes in reading is a second important ability
or skill. William G. Perry has reported a study done with fifteen hundred

Harvard and Radcliffe freshmen to determine their habits of study when presented with a typical chapter in a history text.[1]

In presenting his results, Perry has this to say:

> We asked anyone who could do so to write a short statement about what the chapter was all about. The number who were able to tell us . . . was just one in a hundred-fifteen. As a demonstration of obedient purposelessness in the reading of 99% of freshmen we found this impressive . . . after twelve years of reading homework assignments in school they had all settled into the habit of leaving the point of it all to someone else.

These same freshmen were able to do very well on a multiple-choice test based on the details of the material they had read.

If this purposelessness in study exists among students like those at Harvard, what must be the case with others less able? It might be argued that the moral of the tale is that teachers should give better assignments in which they *tell* students what to look for. But it would seem more important to suggest that by the time young people are freshmen at Harvard, it is high time they know how to set their own purposes. It is obvious that Perry questions whether the students he tested had any real comprehension at all. They could answer multiple-choice questions, but they failed to get, as he says, the "point of it all."

Suppose, for example, that a student is studying a chapter about life on the Southern plantations. The inefficient reader plods straight through the material, often with wandering attention because his goal is only to "read the lesson." Contrast the careful attention to detail, the search for visual imagery of the student who studies the same chapter in order to make a drawing of the plantation grounds. Contrast again the procedures of the student who wants to compare the way of life of the Southern plantation with that in colonial New England. Or, again, the method used by a student whose responsibility is to report on one very specific topic: the duties of the mistress of the plantation. This last student, if he is reading efficiently, will skim rapidly through the chapter until he comes to a paragraph which seems to have a bearing on his special topic, then settle down to read carefully for detail. The student who thus reads with purpose, and its corollary flexibility, has comprehension impossible to the student who merely "reads."

A third basic comprehension skill is the ability to make full use of previous learning in attacking new material. It is "reading readiness" in an extended form.

Jokes sometimes make an adult realize how a child must feel when he has to read something for which he does not have the requisite readiness. The following is supposed to be a story told by Helen Taft Manning about her father.

---

[1] William G. Perry, Jr., "Students' Use and Misuse of Reading Skills: A Report to the Faculty," *Harvard Educational Review,* Vol. 29, No. 3, Summer, 1959

When Taft was recuperating from a spell of illness, he wired a friend of his recovery and remarked that he had just taken a long horseback ride. The friend wired in reply, "How is the horse?"

Whether the reader sees anything funny at all in this story depends entirely upon whether he happens to remember from his previous reading or from pictures he may have seen that Taft was one of the heftiest of our presidents.

It is partly a matter of chance whether a reader happens to have a fact like this stored up in his head, but there is more to it than chance. Many students actually have the background information for full comprehension but fail to realize that they have it and to use it. Associational reading — the act of drawing upon all one has experienced and read to enrich what he is currently reading — is a skill which can be taught.

To summarize to this point: If an analysis is made of what lies at the foundation of comprehension, there seem to be at least three basic skills, (1) the ability to observe and use the varied relationships of ideas, (2) the ability to read with adjustment to conscious purpose, and (3) the ability to make full use of the backlog of real and vicarious experience which almost every reader possesses.

These basic skills are developed and strengthened in part by the kind of questioning which teachers use. Questions must be of the type which clarify thought relationships expressed in the material and which bring into focus meaningful associations with previous reading and experiences. "Thought" questions can turn a superficial test of comprehension into a learning experience.

Suppose, for example, that students have read an account of the Olympic Games. It is obvious that the first and last in the following set of four questions will make pupils use their comprehension skills, while the second and third will merely test their ability to skim or, if the exercise is unaided recall, to remember a couple of facts:

(1)   Why do the Olympic Games today feature a marathon race?
(2)   Who suggested that a marathon be added to the Olympics?
(3)   What is the official distance of the modern marathon?
(4)   Does anyone know of a famous American marathon race? Can you tell
      about it?

The kind of question is important. So, also, is the timing of the questions. Most questions should precede reading rather than follow it. If students knew *before* they read about the Olympics that they were to look for the cause-effect relationship required in question 1 above and that they should be making the associations with previous knowledge called for in question 4, they would read for the account with better comprehension because the questions would guide their reading. Questions asked *before* help students set purposes; questions asked *after* may do little but test.

A second kind of guidance which helps students learn basic comprehension skills involves the application of the directed-reading-lesson pattern of teaching to lessons in the curricular areas such as social studies, science, and literature. Teachers in elementary schools are very familiar with the directed reading lesson, which appears so often in the manuals of basal readers. Applied to a lesson in one of the content areas, it starts with the development of background and purpose. The teacher builds readiness for the new lesson by introducing new vocabulary and concepts and by reviewing materials from previous lessons or from the students' experiences to show them how the new content connects with the old. He also helps them set purposes for study. After skimming through the pages of the lesson, looking at pictures, reading headings, reviewing what they already know about the subject, students are able to answer questions like these:

Is this a lesson we can read rapidly or must we study it carefully? Why?
What are some of the things we should try to find out in this lesson? What
    questions can we anticipate *before* we read?
How can we use this new information?

It is during this first part of the directed lesson that students learn one of the basic skills: How to set purposes for reading.

The second step, silent reading and study, will be effective in proportion to the skill and thoroughness with which students are guided during the first step.

The third part of the lesson is the follow-up, usually some kind of questioning or testing. The type of questions and discussion the teacher uses determines how much students improve in their understanding of thought relationships and how much skill they acquire in making associations between what they are presently studying and the many other things they know — in fact, whether or not they get the "point of it all." Thus two more of the basic skills receive constant practice if the directed-reading-lesson pattern is used.

It is the writer's experience that some secondary teachers react negatively to this procedure. They may feel that it helps the student too much. He ought to be more on his own. The truth is that most students, even some very able ones, are not ready to study alone by the time they enter secondary school; we should be well content if they have acquired complete independence by the time they are ready for graduation. Skillful teachers know how to allow students to take more and more responsibility until one day, for most students not until some time late in senior high school, it is time to introduce SQ3R.[2] SQ3R is a grown-up directed reading lesson. The steps are virtually the same, but now the student is on his own. That Robinson's well-known technique is not more successful and popular stems from the fact that they have been expected to learn and use it before they are ready.

[2] Francis P. Robinson, *Effective Study*, Revised Edition (New York: Harper, 1961).

Teachers need to know what materials are available with which to help students learn comprehension skills. Many reading texts and workbooks have been written, some of them very useful, though, as has been implied earlier, the tendency has probably been to fragmentize the skills and perhaps to confuse both teachers and students by presenting too many *different* skills to teach and learn. Many of the exercises are tests of the application of the skills rather than devices for teaching them. Too often, they consist merely of passages to read followed by questions for students to answer. It is the unusual practice exercise which really shows the student how to see relationships, set purposes, and make associations.

Probably the very best materials for teaching comprehension skills are the regular textbooks in social studies, science, and literature. Because the student knows that the content of these books is important to him, he approaches them with a very different attitude from that with which he does a practice exercise in a workbook. He welcomes the teacher's help in seeing relationships and making associations which guide him in his task of understanding and remembering. Setting purposes for study makes sense to him. Every lesson in every textbook is a potential source for the best teaching of reading skills. Few secondary teachers seem to realize this. They are always searching for something different — something "special." Or, on the other hand, they make the assumption that the mere act of assigning reading in a textbook will insure growth in reading skill. Assigning is not synonymous with teaching. Only when the majority of teachers in secondary schools realize that purposeful teaching of reading skills is necessary in the everyday work of the content fields will the "reading problem" be solved.

What role does library or "individualized" reading have in this process of building comprehension skills? A very important one, but *not* the kind of role which most enthusiasts for "individualized reading" seem to visualize. Every bit of reading which a person ever does is a potential source of background understanding for all the reading he will do in the future. "Reading maketh a full man," said Francis Bacon, and he must have meant full of ideas, full of understandings, full of the background for rich comprehension. Any reader's experience can make this clear. He chooses a book or article on some subject with which he is familiar and reads easily with full and deep comprehension.

Contrast this experience with what happens when a reader undertakes to read a book in a field in which he has had no background of experience or previous reading. He can make no associations; he probably has no particular purpose except the very general one of getting some ideas about this new field; he misses many of the relationships which are obvious to the sophisticated reader in the field.

Here, then, is the reason why a broad program of individualized or library reading is essential to development of comprehension skills, not that it is likely, as some authorities have claimed, that most teachers will be able to do a good job of teaching the skills as a part of the individualized program itself. Rather, through the reading of many books, children acquire the understanding and the background which make the teaching of full comprehension skills possible.

If the skills described here are accepted as fundamental to good reading, teachers must make sure that students themselves understand and accept them. Practice of a skill without the student's understanding of what and why he is practicing leads to success in only a hit-or-miss fashion. Strong motivation, so necessary in learning any skill, springs from two main sources: specific evidence of progress in learning the skill and proof of its practical application. The more teachers share their own purposes and understanding with their students, the more likelihood of success in their teaching.

A Cluster of Skills: Especially for Junior High School*

H. ALAN ROBINSON

The Junior High School is somewhat of a twilight zone as far as sequence of reading skills is concerned. There is little certainty, especially in considering study skills, about where to begin and where to go — developmentally speaking. Possibly such a predicament is valuable and healthy, for the junior high school teacher must then evaluate individual pupils in terms of specific weaknesses and strengths.

Unfortunately, though, even if the junior high school teacher is able to ascertain such weaknesses and strengths, he often does not know how to proceed to capitalize on the strengths and to overcome the weaknesses. If he is a fairly typical teacher, he has not had a single course in the teaching of reading during his days as an undergraduate. One of the recommendations growing out of the recent Harvard-Carnegie study is that "a course in basic reading instruction be required of *all* prospective secondary school teachers."[1]

The junior high school teacher can probably get more help, and in turn be able to give more, if study skills are considered in clusters of small units. The conventional attempts to plot full sequences of skills presents too many concepts at once for the teacher and the student. For example, an "outlining cluster" might include only the following subskills in a rational sequence: reading for details, finding main ideas, changing main ideas to topics, supporting the topics with subtopics and details, labeling with outline form.

There might be individual clusters of skills necessary, however, for complete understanding of some of the subskills mentioned above. For instance, the writer of this article realized that junior high school students had difficulty in finding main ideas or key thoughts in paragraphs. At the time he was a consultant in a junior high school and, with the help of other members of the staff, a "key thought cluster" was devised. The purpose of this article is to present that cluster.

*Reprinted from *Reading Teacher*, 15 (September, 1961), p. 25-28, by permission of the author and the International Reading Association.
[1] Mary C. Austin and others. *The Torch Lighters* (Cambridge: Harvard University Press, 1961), p. 191.

The cluster grew out of the belief that students should not be asked to find the main idea before getting a great deal of practice in learning how to read for details. It is the writer's conviction that poor and generalized comprehension is fostered by the introduction of the main idea concept too early in the learning process. The ability to recognize and formulate main ideas calls for a great deal of reading and thinking maturity. In the final analysis, in order to deal with main ideas or key thoughts, a student must be able to recognize important or key words in sentences, understand basic organizational patterns of written material, draw conclusions, and make inferences.

Step One: Key Words in a Sentence

Hovious' technique of sending a telegram is used to establish the concept of key words as the most important words.[2] Students quickly observe that "Arrive International Airport New York nine Wednesday evening" states the most important words in the sentence, "I shall arrive at the International Airport in New York City at nine o'clock on Wednesday evening." They also learn that, for the most part, the same essential words will be chosen by different persons, but experience may cause some people to choose fewer or more words than others. The person who knows New York City or lives there might only need "Arrive International nine Wednesday evening."

Students should then move on to underlining the key words in sentences taken from conversation. A typical sentence might be, "Please be very careful that you do not damage the brand-new desks." Essentially students will underline "do not damage" or "not damage" "new desks." Once proficiency is established at this level, and students are beginning to realize that they are finding the main ideas of sentences, much more practice should be initiated using sentences from content-area materials. Some students who find it difficult to let go of details may need the individual attention of the teacher for a while. Other students may be given more complex sentences to figure out. During this step, however, all sentences should be isolated and not presented as parts of paragraphs.

Step Two: Key Sentence in a Paragraph

In this step the students first learn that they need be concerned with fewer key words when sentences are treated together in paragraph form. They learn this through the experience of underlining key words in the sentences of short paragraphs. For example:

[2] Carol Hovious, *Flying the Printways* (Boston: D. C. Heath, 1938), p. 163.

A school performs many services for the residents of a community. It offers instructional services for school-age children during the day and, often, courses for adults in the evening. It provides a meeting place for community organizations. It also serves as an active cultural center, for plays, concerts, and lectures are often scheduled.

In this paragraph the sentences are so closely linked that it is not necessary to keep repeating the subject. Students soon realize that they are primarily concerned with verbs and their objects once the subject is established.

The paragraphs presented in this step should be well structured, containing definite key sentences mainly as first and last sentences. One or two of the paragraphs may contain key sentences mainly as first and last sentences. One or two of the paragraphs may contain key sentences placed in other parts of the paragraph.

Students are asked to list the key ideas (groups of key words) they have found in the paragraph. For example, this list might have been written about the paragraph on school services:

school performs many services
offers instructional services
provides meeting place
serves as cultural center.

Students learn to *add up* the key ideas and decide whether or not one of them represents an over-all idea. It happens to be contained in the first sentence of the paragraph. Hence, in this paragraph, the over-all or main idea is contained in a key sentence at the beginning.

Here is another example. The task is a little more difficult because some of the sentences in the paragraph contain two key ideas. Students learn to treat these ideas as separate units in their search for the key sentence.

Everyone saluted as the flag was slowly raised. A smartly-dressed woman cracked a champagne bottle across the ship's prow and named it "Sea Hawk." The order was given, and the "Sea Hawk" started down the ways. A new ship was launched.

Everyone saluted + flag raised + woman cracked bottle across ship's prow + named it "Sea Hawk" + order given + started down ways = new ship launched. Obviously, the key sentence is the last sentence in the paragraph. Key idea + key idea + key idea + the over-all or main idea contained in the key sentence.

Look at this example:

Animals have interesting habits. One of the habits of some animals is to use nature's medicines when they are ill. Deer may eat twigs and the very tender bark of trees. Cats and dogs may eat grass when they are not feeling up to par. Bears often eat different kinds of roots and berries.

Deer eat twigs and tender bark + cats and dogs eat grass + bears eat roots and berries = some animals use nature's medicine when ill. The first sentence in the paragraph serves only an introductory purpose. It may be introducing a series of paragraphs which will deal with interesting habits of animals. It is not, of course, the main idea of this particular paragraph. Hence, in this case, the key sentence is the second sentence in the paragraph.

Step Three: The Main Thought in a Paragraph

After students have completed a great deal of successful practice in working with paragraphs containing key sentences in a variety of positions, they should be ready for this step. At this time they might be presented with a paragraph very much like this one:

> We visited the seals frolicking in the water. Then we paid a visit to the colorful birds in the big new birdhouse. After that we stopped for a Coke and hot dog. Before going home we spent a lot of time watching the funny monkeys.

The students would again be asked to find key ideas. Visited seals + paid visit to birds + stopped for Coke and hot dog + before going home spent time watching monkeys + ? At this point numerous students will point out that there is no *stated* over-all idea.

Students must now make inferences, for the author does not state the key thought in a sentence of the paragraph. The student must look at all key ideas and determine the main idea of the paragraph himself. In this easy paragraph most students, of course, will agree that the key thought is "we visit the zoo," or something similar.

When students have mastered the basic ideas in the three-step cluster of skills using carefully structured materials, normal textbook material should provide application and reinforcement. Students soon become aware of the fact that paragraphs which are parts of chapters in books don't always stand by themselves. One main or key thought may be carried through a number of paragraphs without repetition in each paragraph. Often students will decide on the key thought by noting part of a main idea stated by the author and adding to it through their own reasoning. For instance:

> It is not only radio that has given them a great deal of help. Ballistics experts can tell whether or not a bullet was fired from a particular gun by

examining the bullet under a microscope. Chemists help solve crimes by analyzing blood, dust, cloth, and other materials. Photographers, also, are used in helping police solve crimes. Often photographs, especially when enlarged, reveal clues that the human eye overlooked.

Obviously, in the paragraph above, the key thought is concerned with "people and things that help police solve crimes." Clues can be found in the paragraph, but the reader can also arrive at the key thought through reasoning and the context that preceded this paragraph. Certainly a preceding paragraph, or several, dealt with "radio as it helps police solve crimes."

As students learn to look for organizational patterns in the way material is written, they will gain in ability to comprehend and retain. The teacher can best help the student by "clustering" closely related skills together in a teaching unit and by organizing the steps in a given cluster so well that the student has a series of successful experiences. *Challenge* is of tremendous importance *after* students feel that they have mastered the skill or skills to some degree. For even with the teacher's help in dealing with "clusters of skills," junior high school textbooks will present many challenges.

Concepts From Semantics as Avenues to Reading Improvements *

DAVID COOPER

Since the popularization of Korzybski and Ogden and Richards in the late thirties, teachers have found in semantics a source of theories about language and language behavior which has added a vitality to the teaching of English which often seemed hopelessly buried in the rubrics of grammar and rhetoric. Although the systematic application of the principles of semantics to written and oral expression is generally widely practiced, one of the inconsistencies of the curriculum in English has been the lack of similar application to the development of reading skills. Probably for as long as any of us can remember, we have been deploring the inadequacies of reading instruction in the secondary schools. One of the more popular panaceas is "Every teacher a teacher of reading," but there is precious little evidence of ambitious school-wide programs reaching their ultimate targets, the students. The logical place to focus instruction in reading is the English class, in which all of the language skills can be integrated, and in which all students receive instruction. Such a focus does not minimize the importance of reading instruction in each of the content areas of the curriculum. But to develop an understanding of the ways in which language works in all of its facets — listening, speaking, writing, and *reading* — is a prime concern of the teacher of English. Those aspects of semantics concerned with the relation of words to objects and events in the physical world and with the techniques by which we accomplish our purposes through the use of language suggest approaches through which teachers may help develop reading skills which parallel the development of the other language skills.

The English teacher cannot limit his treatment of language to the field of literature. Most literature should not be subjected to the same kind of scientific analysis as discourse which claims to be factual, logical, and objective. We could destroy the imaginative and emotional appeal of literature if we were to apply to it the usual sematic tests of referential language. On the other hand, the student may need more insights into language than are afforded by the tools of literary

*Reprinted from *English Journal,* 53 (February, 1964), p 85-90, by permission of the author and the National Council of Teachers of English.

criticism in order to decide about a candidate or a political issue after reading conflicting opinions, make an intelligent choice about which product to buy after reading the claims of the sellers, or make other practical decisions which might depend partly upon assessing what he has read. In developing skills in speaking and writing, students are expected to have experiences largely with expository materials dealing with all areas of knowledge, with utilitarian rather than artistic uses of language. Teaching expository reading, therefore, should be familiar ground to the English teacher.

What is needed, then, is not "just the "reading specialist" to work with a limited number of remedial students, but the language specialist, the English teacher to apply his knowledge and training in a program for developing the skills of all students in the reading of non-literary as well as literary materials. The program could begin with the reinforcement of such comprehension and study skills taught in earlier grades as recognizing main ideas and significant details, reading between the lines, following cause and effect relationships, and using text and reference materials efficiently. These skills need to be applied to the increasingly complex material with which high school students are confronted. They are prerequisite to developing the reading skills which are a facet of the maturity in the use of language which the English teacher aims to develop. The "mature" reader may be defined as one who generally

— can deal skillfully with increasingly higher levels of abstraction
— suspends judgment until "all" the facts are in
— distinguishes fact from opinion
— draws inferences from and judges the validity of the ideas presented
— recognizes the author's intention(s)
— compares the views of different authors
— makes judgments concerning the quality, the effectiveness or the completeness of what is read
— draws analogies
— goes beyond specific facts to use past experiences and relational thinking in arriving at an interpretation
— applies the ideas gained from reading to new situations
— applies the material read in the solution of problems[1]

A program for developing maturity in reading might be focused around the following aspects of semantics and related language study: language and reality, the purposes of language, semantic shift, the abstraction process, metaphor, and critical reading.

[1] This definition, though restricted to and expanding upon aspects of reading maturity related to semantic awareness, parallels that of William S. Gray and Bernice Rogers in *Maturity in Reading,* (Chicago: University of Chicago Press, 1956). p. 54-55.

Language and Reality

As students progress through school, they become increasingly dependent upon printed matter divorced from direct experience. They tend to verbalize, to relate what they read only to other words and not to experience. An antidote lies in understanding of the symbolic process – of the relationship between language and reality – and in developing the habit of asking what a word represents in the physical world.

The mature reader is one who responds to words as symbols for things and not as the things themselves, who recognizes that names represent not qualities inherent in the objects, but arbitrary classifications agreed upon by the users. He is aware that a verbal map is a production of what is likely to occur in a relevant context, and not a fixed and complete description of reality. He is on guard against the syntactical structures which suggest that objects bearing the same name are identical, or that sense impressions are qualities of things rather than the author's reactions to them. Students need to be trained to translate the static and elementalistic structure of our language to fit the facts of a world of interrelated and orderly change which science has discovered. They need to avoid the pitfalls of an agent-action, question-answer language which places objects and events in neat, unrelated categories.

As the student deals with greater complexities, with abstract ideas further and further removed from his experience, it is essential that he develop the habits and skills needed to follow the circuitous path back from symbol to referent. He needs to develop an extensive and flexible verbal repertoire to cope with the countless nuances of emotion and thought with which symbols are imbued. He needs to recognize that an infinite variety of responses to a symbol is possible and that the accuracy of his interpretation depends upon his experience with the symbol, the possible referents for it, and upon his familiarity with the author's matrix of experience.

In the classroom, students might find and explain examples of euphemisms and word magic (reacting to a word as if it were a thing: curses "dirty" words, Patriotic labels, etc.). They can give their meanings for selected words and then compare them with those in various dictionaries in an attempt to arrive inductively at the concept of how words get meanings. They can find examples of differing newspaper reports for the same event and try to account for the differences. They can observe and describe commercial products and then compare their descriptions to those of advertisers.

The Purposes of Language

Unless the reader has clearly defined purposes, he will read in a disorganized, unresponsive fashion. The reader is handicapped in this selection of a pace and method of reading suitable to the discourse and to his purposes unless he knows something of how language works. He has a responsibility almost as great as that of the writer in analyzing and evaluating discourse. He needs to be concerned with organizational patterns. In clear writing, the author's organization corresponds to his topics and purposes. Narration calls for time sequence, argument for analytical organization, etc. Transitions are determined by the ways in which the parts or events are related in the realities one is describing, narrating, or explaining. The English teacher needs to provide opportunities for students to practice looking for these organizational clues to the meaning of what he reads. Here is an obvious area in which the teaching of reading skills complements the teaching of composition.

Another responsibility of the reader is to fathom the ostensible purpose for the real intent of the writer. The writer may use cognitive language in persuading people to believe or do something. This may be the case in advertising or in political material which sticks to the facts. The reader needs to be aware of the situation in which a statement is made in order to judge the purpose and effect of language, since the same words in the same grammatical structures may have different functions in different situations. When the student knows how language works he can protect himself from verbal hypnosis. His reactions to the printed word should be critical and intelligent rather than automatic. He needs to recognize that no language is adequate for all time and for all purposes.

In the classroom, students can try to determine the attitudes and purposes of the users of selected words (policeman, peace officer, fuzz), phrases, and longer pieces of discourse. They might reflect on the appeal of specific passages to different readers: emotional, informative, persuasive, esthetic. They can find and analyze examples of material written for different groups of people, but for the same purpose: an election appeal or advertising addressed to farmers, intellectuals, city workers, minority groups, retired persons. They should have practice in reading various types of material for different purposes: for information, to reflect on the effect of a proposal, to understand feelings of others, to be moved, to weigh opposing opinions, etc.

Semantic Shift

Students need to develop a flexibility in interpreting what they read which corresponds to the growing proliferation and complexity of the areas of knowledge which they explore. They need to recognize that words have no fixed meanings and that meanings shift with the contexts of time, place, and situation. In each reading situation they have to be aware of the variables of context in order to determine the writer's meaning for a word. The mature reader selects from a number of related meanings the one which best fits the circumstances, particularly when he is interpreting those high-level abstractions and statements of feeling which tend to elicit stereotyped and emotional responses. If meaning cannot be derived from context, a dictionary may help, provided that it gives a definition within the student's experience. Students need to be able to shift their viewpoints, to carry over into a new set of definitions the results gained through past experience in other frameworks.

The theoretical knowledge of the role of context and of shifts in meaning will not, of course, guarantee sound semantic reactions. Of primary importance is the overlap of experience between reader and writer. However, students can practice reading representative passages to develop awareness of multiple meanings and of the role of context, which should in turn develop an appreciation of the need for experiential background similar to an author's, in order to share his meaning. They might analyze the variations in meaning of the same word found in different contexts: Compare passages in which a contemporary American statesman, a Chinese communist, and a Periclean Greek use the word "democracy." They can find and analyze examples of similar language describing identical phenomena, but which may represent different meanings for different individuals: What makes a particular day "beautiful" for a farmer, a skier, a fisherman, a photographer? They might look for words in print which did not exist or whose meanings have changed in the past fifty years. General semanticists suggest that the device of indexing, to differentiate one member of a class from others, and dating, to indicate that change takes place in time, may be useful reminders that a word never means the same thing twice.

The Process of Abstraction

When we abstract, we attach a label to two or more objects, events, or ideas which have some characteristic in common. Thus a table and a chair become furniture. John Smith and William Jones, who share a skin pigmentation several shades darker than that of their neighbors, are labeled Negroes. These classifications emphasize similarities and leave out differences. But every individual in a given classification differs from every other one and every individual changes over a period of time. Awareness of the process of abstraction and classification may help the reader recognize stereotyped thinking in what he reads and in his own thinking. He may realize that "William Jones, Negro, was jailed last night" makes use of an irrelevant classification, since Jones can be classified in an infinite number of ways.

In the classroom, students might check reports against experience to determine what is omitted, why different people remember different details, and what the possible referents are for the writer's abstract terms. Many high-level abstractions are not obviously reducible to expressions designating individual objects, and it would be futile to pursue every symbol back to every referent, but if students develop awareness of the omission of details in various levels of abstraction they are more likely to be aware that the inference is not the report and that people never say all there is to say about anything. Students can practice writing operational definitions for high-level abstractions, especially those with strong connotations. They might then substitute more concrete and neutral words in selected passages. They can learn to spot statements that fail to recognize that individuals in a group are different and that changes occur. They can evaluate the purpose, validity, and appropriateness of classifications in the material which they read.

Metaphor

The recognition and evaluation of metaphor is another aspect of linguistic sophistication which becomes more important as reading tasks become more difficult. As new areas of knowledge are explored, the writer relies heavily upon metaphor to describe new experiences. The reader, as he is increasingly divorced from direct experience with the subject, must, for maximum understanding, depend upon a clear interpretation of the metaphors employed. The mature reader needs not only to recognize metaphor, but also to assess its applicability, the elements which can be applied to the new situation, and its emotive elements.

Metaphor should be taught as an integral aspect of language, the chief means by which words are given new meanings, and not merely as an ornament of poetry. Even though a metaphor is stated simply, it poses serious comprehension problems for the unsophisticated reader who may lack both the background and the insight into language to reconstruct the experience which metaphor demands of the reader. Students might begin with a recognition and analysis of the literal referent and go on to examine its relationship to what is being talked about. The sports pages are rich sources of metaphors which are easy to trace back to their literal referents: the cog of the infield; Pirates shade Giants; glass jaw; stretch run; casaba clash. In examining a metaphor they must ask themselves which elements have been selected for comparison and which have been left out. They should learn to determine the nature of the parallel relationship which is being borrowed, which elements can be applied to the new situation, and in what ways. They should not assume that relationships exist which the writer does not mean to imply do exist: What characteristics are being compared when we say someone works like a horse, treats her like a dog, or behaves like a pig, snake, rat, or fox? How has the writer employed metaphor to appeal to the emotions?

Critical Reading

Although "critical reading" is a shifting and amorphous term, there is unquestioned consensus that students should be trained to go beyond literal comprehension of what is read to evaluating, organizing, and inferring and drawing conclusions from their reading. The classroom can develop a concern for meaning, rather than mere fact. The student needs to be able to consider the consequences of alternate choices. In order to do this he needs not only accurate information, but freedom from the kind of communication situation in which he is restricted to automatic responses by the nature of the symbols and syntactical patterns with which he is confronted.

Understanding of the relationship between language and reality, of the purposes of language, of semantic shift, of the abstraction process, and of the nature of metaphor are all basic to mature evaluation of what is read. In teaching "critical reading," however, English teachers have customarily concentrated their efforts on training students to

— recognize underlying assumptions
— recognize common fallacies in thinking
— distinguish among fact, inference, and opinion
— distinguish between the connotation of words
— evaluate the adequacy of general statements
— evaluate the dependability of data and the competence of authorities

All of these evaluative skills call for an awareness of how language works. Assumptions are frequently obscured by the nature of our syntactical patterns: "When did you stop beating your wife?" Perhaps the most pervasive fallacy in thinking is that based on two-valued orientation, the either-or, black-or-white way of looking at life. At least part of this elementalistic way of thinking may be ascribed to our language, or labeling habits. We tend to respond favorably to all persons or events which are classified in one way and unfavorably to all persons or events which are classified in another. The subject-predicate sentence pattern permits the reader to internalize the assumption that everything is either A or not A: "You are either for us or against us." It also fails to distinguish, syntactically, between emotive and referential language. "He is a dirty red" and "He is a member of the Communist party."

The English class can be a laboratory in which readers have opportunities to identify and evaluate assumptions, instances of two-valued orientation, statements of cause and effect, stereotypes, and unsupported generalizations. The mature reader makes evaluations on the basis of whatever characteristics he can discover, rather than on the basis of names or classifications, and he makes his evaluations tentatively. He avoids noting only characteristics which agree with his preconceptions and is on the alert for such selectivity (slanting) on the part of the writer. He interprets the writer's connotations for a word while guarding against the imposition of his own connotations.

Language study based on scholarly findings has achieved considerable recognition in the English curriculum in recent years. Curriculum guides and composition textbooks have reflected the growing concern with the relationship of language and thought. As a point of departure for the teaching of reading, the English teacher might apply much of the content of language instruction available in guides and texts. The following composite of language concepts dealt with in four recent series of secondary school composition texts suggests a possible sequence for a reading skills program based on semantics:

Grade 9

The role of context in meaning
Multiple meanings
Kinds of statements

Grade 10

The purposes of language
Distinguishing between fact and opinion
Emotive and referential language
Connotation and denotation
Shifts in meaning
The nature of questions

Grade 11

Recognizing basic errors in thinking
Loaded words
The process of symbolization (symbol and referent)
Abstract and concrete words
Pinning down the meaning of abstractions
Classification
Definition

Grade 12

Levels of abstraction (the abstraction process)
Meaning and experience
The nature of metaphor
Generalization
Recognizing assumptions

Until suitable collections of readings are developed, the teacher will have to rely upon newspapers, magazines, advertising copy, an occasional expository essay found in literature texts, and, for advanced students, such college texts as

Altick's *Preface to Critical Reading* and Leary and Smith's *Thought and Statement.* If we base it upon the study and effective use of language, not only should the English teacher not shy away from teaching reading, but he should welcome the opportunity to deal with this hitherto neglected aspect of his subject.

Factors in Critical Reading *

WILLIAM ELLER AND JUDITH GOLDMAN WOLF

Improvement of critical reading ability is an acknowledged goal of many of the college reading programs in America, and of many courses in freshman English, rhetoric, or communications skills. A number of college reading handbooks — Stroud, Ammons, and Bamman (17),† Glock (3), and Hill and Eller (4), for example — include assorted exercises for the extension of the critical skills, and a few complete textbooks are devoted to critical thinking and reading, usually with considerable emphasis upon logic. Altick's *Preface to Critical Reading* (1) is typical of these texts employed in teaching evaluative skill to college freshmen and sophomores.

Because college-level instruction in reading is usually provided by departments of English and education, the teaching methodologies commonly employed have been developed mainly by specialists from these two academic areas, and the bulk of the published materials have been created by authors who are either English instructors or professional educators or both. Inasmuch as reading teachers with English and education backgrounds tend to be skills-oriented rather than personality-oriented, the programs and materials which they have developed are directed toward the improvement of specific academic reading skills and give very little attention to the psychological, social, and emotional aspects of reading comprehension. Instruction in critical reading when planned by English teachers tends to feature the fundamentals of logic and the numerous propaganda devices against which the reader must learn to defend himself. Reading teachers trained in education departments, on the other hand, are inclined to construct and use exercises which appear to develop skills such as (1) determining the author's probable purpose, (2) gauging the extent of the writer's expertise, (3) detecting inconsistencies between statements of different authors and even within the writings of a single author, and (4) compensating for the known biases of standard publications such as the *Chicago Tribune* and *The Reporter.* Probably no one would argue that it is useless to teach these and other

*Reprinted from *The Philosophical and Sociological Bases of Reading,* Fourteenth Yearbook of the National Reading Conference, Eric L. Thurston, editor, 1965, p. 64-72, by permission of the authors and the editor.
†Numbers in parentheses refer to references at end of article.

skills commonly pursued in college reading centers and rhetoric classes; the question is: Are there some factors in the process of reading comprehension which are so personal that the mastery of the so-called reading skills does not assure the ability to read critically, at least in some types of printed matter?

The experimentation of social psychologists and communication theorists over the past two decades would seem to indicate that the foregoing question must be answered in the affirmative; that relationships between the reader's personality, the portion of society in which he functions, and various aspects of the communicative act have considerable bearing upon the whole comprehension process, including the evaluative acts known as critical reading. It is true that most of this experimentation was not performed with the purpose of checking on the factors which relate to critical reading ability, but the studies subsequently cited appear to have definite implications for reading comprehension in general and critical reading, per se. At the very least these experiments suggest numerous possibilities for research in the evaluative processes of reading comprehension.

Since there are numerous experiments in the psychology of communications which would seem to have implications for teachers of reading comprehension, some organizational scheme should prove helpful to a scrutiny of the research. Perhaps the simplest acceptable arrangement of evidence would be one employing four categories: (1) Who is trying to convey a message? (2) What is the message conveyed? (3) What is the nature of the mode of communication? (4) Who is the recipient of the message? Each of the several studies reported herein will be considered under one of the four questions. Of course, many other investigations could be reported; but the ones cited are representative, it is hoped. For certain of the experiments, contradictory data could be found elsewhere. The discrepancies among studies and the incomparability of some research works are attributable in part to the fact that different experimenters have based their designs upon different theoretical frameworks. Inasmuch as every one of these frameworks is at this point very incomplete, it is not surprising that research workers disagree concerning the interpretation of the findings of others as well as their own.

Who is trying to convey the message? Characteristics of the cummunicator which could be expected to influence the effectiveness or force of the communication are his (1) credibility, (2) prestige, and (3) attractiveness. The first of these has repeatedly been demonstrated to be a factor in communicative efficacy. In 1951, in a frequently-cited study, Hovland and Weiss (7) presented subjects (college students) with four articles, each of which was attributed by the experimenters to a highly credible source for half the subjects. A low-credibility individual was credited with the authorship of each article for the other half of the subjects. Analysis of subject responses indicated that communications attributed to high credibility sources were more often adjudged "fair" or "unbiased" than were the same communications attributed to low credibility writers, and the conclusions were more often considered "justified" when the subjects viewed the authors as of high credibility. Immediately following the reading the indication of change in opinion in the direction favored by an article was three-and-one-half times as great among those who thought they were reading the argument of a highly credible author as among subjects who viewed their author as having low credibility. However, this differential in attitude change did not persist. One month after the experiment no significant differences between groups could be detected. Although Mandell and Hovland (14) in 1952 were unable to establish significantly different changes in attitude among two groups, when one set of subjects thought they were reading the opinions of an author who was "suspect" and the other group viewed its author as "non-suspect", the bulk of the Yale studies of this variable of credibility indicates that a communicator who is perceived as credible or trustworthy is more persuasive than one not so perceived.

Bettelheim and Janowitz (2) mailed anti-Semitic literature attributed to various authors to several dozen male Gentiles. Analysis of responses revealed that the propaganda was more effective if it was attributed to a known Jew. The investigators interpreted this trend as an indication that the readers had regarded the ostensible Jewish authorship as reasonably objective.

In the matter of prestige as a characteristic of the communicator, Kishler (12) reported that the esteem in which Catholic priests were held by his subjects were related to the amount they learned from the motion picture "The Keys of the Kingdom" and to the magnitude of opinion change in the direction of religious tolerance. Kishler added the interesting observation that in this situation the subjects were reacting differentially, not to a genuine priest, but to an actor.

What is the nature of the communication? A number of variables in the content of a communication may be related to its efficacy. One such variable concerns the "sidedness" of a presentation: Is a communication more persuasive if it presents only one side of an issue, or if it presents arguments on two sides? The research on this question is not entirely clear-cut, because the investigators have usually confounded the sidedness variable with some other factor such as the degrees of overt commitment (of subjects) to a certain point of view. However, Hovland et. al; (6) has attempted to summarize the literature with a few basic generalizations: (1) In the long run two-sided presentation is more effective than one-sided when the audience is subsequently exposed to counter-propaganda, regardless of initial opinions; or when the audience initially disagrees with the communicator's point of view, regardless of subsequent exposure to counter-propaganda. (2) One-sided communication is more effective than two-sided if the audience initially is in agreement with the point of view of the propaganda. Klapper (13) modifies these generalizations with the addition of summary statements concerning some interacting variables: One-sided presentations are more effective with persons of limited education; one-sided communications are efficient persuaders of audiences which are required to publicly defend the presented view; and one-sided presentations are more susceptible to "boomerang" effect if the audience suspects that the communicator is "pouring it on" too much.

Somewhat related to the sidedness issue is the factor of order of presentation. Much of Hovland's 1957 volume (3) in the Yale series is devoted to a consideration of the effects of order of presentation and its interaction with other factors. The basic question is: If two different points of view are expressed to an audience, which is more persuasive, the argument presented first or the latter one? At the conclusion of a series of experiments on this primacy-versus-recency problem, Hovland settled upon the following summary statements: (1) If two opposing statements are offered by different communicators, the position stated first doesn't necessarily have the advantage. (2) If communicatees make a public endorsement of one side of an issue before exposure to the opposing side, subsequent presentation of the second side is less effective; hence, there is a primacy effect. However, the anonymous statements of opinion through the use of questionnaires after presentation of one side of a controversy does not significantly reduce the persuasiveness of the second (and opposing) presentation. (3) If both sides of a controversial issue are presented in a single session by a single communicator, there is a distinct tendency for the viewpoints presented first to prevail. However, this primacy effect can be reduced either by interpolating other activities between the two presentations of controversy, or by warning the subjects against the tendency to respond to first impressions. (4) If communications highly desirable to the communicatees are presented first, followed by less desirable messages, there is more persuasion than when the reverse order is followed. (5) Order of presentation interacts with personality type to some extent in that experimental subjects with high cognition need are influenced by communications without regard for the order, whereas those with low cognitive needs demonstrate the law of primacy.

Another continuum which relates to persuasibility is the degree of specificness — as contrasted with implicitness — in the communicator's directives. As a rule, the persuasive effect is greater if the communicator draws specific conclusions rather than permitting the recipients to draw their own, or as Katz and Lazarsfeld summarized in 1955, "the more specific the suggestion which a personal contact makes, the more likely it is that his or her advice will be followed." (11, p. 17)

In at least a couple of respects the emotional quality of message content seems to relate to the effectiveness of the communication. One of them, the emotional-versus-rational appeal factor, obviously interacts with so many other elements in communicative process that present research only begins to describe its role. Weiss (18) presented three types of content information (one each) to his three experimental groups: group E read a highly inflammatory statement designed to arouse aggressive emotion concerning criminals; group R was confronted with a rational treatment containing factual data on the same subject; and group ER read a text which contained both emotional and rational approaches. The emotion content "induced a greater degree of expressed arousal" than the rational material. Because Weiss had administered a personality inventory to his subjects, he was also able to observe that the attitudes of the high authoritarian aggressives in the sample were significantly more punitive than the opinions of those who were low in this trait measurement, after exposure to the communications.

Another facet of the emotional quality of messages to be investigated by a number of workers is the level of fear induced, or the intensity of the threat. One of the oft-cited studies of this facet was done by Janis and Fesback (9), who developed three forms of an illustrated lecture on dental hygiene with three different intensities of fear appeal, the most threatening of which included some rather disturbing views of pathological conditions. High school students who consitituted the experimental samples revealed more conformity with the position on the communication when the fear level was lowest (of the three); that is, the actual dental practices of the teen-agers were modified least in the groups which had been exposed to the strongest – most fear-arousing appeal. Similar results have been derived from experiments which employed varying levels of fear in communications designed to induce subjects to provide themselves with bomb shelters.

What is the nature of the mode of communication? Of the four questions posed earlier, this is probably the least important to the teacher of critical reading skills, since he is concerned only with printed media, at least in his role as reading teacher. Then, too, the printed word is not a very forceful communicative agency in comparison with more personal and lively media, and thus interactions with other factors in opinion formation may be of less importance in the reading setting. At least two major generalizations, however, should be worthy of the reading teacher's notice: (1) The use of multiple media in communication results in greater persuasive effect than the use of a single media; and (2) the more personal means of communication are most effective in persuasion, so that for most recipients of presentations, "in-person" delivery, television and radio achieve more attitude change than reading matter.

What are the characteristics of the recipient of the communication? Manis and Blake (16, p. 225) introduced a recent article with the suggestion that "distorted interpretations of persuasive messages may often result from the recipient's attempt to maintain his existing beliefs in relatively unchanged form. Thus, given the fact that most messages can be reasonably interpreted in a variety of ways, it is assumed that the recipient will select that interpretation which is least challenging to his convictions." The manner in which existing views affect – by resistance or distortion – the acceptance of new opinions has attracted the attention of a number of writers who have investigated it from their differing theoretical bases. Several experimenters have dealt with this phenomenon under the heading of "selective exposure" and one of Manis' (15) 1961 studies illustrates this factor in operation. Three groups of college students, whose attitudes towards fraternities varied, were confronted with a series of short messages about fraternities, half of them attributed to authors of high prestige, and half to writers of low prestige. After reading each passage the subjects attempted to describe fraternities as the author described them, using six evaluative rating scales. When the student readers reacted to the high prestige articles they distorted their reports of the authors' statements in the direction of their own original attitudes; for the low prestige articles there was no relationship between the subjects' views and their judgments of the authors' positions. Thus, if the students felt that the writer of a selection was an important person they tended to displace his position toward their own views of fraternities.

As might be expected, numerous psychologists have mainfested curiosity concerning the relationships between certain personality characteristics of message recipients and their perception of persuasive presentations; however, the research on this relationship has not been as productive of definitive statements as in some of the areas already considered. The Yale Studies, particularly those directed by Janis, have led to a few findings worthy of mention. Janis himself (8) reported that low self-esteem is related to high persuasibility, and vice versa; thus, persons who do not value themselves highly tend to be susceptible to opinion change. Janis and Field (10) found no significant relationship between aggressiveness and persuasibility. Most other investigators have been unable to provide convincing data regarding any such relationship. Richness of fantasy was found to be positively related to persuasibility for males but not for females by Janis and Field. (10)

Group affiliations is another characteristic of the recipient of a communication which has bearing on his persuasibility and comprehension of the message. For three decades social psychologists have known that communications which accord with the general climate of opinion in a group are more likely to be accepted by persons who identify themselves with that group than messages that are at variance with group opinion.

Assorted other characteristics of communicators, their messages, media, and audiences have been explored in the search for factors which influence the moulding and changing of attitudes. The research and conclusions already cited are by no means exhaustive; they are included chiefly to demonstrate that a great variety of factors influence the reaction which an individual recipient may have for a given persuasive communication.

Implications for Teaching Critical Reading

Most of the research which has explored factors and relationships in opinion change was not conducted specifically to aid the teacher of critical reading. In fact, some of it was performed under the auspices of advertising agencies with goals almost diametrically opposed to those of the reading teacher. Further, much of this research in communication psychology did not involve reading as a means of presentation; the subjects' reading was in some instances limited to responses to a pencil and paper instrument after the presentation. Yet certain broad implications seem justified on the basis of the research and theory in these avenues of social psychology.

(1) The conventional academic skills approach to the development of critical reading ability does not even touch upon some of the major sources of "uncriticalness".

(2) Research workers who are also specialists in reading instruction should conduct experiments which parallel many of the studies cited herein. Thus they will learn which of the factors which influence persuasibility in general communication are also important — and to what extent — in the critical reading processes.

(3) At least on an experimental basis some teachers of critical reading should incorporate into their methodologies moderately extensive consideration of the social psychology of communication — the facets of communicator, message and communicatee which influence persuasion and comprehension — in an attempt to improve critical reading skill by arming students with an understanding of some factors which ordinarily cause them to be uncritical. This type of instruction has been provided experimentally for at least a decade by Dr. Ralph H. Ojemann and his colleagues at the University of Iowa, apparently with some success.

(4) Reading comprehension is evidently a much more complicated process than the teaching method textbooks indicate, and must be completely re-considered in terms of the evidence handed over by the social psychologists.

References

1. Altick, Richard D., *Preface to Critical Reading,* New York: Holt, Rinehart and Winston, 1960.
2. Bettelheim Bruno and Morris Janowitz, "Reactions to Fascist Propaganda: A Pilot Study," *Public Opinion Quarterly,* 14:53-60, 1950.
3. Glock, Marvin D., *Improving College Reading,* Boston: Houghton-Mifflin, 1954.
4. Hill, Walter R. and William Eller, *Power in Reading Skills,* Belmont, California: Wadsworth, 1964,
5. Hovland, C. I. (Ed.), *The Order of Presentation in Persuasion,* New Haven: Yale University Press, 1957.
6. Hovland, C. I., I. L. Janis, and H. H. Kelly, *Communication and Persuasion,* New Haven: Yale University Press, 1953.
7. Hovland, C. I., and W. Weiss, "The Influence of Source Credibility on Communication Effectiveness," *Public Opinion Quarterly,* 15:635-650, 1951.
8. Janis, I. L., "Personality Correlates of Susceptibility to Persuasion," *Journal of Personality,* 22:504-518, 1954.

9.   Janis, Irving L. and S. Fesbach, "Effects of Fear – Arousing Communications," *Journal of Abnormal and Social Psychology,* 48:78-92, 1953.

10. Janis, I. L. and Peter B. Field, "A Behavioral Assessment of Persuasibility: Consistency of Individual Differences," *Sociometry,* 19:241-59, 1956.

11. Katz, Elihu and Paul F. Lazarsfeld, "Personal Influence: The Part Played by the People in the Flow of Mass Communications," in J. T. Klapper, *The Effects of Mass Communication,* Glencoe, Illinois: Free Press, 1960.

12. Kishler, John, "Prediction of Differential Learning from a Motion Picture by Means of Indices of Identification Potentials Derived from Attitudes Toward the Main Character," *American Psychologist,* 5:298-99, 1950.

13. Klapper, J. T., *The Effects of Mass Communication,* Glencoe, Illinois: Free Press, 1960.

14. Mandell, Wallace and Carl I. Hovland, "Is There a Law of Primacy In Persuasion?" *American Psychologist,* 7:538, 1952.

15. Manis, M., "The Interpretation of Persuasive Messages as a Function of Recipient Attitude and Source Prestige," *Journal of Abnormal and Social Psychology,* 63:82-86, 1961.

16. Manis M., and J. B. Blake, "Interpretation of Persuasive Messages as a Function of Prior Immunization," *Journal of Abnormal and Social Psychology,* 66:225-230, 1963.

17. Stroud, James B., Robert B. Ammons, and Harry A. Bamman, *Improving Reading Ability,* New York: Appleton-Century-Crofts, Inc., 1956.

18. Weiss, W., "Emotional Arousal and Attitude Change," *Psychological Reports,* 6:267-280, 1960.

Questions for Discussion

1.   If you are teaching in a particular content area, look at the next chapter or story in the textbook. How could a directed reading lesson be built around the material so that both content and reading skill development would be enhanced?

2.   In what ways should the purposes a teacher gives for a reading assignment be related to the question she uses in a discussion of the material with the students?

3.   What do you think of Eller and Wolf's contention that teachers should present findings from the work of social psychologists so that students will understand some factors which do cause them to be uncritical? Do you think this would affect their critical reading skill?

4.   To what extent do you agree with Cooper's definition of a mature reader? Are there any skills or abilities that you would add to his list?

Developing Reading Rate

VII

In the past fifteen years, a great deal of interest in speed reading has been expressed in both professional and popular literature. In some cases, the effect of this interest has been that considerable pressure has been put on secondary schools to develop reading programs concerned only with speed reading growth.

Certainly, few would disagree with the contention that developing proper reading rates in students should be *part* of a comprehensive secondary school reading program. The articles in this section have been selected so that speed reading development can be seen in the proper perspective.

In the first article, Miles Tinker raises and then attempts to answer thirteen different questions regarding the value and limitations of speed reading programs. Tinker, early in the article, distinguishes between the term *speed of reading* and the term he prefers, *speed of comprehension*. He then identifies the type of student he feels can profit from programs designed to improve speed of comprehension.

In another portion of the article, Tinker discusses the research findings on the role of eye movements in reading and relates these findings to the use of various mechanical devices in speed reading programs. He concludes that machines are no more effective than less complicated and expensive classroom procedures.

Don Parker expresses many of the same ideas as Miles Tinker. Parker feels that the basic concept that must be developed in the minds of students is that reading rate must be flexible. An appropriate reading rate depends on the type of material being read and the purpose for which it is being read. Parker does appear to believe that mechanical devices can be of considerable value in increasing the eye spans and thus the reading speed of students.

Helen Grayum directs her attention to one specific rate of reading — skimming. She presents the results of a research study where readers of various ages were asked to skim a social studies selection and then two tests over the content were administered. Those students scoring highest and lowest on the tests at the various age levels were then studied in greater depth.

Uses and Limitations of Speed of Reading Programs in Schools *

MILES A. TINKER

Active interest in speed of reading is prevalent on all sides. School teachers, pupils, parents, business executives, and many others are concerned with how fast one can or should read. This interest is reflected in the writing of professional educators, and of journalists in popular magazines and in newspapers. Commercial outfits throughout the country are capitalizing on this interest as well as intensifying it by their programs to improve speed which they advertise and sell. One example taken from the Santa Barbara News-Press, November 27, 1961 publicized registration for a reading laboratory. It is stated in the article that 1000 words per minute or 100 per cent increase in rate is guaranteed with 80 per cent or greater comprehension. It is also stated that students who take the course read from three to 20 times faster at the end of the course "with the average ranging from 1200 to 1600 words per minute with improved comprehension," and that some students read up to 10,000 words per minute. These claims are not uncommon.

This emphasis upon speeding up reading has a bearing on practices in schools. The teacher feels compelled to develop some program to improve the speed of reading of her pupils. But to organize and carry out a successful program for improving speed of reading in the school, the teacher should know the answers to several questions such as the following: (1) What is meant by speed of reading? (2) When is rapid reading important? (3) What are appropriate rates of reading? (4) Are speed of reading and comprehension related? (5) What role is played by eye movements? (6) Of what value are speed of reading norms? (7) Who should have training to speed up his reading? (8) What are the prerequisites for success of the program for increasing speed? (9) What is the role of flexibility of rate? (10) What should be done to speed up the reading of disabled readers? (11) What is the nature of successful programs to increase rate of reading? (12) What is the value of mechanical aids for speeding up reading?

*Reprinted from *Speed Reading: Practices and Procedures,* Proceedings of the 44th Annual Education Conference University of Delaware, 10 (March, 1962), pp. 9-18, by permission of the author and the Reading-Study Center, School of Education, University of Delaware.

(13) What gains in speed may be expected? The following discussion will provide some information on these questions.

Nature of the Problem

Teachers at all educational levels, elementary school through college, are under pressure to improve speed of reading of their pupils. Concern with speed reading is understandable. The pupil who is able to read material rapidly with understanding has a distinct advantage over a slow, plodding reader. Classroom practice, however, too often results in an overemphasis upon rapid reading per se. In many instances the outcome of this emphasis has been a speed up of reading but with little understanding of what is read. Learning to read effectively depends upon acquiring many skills more basic than speed.

What do we mean by the term "speed of reading?" The only justifiable or valid definition of "speed of reading" is "speed of comprehension." The rate with which words are recognized as words, without reference to whether their meanings and their inter-relationships are understood, is of little or no significance in real life. That is, so-called "reading" without comprehension is not reading. Any useful and adequate definition of rate of reading, therefore, must also take into account how fast printed and written material is comprehended. In this discussion, the term speed of reading means speed of comprehension. Every teacher should keep in mind that rapid reading in itself is not a cause of better understanding. A fast rate of comprehension becomes possible only because the pupil possesses the abilities necessary for clear and rapid understanding.

RAPID READING IS IMPORTANT

The problem of speed in reading seldom arises in the primary grades where children are mastering the mechanics of reading and are learning the basic comprehension skills. Here an appropriate rate can be expected to be acquired as a byproduct of well taught reading. But as a child moves along into the higher grades, an important task of the teacher is to help pupils read at appropriate rates. *Relatively* rapid reading is to be desired in any area, i.e., the reading should be at as fast a rate as the material can be adequately comprehended. While the proper rate of reading mathematics and science is relatively slow, some pupils read such materials at an undesirably slow rate. The goal is to comprehend as rapidly as possible whatever the material.

RELATION OF SPEED TO COMPREHENSION

Unfortunately the exact relationships between speed of reading and comprehension are not firmly established. As pointed out by Tinker (18, 19),† this condition is due to poorly designed experimentation. Speed of reading is

†Numbers in parentheses refer to references at end of article.

fairly specific to the kind of material read. Thus speed of reading easy narrative material bears little or no relationship to speed of reading scientific materials. The only valid procedure is to measure speed of reading and comprehension on the same or strictly comparable material and relate the two scores. When these conditions are fulfilled, the following trends appear: (1) With elementary school pupils, the relationship between speed and comprehension tends to be small (Carlson, 6). Analysis revealed that purpose for which the reading was done, difficulty of the material, and intelligence of the pupils affected the relationship. One is apt to find a higher relationship between speed and comprehension among the more mature readers. In general, more difficult materials and those requiring methodical, slow reading to grasp concepts, reveal little relationship between speed and comprehension (Tinker, 19). With relatively easy materials, the relationship tends to be significantly high.

Choice of Pupils for Speed Training

The best indications from research are that a program to improve speed of reading is advantageous for most pupils who are well advanced in acquiring the basic reading skills, provided speed is not pushed to the point where adequate comprehension becomes impossible. But any general program for whipping up the speed of reading for all pupils in a class is inadvisable. It would seem that the child who has the necessary skills and abilities to comprehend well also has those necessary to read faster.

SPEED TO AVOID DAWDLING

Many pupils at all educational levels acquire a comfortable, meandering way of reading that is considerably below the rate at which they might read with both understanding and pleasure. These habits are a handicap to proficient reading. Such easy-going dawdling permits attention to wander and encourages daydreaming. Pupils cover too little material in a given time. We call it dawdling when the slow progress is not due to any one of the handicapping factors discussed below. In the case of dawdlers, incentives and exercises to promote an appropriately faster rate should be provided.

REMOVE HANDICAPS PRIOR TO SPEED TRAINING

A number of handicapping conditions tend to produce reading at an unduly slow rate. Only when these handicaps are largely overcome is the child likely to grasp meanings accurately and as rapidly as he needs to for a particular purpose, even with special training. It should be noted that *no disabled reader* should receive instruction to speed up his reading until any basic difficulties he may have, have been corrected.

Before a pupil is given speed training, the teacher should be sure that the following prerequisites are fulfilled, i.e., the handicaps are reduced to a minimum.

(1) Without an adequate *sight vocabulary,* a pupil cannot read at an appropriate rate.

(2) *Vocabulary knowledge and comprehension* are essential for rapid reading. An adequate grasp of word, sentence and paragraph meanings facilitates an increase in speed of reading.

(3) Only when a child has mastered *word identification and recognition skills* can he improve appreciably his speed of reading.

(4) *Overanalysis,* or the habit of sounding out a large majority of words encountered, makes rapid reading impossible.

(5) *Minimum use of context clues for word recognition* hinders improving speed of reading.

(6) Unless a child *comprehends phrases as thought units* as he progresses through a sentence, he becomes a slow, plodding, word-by-word reader.

(7) *Vocalizing,* either as whispering, silent articulation of words or mentally saying words to oneself, must be markedly decreased before speed of reading can be improved appreciably.

Program for Improving Speed

To assure success, any program to increase speed of reading must be carefully organized. First of all, the reading status of a child must be favorable, i.e., any handicapping condition must be largely eliminated. Also, the teacher will want to ascertain the speed at which each child is accustomed to read, but this presents certain problems.

Standardized tests are of little practical use for measuring speed of reading. The teacher can only determine the speed level of her pupils for reading the kind of material in the test which usually is easy narrative. Teacher-organized informal tests, employing the kind of material she is concerned with, are most useful. Directions for organizing and using such tests are given in Tinker and McCullough (34) and DeBoer and Dallmann (8). They also describe practice exercises and kinds of material to use.

Tinker and McCullough (34) emphasize strongly the role of incentives and motivation in any program to improve speed. The teacher provides the incentives to develop motivation. *If he lacks a motive for doing so, the pupil will feel little or no urgency to read faster and is not likely to do so.*

The Role of Eye Movements

Educators have been interested in eye movements in reading for over half a century. Surveys of all the research studies (386 titles) published up to 1958 on this subject are given by Tinker (20, 21, 22). Since about 1900, much emphasis has been placed upon the relationship of eye-movement patterns to speed of reading. In reading, the eye makes several stops, each a *fixation pause,* along a line of print. The eye moves from one fixation to the next with a quick jerk known as a *saccadic movement.* While reading, the eyes sometimes move backwards toward the beginning of the line and make fixation pauses to get a clearer view of the material or to re-read it. These backward moves are called *regressions.* When one line is finished, the eyes make a *return sweep* down to the beginning of the next line.

SOME RESEARCH FINDINGS

Brief mention of selected research findings will help to explain the relation between eye movements and speed of reading. In an initial series of investigations, Tinker (23, 24, 25, 26, 27, 28, 29, 30) studied the time relations for eye-movement measures in reading. The findings may be summarized as follows: (1) The saccadic moves between fixations are very rapid and the pauses relatively long. The interfixation moves take only about 6 per cent of the reading time while the fixation pauses take 94 per cent. Thus in reading the eyes are motionless on the fixations a very large proportion of the time. Furthermore, the interfixation moves are so rapid that during them no clear vision is possible. On the average, these moves take about 15 thousandths of a second; the return sweep, about 45 thousandths. In contrast, the average pause duration is about 250 thousandths, or 1/4 of a second. (2) Eye movement measures are reliable. (3) When an adequate experimental design is employed, fixation frequency and perception time (sum of all pause durations) are valid measures of speed of reading. (5) Eye movement patterns also provide information on regularity of the movements (regressions). (6) In most reading, pause duration is fairly constant. But when comprehension becomes involved, pause duration increases and varies greatly. (7) Good readers tend to make relatively few fixations and regressions per line of print. Poor readers employ many fixations and regressions.

Effect of Typography on Eye Movements

In another series of experiments, Tinker and Paterson (13, 14, 15, 16, 17, 31, 32, 33) studied eye movements of subjects when they read printed material set in optimal and non-optimal typographical arrangements. They found significant increases in one or more of the following measures when non-optimal arrangements were read: perception time, fixation frequency, regression frequency and pause duration. Thus, when lines are too long, type is too small, the type face makes words difficult to recognize, the contrast between print and paper is poor, or all-capital print is used, the eye-movement patterns deteriorate. In other words, reading material in non-optimal printing produces eye-movement patterns analogous to those of poor readers.

USES AND LIMITATIONS OF EYE-MOVEMENT RECORDS

The uses and limitations of eye-movement measures have been evaluated by Tinker (23, 24, 30). As already noted, inefficient reading is accompanied by characteristic oculomotor behavior which contrasts with eye-movement patterns of the efficient reader. Difficulties of word perception, word meanings and interpretations are reflected by a relatively large number of regressions and fixation pauses, i.e., the eye-movement patterns deteriorate. This apparent relation between eye movements and reading proficiency was noted 50 years ago and led many writers to conclude that faulty eye movements cause inefficient reading, i.e., that peripheral motor habits are determinants of central processes of perception and comprehension. This belief led to the training of eye movements to improve reading efficiency. Various techniques and machines have been and continue to be used to accomplish this.

So-called ineffective eye movements, however, *do not cause poor* reading. Numerous research studies indicate that eye-movement patterns during reading are symptoms of the central or brain processes of perception and comprehension. They merely reflect the ability of the reader to perceive and interpret what he sees. The changes in eye movements which occur with improved reading proficiency do not mean that the eye muscles (Tinker, 27) coordinate better than before. Oculomotor behavior is very flexible and adjusts readily to any change in the perceptual and assimilative processes involved in reading.

Eye-movement measurement is essentially a research technique and has been very useful in studying the characteristic oculomotor patterns associated with reading. Since research has already shown what the eye-movement patterns of poor, average and good readers are, there is no need to study the oculomotor behavior of school children. And attempts to improve reading by training eye movements are useless or even harmful. The best way to achieve improved oculomotor patterns in reading is to eliminate faulty habits which hinder improvement of speed of reading. These faulty habits have already been discussed. Our conclusion is that *the school teacher need not concern herself with eye movements in any of her work in teaching reading.*

Mechanical Devices. Numerous mechanical devices are vigorously promoted to increase speed of reading through pacing the reading or by increasing the perceptual span. The pacing machines either expose in succession segments of a line of print or guide the eyes line by line down a page of print. Speeds may be varied from slow to fast. Machines to improve span or perception are some type of tachistoscope or short exposure apparatus. Numerals, words and phrases are flashed onto a screen for a fraction of a second.

Value of Machines. The use of tachistoscopic training to improve speed of reading is advocated by many writers. But authors who are recognized leaders in the field, such as Anderson and Dearborn (1), Harris (10), Gates (9), and

Bond and Tinker (4) question the value of such training. And Manolakes (11) in a well-controlled experiment showed that tachistoscopic training had no effect on speed of reading. Evaluation of all the relevant literature (Tinker, 21) suggests that such training is of questionable value. Although tachistoscopic training may not increase speed of reading as such, it can produce other desirable effects. Some of these are: improved visual discrimination of details and forms of letters and words; quick perception of words alone and in phrases; greater attention in perceiving printed symbols; motivation to improve.

In every experiment that has attempted to evaluate the use of pacing machines, the results reveal that they are no more effective in increasing rate of reading than are less complicated but sound classroom procedures. Notable examples are the studies of Cason (7) with third-grade children and Westover (35) with college students. Tachistoscopes and pacing machines are expensive. And too often their use becomes a ritual and tends to overemphasize the mechanical aspects of reading to the sacrifice of proper attention to the more important processes of comprehension and thinking, which are prime essentials of good reading. It would seem that any funds available for purchasing machines might be better used to acquire additional books for the classroom and school library. Nevertheless, reading pacers may be employed advantageously at times, particularly in combination with other methods. Such use may provide quickly a well-motivated procedure to increase rate in reading easy material. And attitude toward reading may improve. But there may be difficulty in transferring the improved rate to more difficult material. As pointed out by Harris (10), the carryover to natural reading situations is sometimes disappointingly small. Whether the favorable effects are due to use of the reading pacer or to an increase in motivation is difficult to estimate.

Flexibility in Reading Speeds

The pupil who tends to read all material at about the same rate, as so many do, is a poor reader. Flexibility in adjusting speed of reading to the kind and difficulty of materials read and to the purpose for which the reading is done is necessary for proficient reading. When flexibility is achieved, and as occasion demands, the pupil can tear along at a very rapid rate or he can employ a moderate rate if that is appropriate, or he can read very slowly, with rereading where highly analytical reading is in order. An appreciable proportion of pupils at all educational levels have not acquired the ability to adjust their speed of reading appropriately.

Flexibility in speed of reading is difficult to teach and tends to be poorly taught in schools. Adequate emphasis should be devoted to teaching this skill at all educational levels from the beginning of the fourth grade on.

Gains to be Expected

As noted above, the first step in organizing a speed of reading program in a school is to reduce to a minimum any faulty habits that may hinder or obstruct gains in speed. When this is done, the teacher can expect practically all pupils to increase their rate with training. There will be marked individual differences in amount of gain. It is no accident that the more fluent readers tend to make the greatest gains. They have an adequate basis to build upon.

In properly conceived and executed classroom programs to speed up reading, a few pupils will achieve relatively small gains, many will make moderate gains, and a few will make relatively great gains in rate of reading. An occasional pupil will achieve exceptional improvement. In the customary school speed-up program, pupils receive a total of 4 to 18 hours of training spread over several days or weeks and divided up into 10 to 30 minute periods. Representative average gains for groups vary considerably: about 17 per cent (Bird, 2), 30 to 35 per cent (O'Brien, 12), 37 to 56 per cent (Brooks, 5), and 39 per cent (Harris, 10). If the training program continues for two to three months, the teacher may expect an average gain in speed of 30 to 40 per cent. Note that these gains are for reading relatively easy materials. The degree to which the gains are maintained or to which they are transferred to reading work-type material is not well established.

Individual gains from training vary greatly, ranging from very little to several hundred per cent. Bond and Bond (3) give data on a 15-year-old boy who improved his rate 230 per cent during five weeks of training. It is not unusual to find occasional cases that double their rate of reading through systematic practice.

In most programs to improve rate, comprehension is maintained at an adequate level, i.e., 75 per cent or higher. However, if speed alone is emphasized, comprehension may decrease. No pupil should be pushed to this stage.

HOW FAST CAN ONE LEARN TO READ?

This is a difficult question to answer, for so many factors affect rate of reading. Published data tend to be for reading fairly easy material. For such material, 400 words per minute is very high for a seventh grade pupil; 600 words per minute is very high and 850 exceedingly rare for college students. It is fairly common for well educated adults to attain (at least temporarily) rates of 500 to 600 words per minute. These high rates are for superior readers. They are not achieved by a large majority of any group. When rates of 1200 to 1500 or more words per minute are cited, one may presume it is for partial reading such as skimming. See Spache's analysis (17a) of such claims.

If a reader is well trained so that he varies his speed to fit the material and the purpose for which the reading is done, he will have many rates for appropriate adjustment to achieve efficient reading.

In summary, we may say that training to improve speed of reading is an essential aspect of the developmental reading program, especially for pupils in the sixth grade and at higher levels. Any speed program should be individualized to fit the needs of specific pupils. And every teacher should keep in mind the appropriate uses and the limitations of any plan to improve speed of reading.

References

1. Anderson, I. H., and Dearborn, W. F., *The Psychology of Teaching Reading.* New York: The Ronald Press Company, 1952.
2. Bird, C., *Effective Study Habits.* New York: Appleton-Century-Crofts, Inc., 1931.
3. Bond, G. L., and Bond, E., *Developmental Reading in High School.* New York: The Macmillan Company, 1941.
4. Bond, G. L., and Tinker, M. A., *Reading Difficulties.* New York: Appleton-Century-Crofts, Inc., 1957.
5. Brooks, F. D., *The Applied Psychology of Reading.* New York: Appleton-Century-Crofts, Inc., 1926.
6. Carlson, T. R., "The Relationship between Speed and Accuracy of Comprehension." *Journal of Educational Research,* 42, 1949, 500-512.
7. Cason, E. B., "Mechanical Methods for Increasing the Speed of Reading." *Teachers College Contributions to Education,* 1943, No. 878.
8. DeBoer, J. J., and Dallmann, M., *The Teaching of Reading.* New York: Holt, Rinehart and Winston, Inc., 1960.
9. Gates, A. L., *The Improvement of Reading,* 3rd ed. New York: The Macmillan Company, 1947.
10. Harris, A. J., *How to Increase Reading Ability,* 4th ed. New York: Longmans, Green and Company, 1961.
11. Manolakes, G., "The Effects of Tachistoscopic Training in an Adult Reading Program." *Journal of Applied Psychology,* 36, 1952, 410-412.
12. O'Brien, J. A., *Silent Reading.* New York: The Macmillan Company, 1922.
13. Paterson, D. G., and Tinker, M. A., "Influence of Line Width on Eye Movements," *Journal of Experimental Psychology,* 27, 1940, 572-577.
14. Paterson, D. G., and Tinker, M. A., "Influence of Size of Type on Eye Movements." *Journal of Experimental Psychology,* 27, 1940, 572-577.
15. Paterson, D. G., and Tinker, M. A., "Influence of Line Width on Eye Movements for Six-Point Type." *Journal of Educational Psychology,* 33, 1942, 552-555.
16. Paterson, D. G., and Tinker, M. A., "Eye Movements in Reading Type Sizes in Optimal Line Widths." *Journal of Educational Psychology,* 34, 1943, 547-551.
17. Paterson, D. G., and Tinker, M. A., "Eye Movements in Reading Optimal and Non-Optimal Typography." *Journal of Educational Psychology,* 34, 1944, 80-83.
17a. Spache, G. D., "Is This a Break-through in Reading?" *The Reading Teacher,* 15, 1962, 258-263.
18. Tinker, M. A., "The Relation of Speed to Comprehension in Reading." *School and Society,* 36, 1932, 158-160.
19. _____ . "Speed Versus Comprehension in Reading as Affected by Level of Difficulty." *Journal of Educational Psychology,* 30, 1939, 81-94.
20. _____ . "Eye Movements in Reading." *Journal of Educational Research,* 30, 1936, 241-277.

21.   _____. "The Study of Eye Movements in Reading." *Psychological Bulletin,* 43, 1946, 93-120.

22.   . "Recent Studies of Eye Movements in Reading." *Psychological Bulletin,* 54, 1958, 215-231.

23.   _____. "Photographic Measures of Reading Ability." *Journal of Educational Psychology,* 20, 1929, 184-191.

24.   _____. "Use and Limitations of Eye-Movement Measures of Reading." *Psychological Review,* 40, 1933, 381-397.

25.   _____. "Reliability and Validity of Eye-Movement Measures of Reading." *Journal of Experimental Psychology,* 19, 1936, 732-746.

26.   _____. "Time Taken by Eye Movements in Reading." *Journal of Genetic Psychology,* 48, 1936, 468-471.

27.   _____. "Motor Efficiency of the Eye as a Factor in Reading." *Journal of Educational Psychology,s, 29, 1938, 167-174.*

28.   _____. "Time Relations for Eye Movement Measures in Reading." *Journal of Educational Psychology,* 38, 1947, 1-10.

29.   _____. "Fixation Pause Duration in Reading." *Journal of Educational Research,* 44, 1951, 471-479.

30.   Tinker, M. A., and Frandsen, A., "Evaluation of Photographic Measures of Reading." *Journal of Educational Psychology,* 25, 1934, 96-100.

31.   Tinker, M. A., and Paterson, D. G., "Influence of Type form on Eye Movement." *Journal of Experimental Psychology,* 25, 1939, 528-531.

32.   Tinker, M. A., and Paterson, D. G., "Eye Movements in Reading a Modern Type Face and Old English." *American Journal of Psychology,* 54, 1941, 113-115.

33.   Tinker, M. A., and Paterson, D. G., "Eye Movements in Reading Black Print on White Background and Red Print on Dark Green Background." *American Journal of Psychology,* 57, 1944, 93-94.

34.   Tinker, M. A., and McCullough, C. M., *Teaching Elementary Reading,* Inc., 1962.

35.   Westover, F. L., "Controlled Eye Movements versus Practice Exercises in Reading." *Teachers College Contributions to Education,* 1946, No. 917.

Reading Rate is Multilevel*

DON H. PARKER

The taxicab driver glanced back through his rearview mirror and ventured a guess: "You must be a college professor?"

"Ugh--Oh, me? Yes, but h---how did you know?" stammered the bespectacled fare as he extricated himself from the academic fog in which he had been mired.

"Oh, I like to try to figure out my passengers sometimes. Could I ask what you teach, sir?"

"Reading."

"Reading! Say, I'll bet you can really read fast. How fast can you read, professor?"

"Sometimes I read about 50 words a minute."

No answer from up front. The professor repressed a mischievous grin as the face in the rearview mirror registered perplexity, then irritation. After a long moment, the taximan ventured another guess.

"Hey, Prof, I'm not sure I heard you right, but I think I read somewhere that the average high-school graduate reads around 300 words per minute."

"You probably did."

"Then how come you only read 50 words a minute?"

"I said *sometimes.*"

"Yes, sir, Prof, I heard you. I didn't mean anything. I was just wonderin'."

"It's about time *everybody* started wondering about what they read about *rate of reading* these days. Some of it is downright nonsense and grossly misleading!" By now the professor was in orbit.

"Indeed, I *do* read at the rate of 50 words per minute sometimes. At other times I read at l0,000 words per minute ....." Like a hound in full cry, the professor had the scent of teaching in his nostrils. Now he poised for the kill. "... and so do *you!*"

"Who me ... read l0,000 words per minute?"

*Reprinted from *Clearing House,* 36 (April, 1962), pp. 451-455, by permission of the author and the editor.

Now the professor had the situation in the palm of his teaching hand. "Yes, *you*. When you pick up your daily paper to scan the front page, you are doing a specific kind of reading. You are reading the headlines and estimating what the article will say. If you think it will say something that will interest you, you may settle down to read it, or you may scan the whole paper, then come back to certain articles. When you're scanning, or *surveying,* the paper you are covering the material at perhaps six, eight, or even ten thousand words per minute."

"Wow! I never thought of that. But by golly you may be right. A newspaper fellow once told me there were about 2,500 words on a newspaper page, on the average. If I took, say, 15 seconds, to survey the page, I could survey four pages or 10,000 words in a minute. Say, that would make you about right, Prof!"

"Naturally. So much for the *survey* type of reading. Now, when you settle down to read an article you've selected during your survey, you may be reading at any number of rates--100, 200, 500, or a thousand or more words per minute."

"How come?"

"Simple. Suppose the article is about the tryout of a new kind of car that floats on a cushion of air as it glides over the ground. You read at perhaps four or five hundred words per minute through the first part of the article. It is easy for you because it tells where the tryouts are to be. You used to drive your old jalopy there when you were a boy. The terrain described is familiar to you. You comprehend the material easily.

"Now you come to the part describing how the engines and blowers work to form the cushion of air. This is all new to you, so you shift your reading into low gear and crawl through that part at, perhaps, only 100 words per minute, or less. Now you come to a part telling the names and titles of all the company officials to be present at the tryouts. You couldn't care less, so you whizz over this paragraph--just to see if there *might* be someone you know. While you are engaged in this kind of *key-word* reading, you may be racing over the material at 2,000 words per minute. Lastly, you come to a short paragraph telling how much such a car is likely to cost and when you can buy one. Again you slow down to a walk; your reading rate may drop to 50 or 100 words a minute."

"Gee, you know, Prof, that's just about the way I drive. Do you think I could learn to read at a lot of different speeds?"

"Certainly. You speed up when the going is easy and you're in familiar territory; you slow down when the going gets rough or when you're on unfamiliar streets. In a word, a good reader is like a good driver. He doesn't move at the same rate all the time; he is *flexible.*"

Our friend the taxi driver is more fortunate in receiving guidance toward more efficient reading than many high-school and college and adult students now taking "speed-reading" courses either in school, in special courses, or by correspondence. "Why?" Because speed-reading courses often give false standards to "live up to." While reading instructors are becoming more aware of the need to stress flexibility in the act of reading, rather than either sheer speed or plodding power, many students are still being told that "x-words per minute" is the mark at which they should shoot to become "a good reader."

There are two serious fallacies here. The first, we have just discussed. There is *no* "best speed." Reading rate is *flexible;* it should be determined by the *purpose of the reader.* Speed reading is *multilevel.* Performance in this area is a function of general intelligence. Individuals differ in their intellectual capacities; therefore they will differ in the extent to which they can (1) learn to use the principles of flexibility; and (2) achieve an actual increase in overall rate of absorbing meaning from the printed page.

By setting artificial words-per-minute speed standards and by failing to allow for individual differences in reading rate achievement as well as in reading comprehension, we may be actually endangering the development of *efficient* reading on the part of many individuals. If 500 w.p.m. is set as the standard for "the good tenth-grade reader," what about the student who can easily reach 800 or 1,000 w.p.m. on the same material? Will too low a standard rob him of a drive toward his true potential? On the other hand, what about the student whose neuropsychological time clock is simply set for a slower pace, yet through persistence he covers equally as much ground as the swifter reader? Would not both the temperamentally faster, as well as the slower student, be better off with the concept of flexibility?

But there is still a third fallacy. Reading is a two-way communication process. One-half of it depends on what the writer sets down; the other half is a function of what the reader brings to the printed page. If the reader does not have sufficient common experiences with the writer, communication can be seriously hampered. Thus, if Reader A meets material in archeology and has no archeological background, he must plod through it. However, the same material may put Reader B in excellent communication with the author. He may move through it "on wings of meaning" because of previous reading or experience in this particular area of interest. Would it be realistic to hold up the same standard of reading rate to these two readers?

What about the present wave of insanity with reference to rate of reading which seems to have swept the country lately? "She Can Teach You to Read 2,500 Words a Minute" screams a headline in a Sunday magazine section of a large newspaper. "Forty Pages a Minute Too Fast?" asks a feature in an internationally famous daily. What does it all mean? For one thing, it could mean that a particular teacher got hold of a particularly brilliant student and helped him learn how to "scan" or "survey" and called it simply "reading." On reading reports such as the two mentioned above, one would do well to ask: (1) How much was this student *supposed* to learn as he read at this rate? (2) What kind of material was he reading? (3) What was the overall intellectual capacity of this student? (4) To what extent can this method be generalized and therefore be taught to all students? With these four criteria in mind, one will hardly be carried away by fantastic speed claims, but maintain a feet-on-the-ground approach to helping students improve their *total reading efficiency* through the concept of flexibility.

If flexibility is the keynote to more effective and efficient reading, how can we teach it?

One of the most useful approaches that has been found is the SQ_3R (Survey, Question, Read, Review, Recite) reading and study formula. Here, much as the taxi driver learned from the professor, the reader first *surveys* what he is to read to establish a general framework on which to build in meaning through the reading step. Simultaneously with the survey step, the reader formulates *questions*. These create a sort of tension which is later relieved during the reading process. Questions also create "memory hooks." Now comes *read*. This is the simple act of reading as we usually think of it. Lastly, the student *reviews* and *recites* alternately and to the degree necessary for the kind of learning required. Robinson[1] was the earliest developer of the SQ_3R methodology. Strang[2] has developed SQ_3R practice material for use by students at both high-school and college levels; the writer has elaborated student practice material[3] based on the work of both.

Must we conclude from the foregoing that nothing can really be done to increase the speed at which a reader may move over a line of type? Not at all. Few, if any, individuals of any age are as efficient as they might be in the *perceptual* behavior related to the art of reading. While considerable is known about eye fixation and eye span, relatively little is done to put this knowledge to work in the classroom.

Underscoring the idea that reading rate is multilevel, students along the whole range of individual differences in learning ability can learn to increase their speed of eye fixation and the number of words they can fixate in a single eye span. Thus, to develop each individual to highest potential, the slow, the average, and the superior student should have this opportunity. Tachistoscopes, filmstrips, and various reading-accelerator devices can greatly facilitate such learning.

However, regardless of whether special equipment is available, the teacher should clearly point out to students what is meant by "eye fixation" and "eye span." These two concepts can be introduced by a simple chalkboard illustration. Take this sentence, for example, and write it on the board:

[1] Francis P. Robinson, *Effective Study* (New York: Harper and Brothers, 1946).
[2] Ruth Strang, *Study Type of Reading Exercises,* Secondary Level, 1956, College Level, 1959 (New York: Bureau of Publications, Teachers College, Columbia University).
[3] Don H. Parker, *The SRA Reading Laboratories,* II, III, and IV series (Chicago: Science Research Associates, 1959).

The newspaper reported that the airplane fell.

Next, rewrite the sentence underneath, spacing as indicated below, and draw diagonal lines to divide into three separate fixations, thus:

The newspaper / reported that / the airplane fell.

Explain that each group of words should be taken in at a single "look." Have the class read each fixation as a single unit, pausing at each diagonal. Point out that these word groups are natural "thought units"--each group tells an idea. The good reader learns to read *ideas* — not words.

Now explain that the eyes see by "fastening" on or "fixating" on the central part of an object and spreading out on all sides of it. Therefore, to see each of these three phrases most effectively, the reader should look at the middle of the phrase or thought unit. His vision will then spread to take in the whole group of words in the thought unit. Illustrate on board, thus:

.

The newspaper

To illustrate fixation point, place a heavy dot over each thought unit, thus:

.   .   .

The newspaper / reported that / the airplane fell.

Have the students move their eyes from dot to dot as you point. After three such trips across the line, you might pass out a paragraph of dittoed material you have prepared to give practice in discovering thought units, marking them off, and moving across dot-marked lines in rhythm. As an added touch for novelty, but also to establish rhythm and the idea of continued forward progression, try having the class read approximately 200 words of material that has been marked off and dotted, to the accompaniment of music! Select a piece of music in which the rhythm is not too fast. Either three-four or four-four time will serve. Read the selection by moving the eyes from fixation to fixation in time with the music.

Now, a last concept. In addition to learning the concept of eye span--reading "thought units" or "ideas" instead of words—and of rhythmical eye movement or progression, the good reader is continually seeking to *increase* the length of his eye span. He is always trying to take in more words at a fixation—to read with "bigger and bigger eyefuls." There is, of course, a physical limit beyond which the vision during one fixation will not spread, but few if any of us have reached this limit. To illustrate increased eye span, write the sentence on the board, thus:

The newspaper reported / that the airplane fell.

A number of workbooks and other tools are available for giving introduction and practice in the foregoing concepts of span and fixation. However, the teacher, with typewriter and ditto, can come up with some interesting and helpful materials for his students.

In what grades should the various speed-reading concepts be introduced? Certainly, the secondary grades, 7 through 12, are safe. By then, in all but the most extremely immature, the ocular-motor muscles have developed sufficiently to respond to such activity.

But now *a word of caution* is in order. While there may be physical readiness among most secondary students for participation in exercises to improve the *perceptual* processes of reading, not all students will have a sufficiently full kit of basic skills in the *conceptual* processes of reading.

If a student does not have a fairly well-developed word-recognition sense, he cannot even read *words,* much less groups of words or thought units. To participate successfully in the relatively high-level activity of training his perceptual processes, the student should have a mastery of both phonic and structural word-attack skills, plus a fairly large sight vocabulary gained from reading in a wide range of interest areas. Too, he should have training in the reading-thinking (comprehension) skills of main idea-detail, cause-effect, like-difference, and sequence-organization.

Lastly, while the above ideas for improving these perceptual skills of fixation and span can be introduced to a class on a one level basis (same material for each), actual practice in these--or in any reading skill--must be conducted on a *multilevel* basis. This means that, beyond simple introduction to the idea, each student must practice in reading material at his own *present functional* level. As every teacher knows, there may be four, five or even six different reading levels in any given classroom, even though students have been "homogenized"!

In summary, reading rate is multilevel because:

(1) Individual students differ in their rate-of-reading capacities.

(2) Individual students bring individually different interest backgrounds to the same reading job; each will have an individually different readiness for communication with the author he is reading.

(3) There is a need for many levels of speed in the reading behavior of each individual. The good reader does not aim at rocket-speed-for-everything reading. Instead, he practices *flexibility* in his rate in accordance with *his purpose* in covering the material.

(4) SQ_3R offers a sound methodology for teaching flexibility in rate of reading where study type of material (not fiction or poetry) is involved.

(5) Something can be done to improve the *perceptual* processes of reading—eye span and eye fixation—PROVIDED the student has a fairly good background of basic skills in the *conceptual* processes of reading (word attack,

vocabulary, comprehension), or is acquiring it systematically in a parallel course. Unless a student possesses a fairly complete "kit" of basic reading skills *before* he begins special training in the perceptual skills of speeded reading, *much damage can be done.*

(6) Training in rate of reading must be on materials of the students' present *functional* reading level. Opportunity to advance in both difficulty levels and speed *when he is ready* should be provided.

(7) The good teacher of reading—be he a teacher of English, social studies, science, math, or a full-time reading teacher—will not hold up to his students false standards of a certain number of words to be read per minute.

Instead, he will make his students aware of all of the above factors entering into improving total reading efficiency.

Skimming in Reading:
A Fine Art for Modern Needs*

HELEN S. GRAYUM

"... and read carefully," students are reminded before beginning work on an assignment. The advice is humdrum; they seem to have heard it always. "Yes, better get all the points." It's bad not to. So, word by word along the lines. . . . Thus, with a goodly portion of students the admonition has long before been accepted as a matter-of-course, and become a standard pattern of response — a habit in reading a page, a selection, or a book. For to them, "reading is reading, and this is the way it is done." The intent of the advice is honorable. Never would it be questioned here if it had a specific and useful meaning to students of reading, and if it did not often imply a constant meticulous attention to details, regardless of the purpose of reading.

Does this procedure meet the need for covering the quantities of material that come our way today in every occupation — materials we must comprehend in varying degrees of thoroughness, *depending upon our purpose?* It is a well-known fact that the quantity of printed matter, both informative and recreational, has multiplied in recent years. There is need for our reading to be at once more extensive and more intensive. Intelligent living demands, on the one hand, a broad scope of knowledge and information which must be, on the other hand, adequate, accurate, and unbiased. In reading all manner of content there must be conscious and deliberate seeking for understanding by surveying, sorting and sifting; by comparing, weighing, and analyzing. Business-man and home-maker, student and farmer, professional man and clerk, tradesman and scientist — for all the task and responsibility for reading has increased.

Furthermore, for many persons time for reading seems to be decreasing. The popularity of digest magazines indicates that genuine reading problems are encountered by significant numbers of adults. With the original articles shortened, simplified, and sometimes interpreted, digests have been produced to meet certain limitations in reading ability.

*Reprinted from *Bulletin of the National Association of Secondary-School Principals,* 39 (September, 1955), pp. 26-34, by permission of the author and the National Association of Secondary School Principals.

Unfortunately, the ability to meet the reading requirements described above is not measured by standardized tests thus far developed. Although the score on any one part of a test and the "average" score on the different parts are inadequate, they may be helpful in indicating certain relevant information. Simply stated, the reading task today consists of achieving a high degree of proficiency in selecting pertinent information and understanding and responding to meaning at a comparatively rapid rate.

Recognition of the need for increased efficiency in reading is not new. For the past fifty years the ability to skim has been suggested with increasing frequency as an appropriate facility for meeting the requirements. For example, in a 1902 issue of *The Atlantic Monthly,* skimming as an ability in reading was recognized and described as follows:

> Skimming and reading are different processes, but skimming is at times a good thing, too; even skipping becomes on occasion a scared duty. . . . Skimming implies the cream, and skipping a foot-hold somewhere. . . . The eye of the skilled reader acts like a sixth sense, selecting the gist of the matter in whatever form it may appear.[1]

In courses of study skimming is often listed at all levels, including the elementary, junior and senior high school, and in college reading manuals, as an ability in reading to develop. Usually it is first designated for the fourth grade, although it is occasionally specified also for the second and third grades.

While frequent references to skimming are found in the professional literature on reading--and to scanning, as well--the meanings ascribed to these words by different writers vary; sometimes the terms are used interchangeably. It is pertinent to note that Webster's Dictionary defines "to skim" as "to read, study, or examine superficially and rapidly; especially to glance through for the chief ideas of, as to skim a book." "To scan;" on the other hand, is defined as "to go over and examine point by point; to examine with care."

As the meaning of skimming lacks agreement among authors, so also do the purposes which they suggest vary widely, ranging from "to skim to find one or more specific facts" to "to get the author's chief message." Little information on teaching this skill is found.

It has long been known that rates of reading among individuals vary enormously, and that degrees of understanding observable especially among students may be markedly irregular. Furthermore, rate and understanding are not always found in inverse relationship. That is, the rapid readers may understand adequately, while the slow, plodding readers may not, although the content is equally familiar to both groups.

---

[1] "Peace in Reading" *The Atlantic Monthly* 90:144, July, 1902.

A Research Study

Little research on the subject of skimming has been done, although related studies are numerous and useful. Therefore, an exploratory study to discover the nature of skimming, its purpose and place as an ability in reading, with implications for teaching, was needed. Twenty-five students in each of six groups took part in the study. The six groups were fourth-, seventh-, and tenth-grade pupils, college freshmen, graduate students, and widely read adults in different occupations. All had intelligence and reading ability that were average or above.

A readably written selection of social studies content which was generally not unfamiliar, with a comparatively light concept load, was chosen for each of the six levels. The chapters selected varied somewhat in length. Each person was asked to skim the selection according to his best knowledge and ability. The time required was noted, but was not limited. Observations were recorded by code and supplemented by eye-movement photographs.

Afterward each student took two tests on the content read, one on general ideas and the other on details to determine form and degree of comprehension when the subjects presumed to be skimming. That is, to what extent did the readers actually comprehend the main ideas and details when skimming, and what was the relationship between the two different types of information. As the criterion of skimming ability for this investigation, a time unit score was obtained by the subject's combined scores on the two tests by the time required for reading.

The next step was to make an intensive study of the five people in each group who had the highest scores, called the "Goods," and the five in each group with the lowest scores, the "Poors." An analysis was made of their comprehension test scores and of their reading techniques as revealed by observation and eye-movement photographs. They were also interviewed to discover their attitudes toward reading and to check with them the observations recorded. Conferences were held with expert teachers on various levels and classroom observations supplemented findings of the study by adding information on points of view and practices in the teaching of skimming.

Results of the Study

Results of the study showed marked differences in ability to skim at each of the six age-grade levels, even though all were average or above in intelligence and in general reading ability. The techniques used by the persons who ranked as superior in skimming ability were characterized by (1) flexibility of rate and (2) individuality.

Example of the performance of college freshmen illustrate the outcome of present procedures of students' learning to skim, the status of ability in skimming at the conclusion of their common school training. Implicit in the descriptions are startlingly candid cues for the improvement of reading instruction. One student representing the "Goods," age 19, with a psychological rating (percentile) of 99, a general reading rating of 97, required eight minutes for skimming the selection, ranged in rate from 600 to 1,380 words per minute, averaged 2.65 words per fixation with 84 per cent comprehension of general ideas and 60 per cent of the details.

In that part of the selection read most slowly, every line was covered with two or three fixations per line, while in the part read most rapidly there were five sweeps across the card of twelve lines, with one or two fixations per "line" across the card as shown by the photographs. In the interview, the student stated that he[2] likes to read; has always read quite a lot. Concerning techniques used, he said that he uses no "special" techniques; does quite a bit of recreational reading at this rate.

Another freshman, representing the "Poors," age 19, with a psychological rating of 85, a general reading rating of 88, required twenty-one minutes for skimming the selection, ranged in rate from 175 to 240 words per minute, averaged one word per fixation with 42 per cent comprehension of general ideas and 70 per cent of the details. The observable manifestations of the mental processes of this student were very different from those of the student described above. In the portion read most rapidly, every line was covered, rereading three lines of the twelve, and regressing many times. Even in the part read most rapidly, every line was covered. This student, too, said that he likes to read, and has always read quite a bit. He reads the first line of a paragraph more carefully than the rest; learned to do that in literature class. He reads about like this when reading "for skimming"; not when reading to get all the details.

By comparison, how do seventh-grade pupils perform? One pupil representing the "Goods," age 12-10, with an IQ of 126, an average reading score of Grade 10.1, required 5.5 minutes for skimming the selection, averaged 357 words per minute, with 86 per cent comprehension of general ideas and 75 per cent of the details. This pupil likes to read and reads quite a bit. He reads stories faster than textbooks.

A classmate, representing the "Poors," also age 12-10, with an IQ of 124, an average reading score of 6.7, required 14.5 minutes for skimming the selection, averaged 135 words per minute, with 59 per cent comprehension of general ideas and 80 per cent of the details. This student likes to read, and reads a great deal when he has time. He usually reads at about this speed if the story is interesting.

A sophomore representing the "Poors," age 15-3, with an IQ of 112, an average reading score of 10.1, required fourteen minutes for skimming the

---

[2] Pronoun "he" implies either masculine or feminine. Statements are indirect quotations.

selection, averaged 207 words per minute, with 33 per cent comprehension of general ideas and 20 per cent of details. This student likes to read, and used to read a great deal. He went over all the lines; slowed up for words he didn't know. He does all his reading about this way except when reading for something in particular; then he reads more carefully.

An examination of the pertinent data of all the subjects who participated in the study (125) showed a general relationship between the scores on the standardized reading and intelligence tests and scores of skimming ability, but with marked exceptions. A high total score on a standardized test did not assure ability to skim. In addition to the fact that subjects of similar mental ability varied widely in their ability to skim, certain instances were noted in which students of lower mental capacity were found to surpass others of higher mental capacity in their ability to skim, according to the tests used. For example, one college freshman with a psychological rating of 85 and a reading rating of 85 required twenty-one minutes for "skimming" the selection with an average rate of 198 words per minute, and 51 per cent correct on the combined tests. Another college freshman with a psychological rating of 77 and a reading rating of 82 required 5.8 minutes for reading the selection, with an average rate of 723 words per minute, and 73 per cent correct on the combined tests.

Growth in the factors of rate and comprehension is observable. The smallest differences in rate and the greatest in comprehension were found in the fourth-grade group, with the seventh-grade group next. At these levels, ability to comprehend and evaluate ideas was a greater determining factor in skimming ability than was rate of reading. In the college freshman and adult groups, circumstances were reversed: the greatest difference in rate and the smallest in comprehension was shown. Here the determining factor in the ability to skim resides chiefly in rate in reading. Understanding has developed while with some readers' rate has remained "immature" and has become relatively inflexible. The "Goods" of all the groups except two, the tenth-grade pupils and the graduate students, in this study were well above the standard speed in reading.[3]

The fallacy of using a slow rate in reading constantly and without discrimination is indicated by the negative correlations between scores on the test of general ideas and time, and scores on the test of details and time. Slight exceptions were shown by the graduate student group in the first instance, and by the college freshman group in the latter instance. There was a tendency toward relationship between the scores achieved by one person on the two tests in each of the six groups except the graduate student group.

The techniques of skimming observed were means of adjusting rate to comprehension, or to thought and response to the ideas. Rather than each being

---

[3]The median rates listed for different grade levels as derived from several standardized tests were listed as follows: grade four, 155 words per minute; grade seven, 215 words; grade nine, 252 words; and grade twelve, 251 words. See Harris, Albert J., *How to Increase Reading Ability,* New York: Longmans, Green, and Co. 1948, 2nd ed., rev. P. 449.

distinctly different from the others they are modifications of the same process, merging gradually from one to the next. The principal classifications were: (1) skipping in various degrees, (2) marked changes in one person's regular reading rate, (3) pausing, (4) regressing, (5) looking back, (6) looking ahead. All were observed at each grade level. With one exception,– "looking ahead," all were employed both by the "Goods" and by the "Poors." However, the frequency and the purposes for which the techniques were used by them were different.

Approximately one third of the subjects, and twice as many "Goods" as "Poors" used some form of skipping. A total of seven variations in form were used, five by the "Goods" and two different forms by the "Poors." The latter either swept their eyes mechanically over a page or skipped a block of content.

There was a difference not only in the forms of skipping, but also in the discernment with which other marked changes in reading rate, as well as skipping, were used for reading certain portions of content. The chief reasons given by the "Goods" for increasing rate, listed in order of frequency, were "familiar," "unimportant," "uninteresting," and "elaboration." The second and fourth items were not mentioned by the "Poors." The reasons given most often by them were that the portion was "uninteresting," and equally frequently, "interesting," "familiar," and "last page of selection."

The chief reasons given by the "Goods" for changing to a slower rate were "thinking," "new, or less familiar," and "important." The "Poors" did not mention the second item. The reasons given most often by them were "interesting," "thinking," "important," and "last page of selection."

The reasons for pausing and regressing were classified as aiding (1) in comprehension, including word recognition and (2) in thinking or responding to thought. "To aid in thinking" was given as a reason far more frequently by the "Goods" than by the "Poors."

Reasons given for looking backward suggested reasons similar to those given for regressing; those for looking ahead either were incidental or suggested uncertainty about the reading task ahead. Both techniques were used more frequently by the graduate student group, whose rate and comprehension of general ideas as shown by the tests given were comparatively low.

While the subjects who ranked as superior in skimming ability used variations of certain general techniques of skimming, they also employed individual details of procedure of their own devise, such as looking for key words or sentences, and finding the main ideas of paragraphs. They drew upon a greater variety of techniques and used them with greater frequency than did the "Poors." In addition they showed excellent judgment in adjusting reading rate to aid in their understanding of the content, and persistence in adhering strictly to the purpose of reading.

The "Poors" were inclined to "read everything in the same way." In the upper age-grade levels particularly, differentiated techniques were described, and they believed were used, when in reality they were not. These students knew the appropriate language about skillful reading but they did not practice it. The merits of "careful reading" were related by several others who read slowly. They did not seem to feel an urgency to achieve the purpose of reading, and were often easily diverted from it, for example, by an amusing sentence or an illustration.

It is concluded that for efficient skimming the mastery of the fundamentals of reading-mechanics, vocabulary, comprehension, and thinking, including especially skill in evaluating ideas presented – appeared to be necessary. Also essential was a constant awareness of the immediate purposes of reading and a constant effort to accomplish it efficiently.

A minor proportion of the subjects used techniques which permitted them to comprehend most of the general ideas and/or chief details in a comparatively short time. The rate for assimilative reading was more frequently employed for skimming purposes. Skimming might be called a form of rapid reading, but implied advanced, or higher-level techniques.

What the Study Showed

This study showed that response to the content is a highly individual matter; minute personal reactions to meaning were reflected in the reading pattern. This was shown, for example, by changes to a slower rate, pausing, or regressing to unusual words, certain emotionally toned words and words or sentences that have particular meaning for the reader. Every individual reads in terms of a background of previously acquired associations to which he now adds and rearranges.

Concepts of skimming, referred to near the beginning of this report, can be grouped into four broad categories, according to the purpose for which the ability was used. The chief purpose of skimming at certain grade levels recommended in thirty representative courses of study, listed in order of frequency of mention, were:

(1)   To find specific information--stressed on primary and intermediate levels, but not at senior high-school level.
(2)   To find pertinent information in a certain book or article – emphasized at all levels, but proportionately more in senior high school.
(3)   To find general ideas – also emphasized at all levels, but proportionately more in senior high school.
(4)   To locate information, such as appropriate books or articles – stressed at all levels.

The value of skimming to get a general picture before reading for assimilation was pointed out by teachers at all levels except the primary. There is need for a more comprehensive view of the meaning of skimming and its uses. Greater understanding of its nature, as well as its uses, would aid teachers in developing this ability more effectively with their students. Interviews accompanying this study revealed that a teacher's own ability to skim appeared to influence the encouragement of this skill. It was suggested that the necessity of reading under pressure might be conducive to skimming. An abundance of suitable reading material at hand is probably an important provision.

The foundation for this ability should be laid when the child is learning to read, and guidance in its development continued judiciously throughout his school career as a part of the whole reading program. Students should be taught how to determine candidly their own purpose of reading, how procedure may vary according to purpose and background of information, and the significance, in time and satisfaction, of using the reading procedure best suited for a particular purpose. A positive attitude toward flexibility of rate is essential. A pattern of rate can become a habit early and easily.

Of prime importance in developing the ability to skim is: establishing the purpose, evaluating the importance of ideas in terms of the purpose, developing flexibility of rate, and encouraging individual techniques which accomplish clearly the purpose of reading. For there must be not only conviction but determination in order, as one seventh-grade pupil put it, "to get the most meaning from the fewest words."

Selected References

Bayle, Evalyn, "The Nature and Causes of Regressive Eye-Movements in Reading," *The Journal of Experimental Education,* 11:16-36.

Grayum, Helen S., *An Analytic Description of Skimming: Its Purpose and Place as an Ability in Reading,* Doctor's Thesis, Graduate School, Indiana University, 1952, 250 pp. typed.

Hamilton, James A. *Toward Proficient Reading,* Claremont, California: Saunders Press, Claremont College. 152 pp.

Harris, Albert J. *How to Increase Reading Ability.* New York: Longmans Green and Co., 1948, 2nd ed., rev. 582. pp.

Huey, Edmund B., *The Psychology and Pedagogy of Reading.* New York: The Macmillan Co. 1908. 469 pp.

Kier, Clarinda, *The Relative Order of Difficulty of Different Types of Skimming,* Master's Thesis, Graduate School, Boston University, 1938, 34 pp., typed.

McQuarrie, Charles W., and Hansen, Bernard I., *"Visual Training: An Aid to Better Seeing,"* in Twelfth Yearbook, pp. 80-82, Claremont College Reading Conference. Claremont, California: Claremont College Curriculum Library. 1947.

"Pace in Reading," *Atlantic Monthly* 90:143-144, July, 1902.

Perry, William G., and Whitlock, Charles P., *"The Right To Read Rapidly,"* *The Atlantic Monthly,* 190:88, 90, 92, 94, 96. November, 1952.

Preston, Ralph C., "The Changed Role of Reading," in *Reading an Age of Mass Communication* pp. 1-18, edited by William S. Gray, College Levels of the National Council of Teachers of English. New York: Appleton-Century-Crofts Co. 1949.

Russell, David H., "The Mature Reader," bul. 4:1, 13-14, *The International Council for the Improvement of Reading Instruction,* Philadelphia: Temple University, January, 1951.

Sisson, E. Donald, "Causes of Slow Reading, an Analysis," *The Journal of Educational Psychology,* 30:206-2;4, March, 1939.
Smith, Dora V., "What Shall We Do About Reading Today: a Symposium," *The Elementary English Review,* 19:244-247, Nov. 1942.
Whipple, Guy M., and Curtis, Josephine N., "Preliminary Investigations of Skimming," *The Journal of Educational Psychology,* 8:333-349, June, 1917.

Questions For Discussion

1.   Can you distinguish three or four different reading rates? For what kind of material and for which reading purposes would each rate be appropriate?

2.   What are some classroom procedures that can be used to increase students' reading rates?

3.   To what extent do you agree with the contention that many of the highly publicized speed reading courses simply teach students to use a S-Q3R approach in a rapid manner?

Developing Reading Skills
in the Content Areas

VIII

In an earlier section of this book, the issue of who should be primarily responsible for teaching developmental reading at the secondary school level was discussed. Most schools have initiated programs through English classes or through the use of special reading classes with the realization that ultimately the responsibility must rest with all content area teachers. In this section, the responsibility of all content teachers is clarified and certain content areas are studied in depth to identify the reading skills needing specific attention.

In the first article, Ruth Strang presents the general rationale for all teachers being teachers of reading. She then distinguishes basic skills that are prerequisite to success in any content field from the general reading skills common to all subjects and the specific skills essential to certain content fields.

Olson reports the findings of a research study where secondary teachers representing seven different content areas responded to a checklist involving their practices relating to reading. In general, the teachers appeared to feel that they did provide for the differing reading abilities of their students although some inconsistencies in responses were noted.

The next three articles are concerned with reading skills needed in the field of English. Margaret Early points out that the English teacher certainly does have responsibilities but not exclusive rights in the teaching of reading. She makes an important distinction between the teaching of reading and the teaching of literature, and she feels that the English teacher must make more use of expository prose materials in developing students' reading skills.

Edward Gordon and John Simmons focus their attentions on the reading skills needed by students to deal with particular literary forms. Gordon concentrates on the novel and suggests that students need to become acquainted with techniques that writers use such as irony, metaphor, connotation, parallelism, and contrast. Simmons discusses the reading difficulties of short stories and poetry.

Social studies material and the reading difficulties it presents is the focus of the article by Helen Huus. She discusses five different aspects of social studies content that makes it difficult to read, and she then presents her suggestions for teaching procedures to help students The articles by Mallinson, Lockwood, and McTaggert deal with reading problems in the science content area. Mallinson presents a set of criteria that he feels should be considered by those selecting science materials for students. He feels the content of various science textbooks may be quite similar but there may be important differences in such respects as vocabulary load and sentence structure.

Lockwood reviews a set of research studies that generally substantiate Mallinson's contentions about the difficulty of science materials and teachers' ability to judge the reading difficulties. McTaggert reports on a research study involving the attempt to validate the use of two readability formulas with health materials.

The teaching of reading in mathematics classes is the topic of the next two articles. Ira Aaron identifies five areas of responsibility that the mathematics teacher should assume in teaching the specialized reading skills needed by students. Call and Wiggin report a study where a successful implementation of the teaching reading skills in mathematics concept was accomplished in a second year algebra class.

The final two articles of this section deal with the teaching of reading skills in industrial arts. Levine, in particular, presents a number of practical suggestions for exercises designed to improve students' reading in vocational subjects.

Developing Reading Skills in the Content Areas*

RUTH STRANG

Many teachers complain, "My students cannot learn my subject because they cannot read." This is true. A large part of school learning is acquired through reading. More important, pupils are not learning how to learn, if they are not learning how to read in each of the content fields.

Proficiency in general reading skills is not enough; pupils need a technical vocabulary and special skills in each of the content areas. Special reading abilities must be developed in each subject. Specific reading skills will not automatically transfer from basal reading programs to special fields. However, specific instruction in the reading of a particular subject matter improves reading in general, because many attitudes and reading skills are common to all subjects.

The reading tasks presented in most content fields are more complicated than those which pupils have faced in the basal reading program. Science and mathematics involve a type of symbolism that is not found in basal reading material, though children are now encountering it early in the "new" mathematics. The reading of literature demands higher levels of interpretation. The study of history requires extensive reading and critical evaluation of many sources and points of view. Although simple forms of these skills should be introduced in the early grades, the more complicated forms must be taught as they become necessary in each subject. It has been proved that specialized instruction in these skills pays off in improved general academic achievement.

Exploration of Reading Skills

One way in which a teacher may learn what reading skills are needed in his subject is by examining his own reading process. Presumably, a history teacher would be the best person to describe the reading skills that pupils need in reading their history assignments. Similarly the science teacher should be able to suggest efficient methods of reading science.

*Reprinted from *High School Journal,* 49 (April, 1966), pp. 301-306, by permission of the author and the editor.

The teacher, however, should check whether his methods are the methods used by successful pupils. McCallister[1] interviewed seventh and eighth grade pupils as they studied science, mathematics, and history to find out what reading skills they were using and what reading difficulties they were having. H. Alan Robinson[2] recently used a similar method with bright fourth grade pupils. To gain an understanding of the methods used by ninth grade pupils in reading poetry, Letton[3] systematically recorded their oral interpretive responses. Rogers[4] obtained similar information about the responses of eleventh grade pupils to a short story. She began with a completely unstructured approach – "Try to tell me everything you thought and everything you felt as you read this story. Just go ahead and talk about the story." She followed this general approach with more specific inquiries about the reading processes that they had used.

To learn which methods are most effective, and how wide a variety of reading skills is necessary in each content field, teachers should study their own successful methods, and those of their pupils, in reading different kinds of materials for different purposes.

Reading Skills Needed in Each Subject

Certain skills are prerequisite to successful reading in any of the content fields. The first of these comprise basic skills – basic vocabulary, basic word recognition skills, and basic ability to get the literal meaning of a selection. The last mentioned ability involves skill in paragraph reading, skimming, and using clues to the organization of a unit of content. Most pupils have not learned these basic skills in the intermediate grades. The junior high school teacher must not only teach them, but help the pupils apply them to the reading of his subject.[5]

Second, there are general reading skills that are common to all academic subjects. Among these are (1) ability to determine, by an initial survey, the structure and purpose of the selection, pick out its main topics, and decide on an appropriate reading approach; (2) flexibility in adapting one's rate and method

[1] James M. McCallister. "Determining the Types of Reading in Studying Content Subjects," *School Review,* 40 (February, 1932), 115-123.

[2] H. Alan Robinson. "Reading Skills Employed in Solving Social Studies Problems," *The Reading Teacher,* 18 (January, 1965), 263-269.

[3] Mildred Letton. "Individual Differences in Interpretive Responses to Reading Poetry at the Ninth Grade Level." Unpublished doctoral dissertation, The University of Chicago, 1958.

[4] Charlotte Dee Rogers. "Individual Differences in Interpretive Responses to Reading the Short Story at the Eleventh Grade Level." Unpublished doctoral dissertation. University of Arizona. 1964, p. 40.

[5] For detailed lesson plans see: Board of Education, City of New York. *Reading in the Subject Areas, Grades 7, 8, 9,* Curriculum Bulletin 1963-64 series No. 6. 110 Livingston Street, Brooklyn, New York 11201: Board of Education of the City of New York. Auditor, Publication Sales Office. Price $1.25.

to the nature of the material and to one's purpose in reading it; (3) a good general vocabulary; and (4) ability to organize the ideas one gains and relate them to one's present knowledge.

Other skills are considered to be of special importance in various subjects. The following are frequently mentioned as essential in reading social studies material:

Locating specific information
Determining the authenticity of sources
Seeing relationships that involve time, and cause and effect
Drawing conclusions
Applying facts gained to the solution of important problems
Using one's background of experience and knowledge
Understanding key words and concepts
Correctly interpreting maps, graphs, and tables
Reading critically to detect discrepancies, propaganda, and bias

In mathematics the following reading skills are considered to be of special importance:

Understanding technical terms and symbols; also common words that have
    special mathematical meanings
Recognizing relationships
Organizing details and processes to find solutions
Evolving procedures for problem-solving

In reading science, one needs, in addition to the general skills, the following:

Interpreting graphs, charts, tables, formulas
Understanding technical words, and the basic Latin and Greek roots and affixes
    from which many scientific words are derived
Using inductive and deductive reasoning
Applying scientific facts to life today

In the reading of literature, many purposes require many different reading skills. Among these are:

Locating and interpreting clues to plot, character, motive
Recognizing the author's mood, intent, and purpose
Understanding connotations, symbolism, and allusions
Visualizing descriptions and dramatic action
Noting cause-and-effect relations and sequences of events

Appreciating the author's style, tone, and rhythm.
Understanding the theme of the selection.

These higher level skills that are needed in various subjects are developed all during the senior high school years.

In addition to these specific skills, the teacher's objectives should also include certain skills, attitudes, and approaches to reading:

To awaken the student's curiosity and give him a desire for more knowledge about an historical character, a scientific topic, a form of literature, etc.
To establish a persistent habit of voluntary reading in the subject — newspapers, magazines, current books, historical novels.
To develop standards of precision and accuracy in reading.
To encourage the student to read with the intent to remember significant ideas.
To develop the habit of reading with a purpose.
To establish the habit of inquiry — reading to discover new thoughts and feelings.

Teaching Suggestions

When he has determined what reading skills his subject demands, the teacher next finds out which skills need to be taught, reinforced, or applied in his particular class. This he may do by means of informal tests, and by noting pupils' responses during the class period. For example, the teacher may select certain paragraphs from the text and ask the pupils to state the main thought of each.

If the pupils prove to be deficient in this skill, the teacher may use the informal test as a basis for instruction. He helps the pupils go through the process of identifying the main ideas. They find some paragraphs in which it is stated in the first sentence, in the last sentence, in other parts of the paragraph; they find instances in which it is not stated at all, but only implied. They discuss ways of identifying the main thought — it is the most general and important idea; the other ideas relate to, support, or explain it. They note different kinds of paragraph structure,[6] and discuss the different purposes that paragraphs serve. Following such a period of testing-diagnosis-instruction, the class will continue to apply their understanding of paragraph construction in every reading assignment.

Senior high school students may delve more deeply into the logic of paragraph reading. They will identify whole-part relationships, cause-and-effect

[6]Ruth Strang and Dorothy Bracken. *Making Better Readers.* Boston: D. C. Heath, 1957, pp. 222-232.

relationships, sequential relationships of time and place. They will note comparisons and contrasts, and coordinate-subordinate relationships. Their awareness of these various types of idea relationships will help them to classify and define words and ideas that occur in the subject, to summarize, make generalizations, and arrive at important principles. This is a high level of critical thinking. It must be taught and repeatedly practiced.

One may easily test a pupil's knowledge of the technical vocabulary of a subject by selecting words from the glossary and asking them for definitions. If the teacher suspects that a pupil possesses greater potential reading ability than he shows in his class work, the teacher may compare his comprehension when reading a passage of similar difficulty.

In the junior high school each teacher may well schedule systematic instruction in each reading skill in which his class is deficient. Without this instruction the pupils will fail to learn the content of the subject.

Each lesson may offer opportunity to emphasize a particular skill, as in the technique illustrated by David Shepherd.

In planning each lesson, the teacher will have two main objectives – knowledge of the subject and reading proficiency. For example, in a biology lesson on the eye, the teacher might have the following objectives:

Knowledge: To teach the parts of the eye and how they function.
Reading skills: To teach methods of reading and interpreting a diagram, and how to use it in connection with the text; to apply previously learned skills in interpreting the title and using the author's clues and other word recognition skills to find the meaning of new words.

In a social studies lesson on the building of new tunnels through the Alps the objectives might be:

Knowledge: When, where, how, and why these tunnels were built?
Reading skills: To apply previously learned skills in paragraph comprehension, and to use the main thought of each paragraph to build an outline of the whole article.

In the lower grades much time is spent in systematic teaching of reading skills. As the pupils become increasingly proficient in these skills, a larger proportion of time is spent in applying them to the reading of each subject. Thus in a single lesson, many reading skills may be applied and practiced. The teacher's concern is to help pupils to read effectively – to use reading as a means of gaining the basic concepts with which they can acquire a growing knowledge and understanding of themselves, of other people, and of the world around them. To accomplish this same end, high school teachers of every subject are also responsible for giving instruction, – i.e., going through the reading process with the pupils, and not just talking about it — in the skills that are required for success in their respective fields. They must also constantly reinforce and apply to their own subject matter the reading skills that the pupils have previously acquired.

Attitude of High School Content Area Teachers Toward the Teaching of Reading*

ARTHUR V. OLSON

The teaching of reading skills in the secondary schools is an educational trend that is receiving increasing emphasis. There seems to be an ever greater demand for trained teachers to develop and teach such programs. Several approaches have been made by secondary schools to initiate programs. The most common approach used is to make the teaching of reading skills an integral part of the English curriculum. Although this appears to be the most common pattern, the most desirable organization would be to have all the subject matter teachers teaching the skills pertinent to their own teaching area.

The major problem in developing a reading program in the secondary school is to enlist the aid of the content area teachers. Even when the teachers are willing to admit the needs for such a program, they are sometimes hesitant to learn anything about the techniques needed to improve the skills. Many of them feel that they just don't have the time to teach both the content and the necessary reading skills. It is possible that some teachers feel they are doing an adequate job of teaching the needed reading skills and therefore see no need for change.

In a study done by Olson and Rosen (1967-68) with the same population of teachers and their principals as discussed in this paper, the following was found:

1.   Female teachers feel they almost always used textbook materials suited to the reading levels of the students. Male teachers felt they did a good job of this but were less positive that they almost always used appropriate materials. The principals felt that the teachers did a much less effective job in suiting the reading material to the reading levels of the students than the teachers indicated they were doing.

2.   Over half of the female teachers felt they taught the reading skills needed for their content area adequately almost always while the male teachers

*Reprinted from *Multidisciplinary Aspects of College-Adult Reading,* Seventeenth Yearbook of the National Reading Conference, George Schick, editor, 1968, pp. 162-166, by permission of the author and the editor.

indicated that they taught them adequately less frequently. The principals felt that the teachers did not do as adequate a job as they said they were doing.

Perhaps of more interest than the differences between the responses of the teachers and the teachers and principals were the contradictions between responses.

Procedure

The author, in order to evaluate the extent to which teachers felt they were teaching some aspects of reading skill development collected the responses of junior and senior high school teachers (N = 585) to a checklist involving their practices relating to reading. In the teacher's responses there were seven content areas represented: English (N = 146), Social Studies (N = 123), Science (N = 102), Mathematics (N = 108), Business (N = 33), Vocational (N = 49) and Foreign Language (N = 24).

The teachers were given a list of twenty practices relating to reading in the content areas (see Appendix A) and asked to put a check in the column which best described their own classroom practice. They were to check Column One if they almost always carried on the practice, Column Two if they carried it on most of the time, Column Three if they carried it on sometimes and Column Four if they seldom or never prescribed to the practice.

Analysis of the Data

Tables 1-5 show five of the items on the twenty-item survey that are most pertinent to this report. The five items shown were significant at the .01 level.

TABLE 1
PERCENT OF TEACHER RESPONSE TO ITEM #1*

	Almost Always	Most of the Time	Sometimes	Seldom or Never
English	89.7	10.3	- -	- -
Social Studies	84.6	15.4	- -	- -
Science	82.4	14.7	2.9	- -
Mathematics	89.8	9.3	.9	- -
Business	90.9	9.1	- -	- -
Vocational	81.6	18.4	- -	- -
Foreign Lang.	62.5	20.8	- -	16.9

*Item #1. Text materials are suited in difficulty to the reading levels of students. $(X^2 = 111.51)$

The complete data for each of the twenty items may be obtained from the author.

Table I shows that all but one (foreign language) group of teachers felt that they almost always suited the reading difficulty to the reading level of the students. The response of the foreign language teachers is not surprising since they are working with a select group of students. Except for the language teachers the vocational teachers indicated that they provided material to a lesse⁻ degree than other teachers.

TABLE 2

PERCENT OF TEACHER RESPONSE TO ITEM #7*

	Almost Always	Most of the Time	Sometimes	Seldom or Never
English	39.7	39.7	15.8	4.8
Social Studies	18.7	32.5	38.2	10.6
Science	22.5	31.4	25.5	20.6
Mathematics	25.2	37.4	25.2	12.1
Business	33.3	27.3	24.2	15.2
Vocational	16.3	26.5	36.7	20.4
Foreign Lang.	54.2	29.2	- - -	16.7

*Item #7. The teacher knows the special reading skills in the subject. ($X^2 = 61.86$)

Table 2 shows that 57.1 percent of the vocational teachers felt that they knew the reading skills needed for their subject sometimes or seldom/never. The social studies teachers, 48.8 percent, responded in the same way. All of the content area showed a wide variation in their responses.

TABLE 3

PERCENT OF TEACHER RESPONSE TO ITEM #17*

	Almost Always	Most of the Time	Sometimes	Seldom or Never
English	16.4	26.7	39.0	17.8
Social Studies	11.4	20.3	42.3	26.0
Science	13.7	15.7	42.2	28.4
Mathematics	2.8	15.0	44.9	37.4
Business	6.1	15.2	30.3	48.5
Vocational	4.1	32.7	32.7	30.6
Foreign Lang.	4.2	20.8	20.8	54.2

*Item #17. Readings from various textbooks are provided for those who cannot read the regular text. ($X^2 = 48.40$)

Table 3 shows that the majority of the teachers only sometimes or seldom/never provided other reading materials for those who could not read the regular textbook assigned to the course.

Table 4 shows that the majority of the teachers felt that they did an adequate job of grouping for differentiated instruction. The foreign language teachers indicated that they grouped almost always or most of the time (91.7 percent). The English and social studies teachers respond in the same way, 87.6 percent and 85.3 percent respectively.

TABLE 4

PERCENT OF TEACHER RESPONSE TO ITEM #18*

	Almost Always	Most of the Time	Sometimes	Seldom or Never
English	56.8	30.8	12.3	- - - -
Social Studies	45.5	39.8	14.6	- - - -
Science	43.1	33.3	18.6	4.9
Mathematics	37.4	49.5	10.3	2.8
Business	30.3	33.3	18.2	18.2
Vocational	30.6	51.0	14.3	4.1
Foreign Lang.	54.2	37.5	8.3	- - - -

*Item #18. Students are grouped within the classroom for differentiated instruction. $(X^2 = 61.68)$

Table 5 shows that the vast majority of the content area teachers felt that they knew the reading level of the textbook(s) they were using almost always. The business training teachers had more variation than any other group.

TABLE 5

PERCENT OF TEACHER RESPONSE TO ITEM #19*

	Almost Always	Most of the Time	Sometimes	Seldom or Never
English	69.9	26.7	.7	2.7
Social Studies	53.7	36.6	8.9	.8
Science	55.9	31.4	6.9	5.9
Mathematics	48.6	43.9	5.6	1.9
Business	54.5	15.2	15.2	15.2
Vocational	51.0	32.7	10.2	6.1
Foreign Lang.	58.3	25.0	12.5	4.2

*Item #19. The teacher knows the reading level of the textbook(s) being used. $(X^2 = 48.69)$

Other items that showed a significant difference (.01 level) in the responses of the seven groups of teachers were: 2, 4, 5, 6, 8, 11, 12, and 15.

Conclusions and Discussion

The results of this study seem to indicate that the teachers generally feel that text materials are suited in difficulty to the reading level of the students, group for differentiated instruction, know the reading levels of the textbooks they use, and know the special reading skills of their content area. They indicated that they generally did not provide other reading materials for those who could not read the textbook. In most of the items evaluated, however, there was an indication of wide variation in responses for teachers within the same content area and between content areas.

Further evaluation of all the twenty items indicates a number of inconsistencies in the responses of the teachers. An example of one inconsistency can be found by comparing the responses on Items One and Seventeen. It appears that the teachers are saying that the reading materials are almost always suited to the reading level of the students but for those who cannot read these materials little or no provision is made. If we couple this with the information from Item Nineteen it appears that the teachers are not as sure about the reading level of the materials they use. The question could be asked, Is it possible to say that we always provide text material suited in difficulty to the reading levels of students and at the same time say we don't provide other textbooks for those who cannot read the regular text? It is of interest to note that when the teachers were asked how they knew the reading level of the text, most of them responded that they got this information from the grade level for which the publisher said the text was appropriate.

Reference

Olson, A. and Rosen C. "An analysis of teacher-principal responses to practices related to reading in the secondary school." *Reading Improvement,* Winter 1967/68.

Appendix A

Practices Related to Reading in the Content Areas

Teacher's Name: -*Subject Taught*: - - - - - - - - - - - -

The twenty practices listed below often are recommended in teaching effectively the special reading skills in the various content areas. Indicate the extent to which this practice applies to your classes. Draw a line around the number that indicated the appropriate response from among the following four:

1–Almost always   3–Sometimes
2–Most of the time   4–Seldom or never

1. Text material used is suited in difficulty to the reading levels of students.   1 2 3 4
2. Students are encouraged through assignments to read widely in related materials.   1 2 3 4
3. At the beginning of the year, adequate time is taken to introduce the text and to discuss how it may be read effectively.   1 2 3 4
4. The teacher is aware of the special vocabulary and concepts introduced in the various units.   1 2 3 4
5. Adequate attention is given to vocabulary and concept development.   1 2 3 4
6. Provisions are made for checking on extent to which important vocabulary and concepts are learned, and reteaching is done where needed.   1 2 3 4
7. The teacher knows the special reading skills involved in the subject.   1 2 3 4
8. The teacher teaches adequately the special reading skills in the subject.   1 2 3 4
9. The course content is broader in scope than a single textbook.   1 2 3 4
10. Assignments are made clearly and concisely.   1 2 3 4
11. Students are taught to use appropriate reference materials.   1 2 3 4
12. Adequate reference materials are available.   1 2 3 4
13. Plenty of related informational books and other materials are available for students who read *beiow-grade* level.   1 2 3 4
14. Plenty of related informational books and other materials are available for students who read *above-grade* level.   1 2 3 4
15. The teacher takes advantage of opportunities that may arise to encourage students to read recreational as well as informational reading matter.   1 2 3 4
16. The teacher helps the poor reader to develop adequate reading skills.   1 2 3 4
17. Readings from various textbooks are provided for those who cannot read the regular text.   1 2 3 4

18. Students are grouped within the classroom for dif-   1 2 3 4
    ferentiated instruction.

19. The teacher knows the reading level of the text-   1 2 3 4
    book(s) being used.

20. The teacher knows the reading ability of the   1 2 3 4
    students from standardized tests, other evaluative
    materials, and/or cumulative records.

Reading:
In and Out of the English Curriculum*

MARGARET J. EARLY

Because reading and study skills are basic to every subject in the secondary school curriculum, English teachers do not have exclusive rights to the teaching of reading. Nor do they want such prerogatives. But they do have responsibilities for understanding the nature of reading instruction in secondary schools, for defining the differences between "reading" and "English," and for giving leadership to schoolwide efforts to improve reading services. As articulate spokesmen for all-school developmental programs, English teachers can dispel the notion that remedial or corrective programs are the answer to all the reading ills in a secondary school. By clearly defining the role of English with respect to reading, they can help other members of the faculty understand *their* roles and assume *their* responsibilities.

Until this decade, the extension of reading instruction beyond the elementary school has been slow, haphazard, and piecemeal. Now, with the aid of state and federal funds, the momentum has increased but secondary programs are still haphazard and piecemeal. Special reading classes are being planned overnight and hastily staffed with inexperienced and untrained teachers, recruited usually from the English department. In such circumstances, confusion and disappointment are inevitable, but there remains at least the hope of learning from mistakes. School systems that began by scheduling special reading classes have become aware of their limitations and are moving now, with the help of ESEA funds, to more broadly based programs involving subject-matter teachers beyond the English department.

Importance of Clarity of Purpose

False starts can be avoided by long-range planning. From the beginning, administrators and teachers should know the dimensions of reading instruction

*Reprinted from *Bulletin of the National Association of Secondary-School Principals,* 51 (April, 1967), pp. 47-59, by permission of the author and the National Association of Secondary-School Principals.

in the secondary school. Its aim is the extension and refinement of skills, habits, and attitudes which have begun to take shape in the elementary grades. How can this extension and refinement be accomplished? In two ways: (1) through direct skills instruction concentrated in reading and English courses, and (2) through the fusion of reading and study skills with subject matter in all other courses. Of the two approaches, logic lies with the second; it makes more sense to "extend and refine" reading and study skills as they are required for subject matter learning. Nevertheless, we can defend direct instruction through reading courses or units of study as an expedient in schools where few teachers are prepared to teach reading-study skills.

Which of these two approaches should receive first emphasis is a point of needless controversy. Obviously, this question of priority has to be settled by the resources available in a given situation. Where a competent reading consultant is available, the approach through subject matter should probably be emphasized. Where there are large numbers of immature readers, and where experienced reading teachers may be recruited or inexperienced ones trained, it would be sensible to begin with direct instruction. Either approach is a safe one so long as the ultimate goal of an all-school developmental program is firmly established with administrators, teachers, and boards of education.

Either approach involves the English department from the beginning because English teachers are responsible for both skills learning and subject matter. If the decision is to emphasize direct instruction, English teachers will have to staff the program, wholly or partially. If the approach is through subject matter, they will have as much to learn as their colleagues about how to teach reading-study skills instead of merely requiring their use.

Direct Instruction

Direct instruction classes are usually labeled "corrective" or "developmental." These labels are relatively unimportant except as they suggest that the major concern in secondary school reading is *not* with the remedial. When we define *remedial* precisely, we limit its application to students of average to superior mental ability who have not learned to read beyond first-grade or second-grade level, even though they have had opportunities to learn. In the average American high school, relatively few students fall into this category. Those who do are likely to be suffering from psychoneurological disturbances requiring specialized treatment. After years of failure they should not in secondary schools be assigned to still another reading class. English teachers and minimally trained reading teachers are not remedial clinicians. The school's responsibility to such severely handicapped students is to help them to learn through channels other than reading, referring them when possible for expert psychological and medical advice.

In center-city schools (and in many rural and suburban schools as well), illiterate or almost illiterate adolescents are found in high school classrooms. These young people do not fit the restricted definition of "remedial" we have just applied. Therefore, they may be appropriately assigned to corrective or developmental classes of limited size, so that teachers can learn to work with them individually much of the time. It is arguable that these youth do not need the skills concentration that is the *raison d'etre* for special reading classes. If, however, the goals and consequently the methods and materials of instruction are reoriented for these pupils, the "extra reading class" is as justifiable for them as for others.

The most optimistic goal for the average adolescent illiterate is that he will become a reader, not a student. This means that the total effort should be to get him to read – anything. Perhaps the worst approach is through textbooks, workbooks, and skillbuilding exercises. (One junior high teacher tells me that mimeographed sheets are more palatable to these pupils than are more legible, better designed workbook pages, probably because the former seem more personalized, even when they are not). If textbooks are ever to be used successfully with these pupils, it will only be after they have learned personally satisfying reasons for reading. Only then will it be possible to develop orderly sequences for word analysis skills and basic comprehension skills.

So far, success stories involving adolescent illiterates are rare. Those that have appeared emphasize the importance of motivation and endorse all kinds of unorthodox materials, from menus and racing forms to hot rod magazines and best selling paperbacks. The program described by Daniel Fader in *Hooked on Books* as achieving varieties of success in a boys' training school in Michigan and the Garnett-Patterson Junior High School in Washington, D.C., breaks with traditions of both reading and English.[1] Apparently, what happens when seeming "illiterates" suddenly begin to read adult magazines and paperbacks is that walls of resistance are shattered and dormant skills are put back into service. The true illiterate has no dormant skills, and for him miracles come more slowly.

Helping Readers Become "Studiers"

Dramatic though they may be, the problems of the adolescent illiterate are not the chief concern of secondary reading instruction. Rather, the main thrust is toward students who have acquired the basic skills which need to be extended and refined. They are competent "general" readers by the criteria of standardized grade-level tests. Our aim is to help these readers become students, that is, "studiers"—persons who learn through reading. When we set up special reading courses for these readers, our reason is that they require more direct

---

[1] Daniel Fader. *Hooked on Books.* New York: Berkley Publishing Corporation, 1966.

teaching, followed up by intensive practice, in how to read and study than is being supplied by the teachers of subject matter courses.

The content of the reading course should be dictated by the needs of the students. We analyze the reading tasks required in studying textbooks; we test students' abilities with respect to these tasks and identify where they need help. On the basis of this skills analysis, we select from instructional materials of varying difficulty those lessons needed by particular students. We provide for practice but only after demonstrations and explanations have made clear how to apply the skill. Frequently this teaching is directed at individuals and small groups, but occasionally all students in a class may need teaching preceding differentiated practice.

The focus on skills development dictates a laboratory classroom, equipped minimally with many short sets of textbooks and workbooks on varying levels, dictionaries and other references, and several hundred paperbacks. Ideally, the room should also be equipped with study carrels, tape recorders and headsets, projectors and viewers, and under some circumstances with a few pacers for improving rate of reading. Extensive equipment will not ensure excellent instruction, but neither can we expect dramatic achievement when the teacher is a "floater," with access to a duplicating machine and a box of skills exercises and little else.

As part of the English curriculum, the goals, methods, and materials of the reading course are similar to those of other English offerings. Periods of instruction are usually shorter, ranging perhaps from two to six weeks of intensive work on reading-study skills, per se. This brief time allotment is compensated for by the fact that English teachers who employ unit methods and laboratory techniques can extend skills instruction to groups and individuals from time to time throughout the year.

Motivation Essential

Skills practice in any endeavor—sports, music, typewriting, reading—must be highly motivated and sharply focused on individual needs. Even so, it can be dull or demanding. Students would rather engage in discussion (often lively but irrelevant), or they would rather escape thinking by listening or pretending to listen, or by a type of reading for pleasure which is more closely akin to daydreaming than to thinking. For teachers, too, skills instruction is more demanding and less interesting than leading a discussion, lecturing, demonstrating, or merely talking. In reading classes, the great temptation is to distribute the mimeographed exercises, get out the skills box, plug in the film or tape recorder, and then escape to the teacher's room for a cup of coffee. No wonder students learn to hate reading classes, even if they like to read.

How can we motivate? This question is often asked in despair by teachers who don't want a usable answer. It is difficult to motivate skills practice unrelated to substantive learning. This is the hurdle we set for ourselves when we organize special reading classes. Since we would not schedule these classes in the first place unless convinced of their usefulness, we must be willing to surmount the hurdle. One way to infuse the skills course with purpose may be to treat it as a course in the psychology of learning, one in which students study themselves as learners. Another way is to teach individuals instead of large groups. Another is to let students see success as they chart their own progress. Nourishing a spark of motivation takes constant attention. The flame can go out while the teacher distributes mimeographed exercises or the student chalks up another failure.

Teacher May Lack Motivation

Perhaps the teacher's own lack of motivation contributes most to failure in skills courses. Just as he needs to offer constant and genuine encouragement to his students, so, too, the teacher needs to have his enthusiasm bolstered. He needs tangible help – materials, ideas, equipment – from consultant and principal. He needs their support in scheduling classes of reasonable size, and in providing time for diagnosis and consultation. Most of all he needs to see progress in the spread of the program throughout the subject classes.

Because skills instruction is a hard job, especially for the novice, many reading classes become something else. In the hands of English teachers they often become extensions of literature courses, weak courses at that.

"Send me an English teacher who knows the difference between teaching reading and teaching literature," pleaded a secondary school principal recently. In too many junior high school reading classes, the bulk of the time is spent in reading novels – in common. When a teacher orders thirty copies of *The Yearling* for a junior high reading class, this is a sure sign that he is unaware of the objectives of reading instruction. (If he orders whole class sets of any textbook, he is doing a poor job of teaching literature, too.)

Of course, we can justify the inclusion of fiction in a reading course as part of "free reading." One of the aims is to get weak students to read whatever appeals to them, and fiction appeals to many as a relatively undemanding exercise of basic reading skills. Wide reading serves an appropriate skills objective: it is a vehicle for developing fluency, adding to vocabulary, and exercising simple comprehension skills such as the ability to follow sequence. But reading fiction does nothing for the development of essential study skills such as relating major and minor ideas,—understanding closely reasoned argument, judging facts, following explanations, and other skills necessary for the assimilation of informative prose.

The study of *how* to read literature can be justified as content for the reading and study skills class only when equal time is allotted to how to read science, history, mathematics, and other subjects. Obviously, equal allotment of time to each subject in the curriculum means that scant attention can be paid to any of them, and thus points up again the need for teaching reading not only in the special class but in every subject area. The teaching of subject-oriented skills in the special reading class sets up an artificial learning situation, takes additional time, lessens the chance that something of substantive value can be learned at the same time that skills are being refined, and puts the burden for the transfer of learning wholly upon students.

English teachers, while claiming to be unprepared to teach reading,[2] assert that they do it all the time. They mean, of course, that they *use* reading in the literature program but are ill equipped to deal with word analysis, basic comprehension skills, and rate of reading – the components they define as "reading." It is the exceptional English teacher who teaches his students how to read imaginative literature. In his disregard of the skills required for reading in his specialty, the average English teacher is no different from his colleagues in other subject fields.

The truly professional English teacher who recognizes his dual role as a teacher of skills and of subject matter distinguishes between reading and literature and gives balanced attention to both. (English teachers of junior high school students or of weaker students in the senior high school give more time to developing reading skills and interests, less time to the study of literature. Teachers of mature students reverse the emphases).

Reading Versus Literature

How do we distinguish between "reading" and "literature" in the secondary school curriculum? Differences are evident in the objectives and in the materials of instruction. The development of reading-study skills requires informative or expository prose as its vehicle of instruction, rather than discursive or imaginative writing. If the fare of the English course is exclusively novels, poetry, and drama, the English teacher can fulfill only one part of his dual role. Fortunately, nonfiction articles and essays are found in most anthologies. If these have been abandoned, the teacher must seek other sources of nonfiction, principally periodicals. Materials do not make the program, of course. But the absence of expository prose proves that reading-study skills are being ignored; its presence indicates at least the possibility of appropriate instruction.

Many reading teachers and supervisors are unaware of any confusion

---

[2] According to the National Interest and the Continuing Education of Teachers of English (Champaign, Ill.: National Council of Teachers of English, 1963), 90 percent of English teachers do not feel well qualified to teach reading.

between reading and literature. They assume that the narrative-type materials which predominate in elementary school — where individualized reading as well as basal approaches have favored narrative materials — should be continued in junior high school, even though by this time students' needs have shifted from general comprehension to study skills. Fortunately, the current trend in elementary reading instruction is to correct the imbalance in materials and in methods of teaching. As more exposition is included in elementary materials and as elementary literature programs become more sharply distinguished from basal reading instruction, the tradition of basing developmental reading on narrative prose will die out.

Confronted with the obligation to teach reading-study skills *and* skills for reading literature, English teachers plead the restrictions of time. In junior high school, time limitations are eased by extra reading classes, double English periods, and core or block-time arrangements. In senior high English classes, the time required for direct instruction will become less as more of the reading-study skills are shifted to the content areas. Elective courses in reading-study skills, especially for college-bound students in grades 11 and 12, are another kind of solution. Nevertheless, many English teachers must still decide what to leave out in order to include reading-study skills.

We suggest a hard look at the efficiency of the language instruction and the inordinate amount of time given to the discussion of literature. Fortunately, new developments in language and literature suggest economies in teaching. (See Harold B. Allen's article in this symposium.) Moreover, new methods of organization, such as team teaching and laboratory techniques, provide more time for skills instruction and free reading than do methods which treat a class of 25 or 30 as an inflexible unit.

Schoolwide Reading Improvement

Leaving reading instruction entirely in the hands of the English department, even one with a supplementary staff of reading teachers, has proved extremely limiting. The resulting program may be effective but limited, or it may be merely an extension of English and not very effective at all. In either case the program falls far short of what we mean by teaching reading in the secondary school.[3]

In schools where reading instruction is truly pervasive, it would be inappropriate to talk about reading "programs." Instruction would be clearly visible and measurable, but it would be so thoroughly integrated with subject learning that it would not show on master schedules. There would be no extra

[3]Olive S. Niles. "Systemwide In-Service Programs in Reading." *The Reading Teacher,* No. 19 (March 1966).

classes and no reading teachers and, except in large urban schools, no special clinics or laboratories. But this pervasive instruction, reaching into every classroom where reading is a medium of learning, would be visible to the administrator who knows what to look for.

For example, the administrator surveying reading instruction in his school would look in every classroom for answers to questions like these:

Do teachers frequently develop concepts and introduce vocabulary *before* students read an assignment?

Do teachers help students to identify the reading tasks required by a particular assignment?

Do they then demonstrate how to apply the necesary skills?

Is attention paid not only to what a textbook says but to how it is said, that is, to the author's choice of words, his sentence structure, and his organization of ideas?

Is the author's purpose examined?

Are comparisons made among treatments of the same subject?

Are students not only encouraged to make judgments but shown how?

Are teachers aware of the different kinds of reading abilities their students possess?

Do they help them to make the best use of their various abilities by providing books and other reading materials on varying levels of difficulty?

Supervisory Leadership Essential

The foregoing questions, by no means comprehensive, suggest what we mean by teaching reading in secondary schools. To initiate and maintain this pervasive instruction in reading requires strong administrative backing and the day-to-day services of a competent coordinator, who may or may not be attached to the English department. Just as scheduling reading classes produces no easy solutions, neither does hiring a coordinator, provided one can be found. But it is well for administrators to recognize the need for schoolwide reading improvement. In large schools, the English chairman's hands are too full to undertake this task even though, if he is competent, he will understand and give support to the movement. The near-impossibility of finding a reading coordinator leads most schools to select one of their own staff, perhaps a reading-English teacher, and to subsidize his further study. We recommend a year if possible of full-time study at a university near enough to his school that its students, teachers, and resources can be subjects of his study.

Educating teachers to teach reading is the main job ahead. State and federal funds have presented us with opportunities for greatly expanding in-service education; what we need now are ideas for spending this money effectively. Among the least effective methods is transplanting the university course intact to the school cafeteria for 15 weekly meetings from 4 p.m. to 6 p.m. Nor is the currently popular plan of bringing in a series of guest lecturers from hither and yon likely to prove any more effective — if by effective we mean producing changes in the classroom. Even lecture courses that are well planned and intelligently presented probably do little more than supply background information, spark interest, and soften the attitudes of recalcitrant teachers, getting them ready to have someone else do the job that needs doing!

Along with or instead of the credit course or lecture series, some schools get the most from their government grants by concentrating attention on a few teachers at a time and freeing them, by hiring substitutes, to work intensively with the reading consultant. For example, three small school systems in central New York have selected key teachers from their secondary school faculties to attend a series of three week-long workshops conducted at intervals during the first semester at a nearby university reading center. Three days of each week are spent in the center in intensive study of reading methodology applied to the teachers' own textbooks; two days are spent in local schools observing preplanned reading lessons in the content areas, in examining other phases of the reading program, and in teaching demonstration lessons to "borrowed" classes. Between the weeks on campus, these teachers spend regularly scheduled days in their own schools demonstrating for each other and for the university personnel who are consultants to the project. In each school, these teachers are becoming the nucleus for subject-centered reading instruction.

The Reading Center staff at Syracuse University has produced a series of 10 films on teaching reading in secondary schools. These films, accompanied by 15 manuals, constitute the core of an in-service workshop to be directed by a school's reading consultant, supplemented perhaps by university personnel. The films are meant as an introductory step in developing an all-school program. Like the customary course, they will prove minimally effective unless followed up by work in the teachers' own classrooms. However, the film package can be used with considerably more flexibility and economy than can the university course. For example, the films may be viewed by a single department, with discussion restricted to the special concerns of this particular group. Teachers study the film content through viewing and reviewing, discuss with each other the implications for their classrooms, turn to the manuals and suggested references for more information, and try out recommended procedures. The films appear to offer another approach to in-service education without straining further the overextended resources of the universities.

Administrators about to embark upon schoolwide efforts to improve reading instruction would do well to study the recommendations made by Olive S. Niles in her article previously cited.

Summary

In an all-school reading program, English teachers have responsibilities comparable to those of other subject specialists. Additionally, they are responsible for the direct instruction of reading-study skills as part of regularly scheduled English courses or in extra classes. In spite of the fact that reading is one of the skills of language which, with literature, constitutes the discipline of English, the majority of teachers of English seem neither better prepared nor more willing to teach reading-study skills than their colleagues on secondary faculties. Because of lack of preparation, English teachers assigned to reading classes tend to teach literature or promote wide reading and to ignore reading-study skills.

There is no standard pattern for reading instruction in secondary schools nor should there be, but readily observable features distinguish excellent from mediocre direct-skills instruction. Chief among these are the attention given to individuals, the diversity of materials for skills instruction, the preponderance of expository prose in skills exercises, and collections of paperbacks and periodicals for wide reading.

Similarly, reading instruction in subject matter classes does not follow fixed patterns, but is easily identified by the ways in which those teachers direct students towards the process of learning through reading.

Schemes for improving reading instruction in the secondary school should probably concentrate first on the preparation of teachers in in-service action programs, since preservice courses are rare and in any case theoretical and introductory. English departments should play leading roles when a whole school faculty undertakes reading improvement. Along with helping others to understand the rationale of a whole school program, English teachers should decide upon the relative emphases to be given direct instruction in reading-study skills and in how to read literature.

The Reading of Fiction*

EDWARD J. GORDON

During recent years the teaching of English has been subjected to a critical and stimulating examination of its objectives. For this long-needed search have come new directions; realistic objectives have revitalized the teacher's thinking. We have moved to a point where we recognize that

> In an unsettled world, our schools and colleges are confronted with the demand that they prepare the student directly for living. He must be helped to develop the intellectual and emotional capacities for a happy and socially useful life. He must be given the knowledge, the habits, the flexibility, that will enable him to meet unprecedented and unpredictable problems. He needs to understand himself; he needs to work out relationships with other people. Above all, he must achieve some philosophy, some inner center from which to view in perspective the shifting society about him; he will influence for good or for ill its future development. To have pragmatic value, any knowledge about man and society that the schools can give him must be assimilated into the stream of his actual life.[1]

There is no part of the curriculum that bears so directly on those problems as literature. Yet there is little evidence that these objectives are being achieved, and the next ten years might well be used for finding ways through which such high purposes might be fulfilled.

The Narrow Concept of Reading

One of the main reasons why there is such a hiatus between hope and performance lies in an overly narrow concept of reading, especially in dealing

*Reprinted from *Bulletin of the National Association of Secondary-School Principals,* 39 (September, 1955), pp. 44-49, by permission of the author and the National Association of Secondary-School Principals.
[1] Rosenblatt, Louise. *Literature as Exploration.* New York: D. Appleton-Century. 1938, p. 5.

with works of fiction. Although we speak of literature as bringing an understanding of others and eventually an understanding of self, there is little hope that such an ideal will be realized until the student learns to "read" the books we teach.

One of our most urgent needs then is for an evaluation of what we mean by "reading." What do we mean when we say that a student is a "good reader"? We are overly concerned with finding out whether a student has "done the work," whether he knows what happened, and too little concerned with teaching him *how* to read. Reading, as a series of skills, is taught in the elementary schools; in the secondary schools it is often merely tested. Books are assigned; questions, usually factual, are asked; and the consequences are only too apparent.

We deplore the comic books, yet us comic book techniques in our teaching: emphasizing plot and superficial chacter study. The result, as David Riesman points out in his study of the Ameri an character, is a comic strip type of reading.

(If) child comic fans read or hear stori that are not comics they will read them as though they were comics. They wi end to focus on who won and to miss the internal complexities of the tale, o morale sort or otherwise. If one asks them, then, how they distinguish the "good guys" from the "bad guys" in the mass media, it usually boils down to the fact that the former always win; they are good guys by definition.

But of course the child wants to anticipate the result and so looks for external clues which will help him pick the winner. In the comics there is no problem: the good guys *look it,* being square-jawed, clear-eyed, tall men; the bad guys also look it, being, for reasons of piety, of no recognizable ethnic groups but rather of a generally messy Southern European frame — oafish and unshaven or cadaverous and over-smooth.

Yet he (the child) is strikingly insensitive to problems of character as presented by his favorite story-tellers; he tends to race through the story for its ending, or to read the ending first, and to miss just those problems of personal development that are not telltale clues to the outcome. . . He cannot afford to linger on "irrelevant" details or to day-dream about heroes. To trade preferences in reading and listenting, he need know no more about the heroes than the stamp trader needs to know about the countries the stamps come from.[2]

What we might do is work out a series of techniques which, having been deliberately taught, would in turn lead to a fuller understanding of a book; and it is with fiction, the most widely read and probably the most poorly taught of all forms of literature, that we must be most concerned. Then we might help the student to achieve some of the more abstract virtues that we as English teachers hope to inculcate.

[2] Riesman, David. *The Lonely Crowd.* New Haven: Yale University Press. 1950. pp. 103-104.

The job will not get done in a question-and-answer search for what happened, or in a consideration of the life of the author. We must teach the book, not *about* the book. The teacher must not give the answers; he must ask the questions. And to ask the right questions, the teacher must be a good reader. As the work progresses, the teacher should become useless; the reader should be able to ask his own questions. It is only then that the student is becoming a reader.

What Does It Mean?

What does it mean to read a piece of fiction? What are the major techniques that an author uses to tell his tale? How do we make out interpretation of the work at hand?

Most important, the book should be seen as a whole, not as a series of chapters read on a one-a-day basis. Why is it put together the way it is? There is no way to judge, for example, why the story begins where it does unless we know the ending. Why are particular characters presented by the author? What is put in? What is left out? On the principle of selection Rosenblatt says

> No one would question that, in the creation of the literary work, the writer does not rarely passively reflect experience as through a photographic lens. He uses his command over words to convey to us an impassioned insight. This has been the selective force at work. Discarding all else, the writer weeds out from the welter of impressions with which life bombards us those particular elements that have significant relevance to his insight. He leads us to perceive selected images, personalities and events in special relation to one another. Thus out of the matrix of elements with common meaning for him and his readers, he builds up a new sequence, or new structure, that enables him to evoke in the reader's mind a special emotion, a new or deeper understanding — that enables him in short, to communicate with his reader.[3]

The communication will not adequately take place unless the reader sees why the particular selection was made. The *why* is the central problem. The unity of a work of art is determined by the effect that the author is trying to produce. If the function of a particular character, scene or setting is not apparent to the student, he has to that extent missed the intention. Or, and this should be apparent too, the book may be poorly written.

[3] Rosenblatt. *Op. cit.,* p. 42.

Specific Teachniques

Turning to more specific techniques, we might add immeasurably to a student's understanding of a book by teaching three major writing techniques: *irony, metaphor,* and *connotation.*

Irony, briefly, is involved in the statement which ostensibly means one thing, yet turns out to mean something else. It is the contrast between what seems and what is. We have the classic example of ironic tone in Antony's oration on the death of Caesar, of an ironic situation in Hamlet's — "Haste me to know't, that I with wings as swift as meditation or the thought of love, may sweep to my revenge."

Quite often irony is the structural principle on which a whole play or novel is built. Oedipus searches for the cause of the plague and so destroys himself. In Odets' *Golden Boy,* Joe Bonaparte gets "on the millionaire express," finds the gold he seeks, and destroys himself. Willy Loman, in *Death of a Salesman,* is driven by the need of being "well liked," yet when he dies, no outsiders come to his funeral. In such instances of dramatic irony a phrase, conversation, or situation may have a double meaning known to the audience but not to the actor or actors. A character's actual situation is one thing, and his idea or interpretation of it is another; the promise that things have for him is at variance with their outcome — they are not what they seem. The contrast is between expectation and fulfillment. It lies in the sense of contradiction felt by the spectator of the drama who sees a character acting in ignorance of his condition.

In subtler types of irony, the author may use the setting as an ironic contrast to the plight of his character, or he may comment on the action with some ironic symbol. When, in *Jude the Obscure,* Jude and Arabella went on their first walk, they stopped at a tavern on the wall of which hung a picture of Samson and Delilah, symbolizing what she was about to do to his career.

Metaphor, the second of our major elements, needs to be taught as much more than a poetic decoration; it is rather a basic principle in the development of language, a central means of communication. In an intercalary chapter of *The Grapes of Wrath,* a turtle crosses the road and is spun on his back by a passing truck; he rights himself and goes on. This incident cannot be passed over as an unrelated anecdote about turtles, but rather a metaphorical statement of Steinbeck's ideas on man and society, on the impact of the "machine age." Hardy's opening chapter in *The Return of the Native* is a metaphorical expression of Fate. Much of the meaning of *Ethan Frome* is conveyed metaphorically in these scenes between Ethan and Mattie, of the breaking of the pickle dish, symbolizing what has happened and what will happen to Ethan's happiness. In *Giants in the Earth,* Beret is continually looking out the east window toward home; Per Hansa, the west window. Finally he dies, still going west.

Through such metaphors, or symbols if you like, the author comments on his story. He adds new dimensions of meaning to what ostensibly is "happening." For example, the setting is often a metaphor: a raging sea, a storm, a heath, a decaying castle. It becomes the author's comment on a seemingly objective scene, or often a reflection of what is happening in the mind of the character.

In some books, metaphor becomes the basic method of conveying the idea. Forster in *A Passage to India* uses the Marabar Caves to comment on the division of men into classes and the evil consequences of such distinctions; this in ironic opposition to the idea that "My Father's house has many mansions," a line quoted by the English missionaries. Then too, Conrad in *The Heart of Darkness* is talking, not so much of the center of Africa as of the blackness of human soul when it becomes purely materialistic. "The horror, the horror" is the summary of a life without love. Often, as in this last example, the whole story is a metaphor.

The third major principle, *connotation*, is the author's way of getting the reader to feel a certain way about what takes place, about the characters, or about the setting. The words or images used in describing the setting, for example, will make the reader feel a certain way toward it. In a description of a room in *Ligeia*, Poe said:

> ... I minutely remember the details of the chamber .... The room lay in a high turret of the castellated abbey. ... Occupying the whole southern face of the pentagon was the sole window — an immense sheet of unbroken glass from Venice — a single pane, and tinted of a leaden hue, so that the rays of either the sun or moon passing through it fell with a ghastly lustre on the objects within. Over the upper portion of this huge window, extended the trellis-work of an aged vine, which clambered up the massy walls of the turret. The ceiling, of gloomy looking oak, was excessively lofty, vaulted and elaborately fretted with the wildest and most grotesque specimens of a semi-Gothic semi-Druidical device. ...

The choice of weather, colors, time, season, shapes, and other details will evoke an appropriate response in a good reader; he may then see the connection between the setting and the total effect of the book. For another example, Gatsby lives in great splendor at the opening of *The Great Gatsby*. We see his house at night; luxuriant and lighted it reflects its owner's values. As the story develops, we get a reversal of roles. The house grows shabbier as Gatsby grows nobler. Fitzgerald throws the light of day, or truth, on the house when Gatsby discovers that the values to which he keyed his life are not working.

There are other, less important but similarly overlooked, reading skills that need to be taught. Parellelism and contrast are much used literary devices. Similarities and differences heighten the effect at which the author is aiming. Laertes is put in a similar position to Hamlet's, a father murdered and revenge indicated. He, however, does sweep to his revenge. Why then does Hamlet delay?

Awareness of these devices explains much that is otherwise irrelevant. The two girls in *Winterset* who babble of their romantic experiences heighten the concept of the love of Mio and Miriamne. The evil of Claggert in *Billy Budd* emphasizes the goodness of Billy. Authors are constantly comparing and contrasting scenes. Ethan Frome and Mattie say their "final" good-by against the setting in which their romance began. Characters, too, can be paralleled: Eustacia Vye with Thomasin Yeobright, Becky Sharp with Amelia Sedley.

Characterization

If we mean to teach novels as an aid to understanding ourselves and others, we must see the links of causality. Plot cannot be considered as merely a series of disconnected events, but rather a chain of cause and effect — one scene linking onto another. The acts of character, too, must be seen as connected to the motivation. Henry James in *The Art of Fiction* says, "What is character but the determination of incident? What is incident but the illustration of character?" In this light we see the suicide of Emma Bovary as the only logical outcome of her life. Or to put the problem another way, does the outcome of the novel grow out of the concept of character presented by the novelist? It does in a good character study.

An understanding of the devices of characterization is also an important reading technique. How do we come to understand people in fiction, and consequently in life. We see what they do, hear what they say, and often know what they think. A student should be taught to make connections between the happenings in a novel and what they show of the characters. As Henry James says further, "It is an incident for a woman to stand up with her hand resting on a table and look at you in a certain way; or, if it be not an incident, I think it will be hard to say what it is. At the same time it is an expression of character. If you say you don't see it (character in that-allons donc!), this is exactly what the artist who has reasons of his own for thinking he *does* see it undertakes to show you." Beyond this we often hear comments on characters, by the author or by the other people in the book. From these disparate elements, we must work out our total characterization.

Yet characterization can take on subtle forms. In *Victory,* Conrad has several people tell the story of Heyst. The first is Schomberg who hates the hero. It is through the development of the story that we find out that Conrad's ideas are not those of Schomberg. Eustacia Vye is partially characterized through things she admires: "Her high gods were William the Conqueror, Stafford, and Napoleon Bonparte, as they had appeared in the Lady's History used at the establishment in which she was educated. Had she been a mother she would have christened her boys such names as Saul or Sisera in preference to Jacob or David, neither of whom she admired. At school she used to side with the Philistines in several battles, and wondered if Pontius Pilate were as handsome as he was frank and fair." Flaubert is more subtle; when we first meet Emma Bovary, she, in order to make some bandages, "tried to sew some pads. As she was a long time before she found her workcase, her father grew impatient; she did not answer, but as she sewed she pricked her fingers, which she then put in her mouth to suck them." Finally, when her father asks if she will marry Charles, Emma promises to signal her agreement by opening a shutter so that Charles, outside, will know the good news. "Charles fastened his horse to a tree; he ran into the road and waited. Half-an-hour passed, then he counted nineteen minutes by his watch. Suddenly a noise was heard against the wall; the shutter had been thrown back; the hook was still swinging." This contrast between the attitudes of Charles and Emma Bovary forms one of the basic patterns of the book.

Then too, characterization should be related to motivation. What makes the person act as he does? What is the level of motivation? Is the motivation so sketchy and of such surface quality that we are unable to predict behavior in a specific situation? Does the major decision in the book come as a surprise? In better books the action grows out of character.

In soap operas and in second-rate novels, we are surprised when something happens. That is, unmotivated acts are constantly taking place. John leaves Mary because he doesn't like the way she does her hair or because she doesn't clean the corners of the living room. However, he suddenly sees the light, returning from the glamorous blonde. But *why?* The level of motivation is so slight that the behavior is neither predictable, nor understandable — and consequently is unrealistic.

These then are just a few of the major characteristics of structure and style in the art of the novel. They are not necessarily the most important qualities to be considered in a novel, but they are too often the most neglected in secondary-school teaching. Most important, they are the means to the ends. We have devised good ends; let us now improve the means. Let us search for worth-while books and read them more profoundly. Then we may be truly dealing with the humanistic tradition.

The Reading of Literature: Poetry as an Example*

JOHN S. SIMMONS

At the outset, let's clarify one or two presumptions. In my opinion the reading of literature is an ability which should be developed with students only *subsequently* in the English curriculum. In order that we make students competent to any degree at all to deal with literary selections *on their own,* we must be assured that *two conditions* are already present: (1) that certain basic reading skills have been assimilated by these youngsters and (2) that they have lived long enough to have accumulated a storehouse of experience to which they can relate the various literary selections they will be asked to read. It is contradictory to ask students who cannot read much of anything to read literature. Furthermore, literature can be enlightening when it sheds *new* light on something on which youngsters have already established some perspective.

Dwight Burton has suggested a highly useful three-step sequence for effective teaching of imaginative literature. To participate fully in any literary selection, a reader must first make an "imaginative entry." That is, he must be able to relate, to some degree, the experience described in the work to that which he himself has undergone. The "to some degree" is a vital factor in this first phase of understanding. The young reader does not have to have literally experienced that which occurs in the story he has read; he need only to be able to call up experiences in the *general* area of the subject represented.

Obviously, then, works must be within the emotional range of the reader in order for him to have any chance of making such an entry. In the light of this, Burton feels that one of the teacher's important functions in promoting empathy between reader and work is to "select" for study those works which offer a legitimate chance for the student to use his experiences as a touchstone for imaginative entry.

Once an imaginative entry has been made, the reader's next concern, in Burton's eyes, is for the perception of meaning or central purpose of the work.

*Reprinted from *Vistas in Reading,* Proceedings of the 11th Annual Convention of the International Reading Association, J. Allen Figurel, editor, 1966, pp. 93-100, by permission of the author and the International Reading Association.

This goal is most consistently and fully achieved by moving from particulars to universals, from the concrete "facts" of the work to the significance that they, taken as a whole, embody. Thus the process of moving toward realization of meaning is necessarily an inductive one. The finding of meaning in literature is a continuous process of predicting what is to come and then testing the validity of the predition by relating it to what the reader finds as he progresses through the work.

The final stage of examination of literature for Burton is that of perception of artistic unity and significance. This perception, he hastens to add, is a level of realization reached by only a relatively small number of students. In other words, many may never participate aesthetically in the total impact of a writer's language. This contention, *I* hasten to add, has been well-corroborated in my own teaching experiences at the secondary level. And one of my greatest frustrations as an observer of literature instruction occurs when a teacher turns to his students at the completion of all-class reading of a given work and asks them to comment on its aesthetic impact — questions such as "How did you like this poem?," or "How did the author's style impress you?" — these without first finding out if they know what went on in the work, where, and when it happened, and to whom! Students cannot savor verbal finesse until they have first dealt with the facts of a work and their relationships, expressed and implied.

Although I find that Burton's concept of inductive literature teaching is very close to my own, I would like to take his three-step process as a point of departure and suggest some ways in which a teacher of literature, using the *forms* of literature in a purposeful sequence, may develop better understanding. Notice that Burton has laid primary emphasis on what the reader must do. The teacher is, more than anything else, a catalyst of literary understanding, interpretation, appreciation. Burton's process would be related to *any* work of literature regardless of its genre. It is my contention that if we as teachers move from one form purposefully to another with our student, it will make the application of Burton's theory a good deal easier, both for teacher and student.

My opening contention in this matter of form is that teachers of literature should consider starting with works of longer prose fiction, that is, novels. My rationale for this contention grows from the feeling that we should pick the student up where he most probably *is*. First of all, longer prose fiction tells a story, and it should be needless to reiterate that the overwhelming majority of young people enjoy stories. Whether they are superior readers, most younger students are quite accustomed to the narrative, whether it appears in printed or in oral form.

To implement most effectively my suggestion of using novels in the early stages of literature instruction, the teacher should find those novels which are conventionally written. As I define it, a conventionally written novel follows a clear chronological order in its development. The action involved in such work is mostly of an outer nature; that is, physical activity predominates, and the reader is clearly aware of this fact. There are few flashbacks; those which are used are clearly identifiable, and the sequence of events is seldom interrupted for a long period of time. Characters are also developed without obscurity. Dialogue is regularly punctuated, and the thoughts of individuals are labeled as such.

There is no need to pursue, I feel, the notion of conventionality in longer works of prose fiction. But the novel does offer us one further advantage as an introductory form of literature. The development during the past thirty years of the well-written junior novel has provided a great *range* of materials for individualizing classroom instruction in the reading of literature. We all recognize the grim fact that not all readers at any grade level read with the same degree of proficiency. In the study of literature, the addition of the junior novel affords the teacher a valuable implement. Moreover, these works most often portray a protagonist in *adolescence,* moving through situations very close to the literal experience of younger or less mature readers. This facet of the junior novel makes imaginative entry possible for a large number of students. It also allows the teacher to choose well-written but easy-to-read selections for students who have trouble in just plain reading. He can use junior novels as a springboard for exploration of more complex works on more mature topics.

Flexibility is something for which we of the teaching gentry all crave. Equipped with junior novels, long but conventionally written novels on more adult topics (the works of Kipling, London, Twain, and countless others, can represent this type), and the kind of longer fictional works that we as college students manfully ploughed through, the teacher can work with students who are at several stages of development.

The short story offers a vehicle with which we can make an excellent transition in moving students from "easier" to more difficult literary forms. (Although, at this point I should like to interject that the term "easy" is a very slippery one when applied to the *reading* of literature – readability formulas don't tell us much of anything about the relative conceptual difficulty of most imaginative works.) While the short story is obviously still *fiction*, exemplary works often contain some special problems of which students will be largely unaware unless they are led to recognize and deal with them. The problem of reading the short story is not aided by the fact that there is considerably less adolescent fiction to be found in this abbreviated form. While there are undeniably some worthwhile collections of junior short stories available today, the great majority of shorter fictional works studied at the secondary level and widely anthologized for that purpose are quite adult and sophisticated. Thus the teacher will frequently find himself faced with the inescapable responsibility of dealing with short fictional works which present one or more significant structural difficulties.

Opening paragraphs in most short stories are crucial to the understanding of the work. With *much* less room to maneuver than his novelist counterpart, the writer of the short story must invest great significance in some relatively sparse and often trivial seeming detail. The student who is not on the lookout for these opening clues will almost invariably develop a confused or distorted idea of the direction in which the work is moving.

Time sequences are juggled about with abandon in modern short stories. Since the writer is typically presenting only a slice of life, he must often "play about with his clock" as E. M. Forster would say, in order to place in sharpest focus those details he wishes to emphasize. The result is often a series of abrupt transitions in scene, unexpected flashbacks, and puzzlingly underdeveloped situations. The student who is used to reading conventionally developed, longer fictional works may be jarred by these sharp turns and bumps in the road.

Further complications exist in short stories, particularly those written within the last fifty years. Freudian influences have led many writers to concern themselves increasingly with the exploitation of the inner nature of man and to devote a good deal of attention to the disturbed person's outlook on life. The result has been a great deal of experimentation with such stylistic devices as stream of consciousness, interior monologue, etc. Students who cannot follow such nuances will obviously have trouble grasping the contribution which certain characters have made to the story as a whole. When writers add conscious ambiguity to the statements, reflections, etc, of their characters, the untrained reader becomes further confused.

Anti-climactic endings add to the difficulty in interpreting significance in short fiction. The student who has read longer, conventionally written prose works becomes accustomed to the piling up of a welter of evidence leading to a decisive climax. He learns to anticipate such inexorably moving plots and thus may be irritated and disconcerted by the ending which offers no resolution or triumphal confrontation. Hemingway's *Killers* has often had this effect on my high school students. They are vexed by the utter futility evinced by the two main characters in the closing lines of the story.

In the light of all of these structural irregularities, the student who would become a careful and ultimately *satisfied* reader of well written short fiction must come to two major realizations. First, he must recognize that most short stories feature *compression* of idea. Much is said in a few words. Much is left for the reader to infer and relate to his own literal experience. A few lines in a short story can evolve a good deal of frequently wide ranging reaction, and ambiguity is always possible in interpretation. It is in the perception by the student of the significance of his compression of *idea and impression* that the reading of the short story can have value as a transitional activity.

Furthermore, because of compression, the great necessity for slow reading of this form must become gradually more evident to the student. He must move away from the casual inspection, the skimming which has probably characterized his reading of longer, conventionally structured novels. He must make meticulous notes of *each* part, regardless of how seemingly insignificant, as it relates to the whole. When the impact of compressed meaning is fully sensed by the student of literature and when slow, careful reflective reading becomes part of his approach, he may then be ready to joust with poetry, the most difficult literary form for him to read.

For several reasons, poetry presents the greatest obstacle to the teacher who would lead his students to the effective reading of literature. One immediate reason is that poetry, unlike prose fiction or drama, does not necessarily tell a story. Much of the poetry which young people must read even as early as junior high school, develops an abstract idea or establishes a proposition concerning human experience. Some poetry is not even idea-centered; it merely creates an aesthetic impression. Consider the effect of Ezra Pound's famous imagistic work "In a Station of the Metro:"

"The apparition of these faces in the crowd;
Petals on a wet, black bough."

The student who is looking for a story in this work is certainly doomed to disappointment. Because the *ways* of so many poems are simply not narrative ones, readers who are unprepared for this fact may well be troubled by a search which goes unrewarded. If you recall, Burton has reminded us that perception of aesthetic impact occurs in only a small minority of readers. In the poem just quoted there isn't really much else to be gained.

A further complication, in the study of this form, is that there is not much range in its difficulty levels. There is little or no *transitional* poetry. While the junior novel which I described a few moments ago has flourished during the past thirty years, the junior poem is still looking for a champion. Most poetry with which students must deal is based on adult situations, represents abstract themes, and is highly complex of structure when compared to the conventionally written novel. Since there is no appreciable fund of adolescent poetry to augment such instruction, the teacher must come to terms, and realistically so, with the reading problems which the medium presents. By "irregularity" I mean that the form of the work is so vastly different from that which students are accustomed to reading that it continues to frustrate a large number of them. It has been my belief for many years, incidentally, that teenage boys do not really reject poetry because it is "fairy stuff" or "fruity;" this opinion, I feel, has become an institutionalized rationalization. The major reason boys retreat from poetry is that poetry is difficult to read, and so many secondary-level boys are inefficient readers. To go further, much of the reason that poetry has failed to interest and relate to young readers in general is that teachers have often emphasized the wrong elements, have compulsively continued to putter about among the metrical ornaments of verse while neglecting to sense and deal with the real reading problems which the form presents.

Of the legion reading difficulties inherent in the poetic form I shall identify and illustrate only a few. What I would ask is that, as I catalog these difficulties, you continue to remember they are almost invariably occurring simultaneously in the work being studied. In other words, several aspects of the reading of a poem are troubling a student *at the same time.*

One obvious structural irregularity is that, in order to create impressions through rhythmical patterns, the appearance of lines of poetry differs sharply from those of prose fiction. In response to the charge that much of his poetry was difficult, the American poet, E. A. Robinson was once quoted as saying, "If they would only read my sentences!" Of course what Robinson has failed to mention was that many of the conventional characteristics of prose sentence structure are missing in poetry. Each poetic line is capitalized. Punctuation is irregular. Thoughts are often interrupted or ended *in medias res.* Lines are ended to accommodate rhyme rather than necessarily to facilitate syntactic flow. In fact, one of a young reader's major confusions in early bouts with poetry may stem from his wish to stay with the lilt of the poem rather than to pursue it primarily for *meaning.*

That's my last Duchess painted on the wall,
Looking as if she were alive. I call
That a piece of wonder, Now: Fra Pandolf's hands
Worked busily a day, and there she stands.
Will't please you sit and look at her? I said
"Fra Pandolf" by design, for never read
Strangers like you that pictured countenance,
The depth and passion of its earnest glance,
But to myself they turned (since none puts by
The curtain I have drawn for you, but I)
And seemed as they would ask me, if they durst,
How such a glance came there; so, not the first
Are you to turn and ask thus.

Now notice what happens when I take a slightly different tack in my reading:
    (Read above passage again.)
When metrical analysis and identification of rhyme scheme become issues of paramount importance in the teaching of poetry to young people, this kind of distorted reading can easily result.

Word order in sentence structure is a vital factor in the transmission of meaning in the English language. The linguists tell us that somewhere between 75-80 per cent of the sentences produced in our language follow the subject-verb-object pattern. Young readers are most comfortable reading sentences written in this pattern. Therefore, the inversion of word order, the abrupt inclusion of single word and/or phrase modifiers, and other such machinations will create reading problems for the uninitiated. Notice in this next poem by Walt Whitman the time it takes the poet to get to the subject of his discourse and the distance he puts between his subject and his verb.

Out of the cradle endlessly rocking,
Out of the mocking-bird's throat, the musical shuttle,
Out of the Ninth-month midnight,
Over the sterile sands and the fields beyond, where the
   child leaving his bed wander'd alone, bareheaded, barefoot,
Down from the shower'd halo.
Up from the mystic play of shadow twining and twisting as if they were alive,
Out from the patches of briers and blackberries,
From the memories of the bird that chanted to me,
From your memories sad brother, from the fitful risings and fallings I heard
From under that yellow half-moon late-risen and swollen as if with tears,
From those beginning notes of yearning and love there in the mist,
From the thousand responses of may heart never to cease,
From the myriad thence-arous'd words,
From the word stronger and more delicious than any,
From such as now they start the scene revisiting,
As a flock, twittering, rising, or overhead passing,
Borne hither, ere all eludes me, hurriedly,
A man, yet by these tears a little boy again,
Throwing myself on the sand, confronting the waves,
I, chanter of pains and joys, uniter of here and hereafter,
Taking all hints to use them, but swiftly leaping beyond them,
A reminiscence sing.

If we were to use a readability index which included the prepositional phrase factor to judge the level of difficulty of this poem, it would probably turn out to be pretty high.

    As in the work I have just read, sentences in poetry are quite frequently of outrageous length. From early reading and writing experiences, we stress with our students the need for control of sentence length. Reasonable sentence length is an important feature of basic reading materials. Most conventionally written prose fiction (I shall exclude the works of such people as William Faulkner and Henry James from this category) is exemplary of attention to control of length of syntactic expression. Not so in poetry. Here is the opening sentence, always a crucial one, from "Paradise Lost" which we all labored with back in the halcyon days of our youth.

Of man's first disobedience, and the fruit
Of that forbidden tree whose mortal taste
Brought death into the World, and all our woe,
With loss of Eden, till one greater Man
Restore us, and regain the blissful seat,

Sing, Heavenly Muse, that, on the secret top
Of Oreb, or of Sinai, didst inspire
That shepherd who first taught the chosen seed
In the beginning how the heavens and earth
Rose out of Chaos; or, if Sion hill
Delight thee more, and Siloa's brook that flowed
Fast by the oracle of God, I thence
Invoke they aid to my adventurous song,
That with no middle flight intends to soar
Above the Aonian mount, while it pursues
Things unattempted yet in prose or rime.

Certainly there are other problems here as well (I ask you once again to remember that all the problems I mention are present simultaneously), but it must be conceded that it takes a trained and aware reader to sustain understanding of the main idea in the sentence I have just read.

Poets also utilize unusual words, dialect, and historical allusions throughout much of their work. The ease of understanding of much verse is further reduced by expressions which appear in crucial places and are of central importance to the poet's purpose. In the third stanza of "Sailing to Byzantium," William Butler Yeats says

To sages standing in God's holy fire
As in the gold mosaic of a wall
Come from the fire, *pern in a gyre*
              (accent mine)

If you don't know ancient Celtic you probably won't understand what the critics tell us is a most important phrase not only in this work but to all of Yeats' poetic thought. Dialect can be particularly troublesome because it seldom occurs here and there but usually permeates the entire selection. In case you have forgotten, here is a slice of a poen by Robert Burns.

When chapman billies leave the street,
And drouthy neibors neibors meet;
As market days are wearing late,
And folk begin to tak the gate,
While we set bousing at the nappy,
An' getting fou and unco happy,
We think na on the lang Scots miles,
The mosses, waters, slaps and stiles,
That lie between us and our hame,
Where sits out sulky, sullen dame,
Gathering her brows like gathering storm,
Nursing her wrath to keep it warm.

Since the poem continues like this for several pages, and I have already demonstrated quite dramatically my ineptness with this stuff, I shall not proceed. It is important to remember, however, that in the study of English literature, dialect abounds in poetry written at least through the 17th century. *And this constitutes the first several months of study in an anthology-oriented senior high school course.* To deal effectively with the Burns poem, you must be able to handle the printed representation of late 18th century Scottish dialect.

Continual use of historical and mythological allusions is characteristic of renowned poets from all eras and of all nationalities. When such allusions are unclear to the student, he often fails to perceive both the idea that the poet is trying to communicate and the force with which it is conveyed. Here are the opening stanzas of Matthew Arnold's "Dover Beach."

The sea is calm tonight,
The tide is full, the moon lies fair
Upon the straits;–on the French coast the light
Gleams and is gone; the cliffs of England stand,
Glimmering and vast, out in the tranquil bay.
Come to the window, sweet is the night-air!
Only, from the long line of spray
Where the sea meets the moon-blanched land,
Listen! you hear the grating roar
Of pebbles which the waves draw back, and fling,
At their return, up the high strand,
Begin and cease, and then again begin,
With tremulous cadence slow, and bring
The eternal note of sadness in.
Sophocles long ago
Heard it on the Aegean, and it brought
Into his mind the turbid ebb and flow
Of human misery; we
Find also in the sound a thought,
Hearing it by this distant northern sea.

Notice that the first stanza is straight, relatively clear description. Slow careful reading should be enough to comprehend both the situation and to infer the *mood*. Arnold, however, sees fit, at the beginning of the stanza immediately following, to allude to a major tragedian from classical antiquity. Thus, if the student doesn't know who Sophocles was and, more important, what his religious beliefs were, that vitally important allusion will confuse rather than clarify. And don't forget, it happens that there is only one such allusion in the poem I just read from. Where would we be in treating "The Waste Land" if we didn't know all truth about Eastern and Western culture through the ages?

Logically, we can next turn to the whole matter of figurative language in poetry which has always presented great obstacles to understanding for all but the most sophisticated of readers. Certainly one of the main problems in reading this form is that poets juxtapose unusual objects and ideas with great frequency. Eliot's comparing of an evening sky with an etherized patient in "The Love Song of J. Alfred Prufrock" is probably by now one of the truly classic examples of this. Whenever meaning is to be conveyed by allusion, a potential problem in communication exists. In setting up his association, the writer hopes that by comparing something less familiar (his main object or idea) with something *more* familiar to the reader, that the former will then become more easily perceived. The real problem exists in the fact that the reader (and particularly the *young* reader) may not be as familiar with the part of the allusion which the writer hoped him to be. Thus, if the reader cannot conjure up a lucid and complete image of an etherized patient, then Eliot's comparison is done for in this instance, and the poet has confused where he hoped to clarify.

Much can be done, I would contend, in the analytical teaching of figurative language to help less mature readers with problems in understanding such as I have just described. If we would teach *metaphor* for what it is, a basic and widespread means of conveying information and ideas, then our students would probably have a better chance to work with it successfully when it occurs in poetry. As S. I. Hayakawa has been saying for years, metaphor is a fundamental component of our language. In everyday speech we juxtapose the unusual for clarification, emphasis, our language. In everyday speech we juxtapose the unusual for clarification, emphasis, variety, humor. We say, "I'm dying to meet him," or "This box weighs a ton," or "They're in another world." Too much time, however, is spent by teachers in identifying terms such as simile, metaphor, and personification purely as ornaments of poetry. Students memorize definitions of them in the works they read. If these same youngsters were shown the omnipresence of metaphor in *their* language and the relationship of the figurative which occurs in everyday discourse to that found in the poetic work, they would probably understand a greater number of the allusions in selections they are assigned to read.

One thing is sure; we must teach the significant place which metaphor occupies in the search for meaning in poetry. There is virtually no poetic language which is totally devoid of the figurative. It is a chief device by which a poet compresses meaning as he crowds a good deal of thought provoking allusion into a superficially simple figure.

As time closes in and coughs when I would expound, I wish to mention one final feature, found in much verse, that if overlooked by the reader will most certainly weaken the impact of the work on him. Most writers of poetry quite often employ single words and patterns of words for the purpose of evoking emotional reaction largely through tonal effects of these words and patterns. Here is a short poem, "Dead Boy," by John Crowe Ramson in which, I believe, we have an example of such a device.

The little cousin is dead, by foul subtraction,
A green bough from Virginia's aged tree,
And none of the county kin like the transaction
Nor some of the world of outer dark, like me.
A boy not beautiful, nor good, nor clever,
A black cloud full of storms too hot for keeping,
A sword beneath his mother's heart-yet never
Woman bewept her babe as this is weeping.
A pig with a pasty face, so I had said.
Squealing for cookies, kinned by pure pretense
With a noble house. But the little man quite dead,
I can see the forebears' antique lineaments.
The elder men have strode by the box of death
To the wide flag porch, and muttering low send round
The bruit of the day. Of friendly waste of breath!
Their hearts are hurt with a deep dynastic wound.
He was pale and little, the foolish neighbors say;
The first-fruits, saith the Preacher, the Lord hath taken;
But this was the old tree's late branch wrenched away,
Grieving the sapless limbs, the shorn and shaken.

If the reader does not respond to the grating, rasping sound made by "old tree's late branch wrenched away" in the next to last line of the final stanza and the quiet closing provided by the sibilants "s" and "sh" in the final line, then, in my opinion, he has missed something. But, it must be remembered that this kind of appreciative reaction may not come to large numbers of students. As teachers, we may help our students through an inductive approach to realize the significance of such juxtaposition for themselves, but we cannot and should not teach by edict. It goes without saying that effective oral reading by the teacher could be a great influence in areas of poetic consideration such as this.

During this discussion I have tried to point out the pitfalls apparent in the teaching of reading of literature in general and of poetry in particular. I hope that by some of my remarks, I have indicated means of dealing with these difficulties. These things we know: that poetry is "hard" in part, at least, because it has a narrow range of difficulty: *i.e.,* most of it is tough to comprehend; further, that meaning in poetry is greatly compressed, thus calling for slow reading, frequent rereading, and much associative activity; also, that poetry is most irregular in structure, that it *looks* different from conventionally printed matter thereby forcing the reader frequently to reconstruct it mentally into "ordinary" dress in order to gain its meaning. And that, finally, the several aspects of difficulty in poetry are usually functioning at the same time, thus adding to the complexity of our teaching task. Maybe, by applying Burton's three-step process of induction, we can help puzzled and discontent students with heretofore baffling works. Maybe by moving systematically from the more conventional to increasingly irregular literary structures, we can assist the student in making the most of his *strengths* in reading. Maybe by using both of these plus a little individual attention, we can lead students to the point where they will say, "Hey, I like this one," and really mean it.

Reading*

HELEN HUUS

The ability to read is a complex process that is basic not only to education in school, but also to the acquisition of many out-of-school learnings. Although the Western World has attained a fairly high standard of literacy, there are still misconceptions regarding the nature of reading.

Reading is not merely recognizing the printed symbols and pronouncing the words correctly; it is not merely being able to reproduce verbatim or in digested or summarized form what the author has stated; it is, as Strang, McCullough, and Traxler state, "more than seeing words clearly, more than pronouncing printed words correctly, more than recognizing the meaning of individual words. Reading requires us to think, feel, and use our imagination. Effective reading is purposeful. The use one makes of his reading largely determines what he reads, why he reads, and how he reads."[1]

If a broad concept of reading is accepted, the line between reading and thinking becomes only faintly drawn. While all thinking is not reading, all reading will require thinking. Where the dividing line occurs is not within the province of this chapter; nor are all aspects of reading discussed here, for some are found elsewhere in this book. Here emphasis is placed upon vocabulary development, rate of reading, formation of relationships, and wide reading.

Reading itself has no content of its own. It is principally a skill or process by which ideas on the printed page become the reader's own. The ideas may be drawn from a variety of fields, as science, history, geography, sociology, anthropology, mathematics, and art. What makes reading important is its function as the vehicle by which the authors of any age communicate their ideas to contemporary and succeeding generations.

Since the social studies courses in schools today draw from many different disciplines and sources, the need for students to be competent readers assumes added significance. So much of the information in social studies comes from

---

*Reprinted from *Skill Development in the Social Studies,* 33rd Yearbook of the National Council for the Social Studies 1963, pp. 94-114, by permission of the author and the National Council for the Social Studies.

[1] Strang, Ruth; McCullough, Constance M.; and Traxler, Arthur E. *The Improvement of Reading.* New York: McGraw-Hill Book Co., 1961. p. 1.

books, magazines, newspapers, pamphlets, government reports, and other printed sources dealing with a wide range of subjects that the student must put his reading skills to use if he is to acquire the background he needs to make judgments and generalizations.

Reading not only contributes to the background of information of the student and gives him practice in using the skills he has, but this background becomes, in turn, the springboard for expanding his knowledge and further enriching him. Thus the dual purpose of information and motivation is served. In addition, attitudes may be developed, reinforced, or changed through reading; and students can become acquainted with the literary heritage and cultivate a lasting interest in personal reading.

The ability to read is important for the student's success in social studies work. According to Fay, at least fourth grade reading ability is needed for social studies reading in the middle grades (four to six).[2] Rudolf found that eighth grade students who had been given specially prepared materials on certain reading skills showed greater gains in social studies knowledge, study skills, and reading comprehension than a comparable group that had no such help.[3] In a study of eleventh grade students of American history, Aukerman found that good history students were better in general reading ability than poor history students, and that social studies achievement and the ability to find the main idea of a paragraph were related to general reading ability.[4] These are but a few of the studies that show the relation between social studies and reading and emphasize the necessity for good reading habits on the part of students.

Problems of Reading in the Social Studies

While there are certain skills and abilities necessary for good general reading — such as word-analysis techniques, vocabulary and paragraph comprehension, and library skills — some of the reading skills and abilities are especially pertinent to the social studies, though many are also important in reading any specialized subject matter. The special applications lie in two directions — in the material to be read and in the reader himself.

THE READING MATERIAL

Most textbooks in social studies make heavy demands on the reader because of the number of concepts introduced in a relatively small space. The

[2]Fay, Leo C. "What Research Has to Say About Reading in the Content Areas." *The Reading Teacher* 8:68-72, 112; December 1954.

[3]Rudolf, Kathleen Brady. *The Effect of Reading Instruction on Achievement in Eighth Grade Social Studies.* Contributions to Education, No. 945. New York: Bureau of Publications, Teachers College, Columbia University, 1949. 72 pp. plus 12 unnumbered pp.

[4]Aukerman, Robert C. "The Reading Status of Good and Poor Eleventh Grade American History Students." *Social Education* 11:351-53; December 1947.

background needed by the reader to interpret briefly noted events, places, and ideas is greater than most students possess, and as a result, difficulties occur. Because the information is not explained or expanded, much of it becomes mere verbalism without images or meaning.

Another reason for difficulty in reading in social studies stems from the rapidly changing nature of the material. What becomes printed today will in a short time be past history. Two difficulties result: the lack of perspective in viewing material that was prepared in the heat of the moment before the long view could be seen, and the fact that the content will soon be superseded by a current commentary. Information regarding prehistoric life is a good example, for as methods of discoveries are made (such as the exposure of the Piltdown man hoax), the previously known facts must be reviewed and reorganized. Yet rarely are clues to the relative importance of ideas given except in the gradations of type faces used in the headings in most textbooks. Students who have access only to limited and out-of-date sources will suffer as a result.

Still a third difficulty with social studies materials is its complicated style of presentation. Sentences are not only packed with information; but may be long and involved; they may use inverted order; or they may include allusions and figures of speech that need interpretation. In addition, the vocabulary load is very high, for many words are used only once or twice and thus do not give enough repetition to become fixed in the student's mind. Furthermore, technical words are often defined in such a complex manner (either in the text itself, in the glossary, or in the dictionary) that it is difficult for students to ferret out the meaning. Shortened forms, such as abbreviations, letters like NDEA or OEEC, or the symbols used in tables, and the new forms accompanying documentation, such as italics, footnotes, and bibliographical citations, need special attention even for good readers. While these problems are not unique to social studies materials, they do pose difficulties for students.

Since social studies material is usually written by experts who are committed to their field of interest, what they put in textbooks is of interest to them but may not be of much interest to students who read it. In the middle grades, the objective approach in the writing is also a departure from the kind of material which most of the pupils have used in learning to read, and consequently adjusting from fiction with characters and story content to factual material becomes another hurdle. The problem is further complicated in that the factual material usually deals with events which are removed from the pupil either in space or time.

Instead of dealing with the here and now or the immediate community, pupils read about explorations of the 16th century, or of colonial America, or of Latin America today. In higher grades, the curriculum includes other areas of the world — the Far East, Australia, Africa — that are remote from firsthand experiences of the majority, and other times — prehistoric man or the age of the vikings — that are difficult for students to conceptualize. Although textbook publishers have made notable efforts to provide interesting, well-illustrated books for social studies, often space limitations restrict that amount of detail and explanation that can be included, and the treatment of the topic is all too brief.

While the inclusion of much graphic material adds to the meaning, it may also pose problems in reading. The legends under the photographs may require deciphering, for often these have been streamlined to conserve space. The references to other pages in the textbook, or to "Fig. 1" (which sometimes is never explained but eventually comes to be interpreted as "Figure 1"), or to maps and charts found on other pages, or to statistics and tabular data need explanation and practice in interpretation if they are to serve their best use.[5]

Thus it appears that many of the difficulties found in social studies reading lie in the materials themselves. Hence, it behooves teachers carefully to select material which will provide for the best understanding by the pupils.

THE READER HIMSELF

Other limitations in reading are inherent in the reader himself – his intelligence, his background of information, his vocabulary and command of sophisticated language patterns, his attitudes and value pattern. The nature of the material to be read demands of the reader sufficient intelligence and background not only to derive literal meanings but also to infer hidden meanings and to make applications from what is read.

Intellectual ability is required for a reader to sift facts from opinion, to analyze the point of view from which the author is writing, to be aware of biases (both his own and the author's), and to recognize when enough facts have been presented that a valid conclusion can be drawn. His background of information serves as a reservoir from which concepts are recognized, recalled, and compared with the content being read in order to make the meaning clear. Practice is necessary to obtain competence in these skills of inference and application, and even students with a high level of intellectual capacity need instruction in order to acquire such competence.

Studies show that readers tend to remember best those facts and ideas that reinforce their own views and to reject or ignore material on other sides of an issue, whether it be political, religious, racial, or ethical.[6] The development of attitudes and the acquisition of information are, to a great extent, dependent upon firsthand experiences. As attitudes are gradually acquired and as value patterns unconsciously begin to take shape with increasing age, young people

---

[5] Other problems involved in learning to read graphic material are discussed in Chapter XI.

[6] Crossen, Helen Jameson. *Effect of Attitudes of the Reader upon Critical Reading Ability.* Chicago: Department of Education, University of Chicago, 1946. 133 pp.; Eller, William, and Dykstra, Robert. "Persuasion and Personality: Readers' Predispositons as a Factor in Critical Reading." *Elementary English* 36:191-97, 202; March 1959.

bring to their reading the products of their heredity and environment – their family and friends, their neighborhood and community, their state and nation. The approach they take, the interpretations they can make, and the ideas they accept or reject are permeated by their feelings and beliefs.

What the reader obtains from his reading and thinking about what is read is difficult to assess completely. Tangible evidence of the effect of reading, however, can be seen in behavior such as willingness to share, improvement in social courtesies, interest in civic improvements, and concern with national and international issues.

If reading is an important means of social studies learning, if the materials for social studies present unique problems in reading, and if the reader is the product of his heredity and past experiences, what can a teacher do to help? The school offers many opportunities for teachers to guide students in developing reading skills as achievement in social studies progresses; especially important are the skills of vocabulary development, rate of reading, formation of relationships, and extension of reading. These skills are discussed in the sections that follow.

Types of Difficulty

Problems in the social studies vocabulary are principally those of pronunciation and meaning. In the first category are the many proper names met for the first time: in primary grades, names like Pilgrim, Puritan, Samoset, Massasoit, Plymouth Colony, Massachusetts Bay, and Elder Brewster; in the middle grades, words like Antarctic, Amazon, Switzerland, Colorado, Illinois, and Arkansas; in junior high, such words as Indonesia, Saudi Arabia, Angola, Committee of Correspondence, and Reconstruction; and in senior high or college, words like Aristotle, Attila, Renaissance, and Byzantine. It matters not at what level the word is first met; correct pronunciation and definite meaning are still required.

In addition to proper names, terms like *shelter, community, patriotic, interdependence, transportation, industrial, guild, conservation, colonization, imperialism,* and many others need to be interpreted. Students need to learn to use word-recognition techniques – context clues, analysis of structure, and phonetic elements-and to check their best estimates against the authority of a glossary or the dictionary. In many schools today, students are given adequate help in learning to unlock words of one syllable, but so many of the words in social studies have more than one. All too many children have no systematic method by which they can analyze multisyllabic words and arrive at a reasonable pronunciation. Giving help on recognition skills is the responsibility of teachers, even of those above the beginning levels; secondary teachers, too, need to check the recognition skills to detect areas of need. This is true even when helps for pronunciation are included in the material.

Students should be helped to recognize known word elements like prefixes, roots, and suffixes; once the word is thus stripped down to the chassis and the framework located, the synthesis can proceed systematically. Take the word "Alhambra," for example: Students can subdivide it into syllables, and those who know that divisions are usually made between double consonants will have no hesitancy. They figure out "Al-ham-bra" and proceed from there. Or take the word "Indonesia": Using the same generalization, the first syllable becomes "In," and the pupil who knows the generalization that a syllable usually ends *before* a single consonant will be able to separate the word into "In-do-ne-sia." If he knows that a syllable ending with a vowel is usually long, he should be able to arrive at a fair pronunciation, which he can check against his own experience or against a glossary or the dictionary.

Teachers who work with grades above the third would be wise to include in their word study the variations in pronunciation due to derivations from Greek, Latin, French, Spanish, or German. Just a few generalizations will aid the student, and the teaching can be done when the various countries are studied for the first time.

For many words in social studies the pupil already has at least one meaning, but not the meaning that fits the situation — words like *branch, cape, mouth, source, range, plain, belt, cancer, gap, pan,* and *quarter.* To extend the pupil's vocabulary so that he acquires additional meanings is both important and necessary. Too often however, both teachers and pupils skip over known words, assuming the meaning to be clear, but pupils who are taught to demand meaning from the very start will check words that appear not to make sense when met in a new context.

To complicate matters still further, some words shift their meanings in the same selection, and the reader must keep abreast of the changes. Most usual of these shifts are the pronouns *it* and *that* which shift their referents, or words like *regular* when applied to winds, mountain ranges, trade routes, or the army.

But the most complicated of the vocabulary problems stems from the myriads of new words — words unknown both in pronunciation and in meaning. Here the reader must apply his word-recognition techniques to acquire pronunciation, then use context to try to define meaning. Later he can check against the glossary or dictionary, or he can use what association he has and continue reading to see if the concept will clarify itself. If he uses the dictionary, he may need to try several of the meanings for "fit" before he finds the one that suits. When the vocabulary load becomes burdensome because of the large number of new words, it is easier for students to skip along, hoping that the meaning will be clarified in later discussions with little effort on their part. This becomes the plight of the slow learner and the poor reader, and eventually, when the vocabulary load has become too large, they simply quit trying to read.

A recent issue of *National Geographic,* a magazine often used in the secondary school as well as in upper elementary grades, contains the following unusual words or phrases in the space of a few pages in an article on New Zealand:[7] "Rotorua," "thermal district," "Polynesia," "cold tussock deserts," "Thames," "Chelsea," "nomad," "after a spell in Spain," "bush," "kauri gum," 'kiwi," "Maori," "Cape Maria van Dieman," "*Heemskerck*," and "Governor General." Some of these terms ("bush," the "thermal," and "spell") are known words whose meanings can be inferred from context. Others, however, such as "tussock," meaning a "tuft of growing grass," are likely to become intelligible only through use of the dictionary. Words like "Cape Maria van Dieman" and "*Heemskerck*" require some knowledge of foreign pronunciation. The necessarily heavy vocabulary load of materials that deal with foreign cultures or time past complicates the process of reading and learning.

To add to the difficulty, there are phrases and abstract terms that require interpretation, such as "the Crown's representative," "flung lonely, as by some giant hand," "a treasure locked in vast ocean," "gift of the sea," "dominion," "sovereignty," and "eating up 2000 acres of good farmland." To make sense from these in context demands attention and concentration, plus bringing to bear the pertinent past experiences.

Practical Aids for Vocabulary Development

Many opportunities for providing direct experience as an aid in understanding the meanings of words and phrases are at hand for the teacher who can recognize them. In the primary grades, classes can take excursions into the community to such places as the bus station, the grocery store, and the airport to see at first hand some of the service units and agencies. On their return to school, the pupils can make charts containing a list of the new words learned, and the charts can be continued as they learn additional words that fit into the same context. Firsthand experiences of this kind also clarify children's concepts of abstract terms and relationships, such as the processes employed in distributing mail or in putting out a newspaper, the work done by various employees, the physical environment in which work is done, and the specialized equipment that is necessary.

While the purpose of the educational excursion may be the same for the various grade levels, the length and complexity of a tour will increase with the age of the students. Even though pupils at all levels may visit the airport, for example, those in the higher grades acquire information in more areas and in greater detail and abstraction, learn more technical terms, and understand more complex relationships, such as the financial aspects or the airport's contribution to community economics, than do children in the primary grades.

[7]Shadbolt, Maurice. "New Zealand: Gift of the Sea." *National Geographic* 121: 465-511; April 1962.

The middle grades also profit from somewhat more complex excursions to the dairy, factory, newspaper offices, and docks, while secondary school students may take a day's trip to a nearby historical site, a museum, a governmental agency, or a city. Some schools have provided student exchanges for several days at a time with another school in another city.

Other types of firsthand experiences that increase meaning vocabulary can be acquired by students at all levels without leaving the classroom. Inviting visitors to come to the class, or having an exhibit relating to units being studied, gives students a chance to hear explanations or see products and specimens that clarify meanings. When they were studying Mexico, one sixth grade class collected a serape, a sombrero, horses made of straw, silver jewelry, glassware, pottery, hand-embroidered blouses, and other objects made by Mexicans. These same objects could have been used by a third grade or a tenth grade for an exhibit of *their* study of Mexico, but the arrangement, the relationships, and the labels and legends for the various items would vary with the purpose and the maturity of the learners.

When firsthand experience is impractical or impossible, simulated experiences that come as close as possible to reality will serve the purpose. The many filmstrips, films, recordings, models, pictures, pictorial maps, graphs, and charts are in this category. Let the teacher add these to put meaning into the printed symbols and to give the student a feeling of actually living in another place or during another era.

Helpful also, and it requires no additional materials, is the use of discussion, explanation, or exposition to clarify and extend vocabulary and meaning. Helping children make associations between what they already know and what is new can aid not only in understanding, but also in remembering, if the presentation has been vivid enough. Teachers should create or locate colorful, clear explanations, examples, and analogies that help the pupil understand new terms, new information, and new ideas, so that these become real enough for him to identify himself with the situations. The teacher will need to decide how many of the terms and ideas in one lesson he should explain and which are the ones most needed by the pupils. The number will depend upon the complexity of the ideas and the rate at which they are introduced, but there is danger of misunderstanding or confusion when too many terms are introduced too fast.

Some teachers get good results in vocabulary development by encouraging pupils to keep individual lists of interesting or difficult words. In the primary grades this might take the form of a picture dictionary, while in later grades it could become part of a larger word-study project where derivations are discussed and related words coming from the same root (*script, describe, conscription, inscription, subscription,* and *scribe,* for example), are listed. Pupils extend their vocabularies by repeated use of new words, and opportunities to utilize them in exercises or in compositions should be provided. Regular use of the glossary and dictionary and special exercises employing aids are other ways to improve vocabulary, and teachers can sometimes use a series of words from social studies as a spring-board. For example, *government, parliament, capital, kingdom, empire, republic, nation,* and *country* are terms that need to be distinguished, and a glossary or the dictionary can be used to advantage to compare the specific meanings and to help children develop accurate concepts.

Junior and senior high school students might construct other lists containing certain types of words, such as "fighting words"; or words connoting speed, prestige, depression, or other emotional reactions. Study of words of this type is basic to detecting how authors create mood or tone in such materials as editorials, advertising, or reports of political activities. Helping students recognize and interpret these is a teacher responsibility that continues through graduate courses.

If students can get meaning from words in context, they have the basic element for interpreting what they read. Without the basic building blocks, however, this skill cannot be developed.

Adjusting or Adapting Rate of Reading

A reader's rate of reading is affected by his mental capacity and basic reading skills, his familiarity with the field of study, and the level of difficulty of the material, as well as by his purpose for reading. Versatile, mature readers will vary the speed according to their purposes. A slight story in a popular magazine will not be read at the same rate as study material in a social studies textbook. Neither will all parts of the newspaper, such as the editorials, the advertisments, or other features that are of interest to the reader at the moment, be read with the same intensity.

Different rates from the fastest to the slowest have been variously labeled, but there appears to be general agreement that there are at least four levels in rate of reading: (1) skimming, (2) cursory reading, (3) study reading, and (4) critical reading.

Skimming

The most rapid kind of reading consists of merely looking for key words in order to locate the exact place where information may be found, to obtain a general survey, or bird's-eye view, of a longer selection before settling down to read it carefully, or to determine whether the selection is relevant to the problem under consideration. Location skimming is used primarily in reference work with dictionaries, atlases, encyclopedias, almanacs, or directories, while survey skimming is used to decide what the framework of the article is and what parts are pertinent to the problem at hand.

For example, teachers can ask students to make a list of topics covered in the sections about Central and Southern Africa found in their textbooks or in an encyclopedia article on Africa, and then to indicate which part of the lesson or article deals with certain aspects of the topic, such as coffee production in Ethiopia, the industries of South Africa, or the importance of Johannesburg or Cape Town.

Even first-graders can skim to find answers to questions on material they have read, to locate specific words on a page, to "find the part that tells. . . " or to review word-recognition skills. Later, elementary school pupils use skimming to locate words in the dictionary, places on maps, articles or sections of articles in the encyclopedia, or to hunt for such elusive data as dates, amounts of money, exact quotations, and the like. They use survey skimming to learn the length of an assignment, to see the general headings of the main parts of the lesson, or to find the part they want to read. In junior and senior high school the same skills are used, only the contents become more varied and increase in difficulty. This is true of nearly every skill in reading that can be mentioned: The beginnings lie in the primary grades, and problems of learning are different in degree, not in kind, from the primary grades through secondary school and college. This is contrary to a widely held but incorrect idea that the process of teaching reading skills moves in a sequence which introduces problems requiring higher levels of thinking at later grades, rather than one which permits the five- and six-year-olds to grapple with these problems at their level of development.

Asking pupils to "look" for the "part that tells. . . " rather than to "read" until they find the "part that tells. . . " is often helpful in getting them to skip around in the print. Suggestions that they use such clues as a specific word (like "lumbering"), capital letters, dates, italicized words, words in quotations or in boldface type, guide words, or headings are also hints that may prove useful to them. In the long run, skimming contributes to good study habits, for it saves wasting time and energy on irrelevant material and facilitates the location of pertinent information.

Cursory Reading

Cursory reading, also, is used at all grade levels. In this type of reading, pupils read a selection through once as rapidly as they can, skipping over unknown words and pressing on to obtain a general overview or the main idea. This is akin to skimming but requires the reading of main units in more detail than skimming does. Cursory reading is also useful as a review of previously read material in order to make a summary, to generalize, to validate impressions, to check on the main idea, to formulate questions on the material, or to determine the relevance of the whole to the problem at hand. When pupils have trouble in acquiring the necessary rhythm to "scoot along" in cursory reading, it may be helpful to give them much easy material spaced in thought units or to have them pick out the thought units or groups of words in a selection that may be seen at one look.

Primary grade children use this type of reading when they read to dramatize a story, when they reread to choose their favorite story, or when they read to formulate questions of their own. Middle-graders often utilize cursory reading as the first step in their study, as recommended by the "Survey, Question, Read, Recite, Review" (SQ3R) technique. In secondary school, and to a greater degree in college, the rate of reading becomes increasingly important as the assignments increase in length. Students with poor word-recognition techniques, who are word-by-word readers, and who lack a background of experience necessary for easy comprehension will find their rates of reading much too low for academic success or efficient study habits. Practical exercises in word attack, phrase reading, and firsthand experiences or browsing in well-illustrated books, looking at informational films and using other visual aids are ways to improve reading rate indirectly. Once basic skills are attained, timed reading aids in increasing speed, but unless basic skills are established first, reading under the pressure of time will not bring the desired result in speed without loss of comprehension.

Study Reading

Study reading is a third type of reading to which rate must be adjusted at any grade level. This type of reading is done to obtain the greatest possible understanding, such as reading to visualize a scene, to comprehend directions, to follow an argument, to make an outline, to prepare a play, to get information for making a mural, to write entries for a fictitious diary, to take an open-book examination, or just to remember and organize what has been read. Teachers can have young children draw a scene that is described in the story; older pupils can construct dioramas, from miniature size in a shoe box to the almost life size demanded for stage scenery.

Most of all, however, students need to be able to read with optimum speed and concentration as they prepare their daily class assignments. In the middle grades, pupils can be helped to note how the structure they found as they were skimming the selection is completed with explanation, elaboration, and example, and how the parts fit together to make the whole. They can perceive how events build up to a climax — whether it be a revolution, a new discovery, or the fall of an empire — then list the significant events in order to see the gradual, logical progression. With such understanding, making an outline is merely putting these ideas down in written form according to a prescribed pattern. Without this understanding, outlining becomes merely a confused listing of topics identified by numbers and letters.

Many activities that follow from reading can be accomplished only when pupils have paid attention to the details in the lesson and have remembered them. This type of reading is an essential tool for effective study, and unless it can be done with enough ease and speed to keep abreast of assignments, achievement will suffer.

Critical Reading

Critical, or reflective, reading proceeds at the slowest rate of all, for here the reader pauses to recall and associate, to reflect and compare, to ponder over an apt saying and appreciate the author's purpose. This kind of reading is typical of readers who savor what they read and hesitate to quit, for they are truly making what they read their own.

Critical reading begins in the primary grades when children are given a chance to relate what they read to their own experiences. They compare the farms in the stories with those they have seen, or the contributions of community helpers with their own policemen, firemen, and postmen. Even at this level they can use several sources for their information, note similarities and differences, and decide which book gives them the clearest and most complete and interesting information.

In the later elementary grades, pupils can note relationships, images, or feelings identified by allusions and references like *Spice Island, Kaiser, Caesar, czar,* and *the bread basket of America.* In secondary schools, as students delve into the whole realm of adult writings, they are faced with even more complex patterns of style. Secondary school students, too, need to track down allusions, to note the emotional appeal of words like *colossal, incredible, elegant, infallible, extravagant, restless, oppressed, poverty-stricken,* and *harsh,* and to recognize the author's point of view and purpose. Is he trying to convert or debunk? Is he presenting factual information or only his opinion? Is his style direct and straightforward, or is he writing "tongue in cheek?" These are only a few of the kinds of analyses that critical reading requires. Others are discussed in the following section.[8]

In each of the four types of reading discussed above, teachers should encourage students to read at their optimum rate without comprehension loss. While improvement of rate of reading is not the crucial skill in the elementary school that it becomes in secondary school and college, nevertheless attention to the four types of reading and the purpose of each should aid a student in adjusting his rate for each purpose which, in turn, should improve his study habits.

[8] See also Chapters III and V.

Forming Relationships

Basic to the acquisition of concepts through reading in social studies or in any field of study is the ability to recognize the way in which the material is organized, whether in sequence or logically, and to see the relationships that are stated directly or implied; to analyze connections between events so that inferences can be made as to cause and effect; to form mental images of space and distance; to recall and make judgments from the perspective gained by combining past experiences with present knowledge; and to see similarities between what is read with what has been previously experienced or determine what can be applied to present-day life. The remainder of this section describes a few ways by which such relationships can be developed.

RELATIONSHIPS INHERENT IN ORGANIZATION

Unlike stories typically found in many basic readers, social studies content may be written in an objective, reportorial fashion, which presents an account of events as they occurred. In the lower grades, pupils can obtain practice in understanding the idea of sequence by retelling stories or events in order, by giving directions, and by making picture charts, flow charts showing events in a series, or time lines with appropriate notations in the right segments. Children's understanding of chronology is thought to develop relatively slowly, and it is not until the child is 11 or 12 that he begins to have a clear notion of chronology, and then only for a limited span. Time lines in the fourth grade do show pupils relative position, but the relation between the early explorations and the late 19th century is still quite vague to most of them.

In lower grades, studying a specific period, such as "Pioneer Days in the Middle West" or "Children of Colonial Days," helps pupils obtain a feeling of what it might have been like to have lived then, and to realize that the people who did live then are not necessarily to be pitied or envied, but rather to be understood. When the period being studied can be related to the child personally, perhaps to his own family or to the local area, a firsthand connection of this kind can be most useful in concept development. By secondary school age, some students may be sufficiently interested in family genealogy to trace their own heritage and relate it to historical development.

As the pupil gradually fits together the pieces of history he has been studying, he assembles in the mosaic of his memory a picture of the development of civilization. By the time he reaches high school and college, not only should he understand the chronological development of various segments of the world, but he should be able to see the cross-sectional view as well.

The logical development of an idea by the building-up of a reasonable line of argument can be begun with materials for the primary grades and continued on to adult books. Students can tell whether main ideas succeed each other in proper order, whether one idea evolves from the preceding idea, whether all ideas are substantiated, explained, or expanded with appropriate detail.[9] It should be emphasized, however, that the beginnings of the concept underlying logical organization can be started even before children learn to read — as they classify objects and ideas at home or in kindergarten. In the first grade, children can make simple outlines of main ideas in one column and the appropriate details in another column, by helping make a group outline, or by making a mental outline of the three (or more) things to say when given a chance in "Show and Tell."

Primary grade children, like older ones, can also write sentence or short paragraph summaries, and can note signals like *first, second,* and *third* that give warning when the author is about to make a shift. Later on, such signals include words like *next, then, another, finally, moreover, yet, still, at last, meanwhile, furthermore,* and *later.*[10]

In secondary school, even more subtle hints of shift in topic can be pointed out, such as the phrases *on the other hand, in addition to, opposing this,* and *in contrast to.* Individual students could be encouraged to keep a list of such phrases, or the class might compile a master list from their collective efforts.

CAUSE-EFFECT RELATIONSHIPS

Seeing the connection between events and results is basic to the interpretation of facts in the social studies. Such relationships may be chronological, and students at any age can make double-column charts lining up events on one side and results on the other, or make a list of events as they build toward a climax.

Beginning in the middle grades, an understanding of cause and effect in geography can result from studying a physical map and noting how features such as terrain, coast line, drainage basins, and relative location may be helpful in predicting population centers, occupations the land can support, and what product will probably be available for trade. With the addition of temperature, rainfall, and prevailing wind data, students should be able to make even more accurate predictions, which can then be checked against political maps and industrial and commerical statistics. Making such an analysis of a map not only gives students practice in seeing relationships, but also shows them a method for making logical deductions from data and for interrelating several items of data in order to arrive at a conclusion.

[9]See Chapter V, which treats this topic more fully.
[10]Cansler, Gleamon. "Readiness for Reading in Content Fields." *The Reading Teacher* 8:73-77; December 1954.

SPACE-AND-DISTANCE RELATIONSHIPS

The relationships of space and distance, both on the surface of the earth and in the atmosphere, also come within the scope of social studies content. The beginnings of these concepts can be found in the lower grades as pupils compare the distances they travel to school, to the shopping center, to church, or to the city. They make maps of local neighborhoods, put these on the floor and suddenly see their community as a whole. Later, they study road maps, physical and political maps, product and rainfall maps, and maybe even hydrographic and astronomical charts, and compare distances on these with what they already know. They build mental images of space but not always too clearly: even adults have difficulty in grasping how far away the sun, moon, and planets really are, or the relative distance between San Diego and Seattle as compared with that between New York and Minneapolis. Such a simple technique as using a piece of string and a globe can show the reason why a great circle route appears curved on a flat map. Using maps with various projections and comparing distances with those on the globe helps students understand the distortion inherent in most flat projections. All of these activities aid students in their acquisition of ideas about space and distance.[11]

RELATIVE IMPORTANCE OF IDEAS

Determining the relative importance of several main ideas found in a selection or judging which of several causes are the crucial ones requires not only an effective reading approach but intelligence as well. Primary grade children have practice in this when they first choose main ideas in stories heard or read, then line up the ideas in sequence and decide what the story is about. They also have experience in placing concepts in more general categories: so "community" may be a larger grouping than "town" or "farm," and "city" is a larger grouping than "neighborhood" or "shopping center."

At higher grade levels, importance may be determined by having students analyze events and decide the "point of no return" in the procession toward a goal or action. In retrospect, students can interpret and speculate on what might have happened. For example, suppose Marco Polo had not gone to China: How long might it have taken to create widespread interest among Europeans in products from the Orient?

Relative importance may be judged in another manner by reading accounts from more than one source and noting which events are always mentioned and which are sometimes omitted. Frequency of mention does not necessarily indicate importance; yet the very fact that several writers deem an event of sufficient consequence to be elaborated does aid students in judging importance.

---

[11]These and other aspects of developing skill in understanding concepts of place and space are discussed in Chapter IX.

Such comparisons can be started in primary grades as pupils pursue a unit using several sources, including both trade books and textbooks. The learning can be carried forward through elementary school, secondary school, and into college as students read widely and compare. It is only from such a background that valid techniques for judging importance can be fostered, and teachers should aid students in developing a perspective from the limited view they possess.

APPLICATION TO PERSONAL EXPERIENCE

Still another way of seeing relationships is to apply what has been read to personal experiences — for validation, assimilation, enjoyment, or utilization. Young children read stories of airplane trips, relate these to their own experience with airplanes and airports, then build the images into a mental framework in which each individual may visualize sequence along a kind of horizontal time line, with specific reference points of significance to him, or on a vertical pattern with steps or stages progressing upward according to defined levels — perhaps by centuries or decades, or according to significant events like grandmother's golden wedding, the first voyage of Columbus to the New World, or the fall of Rome. As new information is acquired, it, in turn, is stored away in its proper place for future reference.

Young children and immature learners need more concrete experiences and utilize inductive reasoning more than do older children and mature learners, who can shift to the abstract and to deductive approaches.[12] As the child progresses through school, he becomes increasingly independent of firsthand experience as the basis for building concepts and begins to deal with symbols and abstractions. With increasing age and conscious application the ability to relate expands, so that by adolescence he can relate not only to himself, but also to the larger group and to society.

Learning to make sequential, logical, cause-effect, and space relations and to determine their significance and application are important tasks of reading in the social studies, for otherwise many facts would remain unordered and the impact of their interactions would be lost or misinterpreted by students.

Expanding Concepts

One of the best ways to expand the concepts of students and to enlarge their store of information is to promote wide reading from various sources. The unit method provides this and encourages pupils at the start to read in order to learn enough to raise pertinent questions for study. Thus in introducing a unit at any level, it is good procedure to provide for browsing materials that will aid students in formulating their questions. Answering these questions becomes, in

[12]Vinacke, W. Edgar. "Concept Formation in Children of School Ages." *Education* 74:527-34; May 1954.

turn, the purpose for further reading. This arouses interest which sparks additional reading, raises other questions, and the circle continues until the unit is culminated.

Students read many types of material – biography, fiction, almanacs, journals, newspapers, textbooks, reports, government documents, for example. They compare and relate, they judge quality and style, they analyze and organize. Then they synthesize their findings and share what they have found through oral reports, written compositions, booklets, articles, murals, charts, graphs, slides, or other 'pictorial means, and in turn receive the benefit from the work produced by their fellow students.

Many beautiful library books contain the human elements, the story detail so often lacing in a paragraph of text that dismisses a decade in one sentence.[13] Students at all levels, of all abilities, need books that give them a chance to identify themselves with ancient Rome or Norman England, or with the inhabitants of present-day Lebanon or India. It is books such as these that form the woof of the tapestry woven into the warp of the text. And beautiful illustrations not only give aesthetic satisfaction, but often clarify meanings as the student reads.

Perhaps the most lasting value, however, is the development of a liking for books and of the habit of reading that persist long after students leave school. Such permanent use of reading, wisely done, is one of the major reasons for teaching reading and the interest engendered through wide reading in social studies offers one spur to continual use of books.

Summary

Reading *is* important to the social studies. The broad concept of reading requires not only that the reader obtain the literal meanings, but also that he interpret and apply what he reads. The developmental reading program is concerned with the basic skills of word recognition and full comprehension; but there are special applications that must be made to reading in the social studies because of the number and compactness of concepts introduced, the relative importance of the ideas presented (often with no clue), the objective and symbolic style of the language used, and the lack of appeal of the content to

[13]Carpenter, Helen McCraken, and Gaver, Mary Virginia. "Making History Live Through Reading." *Interpreting and Teaching American History.* (Edited by William H. Cartwright and Richard L. Watson.) Thirty-First Yearbook. Washington, D. C.: National Council for the Social Studies, a department of the National Education Association, 1962. pp. 398-414; the World History Bibliography Committee of NCSS, Alice W. Spieseke, Chairman. *World History Book List for High Schools: A Selection for Supplementary Reading.* Bulletin No. 31. Washington, D. C.: National Council for the Social Studies, a department of the National Education Association, 1959. 119 pp.: and Huus, Helen. *Children's Books To Enrich the Social Studies: For the Elementary Grades.* Bulletin No. 32. Washington D. C.: National Council for the Social Studies, a department of the National Education Association, 1961. 196 pp.

some students. The main avenues to improvement in reading discussed in this chapter are the development of vocabulary, the improvement of rate in relation to purpose, the formation of various types of relationships, and the expansion of concepts through extended reading.

If teachers help students catch the spirit of people down through the ages and in the world today, if history and geography are changed from cold facts to human beings continually striving toward progress, and if through reading, each student begins to realize his own place in this continuum of civilization, then truly reading has made its contribution.

Suggestions for Further Reading

Govell, Harold M. "Reading and the Social Studies." *Social Education* 21: 14-16; January 1957.
> This report of a study of the characteristics of good and poor readers of social studies material at the eleventh grade level list nine points of difference between them. Several ways by which teachers can work to improve the reading ability of students, as implied by this study, are also included.

Dallolio, Helen Carey. "Trends in Geographic Content-Re-Emphasizes Difficulties in Reading." *Journal of Geography* 58: 144-49; March 1959.
> Difficulties of vocabulary, concept formation, and problems of location and distance and of organization are discussed. Some suggestions for helping pupils overcome these difficulties are given, especially in the section on organization.

Fay, Leo; Horn, Thomas; and McCullough, Constance. *Improving Reading in the Elementary Social Studies.* Bulletin No. 33. Washington D. C.: National Council for the Social Studies a department of the National Education Association, 1961. 72 pp.
> Nine questions often asked by teachers from the chapter titles of this pamphlet. The answers give suggestions for coping with individual differences, utilizing the textbook effectively, teaching the use of charts, graphs, maps, pictures, reference books, and library resources, and helping pupils develop good reading and work-study skills so that they become thoughtful, critical readers.

Gross, Richard E., and Badger, William V. "Social Studies: Reading in Relation to the Social Studies." *Encyclopedia of Educational Research.* Third Edition. (Edited by Chester W. Harris.) New York: The Macmillan Co., 1960, p. 1310.
> This section presents a summary of research studies relating to the reading of material in social studies. It is most useful as an overview and for locating specific studies pertinent to a problem.

Harris, Albert J. *Effective Teaching of Reading.* New York: David McKay Co., 1962, Chapter 12.
> Chapter 12, which is devoted to the development of efficiency in functional reading, deals with skills in locating information, reading specific subject matter, and organizing and summarizing and with the effective use of these skills.

Heilman, Arthur W. *Principles and Practices of Teaching Reading.* Columbus, Ohio: Charles E. Merrill Books, Inc., 1961. Chapter 8 (pp. 268-98) and Chapter 9.
> The last part of Chapter 8 includes many ideas for teaching reading in the intermediate grades that can also be adapted for use in the secondary school, such as the development of concepts and pronunciation, improvement of the rate of reading, and development of skills. Chapter 9 defines the prerequisites for critical reading and includes a section on "What the School Can Do."

Preston, Ralph C.: Schneyer, J. Wesley; and Thyng, Franc J. *Guiding the Social Studies Reading of High School Students.* Bulletin No. 34 Washington, D. C. National Council for the Social Studies, a department of the National Education Association, 1963. 79 pp.

Discusses importance and need for guidance of reading, together with techniques for meeting individual differences for improving comprehension of social studies textbooks and for stimulating wide reading of nontext materials.

Strang, Ruth, and Bracken, Dorothy Kendal. *Making Better Readers.* Boston: D. C. Heath and Co., 1957. Chapters 3 and 5.

Chapter 3 includes suggestions for teaching paragraph comprehension, outlining, word meanings, and critical reading at the high school level. Chapter 5 applies reading techniques to various subjects in the high school curriculum. While only one section (pp. 220-42) relates specifically to social studies, other suggestions in the chapter may also be adapted and applied to this field of study.

Reading and the Teaching of Science*

GEORGE G. MALLINSON

At the outset it should be emphasized that no effort is being made to support or reject the use of textbooks or other materials in teaching science at any level. Rather, the purpose of this report is to deal with such published materials as they may be related to the reading problems in science teaching.

It is, of course, well known that the reading problems ramify into all subject-matter areas in the public school, not only in the communications program. Since some types of reading materials are used in all areas, it is obvious that the quality of the materials is of little import if the student is unable to read them. The aim of reading instruction for any field is not merely to teach the student to recognize, spell and be able to define the appropriate vocabulary. Rather, the aim is to teach the student to understand the ideas that are encompassed by the verbal symbols. In other words, the terms "reading" and "understanding" have almost identical connotations.

There is, of course, a great deal of debate with respect to the scope of the reading skill needed to understand the subject-matter of an academic field. The research is inconclusive as to whether reading skill is specialized in terms of the specific subject matter involved or whether it is a general skill. Probably, it is a function of both. The writer believes that student achievement in a field depends at least partly on a general factor of reading ability, and the skill of reading specific subject-matter depends on the understandings the student develops. This report is prepared with these interlocking assumptions in mind.

Reading and Understanding

If reading were merely word recognition, spelling and definition, textbooks for reading would differ greatly from those now in use. For reading programs from the kindergarten through ninth grade, one would develop ten

*Reprinted from *School Science and Mathematics,* 64 (February, 1964), pp. 148-153, by permission of the author and the Central Association of Science and Mathematics Teachers.

dictionaries with graded vocabularies, containing appropriate review. The student would be expected merely to "learn the words." Such a view of reading is similar to an experience the writer had a number of years ago with a University colleague. This colleague disparaged contemporary reading instruction and claimed that any child three years old could learn to read. As evidence, he requested his three-year old to select a child's book from one of the book shelves in the living room and bring it to him. The father opened the book, pointed to a line, and requested the child to read, which the child did. This was repeated with several other books, the father beaming at the result. At the end of the demonstration, the writer asked the father for the opportunity to try an experiment with the child. He asked the child to select another book from the library, open to a page, and begin reading. When the child had completed the page, the writer said, "You surely are smart! I'll bet you can read the next page without even turning to it." The child did rattle off the contents of the next page. It is doubtful that it is necessary to point out the implications on the experiment.

Simply, one may say that a person can read, if on scanning the verbal material, the matrices of the ideas intended by the author are developed in the mind of the reader. The development of such a matrix depends on two fundamental components:

(1) An adequate understanding by the reader of the meanings that the verbal symbols should evoke.
(2) A mental organization of these meanings by the reader into the intended matrix.

The manner in which the material is prepared obviously influences the development. Thus, it behooves an instructor to determine whether the materials being used are appropriately designed.

Production of Reading Materials for Science

Some persons seem to believe that textbooks and other reading materials for science generally are produced haphazardly. There is little question that the "frantic determination" to "do something about science" in the past few years, made it possible for many "fly-by-night operators" to publish and sell shoddy materials of all types. The proportion of the material now available for science teaching that is of low quality is not a matter of concern here. It is the writer's experience, however, that the reputable book companies that produce textbook materials, and those who have had long experience in the trade field, generally publish materials that are of high quality. It is reasonable to suggest that the various factors involved in production should be understood by those who are trying to decide whether or not textbooks or tradebooks should be used. Otherwise, valid judgments are almost impossible. Some of the factors are discussed in the sections that follow.

Content

In general, in textbooks published within two or three years of one another, the content does not vary greatly. About 90 percent of the content of any one textbook appears in the others. This does not suggest that the topics are given the same emphases, or that the subject matter is organized the same way. It does suggest, however, that a perusal of the indices will evidence a great deal of commonality. Both textbooks and tradebooks of reputable publishers that have recent publication dates may be assumed to be reasonably and accurately up-to-date, and contain material of contemporary significance. As of the original publication date they may be expected to contain subject matter within six (6) months of being current. Occasionally, minor slips may occur, but these are generally rare in the publications of reputable companies. In general, therefore, an examination of published material for use in teaching may better be directed toward the desired organization and factors related to reading, than to an extensive survey of content.

Vocabulary Load

The vocabulary found in any textbook or tradebook (or for that matter any published material) may be categorized as technical or nontechnical. Obviously, any book designed to introduce the student to new material will contain an unfamiliar specialized vocabulary that the student is expected to learn. This unfamiliar, or technical, vocabulary consists chiefly of those words that a student would be unlikely to use in his lay conversation, but would need to use if he were to understand or discuss the topics under consideration. Any book should be evaluated to determine whether or not these new terms are identified, and if so, whether they are presented so that their understanding is enhanced. When such terms are introduced, the adjacent discussions should make their meanings and implications clear so that the students can use them with a reasonable degree of familiarity in the paragraphs that follow.

There is some major controversy about the non-technical vocabulary to be included in basic materials used for teaching. The nontechnical vocabulary consists of those terms that are used in lay conversation. There are some who suggest that the student should be expected to broaden his non-technical vocabulary while he is learning the new material, such as science. Others suggest that the challenge for understanding should be directed toward the student's development of the science. Others suggest that the challenge for understanding should be directed toward the student's development of the science concepts in the related reading material, not toward learning to read. According to this latter view, the level of the non-technical vocabulary should be one-half year to one year below the students for whom the book is designed. It is impossible to prove that one viewpoint is more defensible than the other. It is the opinion of the writer, however, that the challenge should be with the technical vocabulary and the science concepts, not with the non-technical vocabulary.

A number of studies have been undertaken recently with respect to the number of terms that may be suitably introduced at any level. The task has been extremely difficult. The broadening of a students' experiences through television and other media of communication have no doubt increased the apperceptive mass of contemporary students, so that the appropriate vocabulary load today is probably greater than that of two decades ago. Nevertheless, extreme caution should be taken in "piling it on" merely to "raise standards." It is quite possible to confuse the modern child who has a high level of sophistication or an adolescent who has a more mature intelligence with a vocabulary that is presented "for its own sake." The average child of today probably cannot lift a greater load or carry it further up hill than a child of twenty-years ago. He merely starts the journey from a higher altitude.

Sentence Structure

It is obvious that factors other than vocabulary load are related to the reading difficulty of a book. A book with a minimal vocabulary load may be extremely difficult to read because of long involved and/or obtuse sentences. Sentences can be written with three or four ideas each of which requires digestion, not just verbal recognition. Such sentences can be unduly difficult even with "easy terms." Materials should be written so that the sentences contain but one major idea and seldom more than one contributing sub-idea. Sentences that contain several major ideas and several supporting ideas are likely to be difficult for even sophisticated readers, particularly when the material is unfamiliar.

At this point a word of caution should be injected. There is an ill-founded belief that teachers are generally capable of inspecting a textbook and determining the level of difficulty from the structure of the sentences. In fact, a statement was made at one national convention by an allegedly renowned reading expert that, "Any good teacher can tell the level of reading difficulty of a book by looking at it." Several research studies indicate clearly that such evaluations of the level of reading difficulty of reading materials by reading experts vary greatly, and the opinions of teachers vary a great deal more; often by as much as nine grades. Any analysis of the "gestalts" of the structures of sentences in books should be made with a reading formula such as the Flesch, Lorge or Dale-Chall. These have been found to yield quite consistent results when they have been used to measure the level of difficulty of reading materials.

Illustrations

The problem of preparing published materials is having too little material to fill the pages. Ordinarily, four to five times as much material could be included if space were available. For example, in a typical textbook approximately 20% of manuscript pages are used in end-of-chapter and introductory materials. Also, some concepts can be presented effectively only through illustrations. Thus, with the vast amount of material that must be discarded in producing a book, illustrations must contribute as much to the reading as the text. Consequently, the persons selecting the books or other published materials should examine the illustrations carefully to determine whether or not they extend the reading materials and/or develop additional concepts rather than merely duplicating the text or "providing attractiveness." The responsible persons should read selected pages carefully to determine the extent to which the illustrations are integrated with the reading material and contribute to the understanding of the concepts. If the illustrations are not so integrated they may have a negative distracting effect.

Interest Level

It is obvious that the interest level of a book depends to a great extent on the contemporary characteristics of the topics being presented. It depends, also, on another factor which is difficult to measure; the degree to which the text is written in an interesting style. Whether or not a book may be interesting is largely determined by the subjective judgment of the reader. In one sense, the interest level depends on the use of words that are familiar to the student which provide vivid descriptions. The level of interest depends, also, on the number of striking familiar analogies that can be used to extend the understandings. In a sense, the reviewer must say to himself, "If I were the age of the student, would I like it?" Perhaps some students might be consulted.

The Role of Pedagogy

The pedagogy involved in assuring proper reading accomplishment in an area will not be discussed here, since it would involve far too much space. However, the author believes that some basic materials, without regard for what they may be, are more satisfactory than a miscellaneous assortment. Obviously, supplementary materials should be included, also. However, while instruction should obviously be individualized, it cannot practicably be individualized if each student is in a different classroom in different counties. The same is true with the published materials that are selected. There should be a reasonably basic foundation of subject-matter that all students, except for a few, may reasonably be expected to acquire. The extension of these basic materials to provide individualization cannot be accomplished by means of an assortment of textbooks, since the vast proportion contain about the same material in somewhat different organizations. Tradebooks are more restricted in their coverage, very considerably in their level of presentation, but delve deeply into topics. These materials do enable students to explore their areas of interest "on a solid foundation." These may serve well in extending the basic material.

Whether the analogy is satisfactory or not, one does not expect every student to climb to the same height on the same flagpole, but every flagpole climbed should be "stuck in the ground."

Summary

The writer does not wish to suggest that all of the problems related to reading and the teaching of science have been covered. They have not. However, the points described herein are probably among the more important that need to be considered when the reading problems and science teaching become matters of concern.

Research on Problems in Reading Science*

J. BRYCE LOCKWOOD

The Purpose

The purpose of this report is to summarize the findings of research studies dealing with problems in reading science and to suggest some of the implications of these investigations.

Methods Employed

A search was made through the literature to locate research studies dealing with problems related to reading science. While a great deal of research has been done in the area of reading in general, few studies dealing specifically with problems in reading science have been undertaken. Hence, all the published studies that were available in the literature were included in this investigation.

The studies that were located were then classified under the major headings to which they seemed to belong.

STUDIES INVOLVING THE DEVELOPMENT OF SCIENTIFIC VOCABULARY

Two published studies dealing with the problem of development of scientific vocabularies for use in textbooks for science were found. One of these by Curtis[1] is a monumental study that seeks answers to five questions:

(1) Are the vocabularies found in textbooks of science actually too difficult for the pupils for whom the books are intended?

(2) Is there some definite and readily determined level of vocabulary in present textbooks of science which marks a sharp increase in difficulty of

---

*Reprinted from *School Science and Mathematics,* 59 (October, 1959), pp. 551-556, by permission of the author and the Central Association of Science and Mathematics Teachers.
[1]Curtis, Francis D., *Investigations of Vocabulary in Textbooks of Science for Secondary Schools.* Boston: Ginn and Company, 1938. pp. viii + 127.

comprehension by the pupils, and which, therefore, is the level at which simplification of vocabulary in such textbooks should begin?

(3)   Is the difficulty which pupils encounter in reading textbooks of science attributable, to any considerable extent, to non-scientific, and hence non-essential, vocabulary?

(4)   Do present textbooks of science provide adequately for the mastery of essential vocabulary through definition and repetition?

(5)   What are important terms which should be mastered in the various courses of science?

The data for the study were obtained from one hundred master's theses completed under the direction of the author.

In general, lists of words were obtained by examining the glossaries of textbooks for general science, biology, chemistry, and physics. The word lists thus assembled were compared with the lists of words assembled by others such as Thorndike.

The words were then submitted to qualified teachers in order to determine their values for inclusion in the respective courses. From the data thus obtained, lists of essential and desirable words were developed. Curtis found that:

(1)   Both the technical and the non-technical vocabularies of textbooks of general science, biology, chemistry, and physics are too difficult for the pupils for whom the books are written.

(2)   There is insufficient provision in such textbooks of science for repetition of difficult scientific terms and non-technical words.

(3)   Too large a percentage of the difficult words found in such textbooks of science are non-scientific or non-technical words.

(4)   Too small a percentage of the scientific terms that are introduced into such textbooks of science are defined.

(5)   Not infrequently the definitions of scientific terms fail to appear in the textbooks until the terms have been used more or less extensively in earlier parts of the books.

Mallinson[2] conducted a study, using techniques similar to those of Curtis, for the purpose of developing a scientific vocabulary for general physical science.

A list of words was compiled through the use of textbooks, courses of study (state, county, and city), and theses dealing with the area of general physical science. The list was then submitted for evaluation to a jury of forty-four persons all of whom had written textbooks, or articles on general physical science, or who had helped develop courses of study in that area.

---

[2]Mallinson, George Griesen, "The Development of a Vocabulary for General Physical Science." *The Twelfth Yearbook of the National Council on Measurements Used in Education, Part II,* a Report of the Meeting held in Cleveland, Ohio, April 1955, 6-8.

The result is a list of four hundred words considered to be essential vocabulary for general physical science plus two hundred words considered to be desirable vocabulary for general physical science.

The list of terms may well be of value to those developing curriculum materials for courses in general physical science.

STUDIES INVOLVING THE DETERMINATION OF THE LEVEL OF READING DIFFICULTY OF TEXTBOOKS FOR SCIENCE

Mallison and his co-workers [3,4,5,6,7,8, 9,10] conducted a series of studies in which similar techniques were used to determine the levels of reading difficulty of textbooks for the areas of elementary science, junior-high-school science, general science, general physical science and earth science, high-school biology, high-school chemistry, and high-school physics.

Since an analysis of all of the text material in all the books was impractical, a modification of the Flesch formula was used in the investigations.

It was decided to select for analysis from each textbook one sample passage for each one hundred pages or fraction thereof, but not less than five passages from any one textbook.

The number of pages in each text was computed by counting from the first page designated by an arabic numeral to the last page of the last chapter. Pages on which were found chapter headings, supplementary activities, and questions were included in the count. The pages on which were found the indices, glossaries and tables of contents were excluded.

[3] Mallinson, George Greisien, Sturm, Harold E., and Mallinson, Lois Marion, "The Reading Difficulty of Textbooks for General Physical Science and Earth Science." *School Science and Mathematics* LVI (November 1954), 612-6.

[4] Mallinson, George Greisen, Sturm, Harold E., and Mallinson, Lois Marion, "The Reading Difficulty of Textbooks for General Science." *The School Review,* LX (February 1952), 94-8.

[5] Mallinson, George Greisen, Sturm, Harold E., and Mallinson, Lois Marion, "The Reading Difficulty of Some Recent Textbooks for Science." *School Science and Mathematics,* LVII (May 1957), 364-6.

[6] Mallinson, George Greisen, Sturm, Harold E., and Mallinson, Lois Marion, "The Reading Difficulty of Textbooks for High-School Biology." *The American Biology Teacher,* XII (November 1950), 151-6.

[7] Mallinson, George Greisen, Sturm, Harold E., and Mallinson, Lois Marion, "The Reading Difficulty of Textbooks for High-School Chemistry." *Journal of Chemical Education,* XXIX (December 1952), 629-31.

[8] Mallinson, George Greisen, Sturm, Harold E., and Mallinson, Lois Marion, "The Reading Difficulty of Textbooks for High-School Physics," *Science Education,* XXXVI (February 1957), 19-23.

[9] Mallinson, George Greisen, Sturm, Harold E., and Patton, Robert E., "The Reading Difficulty of Textbooks for Elementary Science." *The Elementary School Journal* L (April 1950), 460-3.

[10] Mallinson, George Greisen, Sturm, Harold E., and Mallinson, Lois Marion, "The Reading Difficulty of Textbooks in Junior-High-School Science." *The School Review,* L (December 1950), 536-40.

The number of pages thus computed in each textbook was then divided by the number of samples to be taken from the respective textbook. In this way each textbook was divided into sections of equal numbers of pages. A page was then selected from each of sections by using the table of random numbers.

A one hundred word sample was taken from each page thus selected by counting from the first word of the first new paragraph on that page. If the page contained no reading material, the sample was taken from the next page that did. The legends under the illustrations on the pages thus selected were disregarded. These samples were then analyzed using the Flesch formula.

In general, the data obtained from these efforts seem to suggest that the following conclusions are valid:

(1)   The levels of reading difficulty of many textbooks in all areas of science are too advanced for the students for whom they are written.

(2)   The differences between the levels of reading difficulty of the easiest and most difficult textbooks in all areas of science are significant.

(3)   In some textbooks of science whose *average* level of reading difficulty seems satisfactory there are passages that would be difficult for some students in grade levels above that for which the book is intended.

(4)   There is a great deal of variation among the levels of reading difficulty of textbooks designed for the same field of science.

(5)   Earlier passages in textbooks of science are not likely to be less difficult than passages found later in the books.

(6)   Many textbooks of science contain non-technical words that could be replaced with easier synonyms.

(7)   Recent textbooks in science are as variable and are likely to cause as much difficulty as earlier books analyzed.

(8)   The level of reading difficulty of textbooks of science appears to be a valid criterion for the selection of textbooks of science.

Although the studies carried out by Mallinson were completed many years later than those of Curtis, the results from them are similar. This would seem to indicate that little use was made of the earlier studies in improving the readability of textbooks in science.

In a study conducted by Crooks[11] the level of reading difficulty of textbooks in college science was investigated. The techniques used in this study were similar to those used by Mallinson in that use was made of the Flesch formula. However, the method of selection of samples was not specified.

Seventeen of the books selected for use in the study were in the areas of general biology (eight books), zoology (four books), botany (two books),

---

[11]Crooks, Kenneth B. M. and Smith, Charles H., "The Reading Problems in College Science Instruction." *Science Education,* XLI (February 1957), 54-7.

anatomy and physiology (two books), and bacteriology (one book). The other books examined were one each in the areas of physical science, chemistry and physics.

The results of this study seem to indicate that all the books, as judged by the Flesch Human Interest Scale, are "dull." Eighteen of the books analyzed were found to be difficult according to the Flesch Scale, while two were found to be fairly difficult. Later editions of these books judged to be fairly difficult were found to rate as difficult.

While the results of this study seem to indicate that the results found by Mallinson at the elementary and secondary levels are also true for the college level, it should be pointed out that one textbook from a particular area is hardly representative of all textbooks written for use in that area.

STUDIES DEALING WITH THE ABILITY OF TEACHERS TO ESTIMATE THE READING DIFFICULTY OF SCIENCE TEXTBOOKS

Two studies were found in this area, one by Herrington[12] and a follow-up study by Mallinson and Holmes[13] in which similar techniques were used.

Herrington conducted a study to determine whether the measurements made with readability formulae of the reading difficulty of certain passages from textbooks for elementary science are more consistent than estimates made by reading experts of the reading difficulty of these same passages.

In the study, samples were taken from Mallinson's studies of textbooks designed for grades four through eight. One hundred and ninety-nine samples from thirty-nine books were used in all.

Twenty-one of the one hundred and ninety-nine samples were selected at random and sent to twenty-six teachers classified as "reading experts" or "specialists in reading" in certain of the larger midwestern cities. These samples were accompanied by instructions for making estimates of the level of reading difficulty of the passages. The same passages were then evaluated, with respect to level of reading difficulty by the Flesch, Lorge, and Dale-Chall formulae of readability.

The results obtained by the readability formulae and the teachers' estimates were then compared. In general, the results indicate the following:

(1)   There is a great difference between the consistency with which the reading formulae evaluate the grade level of difficulty of the samples, and the

---

[12]Herrington, Roma Lenore, "An Investigation of the Consistencies With Which Readability Formulas Measure and Reading Experts Estimate the Reading Difficulty of Materials for Elementary Science." Unpublished master's thesis, Western Michigan College, Kalamazoo, Michigan, May 1956, pp. iii+41.

[13]Mallinson, George Greisen and Holmes, Roma Herrington, "A Study of the Ability of Teachers to Estimate the Reading Difficulty of Materials for Elementary Science." A mimeographed report presented to the convention of the National Council on Measurements Used in Education, St. Louis, Missouri, February 25, 1958.

consistency with which the reading experts evaluate the grade level of reading difficulty of the samples.

(2)   Readability formulae measure grade levels of reading difficulty of science materials with much more consistency than reading experts estimate grade levels of reading difficulty.

(3)   The evaluations made for higher level materials by both formulae and experts tend to be somewhat less consistent than those for lower level materials.

(4)   Teachers should have some method for evaluating materials as to reading difficulty which is more objective than their estimates.

In the study by Mallinson and Holmes cited above, the procedure used in Herrington's study was repeated, except that two elementary teachers in each of the school systems in which the experts were employed were requested to undertake the task of evaluating the sample passages.

The results were tabulated according to grade level of difference between the highest and lowest measurements or estimates of the level of reading difficulty of a sample, together with the number of samples for which that difference was evident.

The results indicated that the median difference for measurements by reading formulae is 1.0 years; for reading experts' estimates, 3.0 years; and for elementary teachers' estimates, 4.0 years. It was concluded that the use of reading formulae is justified, at least in so far as textbooks for elementary science are concerned.

STUDIES DEALING WITH THE SELECTION OF SCIENCE TEXTBOOKS

It should be pointed out that the quality of a textbook is related to a number of factors. The studies summarized earlier indicate that an important criterion in the selection of science textbooks is the level of reading difficulty. Among other criteria are style of writing, organization of material; clarity of presentation; quality of illustrations; value of supplementary activities; and provisions for individual differences. Hence, it would seem that research related to the selection of reading materials falls within the province of this report. In one of these research investigations an evaluation scale for the selection of high-school science textbooks is proposed by Vogel.[14]

The scale is organized around ten general headings: qualification of the author; organization; content; presentation; accuracy; readability; adaptability; teaching aids; illustrations; and appearance. The scale is interpreted in numerical terms for convenience.

[14]Vogel, Louis F., "A Spot-Check Evaluation Scale for High-School Science Textbooks." *The Science Teacher,* XVIII (March 1951), 70-2.

A similar scale has been proposed by Burr [15] that is organized around eight general headings.

In an article, Mallinson[16] suggests several points that should be considered in the selection of textbooks for science. These points are as follows:

(1)   The number of technical terms used in a textbook should be considered with regard for the "normal" increase in all vocabulary for a given grade level.

(2)   The technical terms should explain adequately the scientific meanings that are to be developed.

(3)   The technical words selected may include many that are nonessential to an adequate understanding of science at a given level. Further, many essential terms may have been omitted.

(4)   A careful analysis should include the use of a word-count system such as that of Buckingham and Dolch or a formula such as that of Flesch.

Summary

In summary, it could be stated that authors and publishers of textbooks for science might well take cognizance of the research that has been done on problems in reading science.

[15]Burr, Samuel Engle, "A Rating Scale for Textbooks." *The Journal of Education,* CXXXII (May 1949), 138-9.
[16]Mallinson, George Greisen, "Some Problems of Vocabulary and Reading Difficulty in Teaching Junior-High-School Science." *School Science and Mathematics,* LII (April 1952), 269-74.

Measuring the Readability of High School Health Texts*

AUBREY C. McTAGGART

The Concept of Readability

What is readability? According to Webster's Dictionary, (1)† "readable" means "legible. . pleasing, interesting, or offering no great difficulty to the reader. . . that can be read with ease." Thus, as pointed out by Chall, (2) when a book reviewer states that a book is readable, he may refer to its legibility, its ease, its power to interest, or some combination of these qualities. Dale and Chall (3) pointed out that in the broadest sense, readability could be considered as the sum total of all those elements within a given piece of printed material that affect the success that a group of readers will have with it. This success means the extent to which they understand it, read it at optimum speed, and find it interesting.

But for all the fifty or so measures that have been developed to evaluate the probable success a reader may have with a text, we cannot turn to them for the final answer. There is no magic in readability formulas. They merely analyze elements in the reading material and we make predictions from them. A readability formula gives only an estimate of difficulty. The true test of readability is whether the material can actually be read by people of a given reading ability.

The idea underlying readability measurement, according to Chall, (4) is simply the appropriate matching of reader and printed material. The assumption here is that readers differ in their ability to read and that the printed material in turn varies in readability; that is, in the amount and kind of ability required to read and understand it. Thus, we can say that the purpose and value of readability formulas is to predict and control difficulty and to furnish a tool for matching reading materials to the reader.

Since there are many formulas available for determining the reading difficulty levels of printed materials, teachers, librarians, and textbook

*Reprinted from *Journal of School Health,* 34 (November, 1964), pp. 434-443, by permission of the author and the American School Health Association.
†Numbers in parentheses refer to references at end of article.

committees are often at a loss about which one to use. Some formulas may be more suitable than others for determining the reading difficulty levels of certain types of reading material. (5) If so, there is a real need to determine the most appropriate formula to use with health textbooks.

However, from a scientific viewpoint, a given formula is applicable only to material similar to the criterion on which it is based. (6) Too often this fact is forgotten, which has led to criticism of a formula when, actually, the fault lay in its application to a type of material for which it was not designed.

Two measures that are widely used today are the Dale-Chall readability formula (7) and the revised (1948) Flesch Reading Ease formula. (8) The Dale-Chall formula depends on a word list, and the Flesch formula on a syllable count to aid in determining difficulty. They are both based on the same criterion, the McCall Crabbs *Standard Test Lessons in Reading.* (9) These lessons were intended for use in grades three through seven. The question that concerned the writer was this: How valid are these two formulas when used on high school health texts?

In the original presentation of their formula, Dale and Chall offered evidence of its validity in predicting difficulty of social-studies and health materials. Thus, although it would seem that the Dale-Chall formula should be suitable for use with health materials, the writer felt that it would be worthwhile to check this point experimentally, using recent high school health texts.

In the original presentation of his formula, Flesch presented evidence of its validity with adult magazines. However, we cannot assume that it would be a valid measure of the difficulty levels of high school health textbooks. Thus, this study attempted to evaluate both the Flesch and the Dale-Chall readability formulas as objective aids in selecting high school health texts.

The specific purposes of this study were:

1.   to compare student comprehension of selected health passages of 7th-, 9th, and 12th-grade reading difficulty levels as estimated by a) the 1948 Flesch formula and by b) the Dale-Chall formula.
2.   to determine the effect of health knowledge on students' comprehension of selected health passages.

General Design of the Experiment

Nine classes of ninth-grade students were used in this study. They were given the *Kilander Health Knowledge Test,* (10) and divided into good and poor health knowledge sections. Each of these sections was then randomly divided into three main groups. Students in each of these three groups were matched on the basis of intelligence and reading ability. Intelligence was determined by the Henmon-Nelson Tests of Mental Ability, (11) reading ability by the *Diagnostic Reading Tests* (12).

TABLE I
GENERAL DESIGN OF THE EXPERIMENT

Group	Reading Difficulty Levels	Health Knowledge	
		Good	Poor
A	12th Grade (Experimental)		
B	9th grade (Control)		
C	7th grade (Experimental)		

Nine health passages were used in the Flesch comprehension test, and a different nine health passages were used in the Dale-Chall comprehension test. These passages of approximately 250 words each were selected from current high school health textbooks.

Control Group B read the nine health passages as they were found in the textbooks (9th-grade level). Experimental Group C read the same nine passages, but in a rewritten form which made them easier to read (7th-grade). Experimental Group A read the same nine passages rewritten to make them more difficult (12-grade). Comprehension of each group was determined by the students' ability to answer questions after reading the health-passages. Group comparisons were made by comparing the mean comprehension scores for each of the above cells in Table 1.

The Population

Ninth-grade students from the Rantoul Township High School in Rantoul, Illinois, were used as subjects in this study. Time for the experiment was taken from the students' Freshman science classes over a period of two months during the spring of 1961. Nine freshman classes (257 students) were involved. The students in the sample were arranged in heterogeneous groupings so that a variety of ability was found in each class. Since all students were required to take Freshman Science, it was assumed that this sample could be considered as typical of the 9th-grade students in Rantoul. The fact that an air force base was located at Rantoul is also noteworthy. This meant that many of the students in the Rantoul Township High School were from other states and were at Rantoul because their fathers were assigned to that post. Thus, this particular sample probably represents students from a wider geographical area than a sample taken from a high school that was not located near a service base.

To take the health passage comprehension test, a student had to meet certain requirements. He must:

(1)   Have been a ninth-grader.
(2)   Have taken the reading test.
(3)   Have taken the health knowledge test.
(4)   Have taken the intelligence test.

These requirements reduced the number of students used in the final portion of the experiment to 210 for the Dale-Chall section and 208 for the Flesch.

The Health Passage Comprehension Tests

Each comprehension test (the Flesch and the Dale-Chall) was made up of nine health passages dealing with a variety of health topics from widely used modern high school health textbooks. Passages for the Dale-Chall portion of the experiment were selected and evaluated for reading difficulty by using the Dale-Chall readability formula, and the passages for the Flesch part of the experiment by using the 1948 Flesch formula.

The main requirement to be satisfied in choosing passages was that of independence. This is, passages were used that could be comprehended without the help of visual aids, such as diagrams, charts, and the like.

Since 9th-grade students were used in this study, passages chosen were at the 9th-grade level and constituted the control passages for Group B. These passages averaged approximately 250 words in length and were left as they were found in the textbook.

Authors of both formulas have made definite suggestions for improving the readability of written work. The suggestions of Flesch were used in rewriting the passages for the Flesch section of the experiment and the Dale-Chall suggestions for that portion of the experiment. Technical health terms that were included in the glossary of the texts sampled were considered essential and were not changed when the passages were rewritten.

One comprehension test was based on the content *common* to each of the three versions (i.e. 7th-, 9th-, and 12th-grade levels) found in the Flesch section of the study; the other was based on content *common* to the three versions in the Dale-Chall section. This meant that students in Group C reading the 7th-grade version would answer the same questions as those in Groups B or A, reading the 9th-or 12-grade versions respectively. Each comprehension test was composed of 38 questions based on nine health passages taken from current high school health texts. Unknown to the students, the first passage in each text was a practice passage to introduce them to the testing situation.

After the directions were read, the students were allowed 32 minutes to read the test passages and answer the questions based on those passages. This time limit was determined on the basis of a pretest. The students were allowed to refer back to the test passages as many times as they wished, but they were advised to answer the questions on the basis of their first reading if at all possible. The number of correct responses to the items on the test was taken as the comprehension score (total possible: 34) which was used in determining whether or not significant differences existed between groups.

The following passages are samples* taken from the Dale-Chall Comprehension Test; they illustrate the three levels of reading difficulty.

Passage 1: Reading Difficulty Level, 7th Grade

Malaria is a disease that is caused by a tiny one-celled animal called a protozoan. This protozoan is carried by the female Anopheles mosquito. (The male drinks the juice of flowers.) When the mosquito bites a person, she puts in some of her saliva and the germs along with it. Each germ works its way into a red blood cell, grows, and divides to form new germs. These sometimes break out of the red blood cells. When this happens, the person has a chill and then a fever.

Malaria seems to recur, or become chronic. This makes a person less able to carry on properly. Over 300 million people all over the world are bothered with malaria, with about 3 million deaths each year.

Malaria was one of the greatest health problems in World War II in the Southwest Pacific. The drug quinine was first used to fight the disease. When people became short of this drug, Atabrine was developed.

Passage 2: Reading Difficulty Level, 9th Grade

The word malaria means bad air. The disease got its name because people recognized that something in the night air gave them the sickness. The something that carries the protozoa that cause the disease is the female Anopheles mosquito. (The male drinks the juice of flowers.) When the mosquito bites a person, she injects a little of her saliva and the germs along with it. Each germ burrows into a red blood cell, grows and divides to form new germs. When these break out of the red blood cells, the patient has a chill and then fever. The disease tends to recur, or become chronic, and it undermines the efficiency of the victim. Over 300 million people are affected each year throughout the world, with about 3 million deaths.

Malaria was one of the greatest health problems in World War II in the Southwest Pacific. The shortage of quinine led to the development of Atabrine, which in some ways is thought to be even more effective than quinine itself.

Passage 3: Reading Difficulty Level, 12th Grade

A parasitic protozoan, one of the notorious members of the animal kingdom, is responsible for the disease called malaria. The word malaria means bad air, and the disease got its name because people recognized that something in the night air was responsible for the sickness. The something that transports the protozoa that cause the disease is the female Anopheles

*To save space, only a portion of each passage is presented.

mosquito. (The male mosquito drinks the juice of flowers.) When an infected Anopheles mosquito bites a person, she injects some of her saliva into the victim and in this way deposits the malarial parasites into the blood stream. The parasite undergoes certain changes, burrows into the red corpuscles, and eventually produces a number of "daughter" parasites. When these break out of the red corpuscles, the victim suffers chills, high fever, sweating and general weakness. The disease tends to become chronic and it undermines the efficiency of the victim. Over 300 million people are affected each year throughout the world, with approximately 3 million deaths resulting. Malaria was a tremendous health problem in World War II in the Southwest Pacific. Atabrine, which was developed because of the shortage of quinine, is in certain ways considered to be more effective than quinine itself.

Validity of the Comprehension Tests

Acting on the advice of Dr. J. T. Hastings,* three methods were used to validate the health passage comprehension tests used in this study:

1. *Judges' Opinion.* Six specialists were used in this phase of the validation process, three in the field of reading and three in the field of health and safety. They were asked to decide whether a student who answered the questions as keyed had a better understanding of the passages than a student who did not answer the questions as keyed. Their opinion was also sought on such matters as clarity of directions, readability of questions, mechanical aspects of the tests, and general face validity.

2. *Outside Criterion.* A 9th-grade class from Rantoul High School, that did not participate in the actual experiment, was used in this phase of the validation process. Results of the comprehension tests on this 9th-grade class were compared to a teacher's estimate of their ability. The teacher in this case had taught these students for seven months and should have been able to assess their ability.

3. *Oral Problem Solving.* A teacher was asked to choose six 9th-grade students: two with superior ability, two with average ability, and two with below average ability. These students were then given the comprehension tests and asked to "think out loud" while answering the test questions. This gave the writer considerable insight into the difficulties they encountered.

The comprehension tests were revised on the basis of information obtained by the above methods, and were submitted to members of the writer's dissertation committee for approval before the actual testing began.

*J. T. Hastings, Technical Director, Evaluation Unit of the Bureau of Educational Research, University of Illinois.

Statistical Procedure
Reliability

The reliability of both comprehension tests was determined by the method suggested by Thorndike. (13) He points out that for research projects time for the administration of an equivalent form of the test is often not conveniently available. In the interests of economy, in this study it became desirable to set up procedures for extracting an estimate of reliability from a single administration of a single test.

Each of the two tests in this study was composed of eight passages followed by 34 questions (questions on the practice passage were not scored). Each test was divided into two half-length tests on an odd-even split and the scores correlated to determine their reliability. This correlation gave the reliability, not of the full test, but of one only half as long. The reliability of the full test was determined by the Spearman-Brown formula. (14)

Analysis of Variance

The analysis of variance procedure was used to test for significant differences between the several sets of independently derived experimental samples to see whether they could or could not have arisen by random sampling from the same population. An "F-ratio" was obtained which was checked against tabled values at the five percent level of significance to determine whether or not there was an overall significant difference between the groups.

An F-test alone, however, falls short of satisfying all of the requirements involved. When it shows an overall significant difference between the groups, it does not indicate which of the differences among the treatment means are significant and which are not. To provide this information, the new multiple range test proposed by Duncan (15) was applied to the data.

Findings

Tables II and III are presented to give a graphic illustration of the findings. The numbers in the tables indicate the mean comprehension scores of the approximately 35 students in each cell. The arrows connect groups between which significant differences exist.

When comparing column means, we see that students with good health knowledge scored significantly higher than students with poor health knowledge.

In the good health knowledge section, significant differences were observed between groups reading at the 7th-and 12th-grade level and also between those reading at the 7th-and 9-th grade level. In the poor health knowledge section, however, no significant differences were observed.

TABLE II

SIGNIFICANT DIFFERENCES ON THE FLESCH HEALTH PASSAGE
COMPREHENSION TEST AT THE FIVE PERCENT LEVEL

Group	Reading Difficulty Levels	Health Knowledge		Row Means
		Good	Poor	
A	12	27.17	19.68	23.32
B	9	26.41	21.26	23.94
C	7	28.94	22.55	25.69
	Column Means	27.44	21.11	

TABLE III

SIGNIFICANT DIFFERENCES ON THE DALE-CHALL HEALTH PASSAGE
COMPREHENSION TEST AT THE FIVE PERCENT LEVEL

Group	Reading Difficulty Levels	Health Knowledge		Row Means
		Good	Poor	
A	12	26.00	15.61	20.59
B	9	24.97	18.69	21.74
C	7	27.18	21.00	24.13
	Column Means	26.05	18.31	

When comparing row means, which include both good and poor health knowledge sections, we find significant differences between groups reading at the 7th-and 12th-grade levels, and also between those reading at the 7th and 9th-grade levels.

As with the Flesch Comprehension Test, when comparing column means, we find that students with good health knowledge scored significantly higher than students with poor health knowledge.

In the poor health knowledge section, significant differences were observed between groups reading at the 7th-and 12th-grade levels and also between those reading at the 9th-and 12th-grade levels. In the good health knowledge section, however, no significant differences were found.

When comparing row means, we find, as we did with the Flesch Comprehension Test, significant differences between groups reading at the

7th-and 12th-grade levels, and also between those reading at the 7th- and 9th-grade levels.

Conclusion

1. The Flesch and the Dale-Chall readability formulas had essentially equal validity when used to determine various levels of reading difficulty for the respective comprehension tests. In both tests, differences in student comprehension occurred that were significant over a two-grade range.*

2. Students in the good health knowledge section made significantly better scores on both the Flesch and Dale-Chall comprehension tests than did students in the poor health knowledge section.

3. The Flesch readability formula was more effective, than the Dale-Chall formula in assessing the reading difficulty of high school health textbook material material for students in this study who had good health knowledge scores.

4. The Dale-Chall readability formula was more effective than the Flesch formula in assesing the reading difficulty of high school health textbook material for students in this study who had poor health knowledge scores.

5. The procedures recommended by Flesch and Dale and Chall for increasing the readability of reading materials were effective. When the comprehension scores of all students in this study were compared, those reading the most difficult passages made the lowest scores and those reading the easiest passages made the highest scores, although these differences were not always significant.

6. Essential technical health vocabulary, and basic health concepts and topics need not be sacrificed when making high school health textbook passages more readable. These aspects are not changed when the original (9th-grade) versions were rewritten to the 7th-and 12th-grade difficulty levels.

Discussion

The readability formulas used in this study have certain limitations which should be mentioned here. It is well known that they do not take into account such important aspects of readability as organization, conceptual difficulties, the nature of the content, or physical features of the material, such as size of type, illustrations, etc. They measure only factors related to style as a determinant of reading difficulty.

*However, only experimental validation was used in this study. Evidence of validity of readability techniques also comes from (1) original presentation of the readability formulas, and (2) cross-validation studies.

However, in spite of their limitations, readability formulas have been used to appraise the reading difficulty of printed materials in the mass media, government bulletins, and forms, industrial bulletins, manuals, house organs, and in adult and formal education, including high school health textbooks.

Another use of readability formulas that will be explored more fully in the near future is in the area of programmed learning. Here the student is usually working alone, and it is thus imperative that he completely understand the concepts presented. In a classroom situation, teachers spend much of their time explaining and elaborating on textbook material. Such assistance is often not possible in a programmed learning situation, where the individual student progresses at his own rate.

The importance of the textbook, however, cannot be overlooked. In 1955 Cronbach (16) stated: "At the center of the present-day educational scene in America is the textbook. It takes the dominant place in the typical school from the first grade to the college." Apparently, school achievement is higher when good textbooks are readily available. (17) Indeed, the feeling is rather common now of the need for multiple texts in a given subject area, each at a different level of reading difficulty. (18, 19, 20)

While we might wish that teachers would place less dependence upon the textbook, it is still the main foundation in our present educational system. Michaelis and Tyler (21) conclude that there is a need for extended study of the readability of various types of materials intended for use in the public schools. Bond and Tinker (22) comment: "To require a pupil to read a book he cannot read with understanding will only result in confusing him. . . "

To communicate means "to share. . .to make known." (23) Thus, the primary purpose of writing should be to communicate, and the principles of readability are important in all communication. The writer is interested in communication in health education, and particularly in high school health textbooks. The increase in textbooks in recent years has brought a corresponding increase in health texts, and with it the attendant problems of selection. Teachers are now expected to share the responsibility for textbook selection, and for good reasons. The teacher is in an excellent position to know his own needs and those of his students. He is the one who must directly use the textbook and integrate it into the classwork as an expression of his own teaching aims. Thus, we have the text as the core of instruction and learning, plus the realization that the classroom teacher is sharing an increasingly important part in its selection.

Research has shown that many widely used modern health tests are too difficult for the grades in which they are used. (24). The present study has shown that students who read the most difficult materials scored lowest on comprehension tests, and those reading the easiest materials scored highest. If such differences in comprehension can be found in nine passages of an experimental study, we can assume that there would be even more striking differences after students had worked with a given text for a whole semester. We know that students vary considerably in their reading ability — sometimes over a five-grade range. The obvious inference here is that the average and poor readers in a class are not going to obtain the maximum benefit from their texts. They will be so concerned with the reading task that they will not be able to focus properly on the ideas of the author.

This situation can be improved by careful text selection, using all criteria that are available. One criterion that should be considered is reading difficulty as determined by a valid readability formula which can effectively supplement subjective judgment. The author suggests that health teachers use readability measures such as the Dale-Chall and Flesch formulas. These measures are not difficult to apply and can provide an objective evaluation of reading difficulty.

Let's remember that the health text is for the student, and try to have some matching of his reading ability with the reading difficulty of the text.

References

1. Gove, P. G. (Ed.) *Webster's Third New International Dictionary.* Springfield, Mass.: G&C Merriam, 1961, p. 1889.
2. Chall, Jeanne S., *Readability: An Appraisal of Research and Application.* Columbus: Ohio State University, Bureau of Educational Research, 1958, p. 4.
3. Dale, E., and Jeanne S. Chall, The Concept of Readability. *Elementary English,* 1949, 26 p. 23
4. Chall, *Readability: An Appraisal. . . ,* p. 9.
5. *Ibid.,* p. 164.
6. *Ibid.,* p. 35.
7. Dale, E., and Jeanne S. Chall, A Formula for Predicting Readability. *Educational Research Bulletin,* 1948, 27, 11-20, 37-54.
8. Flesch, R., A New Readability Yardstick. *Journal of Applied Psychology,* 1948, 23, 221-233.
9. McCall, W. A., and Lelah M. Crabbs, *Standard Test Lessons in Reading.* New York: Teachers College, Columbia University, Bureau of Publications, 1926.
10. Kilander, H. F., *Kilander Health Knowledge Test.* Form Bm, Evaluation and Adjustment Series. Chicago: World Book, 1951.
11. Henmon, V. A. C. and M. J. Nelson, *Henmon-Nelson Tests of Mental Ability,* form B for grades 9-12. Chicago: Houghton Mifflin, 1958.
12. Committee on Diagnostic Reading Tests, Inc., *Diagnostic Reading Tests,* Survey section, form A. New York: Author, 1952.
13. Thorndike, E. L. Readability, in E. F. Lindquist (Ed.) *Educational Measurement.* Washington, D.C.: American Council on Education, 1951, p. 579.
14. *Ibid.,* p. 580.
15. Duncan, D. B., Multiple Range and Multiple "F" Tests. *Biometrics,* 1955, 2, 1-42.
16. Cronbach, L. J. (Ed.) *Text Materials in Modern Education.* Urbana: University of Illinois Press, 1955, p. 1.
17. Simonson, Mildred R., How To Choose a Textbook. *Minnesota Journal of Education,* 1959, 39, p. 18.
18. Hoyman, H. S., and A. C. McTaggart, The Readability of Modern High School Health

Texts. *American Journal of Public Health and the Nation's Health,* 1960, 50, 1889.

19.   Simsonson, p. 18.
20.   Lanomaroine, Virgil, Textbooks Can Make a Difference, *Midland Schools* 1959, 73, p. 211
21.   Michaelis, J. U., and F. T. Tyler, A Comparison of Reading Ability and Readability. *Journal of Educational Psychology,* 1951, 42, p. 498.
22.   Bond, G. A., and M. A. Tinker, *Reading Difficulties, Their Diagnosis and Correction.* New York: Appleton-Century-Crofts, Inc., 1957, p. 351.
23.   Gove, p. 460.
24.   McTaggart, A. C., The Readability of Health Textbooks, in C. H. Veenker (Ed.) *Synthesis of Research in Selected Areas of Health Instruction.* Washington: National Education Association, 1963, p. 138.

Reading in Mathematics*

I. E. AARON

Competences needed for successful reading of mathematical materials may be classified into two broad categories. The basal reading abilities, necessary for all types of reading, include the mechanics of word attack and comprehension. The reader of mathematics, in addition, must have the specialized reading skills unique to mathematics.

The mathematics teacher has five areas of responsibility in teaching the specialized reading skills and understandings of his subject. These responsibilities are to develop (1) the mathematical vocabulary, (2) the concept background necessary for understanding ideas presented in mathematics publications, (3) ability to select skills and rates appropriate for the materials being read, (4) proficiency in the special reading tasks of mathematics – reading word problems, equations, charts, graphs, and tables, and (5) skill in the interpretation of mathematical symbols and abbreviations.

Developing the Mathematical Vocabulary

Arithmetic, algebra and other areas of mathematics have their own technical vocabularies. To read mathematical materials with understanding, students must know the technical terms used in them. The teacher of mathematics – not the English, social studies, science, or reading teacher – has the responsibility for developing this special vocabulary. This vocabulary is at the heart of the subject and must be taught thoroughly.

Mathematics texts are filled with technical words. The student encounters such words as *addend, circumference, factors, decimal, diagonal, exponent, integer, isosceles, perimeter, perpendicular, quadrilateral, quinary, ratio, reciprocal, trapezoid, and volume.* A study of five consecutive pages in almost

*Reprinted from *Journal of Reading,* 8 (May, 1965) pp. 391-395 by permission of the author and the International Reading Association.

any mathematics text will reveal a heavy vocabulary load. Often several new words are introduced together because they are related to an operation being taught. This creates more difficulty for the student unless the teacher helps him before he reads to understand something about the meaning of the words. The length and intensity of the teacher's explanation should be governed by the clarity of the presentation in the text.

The reader's confusion is increased by the fact that some words already known are met again in mathematics, but this time with an entirely different meaning. These include such words as *acute, axis, braces, chord, cone, cylinder, face, natural, primer, radius, rational, ray, scale, set,* and *square.*

Some students have trouble with difficult vocabulary in mathematics because explanations in the text or by the teacher assume incorrectly that they know the less complex vocabulary. The definition of *reciprocal,* may be presented as "multiplicative inverse." Interpreting this correctly depends on much knowledge, despite the inclusion of only two words in the definition. The newer textbooks often include reviews of the more elementary terms involved in the new operation, sometimes suggesting that the teacher review these concepts with the students before he introduces the more complex terms.

The student also meets many words not mathematical in nature but which are used to present problem situations. Word problems in arithmetic and algebra are cast in different settings. Those centering around banking use "bank vocabulary," as *teller, cashier, bank statement, check,* and *deposit.* Problems involving satellite flights include words such as *trajectory, astronaut, cosmonaut, jet stream,* and *capsule.* Words used in problems centered around the sale of flowers include *florist, bulbs, jonquil, tulips,* and *camellias.* A discussion of the meanings of such words helps to enlarge the student's general vocabulary.

Developing Concept Background

What a reader takes with him to the printed page determines, in large measure, what he gets from the page. The more he knows about a subject, the more he can get from reading about it. One of the jobs of the mathematics teacher is to give the students some understanding to take with them to their reading of assignments in mathematics.

Relating the new topic to one previously studied helps to strengthen the background of understanding. The teacher may briefly review related units as a transition into the new material. When students are found to be deficient in the understandings basic to mastery of the new content, the teacher must take the necessary time for building the background before launching the new topic.

Some building of concepts will come before reading; some will come afterward. How much help the teacher gives before reading will depend upon the knowledge the students already have and how much explanation the text offers.

Developing Ability to Select Appropriate Techniques for Reading Mathematics Materials

Reading mathematics, in most instances, is a slow and thorough process. Every word, every numeral, every symbol carries crucial meaning. Problems are "cut to the bone," with no wasted words. Mathematics calls for intense concentration. The reader must understand completely if he is to accomplish the mathematical task set up for him. His thought process is interrupted constantly as he moves from one brief exercise to another in a text. Seldom does he meet more than one page constructed around the same theme. Suddenly, in the middle of the page, word problems may change to computation problems. Re-reading is often necessary.

The mathematics teacher needs to know these special problems inherent in mathematics materials, and he must prepare the student for meeting them. At the beginning of the year and at appropriate later times, how to read text materials effectively should be discussed with the students.

Many of the basic comprehension skills are employed in reading mathematics materials with understanding. Following directions, drawing inferences and generalizations, and evaluating critically are very important. As the student reads, he orders his thinking. He selects and discards in terms of the nature of the problem.

Though teachers work on following directions in many subjects, mathematics offers unusually good opportunities for furthering the development of this basic comprehension skill. Almost every page contains at least one set of directions to be followed, and some pages contain several directions for the readers. Teachers must help students to develop exactness in following directions. Some students have developed an attitude of "If I come close to it, I've done the job." This attitude is fatal in mathematics. When students misinterpret directions, teachers have a tendency to correct them verbally because it is quicker and easier. Having such students re-read the directions and standing by to give just the bare amount of help needed is a much more effective way to teach. This places the burden where it should—on the learner.

Developing Proficiency in the Special Reading Tasks in Mathematics

Students must be given help in reading word problems in arithmetic and in algebra. Most teacher's guidebooks offer ways of working problems. Though the words used and steps do not coincide exactly, the overall patterns are similar. They usually include the following:

(1)   Reading the problem quickly to get an overview.
(2)   Re-read the problem, this time at a slower rate, to determine what facts are given.

(3)   Think of the specific question to be answered.
(4)   Think of the order in which the facts are to be used in answering the question raised in the problem.
(5)   Think of the operations required for solving the problem.
(6)   Estimate an answer that seems reasonable.
(7)   Work the problem by performing the appropriate operations.
(8)   Compare the answer with the estimated answer.
(9)   Go back to the first step if the answer seem unreasonable.

When a table, graph, chart, or other illustration is first included in text material, the teacher must teach students how to read it and give follow-up practice for permanent learning. He must also help the students to develop the habit of taking the necessary time to study these aids because they are vital parts of the reading matter and must be read.

The reading of equations is vitally important in mathematics. Students may easily memorize "meaning" instead of understanding. In elementary algebra, for example, the student may meet an equation such as $X + 5 = 7$. In solving this equation, the student who reasons that "you take the 5 across the equals sign and thus change it to a minus; therefore, the answer is 2" may get the correct answer, but he missed completely the meaning involved. When the teacher allows a device such as this to be used to the exclusion of what actually is happening, he is doing a disservice to the learner. He should insist upon understanding. Taking the time to think through "subtracting equals from equals" will assure comprehension of the concept.

Developing Skill in Interpreting Mathematical Symbols and Abbreviations

Symbols play an extremely important part in mathematics from the very beginning. The mathematics teacher is the person who has the responsibility of teaching the students in his classes to interpret these symbols correctly. As these symbols are encountered in mathematics, they should be explained thoroughly to students. Checks are necessary to insure thorough learning, and if testing or observation reveals that some students still do not know these symbols, re-teaching should occur. At the beginning of the year, the teacher may prepare a test on symbols taught at lower levels to be administered to the students. The teacher should then review those symbols not known.

Mathematics symbols sometimes involve understanding an operation. For instance, what we mean by adding is involved in the plus symbol; what we mean by subtraction is involved in the minus symbol. When a student encounters the Greek letter "pi" as a symbol representing one element in the circumference formula, the teacher may introduce this as an apparently arbitrary constant, or he may take the time to have the student measure, first the diameter, then the circumference, which is approximately three times the diameter. An explanation that precise measurement would show the circumference to be 3.1416 times the diameter would follow naturally. If such understanding has not been gained in the elementary school, the high school teacher must do the necessary remedial work.

The high school teacher may have to re-teach many abbreviations encountered in mathematics. Words such as *quart* and *miles* are usually spelled out in work problems and abbreviated in number problems. When abbreviations are not understood, the teacher should take the necessary time to teach them thoroughly.

Helping the Excellent and Poor Readers in Mathematics

In addition to teaching the special reading skills related to their subject, mathematics teachers also have another responsibility. Some students in the typical classroom are sufficiently disabled in reading to find the reading of texts on their grade level extremely difficult or almost impossible. Then there are some who find very little challenge in grade-level texts because they are such excellent readers and because they have excellent backgrounds in mathematics. The subject-matter teacher must be concerned with bringing these students into contact with mathematics materials that suit their varied reading levels.

The good reader who needs more challenge may be encouraged to build greater depth in the subject. More advanced treatments in other texts and use of reference materials are two possibilities for these students.

The poor readers present an entirely different problem. The teacher's challenge here is to locate material in mathematics – and on the topics being studied – that the student can read, if such materials are available. Students who are average and above in intelligence but are poor readers often can understand the mathematical concepts if they do not have to read about them. For these students, the teacher may depend less upon reading and more upon other avenues of learning. Word problems may be rewritten, or they may be read to the students. In addition to this help in mathematics classes, somewhere, somehow in the school day, somebody should devote some time to teaching these poor readers the basic skills they lack in reading. Poor readers cannot be expected to unravel word problems they meet in books if they cannot read well.

Summary

Teachers of mathematics must assume responsibility for teaching those special reading skills necessary for reading mathematics effectively. These reading needs, growing out of the nature of mathematics, must be met through teaching materials that are neither too difficult nor too easy for the students. Systematic attention to the development of the specialized reading skills in mathematics will result in better readers—and in higher achievement in mathematics.

Reading and Mathematics*

RUSSELL J. CALL AND NEAL A. WIGGIN

The teaching of the general topic of solving word problems in mathematics is often a topic of discussion at meetings of mathematics teachers. In an effort to collect data which might suggest areas for curriculum revision and improvement, the study described in this article was conducted by Dr. Russell J. Call, Chairman of the Mathematics Department at Winnacunnet High School, Hampton, New Hampshire, and Mr. Neal A. Wiggin, House Coordinator at Hampton.

The purpose of the experiment was to determine whether there is some correlation between a student's ability to solve word problems in second year algebra and the presence or absence of special reading instruction. In particular, the experiment hoped to show that the instruction in reading would contribute to the development of skills in solving word problems.

Before any experiment is carried out, there ought to be some clear understanding of the learning theory involved, in order to discover whether or not the instructional techniques and the inferences make sense psychologically. The premises upon which this study is based are not inconsistent with Gestalt psychology.

The first step was to define the problem which we hoped to solve. We noted that students who had a high degree of proficiency in performing mathematical operations were considerably less proficient in solving word problems. There is obviously some different factor or factors at work in such situations. To state unequivocally that the problem is one of reading is risky or highly suppositious; of particular interest is the fact that students who can read all the words still have difficulty in solving the problem. Thus, the source of trouble is not entirely vocabulary, since all could identify the words and define them. What, then, is the problem? It may be that lack of reading comprehension is involved, since we know that there can be considerable discrepancy between vocabulary scores and comprehension scores on standardized reading tests.

*Reprinted from *Mathematics Teacher*, 59 (February, 1966), pp. 149-157, by permission of the authors and the National Council of Teachers of Mathematics.

Words are linguistic signs which call up or reactivate a memory trace; they are symbols of concepts. In and of themselves, words are nothing; they derive their meanings from the context in which they are found. The mathematical context is, or, may be, quite different from some other context. Thus, mathematics reading presents some special denotations — denotations which must call into play the proper traces if inhibition is to be minimized. The technique, then, must be such that conceptualization provoked by the words must be consonant with the mathematical context. It becomes a problem akin to translation, as the sample lesson plans will show.

We settled upon the following experimental method because of its practicality within our school. First of all, one of us, Dr. Call, is a teacher of mathematics. The other, Mr. Wiggin, is a teacher of English with some specialization in the field of reading. It might, then, be possible to select two classes of comparable abilities and use one group as a control and the other as an experimental group. The next question is to consider at what level the experiment should be conducted. We decided upon a course in second year algebra. (1)† Students in second year algebra are usually among our better students, both in mathematics and in other subject areas; thus we might reasonably expect that there would be less likelihood of widespread reading deficiency or widespread deficiency in mathematics classes, for instance. (2) Since one of us, Mr. Wiggin, had never studied second year algebra, even in high school, we concluded that this would be desirable for the reason that the instruction given in Mr. Wiggin's section would not benefit from any great familiarity with methods of teaching mathematics; thus any significant results would further emphasize the reading factor, rather than a difference in mathematical approach. (3) Lastly, as a matter of practicality, it would be easier to schedule classes on this basis, since the comparability of groups was less likely in other mathematics courses in the school.

Certain information necessary in the development of the experiment was already available in guidance files. For example, we needed to know what factors in intelligence and aptitude, as well as in previous achievement, might have a bearing on our experiment, particularly as it applied to establishing comparability between the groups. After compiling the available data, we "paired off" a student in the control group with a student in the experimental group. In this way, we could establish individual, as well as group, comparability.

The instruction in both groups lasted for ten days. During that time neither teacher consulted with the other relative to methods in use. This precaution may not have been necessary, but we had concluded that it might be possible for either of us to be influenced by what we knew was taking place in the other class.

There is one other factor which we wished to overcome as much as could be reasonably expected; that is what is known as the Hawthorne effect. In

†Numbers in parenthesis refer to references at end of article.

substance, what the Hawthorne effect means is that a noticeable difference is likely to occur in any experimental situation wherein the subjects are aware that they are involved in an experiment. To avoid this problem, we agreed that Dr. Call would inform the group which Mr. Wiggin was to teach that he (Dr. Call) had some important work to do in the next two weeks and that Mr. Wiggin would be standing in. Thus, neither group knew that an experiment was under way.

The instruction began, and during the period of the experiment we compiled the data. We had to be sure that we had a way to measure the results. No standardized test has been constructed which is designed to measure the results, or the kinds of instructional outcomes, which we were expecting. Thus, we had to resort to teacher-made tests. Both of us contributed items to the test, but neither was aware of what the other was including in the test. This was done to prevent any conscious, or unconscious, effort to "teach for the test."

The basic text in use was *Second Course in Algebra* by Arthur W. Weeks and Jackson B. Adkins, published by Ginn and Company in 1962. For the experiment, we taught Chapter 3, "Systems of Linear Equations, Word Problems." No new procedures were employed in the control group, and an effort was made to keep the instruction as much like that of usual procedure as possible.

Following are two sample lesson plans from the experimental group. The principle is, in general, this: Words are just symbols with a variety of meanings until they appear in context. Thus, they derive their meaning from the whole of which they are a part. We need, then, to examine the whole first before we begin any analysis of the parts. Secondly, we should note that 5 is a symbol for a concept which may be represented by the fingers on a hand, the toes on a foot, by the tabulation sign $/////$, by the Roman numeral V, and by the word "five". Naturally, the same concept may be represented in other ways as well. The important factor to remember is that sounds, words, and mathematical symbols may represent the same concept. More specifically, the word "equal" and the mathematical symbol "=" are represented in problems in a variety of ways. We have to examine the whole problem, and then we have to study the parts to determine which words represent concepts that may be translated into mathematical signs. Note that in a rate-time-distance problem, "equal" is sometimes expressed as ". . . the same distance," ". . . the same speed," and so on. Also, the equal concept sometimes appears in many subtle ways. For example, we have a problem in which a man leaves his home at some given time and another man leaves his home at a later time. At some point, the second overtakes the first. Here we have to learn to observe relationships. The second man traveled less time (represented by a minus sign), but traveled the same distance (represented by an equals sign). Thus, we see that the expression "over-takes" is here equivalent to "equal," and the term "later" indicates "less" and is represented by "minus." We are not presuming in these paragraphs to present the step-by-step procedure used in the classroom. These explanations will give the reader some insight into the complex factors in reading which we believe influence the success or failure of the student attempting to solve word problems.

Lesson Plan 1

What is a mathematics problem? When most people think of numbers or numerals; they think of computations – of addition, subtraction, multiplication, square roots, and so forth. There is no question that these are parts of mathematics. These factors are operations. They are, in fact, pure mathematical concepts, which, in and of themselves, are useless.

Mathematics, to be of use, must be capable of application, and must be applied. Now, how do we apply mathematics in life? We are confronted with some kind of situation which must be resolved by the use of mathematics. It is not enough to know how to perform the operations. We must know which operations apply to a particular situation.

Suppose that I want to lay out a baseball diamond. I must know something of the standard measurements of baseball diamonds, and I must know how to construct 90 degree angles and how to find a point 60½ feet from the vertex of an angle and equidistant from two points located on the sides of the angle 90 feet from the vertex. In other words, I need to know what the situation requires and how to perform the operations in resolving it. It does me no good at all in this situation to know how to construct a square, if I don't know how long each baseline is and how far the pitcher's mound is located from home plate.

In any situation where mathematics is to be applied, we need first of all to acquire the data involved; it is necessary to find out such things as what the following are: 90 feet, 60½ feet, right angles, and so forth. Then we must perceive the relationships between items; then we must proceed with the operations. It is not possible for us in the classroom to set up sample situations for everyone to carry out. That is, the real application of mathematics cannot be taught in class because of physical limitations. Yet, if mathematics is to be of use, we must teach the practical applications of it. If we can only perform the mathematical operations, we are a very poor substitute for a machine, because one machine can outperform many of us humans.

What I am saying, in other words, is this: If you think that the value of studying math lies in the ability to compute, you are wasting your time. Machines have already replaced you. You are training to do a job that doesn't exist. Thus, we must find a suitable substitute for practical situations in order to learn the principle involved in applying mathematics.

The best means we have at present is the word problem. Instead of confronting you with a real situation, we describe the situation to you. From our description of the problem you must decide what computations to make; then you must make them.

My job in the next few days will be to see if I can help you learn to apply mathematics. I shall not de-emphasize accuracy in performing computations; but I shall place in the number one position the learning of "what" to do; how well you do it will take second place.

If industry can find a man who is poor at computation, but an expert at discovering what computations need to be made, he'll never be without a job. A machine can do the computation. It can't do the first job.

Any subject or field has its special vocabulary. If you are to be able to solve word problems, you must know the terminology of the field. When I say "know it," I don't mean "recognize it." I mean that you must be able to paraphrase it and give an example of it. This is the only way we can determine whether you understand the terminology you are using. Today's lesson will be partly devoted to some terminology. At the same time we will learn to make the computations which are necessary for the kind of problems which we are about to study. *First Degree or Linear Equation:* Define "Linear" (having to do with a line). A solution is equal to a pair of values of x and y which make the statement true. The equation has an unlimited number of solutions. It is represented by a line on a graph. The conditions of a problem may be represented by two equations in two variables. Then the solution must satisfy the conditions of both equations.

$$y = 3x - 4$$
$$8x + 2y + 1 = 0$$

When they have one common solution the equations are referred to a system. The process of finding the common solution is called "solving the system of equations." If the two equations are contradictory – if they do not have a common solution – we say the system is inconsistent. (*Illustrate*) If the two equations are equivalent, a solution of one is also a solution of the other. This kind of system is called "dependent." (*Illustrate*) At this point, let's practice a few solutions using two different methods. (*Assignment*)

Lesson Plan 2
Reading the Mathematics Problem

What often happens in a problem is that students supply an answer other than the one required. Look at the problems in Exercise A-2 on page 32. What does the problem ask for in numbers 18 and 19? (The authors are asking "how many pairs of values," and not "what are the values." The less discriminating reader may supply the actual value rather than the number of pairs.) In number 19, we are asked to express x in terms of u. This is analogous to expressing a given sum of money in terms of dimes or nickels. We are really asking: "How many u's make an x?" The second part of the problem asks us to find the value of u when x is given a definite value. When we give a value to x, we are applying a condition to x. We must then find the value of u which will satisfy this condition. (Students need to learn to recognize from the words the condition or conditions which apply to the situation.)

Number 22 has a strange wording. What is asked for? What must we supply for a correct answer? (Values of x and y which will satisfy the conditions expressed by all three equations.) What do we call these systems which have a common solution? (Dependent systems.)

Do Exercise B, problem 1, page 32. Note that a solution of the equation is an answer to the problem.

Note that in problem 2, solutions to the systems of equations are not answers to the problem.

In number 4, the wording is difficult. Restate the problem in your own words so that we know that you understand what is asked for. (Possible answer: We have to find some whole number value of y. There is probably more than one value of y. The one we select will have to give us a value of x that is less than 1.) What are the conditions which apply to y? (It must be the smallest whole number which will make x have a value less than 1.) What are the conditions which apply to x (It must be smaller than 1.)

What is asked for in number 6, on page 33? (This problem is stated in a negative fashion: "Show that no pair of values of x and y satisfies the three equations. . . " We must show that this system of equations is inconsistent.)

What is the condition applied to the equation system in number 7? (Find the value that a must have if the three equations are to have a common solution.)

What is asked for in number 10? Note that we ask how many solutions, not what is the solution. Restate each part of the problem in your own words. What is the mathematical sign indicated by "the sum off"? What word represents the minus sign? (Difference) What sign is indicated by the word equal? How many different conditions apply to a? to b? to c?

What conditions apply to x in number 11?

What conditions apply to y? Note that these are simultaneous conditions.

The foregoing may be of some help in understanding the nature of the instruction in the experimental group. In all cases, the purpose was to get the meaning from the context by seeing the relationship between the parts and the whole. Mathematical signs are symbols of relationships, as well as of operations. Thus, the meaning is not readily translated from words to mathematical symbols until the relationships between the parts are clear. So much for procedure! A seven-question test was administered at the end of the experiment. The first two items were systems of equations; the last five were word problems. The first three tables indicate some of the more useful data.

Table 2 shows the initial analysis figures. Since we are dealing with reading comprehension as well as with mathematics, we have taken into account both the number of problems correctly solved and the number in which the procedure was correct but computational errors led to a wrong solution. It is reasonable to assume that if the student translated the reading into the correct mathematical equation, he understood the problem. From that point on, if he made an error, we counted the procedure correct, but the answer wrong. For our purposes, it seems important to know some comparative data on what pupils did on the reading, as well as upon the computations. Thus we discover, in addition to the above data, that in the control group 63 percent were not able to solve any of the problems correctly, and 42 percent did not have any of the procedures correct; in the experimental group, however, only 20 percent got no correct solutions, and only 6 percent were unable to get any correct procedures.

The discriminative power of a test item is represented by the difference between the number of above-average and below-average pupils answering it correctly. These numbers are converted into percentages of the total group. Above-average and below-average are determined by the performance on the total test, and have nothing to do with external data. Thus, on item 3, eleven of these who scored in the upper half on the test also got item 3 correct, whereas only three of those who scored in the lower half got that item correct. According to J. Raymond Gerberich, in his book, *Measurement and Evaluation in the Modern School,* items are usually rated satisfactory individually when they have indices of discrimination of at least 10, but the average of such indices for all items in a test should probably be above 10, preferably around 15. The average here is 18.6.

Item difficulty is usually expressed as the percentage of pupils in the above-average and below-average groups combined who answer the item correctly. Thus, the number of correct answers to each item is divided by the total number of pupils in the group to obtain the index of item difficulty. In general, items ranging from 30 to 90 percent of correct responses with an average of 70 percent, are considered acceptable in difficulty for objective classroom tests. However, we should note that if a test is to measure effectively, there must be some items of very low discrimination power and/or difficulty in order to reach the poorest performer and the best performer. The average here is 27 percent. There is nothing here to indicate that the items constructed by one teacher were easier than those constructed by the other.

Additional data appear in the tables that follow. In order to be as objective as possible in all conclusions, we have exerted every effort to show that the results might have come from some source other than the type of instruction used. The evidence, however, seems to be over-whelmingly in favor of the instructional techniques employed in the experimental group!

Since a number of variables are involved in this experiment, it was necessary to examine the results with the variables controlled. For example,

TABLE 1

ANALYSIS OF A FREQUENCY DISTRIBUTION OF WORD PROBLEM TEST SCORES
OF 44 STUDENTS IN SECOND YEAR ALGEBRA CLASSES:
ARITHMETIC MEAN AND STANDARD DEVIATION

Raw Score	Frequency (f)	Deviation (d)	fd	fd^2
13	0	9	0	0
12	2	8	16	128
11	0	7	0	0
10	1	6	6	36
9	3	5	15	75
8	4	3	12	36
7	5	2	10	20
6	2	1	2	2
5	4	0	0	0
4	6	−1	− 6	6
3	4	−2	− 8	16
2	5	−3	−15	45
1	2	−4	− 8	32
0	6	−5	−30	150
	44		− 6	546

A.M.: 4.86
S.D.: 3.52
Median: 4

Approximate reliability coefficient of test, based on arithmetic mean, standard deviation, and number of items is .60.

The number of items used to compile these data is 18. Though there were only seven questions, there were 18 separate items which we scored.

TABLE 2

DATA ANALYSIS SHEET

(Figures based on 19-member control group and 25-member experimental group)

	Control Group	Experimental Group
Number of problems correct	12	46
Number of procedures correct	24	69
Average number of problems correct	.63	1.8
Average number of procedures correct	1.26	2.6

TABLE 3

DIFFICULTY AND DISCRIMINATIVE POWER OF TEST ITEMS FOR 44-PUPIL DISTRIBUTION

Item Number	Number Correct		Sum	Upper-Lower Difference	Index	
	Upper Half	Lower Half			Difficulty	Discrimination
3	11	3	14	8	31	18
4	16	2	18	14	41	31
5	14	3	17	11	38	25
6	8	1	9	7	20	15
7	2	0	2	2	4	4

This table is listed for the purpose of determining whether the test items constructed by one teacher were any more difficult than those constructed by the other. There might be a possibility that the teacher of reading had made the items so that they were more readily understandable by the pupils. If this were so, both groups should have performed better on those items. The data do not seem to indicate this.

TABLE 4

COMPARATIVE SCORES USING READING LEVEL AS A CONTROL

	Control Group	*Experimental Group*
1.	0	1
2.	2	8
3.	9	4
4.	4	2
5.	4	9
6.	8	9
7.	0	8
8.	7	7
9.	4	12
10.	0	3
11.	5	10
12.	7	5
13.	2	7
14.	3	6
15.	7	5
	62	96
A.M.	4.14	6.4

These scores are paired on the basis of the Cooperative Reading Test "Level" score, with not more than three points variation between scores. The actual average variation is 1.3 percentile points. Only 40 percent of the control groups scored above the 4.86 mean of the two groups combined; 73.3 percent of the experimental group scored above this mean.

since this was an experiment in the teaching of reading to a mathematics class, the reading ability of the subjects needed to be measured; then we paired off the subjects, one from each group, on the basis of the level of comprehension as measured by the Cooperative Reading Test. The pairs do not vary more than three percentile points; in fact, the average variations between pairs was 1.3 percentile points. Thus, for all practical purposes, it can be assumed that the reading levels were the same. Table 4 shows the results of this comparison. The two columns show the test scores on the math achievement test when the reading level is controlled. The mean score of the control group was 4.14, whereas the mean score for the experimental group was 6.4. To further solidify the significance of these results, we made a similar comparison using the verbal score of the DAT. This was done to discover whether those in one group had a greater aptitude for learning material presented in a verbal manner as opposed to a mathematical manner. If the experimental group had had a greater aptitude for verbal material, the results would have been inconclusive. Table 5 shows the comparison of the math achievement scores when this verbal factor was controlled. The mean score of the control group was 3.5; the mean score of the experimental group was 5.3. Since the pairing was done with no more than three percentile points between any two subjects (actual average variation was 1.8 points), we can assume, for all practical purposes, that there was no difference in verbal aptitude between the groups.

TABLE 5

COMPARATIVE SCORES USING VERBAL SCORE OF DAT AS CONTROL

	Control Group	*Experimental Group*
1.	0	7
2.	2	4
3.	9	3
4.	0	8
5.	4	4
6.	4	2
7.	8	6
8.	0	3
9.	7	1
10.	4	9
11.	0	4
12.	5	3
13.	7	5
14.	3	9
15.	0	12
	53	80
A.M.	3.5	5.3

These scores are paired on the basis of the verbal score from the DAT, with not more than three points variation between scores. The actual average variation is 1.8 percentile points. 33.3 percent of the control group fall above the 4.86 mean; 46.6 percent of the experimental group fall abve the 4.86 mean.

Another factor which had to be examined under controlled conditions was the aptitude of each group for mathematical reasoning. Obviously, if one group was better than the other in this respect, the result could not then be attributed

TABLE 6

COMPARATIVE SCORES WHEN DAT QUANTITATIVE SCORE IS CONTROLLED

	Control Group	Experimental Group
1.	0	3
2.	2	8
3.	9	7
4.	0	4
5.	4	1
6.	4	9
7.	8	6
8.	0	8
9.	7	9
10.	4	2
11.	5	6
12.	7	7
13.	2	12
14.	3	5
15.	0	2
16.	7	5
	62	94
A.M.	3.9	5.88

These scores are paired on the basis of the Quantitative Score from the DAT, with not more than three points variation between scores. The actual average variation is .4 percentile points. 37.5 percent of the control group fall above the 4.86 mean; 66.6 percent of the experimental groups fall above the 4.86 mean.

to the difference in instructional techniques. Table 6 shows the comparison when the pairs are controlled on the basis of the quantitative score from the DAT. Pairings were so nearly identical that the mean variation on the quantitative score between each set was .4 percentile points. We were able to match sixteen pairs of students in this manner. Note that the experimental group did considerably better, with a mean score on the mathematics test of 5.88, whereas the mean score of the control group was 3.9.

Finally, we made a similar pairing on the basis of I.Q. scores from the Otis Gamma. Here we are able to match fifteen pairs, with an average variation of 1.6 points. Insofar as measurable intelligence is concerned, this is considerably closer than we had hoped to get. Thus, for all practical purposes, the groups were identical in intelligence. Again, the control group scored lower than the

TABLE 7
COMPARATIVE SCORES WHEN I.Q. IS CONTROLLED

	Control Group	*Experimental Group*
1.	0	4
2.	2	4
3.	9	8
4.	0	9
5.	4	2
6.	8	12
7.	0	3
8.	0	8
9.	0	7
10.	0	8
11.	5	10
12.	7	4
13.	3	3
14.	7	5
15.	1	7
	46	94
A.M.	3.1	6.2

These scores are paired on the basis of I.Q. scores on the Otis Gamma, with not more than three points variation between scores. Actual average variation is 1.6 points. 33.3 percent of the control group and 73.3 percent of the experimental group fall above the 4.86 mean.

experimental group. In fact, the mean score is doubled by the experimental group. No matter how you slice it, the results point to a better response by the group which was taught reading.

Let us summarize the experiment and see what tentative conclusions can be drawn. Two groups were taught the same unit in second year algebra, a unit involving linear equations and word problems. The control group was taught by an experienced mathematics teacher, chairman of the mathematics department at Winnacunnet High School. The experimental group was taught by an English teacher with a limited amount of training in the teaching of reading and with no training in the teaching of mathematics. In fact, he had never had a course in Algebra II. The major difference in instructional techniques was the fact that the experimental group was taught to get the meaning from the words and translate it into mathematical symbols. This was done more in the manner of the teaching of reading than that of the teaching of mathematics. The results seem to indicate that the experimental group did better, even when reading abilities and mathematical aptitude were controlled. We make the following inferences from the data acquired:

(1)   There is some merit in teaching special reading skills for the solution of mathematical problems.

(2)   Even very good readers, as measured by the Cooperative Reading Test, have difficulty in the interpretation of the kind of reading found in word problems.

(3)   Part of the difficulty which teachers encounter in the teaching of mathematics comes from a special kind of reading disability which does not appear on standard measuring instruments.

(4)   Part of the difficulty which teachers encounter in the teaching of mathematics is that they are not equipped to teach reading.

(5)   If by teaching reading, instead of mathematics, we can get better results, it seems reasonable to infer that the competent mathematics teacher might get considerably better results if he were trained to teach reading of the kind encountered in mathematics.

We also suggest that this experiment has some cogent implications for further testing. An experiment done on a much larger scale might be of significant value in making recommendations for the improvement of teacher education and in-service training. It is time we took note of the necessity for studying relationships between disciplines where no relation has seemed apparent. The experiment further points up the need for a fundamental, but good, developmental reading program in which a trained reading specialist can help to prepare materials which will improve reading skills in all subject areas. All our classes have textbooks; all our students are expected to be able to read them; yet, in the vast majority of cases, not even the high school English teacher has had any training in the teaching of reading skills. How, then, may we expect the student to come from the elementary school and continue to improve his reading skills when he is offered no instruction for that purpose? This study has shown that mathematics is one such area where reading instruction may be enormously beneficial.

Reading Improvement in the Industrial Arts Class*

MALCOLM HEYMAN AND RICHARD HOLLAND

There is virtually no area of life in modern society in which success can be achieved without the ability to read. As human beings we all need a sense of some achievement, some measure of success. Absence of success in school quickly brings frustration, and success for the student is *totally* dependent on his ability to comprehend the written word with as much ease as he does the spoken word. If he does not, failure is his lot every turn of the way.

Repeated failure contributes strongly to the degeneration of the student's self image and ultimately it can destroy the self image entirely. Some students fail to accept the fact that they have come to a dead end and become truants, and finally drop-outs. Others continue to attend school but try to gain their much needed recognition by others through anti-social behavior. Such a student becomes something like the clownish oaf of old-time burlesque shows who tormented his fellow players with pranks and foolish tricks for the amusement of the audience. Our nonachieving student comes to school to gain victims for his antics--teachers--and an audience--his fellow students. Outside, as a truant, he has neither. In a sense this anti-social behavior is achievement for him and perseverance in this behavior can even bring success, of a sort. Thus we have the returnees of reform schools and youth correction houses admired as neighborhood heroes.

In *The Journal of Industrial Arts Education,* March-April, 1965, D. Neslo's article, "Ground for Salvage--Not for Dumping," clearly dramatizes a situation all too familiar to shop teachers. He shows us one of these typical behavior problems undergoing a guidance session with his principal, the final outcome of which is his placement in a shop class in lieu of academic classes for which he was ordinarily scheduled. This situation is so common that it has simply become one of the realities industrial arts teachers just accept. However, industrial arts teachers must not, as Mr. Neslo concludes, take this as an indication of debasement either of themselves personally or of their professional standing in

*Reprinted from *Journal of Industrial Arts Education,* 25 (January, 1966), pp. 48-49, 58, by permission of the author and the American Industrial Arts Association.

the community of education. It is instead a challenge and a demanding responsibility.

Should the industrial arts teacher deal with these students as ne'er-do-wells and do no more than assure that their time and hands are occupied with purposeless tasks, the industrial arts class will indeed become a "dumping ground." However, it can be a place where a return to a full life of learning can begin and hope for meaningful achievement can be renewed. To do this the teacher must consider these students' most important and basic need, in school life and in later life as well — *reading.*

The Foundations

A shop program designed with reading as a main part of the class activity and with reading improvement as its ultimate aim can be implemented very easily. Perhaps some will challenge this with the argument that an industrial arts teacher is not a reading teacher and should keep hands off this area since he lacks the background and training necessary for the job, or another argument against reading training in shop class might be that it is not the responsibility of the industrial arts teacher; students should get their reading instruction in English and reading classes. If, however, we are to be realistic about the situation faced by many industrial arts teachers today, most especially in large urban schools which draw from deprived communities, the job goes far beyond teaching the immediate subject we are trained for. A Peace Corps volunteer would not teach a foreign peasant just how to irrigate the ground and the use of tools; he would also spend time teaching him to write. Our approach with our own should be the same. When dealing with students retarded in reading, we all become in effect reading teachers—academic, industrial arts, health education, and home economics teachers alike. In meeting the problem of making up for a lack of training in the teaching of reading, help can readily be obtained from those teachers in the school whose backgrounds do include such training. A program where the industrial arts department is coordinated with the remedial or corrective reading division in the school is ideal since one department can help the other.

One of the most important responsibilities of the industrial arts teacher is to keep his shop abreast of the times. It should be, in curriculum and equipment, a true and undistorted reflection of practices and material used in current industry. Tools, materials, methods, techniques must be up to date; but in a society such as ours where industry and the most basic trades change and improve their methods and materials rapidly, keeping up to date becomes quite a challenge. The solution to this problem can be found in part in industry itself. And this solution, we are glad to relate, serves both the immediate need of the industrial arts teacher and the purpose of reading improvement. It is simply to take advantage of the availability of publicity materials provided by almost all companies and corporations in private industry. The literature of industry – its catalogs, manuals, brochures, and even printed directions for use of products – is a valuable source of information on current trends in industry so far as both methods and materials are concerned. Such literature is easily obtainable from most industrial organizations on request since it serves their purpose of public relations and ultimately may be a way of selling a future customer on their products, since many of the students will hopefully enter the various industrial fields as tradesmen themselves.

Remedial Reading Coordination

Close coordination on this project with a teacher having remedial reading training is highly recommended. With his help brochures and booklets can be evaluated so far as level of reading difficulty is concerned, lessons in vocabulary and comprehension can be constructed, and the possibility of a carry-over to the corrective reading class of the motivation and work done on these materials can be made available to him. A list of companies which have made such materials available to the writers at Alexander Burger Junior High School 139, Bronx, New York, follows this article. We are sure that any industrial company would reply favorably and generously to a teacher's request. We offer these names as a starter since they have already shown their willingness to help in this area and have supplied us with an abundance of valuable materials. May we further suggest that you state your purpose for wanting the materials in your letters.

Woodworking Project

The preceding project can, of course, be applied to any industrial arts class. Here is a suggestion for a specific industrial arts class—the woodworking shop. With this type of project, we hope to stimulate a desire to follow up what has been done in shop with a good deal of reading.

It is with this hope that we suggest the "mobile class library project." It involves the construction of several mobile bookcases which fold closed and have handles to allow them to be carried from one class to another. Each bookcase should be designed to hold only one type of book: e.g. biographies, fiction, travel, science fiction, etc. In addition a frame should be attached to the outside of the case for some sort of schedule on which teachers may reserve the library for particular classes during the week. This project is particularly ideal for overcrowded schools where teachers have "traveling programs."

Phonic Exercise Board

A third and more elaborate project we might suggest is an electric phonic exercise board which would involve the wood shop and the electric shop. A simple version of such a board could be constructed from an old typewriter and a honeycombed box covered with glass, each pigeonhole in the box containing a separate light bulb with a separate lead out wire. Different colors of contact or other adhesive paper is cut to duplicate the letter keyboard on the typewriter, one letter falling over each pigeonhole with a light bulb on it. The lead out wires are then affixed to each key of the old typewriter and an electrified metal plate put over the platen of the typewriter. When the key is pushed and touches the platen, the corresponding hole behind the proper letter should light (see illustration for an idea of how this practice board looks).

A reading teacher could use such a board to teach different phonic elements such as digraphs and consonant blends, or it could be used to teach spelling. Of course, it would have little use other than with severely retarded children but the motivation is very high and it could be adapted to other uses, even the teaching of the touch system in typing classes.

These few suggestions are offered merely as illustrations of how the industrial arts classes can play their part in the all-important role of leading underachievers back to the fruitful and rewarding experiences in school which have been unavailable to them because of poor reading.

Companies Which Have Provided Materials and Literature:

The Irwin Auger Bit Company, Wilmington, Ohio.
Radiant Lamp Corp., Newark, N. J.
The Rigid Tool Company, Elyria, Ohio.
Nye Tool Company, Chicago, Ill.
Skil Corporation, Chicago, Ill.
Killark Electric Manufacturing Co., St. Louis, Mo.
International Association of Electrical Inspectors, Chicago, Ill.
Rome Cable Division of Alcoa, Rome, N. Y.
General Motors Corporation, Warren, Mich.

Republic Steel Corp., Cleveland, Ohio.
The Wiremold Company, Hartford, Conn.
The Electric Storage Battery Company, Cleveland, Ohio.
The General Electric Company, New York City
Gould-National Batteries Inc., Trenton, N. J.
Champion Lamp Works, Lynn, Mass.
Kraloy Plastic Pipe Co., Inc., Santa Ana, Calif.
The Okonite Company, Passaic, N. J.
The Crescent Tool Company, Jamestown, N. J.
National Association of Manufacturers, New York City.
Sonotone Corporation, Elmsford, N. Y.
Western Union Telegraph Company, New York City.
American Association of Battery Manufacturers, East Orange, N. J.
The Steelduct Company, Youngstown, Ohio.
National Electrical Products Corp., Pittsburgh, Pa.
Union Carbide Corporation, New York City.
Allis-Chalmers Research Laboratories, Milwaukee, Wis.
Consolidated Edison Company, New York City.
Kester Solder Company, Chicago, Ill.
New York Telephone Company, New York City.
Mathias Klein and Sons, Inc., Chicago, Ill.
Sandvik Steel, Inc., Fair Lawn, N. J.
J. H. Williams and Company, Buffalo, N. Y.

Solving Reading Problems in Vocational Subjects*

ISIDORE N. LEVINE

Many teachers of trade subjects in the vocational high schools are convinced that their students can't read. The pupils show their inadequacies by being unable to cope with the texts provided for them. They indicate their limitations by their failures on the final written examinations. They are unable to read the job sheets that can be crucial in daily shop work. Every teacher would like to see some improvement in this deplorable situation.

Some shop teachers feel that reading is the job of the teacher of English. He teaches spelling, composition, vocabulary and literature – all the elements comprising the study of reading. Why doesn't the English teacher do his job well enough to solve the reading difficulties the students experience in other subjects? Perhaps the language arts teacher would assume such responsibility if he were certain he could do the work required. However, mere willingness to teach "reading" does not solve special problems to be met in instructing pupils in the art of getting meaning from a page of trade information.

Specialized Vocabulary

What are some of those problems? Suppose we take electric wiring as a possible trade subject for teaching reading. The class in English is taught to recognize the words "splice," "junction," "tap," "tee," "knotted," "pigtail," and "Western Union." The dictionary definitions of these words are as follows:

> *splice* – joining of ropes or timbers by overlapping.
> *junction* – joining or being joined, station.
> *tap* – (1) strike lightly (1) a stopper or plug (3) tool for cutting internal screw threads.

*Reprinted from *High Points*, 43 (April, 1960), pp. 10-27, by permission of the author and the editor.

tee – a mark from which a golf player starts, a little mound of sand and dirt.

knotted – (1) joined (2) tangled. (There are eight other definitions the teacher of English could rule out as being unrelated to electrical work.)

pigtail – braid of hair hanging from the head.

Western Union – a telegraph company.

The final electrical wiring examination includes this typical question:

> To make a splice in a junction box where a number of wire leads are to be joined, the best splice to use is the (a) tap or tee (b) knotted tap (c) pigtail (d) Western Union.

No combination of definitions will yield a solution to the problem for the ambitious teacher of English. We can go farther and say that even accompanying illustrations for each of these splices would still leave the language arts instructor feeling that he was teaching an unfamiliar language.

Lest some teachers suppose that the electrical trades have the only occupational information the English teacher cannot read, we will take an example from the radio and television field. A recent final test in that subject carried this question:

> In a 100% modulated AM transmitter the modulator varies the carrier (a) from zero to the strength of the carrier, (b) from zero to twice the strength of the carrier, (c) from zero to half·the strength of the carrier, (d) does not vary.

As an English teacher, the writer cannot help admiring any pupil who has the knowledge and understanding to read the above intelligently – not as an academic studies teacher would read it, that is, with correct pronunciation, phrasing, inflection and emphasis, but with the meaning necessary to arrive at a correct answer and to be able to explain the reason for such selection.

As a matter of fact, the above passage takes the writer back to his high school Latin study days, when he could "read" the orotund phrases of Caesar's Commentaries with little inkling as to what that ancient was trying to communicate. In the case of radio and television, there is no Latin "pony" to help understand the above question. We can go farther here and state that no application of the thousand and one skills of reading so exhaustively described in the new Board of Education Curriculum Bulletin, "Reading Grades 7-8-9. A Teacher's Guide to Curriculum Planning," can be of any help here. Reading the above properly means studying the subject.

Perhaps other examples from the trade subjects will make this situation even clearer. In the pamphlet on "Machine Shop Practice for Vocational High

Schools" (Curriculum Bulletin #10-1954-1955 Series) on page 82, we find the following in part:

Unit — How to Turn Tapers by the Offset Tailstock Method
Topic — Checking Offset with Dividers
1. Set the legs of the dividers to the required offset. Adjust set-over screws until the distance between the index line on the base and the index line on the tailstock body corresponds to the setting of the dividers.

Here the teacher of English is not too puzzled since the number of technical references is limited and there is an accompanying series of illustrations with the directions. But after calling out the words and studying the drawings we are still far from a complete understanding of this first step. These directions are not meant to be read and discussed. They are useless without the equipment to which they can be applied as far as instruction is concerned.

Another illustration from still another trade will throw light on still another facet of this problem. In the course of study called "Hairdressing and Cosmetology for Vocational High Schools" (Curriculum Bulletin #8 — 1952 — 1953 Series) we note the Instruction Sheet on page 85 includes this series of steps:

Facial Massage

Steps in Facial

(1) Apply cleansing cream	(6) Remove massage cream
(2) Give manipulation for cleansing	(7) Apply astringent
(3) Remove cream	(8) Apply powder base
(4) Apply massage cream	(9) Apply makeup
(5) Give massage manipulation	

Points to Remember

Apply cream with an upward and outward movement.
To remove cream dab at it lightly with tissues.

As a male teacher of English it might be a little embarrassing to study this with a class of girls, but there would be little difficulty in interpreting and understanding the words. Here at last is a trade sheet we can read. But, would it be wise to take the time in the English classroom for this? Like Shakespeare's plays, these directions are not meant to be read aloud only. They are supposed to be *acted* out and certainly not in an English room except in pantomine. And further, the trade of cosmetology has its own foreign language. Among the terms to be studied by a language-arts teacher determined to give proper reading guidance in this occupation are included:

free edge, keratin, lunula, nippers, oil glove, pledget, French twist, effilating, sebum, bias wave, reverse roll, cuticle of hair

and hundreds of others which take years to learn properly.

Vocations and the Language Arts

We have not discussed some of the implications of the English teacher's efforts to teach the reading of vocational subjects in the language-arts class. The woodworking boy who wants to know why his English teacher is taking the time to have his students read the expressions below would be compelling us to reexamine our goals in vocational education:

Explain how to make a mortise on a leg.
List the first five steps in squaring a piece of wood to size.
Draw a marking guage.
Name five different types of lines used in making a drawing.
Give three uses of the hack saw.
Draw a combination square.

Do we want our vocational students to have a restricted curriculum involving trade experiences exculsively? Would any teacher of English accept appointment to a vocational high school knowing that he would be expected to familiarize himself sufficiently with the trades taught in that school to be able to teach the reading matter of those shops?

In desperation some shop subjects chairmen might suggest that the English teacher should interest himself in the trades of the school. They may not be impressed with the argument that the teacher of English selected his subject just as the trade teacher did, that is, because of a personal interest or talent in that field of study. Nor may it be important that the language arts instructor spent many years studying and preparing for the teaching of literature and composition. However, we may well ask such chairmen whether we have the right to deprive the vocational high student of his share of appreciation of the cultural products of writers in every field of literary expression.

The shop teacher presented with this situation might adopt one or both of the attitudes below:

(1)   The English teacher should teach pupils to recognize words, not teach the meaning of the words in a technical sense.
(2)   The English teacher should teach pupils the general skills of reading, such as selecting main ideas in a paragraph, reading for details, skimming,

reading in phrases, reading with a purpose, reading to understand and follow directions, and many others; in sum, to develop those skills which some experts claim can be transferred from one type of reading matter to another.

Word Recognition in Context

In answer to the first view, teachers of English claim that they are doing their utmost to assist students to use the various skills of word recognition when these skills are needed in the reading of literature in the language arts classes. For example, in the study of O. Henry's short story, "Gift of the Magi," the pupil meets the phrase "imputation of parsimony" in the first paragraph. The teacher will help the students analyze the parts of each difficult word (*im-pu-ta-tion*) (*par-si-mony*) where such analysis is needed. Then he will go on to discuss with the class the meaning of this phrase in the complete picture of that first paragraph. He will select as many such word groups for study as he thinks are material for the appreciation of an O. Henry story, with the hope that the student will be stimulated to look up such phrases as, "instigates the moral reflection," "with sniffles predominating," "on the lookout for the mendicancy squad," and numerous others.

If the trade instructor were to suggest that the English teacher take the opportunity to teach such word recognition skills using the technical terms of the shops, the answer would be that this learning activity would be a waste of time for teacher and student. As we have seen above, the English teacher does not merely analyze the word elements in "imputation of parsimony." What is more important is that he spends valuable class time discussing the meaning of the words as used in *that paragraph* of the story. If the teacher of English were merely to attempt analysis of the oral elements of the technical terms, he would be giving little assistance to the shop teacher anxious to have his students read for understanding. The pupils could call out the words from the examination of radio as smoothly as the teacher and still be no farther into reading the question than when they first started the analysis of words like "modulating."

Transfer of Training

Going on to the suggestion that the English instructor train students in the general skills of reading other than word recognition, it can be said that such practice is given in most English classes in the vocational high schools. Most schools are equipped with reading workbooks which are used to develop the general reading skills used in informational reading. However, it has yet to be determined that any such training can be carried over into the other fields of study included in the vocational school curriculum.

Let us take an example from such workbooks to reveal the possibilities of transfer of training in reading. One of the many such used in the high schools in the Scott, Foresman text called "Basic Reading Skills for High School Use" (Revised Edition, 1958). Included in this text are 18 sections, each devoted to a different reading skill such as Main Idea, Summarizing and Organizing, Word Analysis, Phrase and Sentence Meaning, etc. Suppose we turn to the section called Relationships (cause-effect, sequence). Within this section are included twelve reading selections varying in length from 150 to 1,700 words. The titles of these passages indicate that two of them are stories (A Fish Story, Old Three Toes), nine are informational essays (The Dust Storm, The Flood, The First Basketball Game, Fire-Boats to the Rescue, It's the Ham in Them, The Giants of the Galapagos, Who Is Handicapped?, and Collecting Animal Tracks) and one is a biographical sketch (Thirteen). Students are asked to read these selections and answer questions specially prepared to develop the ability to see cause and effect relationship and sequence of ideas in stories.

It is doubtful that a student who has read all these selections and scored a high percentage of correct answers is any nearer to understanding his trade text or has become more skillful in seeing cause-effect relationships in his radio work. The thinking processes to be used in these selections are not the same reasoning skills to be applied to the trade subjects. To be specific, a reading of the most technical of these essays, "It's the Ham in Them," which is concerned with amateur radio operators, is followed by such nontechnical deductions as these:

(1)   Why might a shut-in enjoy operating a "ham" radio outfit as a hobby?
(2)   Why would "ham" radio operators be valuable in any community in an emergency?
(3)   Why might being a "ham" be valuable to you as an individual?

Compare these questions with the following appended to chapters from the text "Elements of Radio" by Abraham and William Marcus (Prentice-Hall, 1952):

(1)   Why cannot the magnetic field of an electromagnet be used to send wireless messages in a practical manner?
(2)   Why must a reproducer be used in a radio receiver?
(3)   Why must a receiver have a detector?

The first set of questions can be answered without reading the text if one knows, as is explained in the first sentence of the paragraph, that a "ham" is an amateur radio operator. The latter set of questions carries no clue to the answer without the reader's having some previous knowledge and information to be obtained only in a graded course of study such as a trade subject curriculum provides.

The writer believes that most authorities who assume transfer of training in reading skills fail to take account of the cumulative knowledge of technical words and phrases needed to draw meaning from a paragraph in a textbook.

To be specific, when an English teacher uses a workbook such as "Unit Drills for Reading Comprehension" by R. Goodman (Keystone Education Press, 1955) with its 45 paragraphs and accompanying thought test questions, he is supposing that the student brings to each selection only a general knowledge of things. In fact, the pupil is expected to confine his thinking to the items in the paragraph. Thus, in the paragraph below (Paragraph 2, page 27):

> If you watch a lamp which is turned very rapidly on and off, and you keep your eyes open, persistence of vision will bridge the gaps of darkness between the flashes of light, and the lamp will seem to be continuously lit. This optical afterglow explains the magic produced by the stroboscope, a new instrument which seems to freeze the swiftest motions while they are still going on, and to stop time itself dead in its tracks. The magic is all in the eye of the beholder.

The thought questions bearing on this selection are:

The "magic" of the stroboscope is due to (1) continuous lighting, (2) intense cold, (3) slow motion, (4) behavior of the human eye, (5) a lapse of time.
"Persistence of vision" is explained by (1) darkness, (2) winking, (3) rapid flashes, (4) gaps, (5) afterimpression.

We will note two points here. First, the author has included no technical terms or phrases which he has not explained, or which could not be found in an ordinary dictionary. Second, there is no graded block of knowledge on which this paragraph depends for clarity of understanding.

Turning to a textbook in the trade, the above-mentioned text on elements of radio, let us study some typical paragraphs:

> All the above methods of communication suffer from one common fault; they are useful only over comparatively short distances, a few miles at best. (p. 1)
> Having mastered the theory of the crystal receiver, we are now ready to go ahead. If you have constructed the receiver described here and "listened in" on it, you must be aware that the crystal detector has shortcomings. First of all, it is difficult to manipulate. Not every spot will work. You must move the catwhisker about for some time before you touch a spot which enables you to hear radio signals in your phones. (p. 100)
> The problem, therefore, is to devise a system that will build up the signal before it reaches the detector. (p. 200)

But corresponding points on each vertical arm are struck simultaneously and, therefore, the electrons are set flowing these arms in the same direction at the same time (*up* in **Fig.** 199) and with equal pressure. Since the electron streams in each of the vertical arms are equal and flow toward each other, these streams cancel themselves out; hence we have no electron flow into the receiver, and, therefore, nothing can be heard. (p. 300)

You will notice in Figure 281 that in both curves the electromotive force and current reach their maximum in the same direction at the same time and are likewise at zero at the same time. When the electromotive force and current have this relationship to each other, we say that they are *in phase.* (p. 400)

On the other hand, the further up we go, the rarer the air gets — that is, there are fewer molecules in any volume. Beyond a distance of 200 miles from the earth's surface, there probably are so few molecules that ionization is virtually nil. So we see that the ionosphere is a layer or region beginning at about 60 miles beyond the surface of the earth and extending about 200 miles beyond the surface of the earth. (p. 500)

If some of the voltage from the bottom end of the coil is fed through a small variable capacitator (Cn), called a neutralizing capacitator, onto the grid of the tube, neutralization is achieved. The neutralizing capacitator controls the amount of voltage so fed to insure that it is just enough to neutralize that arising from the capacitance of the electrodes. Since this neutralizing voltage comes from the plate circuit, this method is called *plate neutralization.* (p. 600)

This continues until a whole series of bright spots, corresponding to the outline of the shore, have appeared on the screen of the tube. Since the screen of the cathode-ray tube is of the high-persistence type, the bright spots will remain for some time after the sweep has moved on to other angular positions. The result then would be a picture of the area surrounding the ship, whose position is indicated by the center of the screen. (p. 689)

Certain points should be made with respect to these paragraphs. The first paragraph is a sentence which has meaning only when read with the previous related sentences. The second paragraph notes the existence of a body of knowledge which must be brought to bear on subsequent pages for proper understanding. The third paragraph is again a sentence which states a problem developed at some length in previous paragraphs. It has little meaning in isolation, but is necessary for summation. Paragraph four refers to an illustration and demands a special type of reading rarely found in workbooks used in the English class. Here, the pupil's eyes and thoughts must shift from print to picture, a skill developed by comicbook readers but not usable for this text even by the most avid devotee of this art form. The fifth paragraph develops a technical term which may be the key to future pages in the book. Unfortunately the authors do not include this item in the index. Paragraph six leads the reader to believe that the authors are no longer discussing elements of radio. It contains a number of concepts which are clear only to a student of previous pages. The seventh paragraph would probably be double talk to most students in their third year of science. The last paragraph appears easy to understand, but it has a few terms which may or may not be keys to proper understanding of the passage: e.g., "cathode ray tube," "high persistence type," "sweep" and "angular positions." The writer is not sufficiently conversant with the ideas to decide whether those technical words are the solution to the meaning of the paragraph. He is in the same position as an individual who has read a paragraph in a novel and attempts to compare his understanding of it with that of a person who has read the complete narrative. A typical example of this would be the following:

> Tom went to bed that night planning vengeance against Alfred Temple; for with shame and repentance Becky had told him all, not forgetting her own treachery; but even the longing for vengeance had to give way soon to pleasanter musings, and he fell asleep at last with Becky's latest words lingering dreamily in his ear — "Tom, how could you be so noble!"

A junior high school pupil who has read *Tom Sawyer* with understanding would be able to explain that paragraph more clearly than a college student who had never taken the opportunity to follow the adventures of that Mark Twain hero. There is little to indicate the true age, character, or motives of the individuals mentioned. The college student would not know what Becky's "treachery" encompassed, or what "planned vengeance" included.

Guided Growth in Reading

If then, we come to the conclusion that the English teacher cannot help teach reading in the trade subjects, what other solutions are there to our problem? Let us examine the conclusions of some authorities on the subject.

1. Mr. Herman Hall in his book, *Trade Training in School and Plant* (Century Company, 1930) has this to say about the problem:

> As far as the writer knows there are few if any textbooks that are likely to be of service to the trade instructor in his teaching. There are many books which may be valuable if used as reference books for occasional use in connection with some definite job.
>
> The academic instructor in the high school has all too often "gotten by" in his work with the help of a well-written textbook used as a sort of crutch to hold him up. Such instructors are prone to assign "pages so-and-so for tomorrow's lesson." If the instructor himself learns those

pages, or even contrives to have them before him, he can sample his learner's ability to repeat the material contained in the pages. Such teaching will not meet the objectives of trade instruction.

    . . . Textbooks as such have little place in trade education . . ."

    2. "Guideposts in Vocational High School," a pamphlet issued by the Board of Education in 1946 states:

    Teachers of all subjects, especially English, should guide the student's growth in reading. (As we have seen above, teachers of English in most vocational high schools have taken practical steps to follow that suggestion.)

    3. *Methods of Teaching Industrial Subjects* (Gerald B. Leighbody, Delmar Publishers, 1946) decries this practice:

    Some teachers follow the practice of assigning pages in text or reference books to be studied outside of regular school hours. The mere reading of material is no guarantee of comprehension or retention.

    4. In the bulletin of June 1952 entitled, "Instruction in English and Speech," (page 57) it is stated that,

    It is the opinion of the committee, however, that the problem of reading cannot be solved by the teacher of English in isolation. English is to a degree a tool subject; so to a degree are other subjects. It cannot be assumed that because teachers of English teach vocabulary, pupils will know the meaning of all words, or will understand the special vocabulary and concepts of other subjects. All departments must know the factors involved in the reading process and must take direct application of the skills which are taught in the English class.

    5. The authors of "Machine Shop Practice for Vocational High Schools," Board of Education Curriculum Bulletin #10, 1954-55 Series, have this to say about the problem:

    The systematic use of instruction sheets helps students learn to read and follow written directions. (page 71)

    Mention of references is one means of stimulating curiosity about the subject matter and of leading pupils to subject matter that will supplement instruction. However, on the instruction sheet or otherwise, the teacher should suggest only reading that is available and within the student's comprehension. (page 81)

    It is necessary to bear in mind that many pupils have difficulty in getting information and direction from the printed page; they prefer to depend on spoken language. However, the ability to follow written material is an important part of the equipment of the machine shop worker. . .

Show the pupils exactly how to use the various instruction sheets. For example, if you are conducting a demonstration, have a pupil read aloud the steps of the operation while another pupil performs each step. (page 87)

The writer is of the opinion that we should reject the advice to use little or no reading in the shops. On the other hand, few trade instructors have the time or energy to become reading experts.

Shop Teacher and Reading

For the shop teacher, fundamental reading tasks are involved in the job sheets which guide the pupil's work from day to day. Such instruction sheets can be made the subject of reading instruction with profit to both teacher and student. As to when such instruction can take place, it seems wise for such purposes to use the shop information period when demonstrations, lectures and discussions are an important part of the procedure.

There cannot be a blueprint for every type of reading lesson in shop subjects, or academic studies, for that matter. However, it seems to the writer that a carefully thought out lesson should contain some or all of the following steps:

(1)   Motivation for reading.
(2)   Study of difficult words and concepts.
(3)   Oral reading of the selection.
(4)   Discussion and questioning for understanding.
(5)   Application of knowledge gained.

Let us apply these steps to the teaching of the job sheet on page 82 of the Board of Education Bulletin "Machine Shop Practice for Vocational High Schools." (The first paragraph of that job was quoted previously.)

After the teacher has explained and demonstrated the required processes orally with the use of appropriate equipment, the attention of the class is turned toward the blackboard where the teacher has written the key words of the job. Among these would be included such phrases as the following:

(1) required offset   (4) tailstock body
(2) set-over screws   (5) index line
(3) corresponds to the setting   (6) tailstock assembly

(7) toward the headstock

(8) adjust set-over screws

(9) amount of offset

(10) inside caliper

(11) caliper setting

(12) secure the tool post

(13) compound rest

(14) extends far enough

(15) lighten spindle lock

The meaning of each of these phrases may be checked by student demonstration or verbalization. Thus in teaching setover screws, the instructor might have the pupil point to the equipment part and give its function if that is an important part of the learning. This helps concentrate attention on the appearance and spelling of key words. The teacher can take one or two of these words for study of correct spelling by erasing them and having a student write them in again. The rest of the class can be ready for corrective work if necessary.

After these are studied, the teacher reads the sheet orally, or has a capable student read it while the rest of the class follows the reading on their own sheets. Despite the emphasis on silent reading in our schools today, there are immediate values to be derived from reading the job sheets aloud. Just as in the study of a poem the English teacher dwells on the oral reading of the verses for rhythm, color and expression, similarly the trade instructor can read for pronunciation, phrasing and emphasis.

The lesson can be closed with a series of questions designed to develop various reading skills. Many job sheets have such prepared questions, but the teacher may wish to use his knowledge of the needs and capacities of his students to formulate his own tests of understanding. The teacher might thus ask his students,

(1)   Where would the caliper setting be taken from?

(2)   How far should the set-over screws be adjusted?

It is possible that neither of those questions would be of concern to an instructor. The writer cannot claim a knowledge of the subject sufficient to decide the points of emphasis on this particular job.

The results of this learning period can be tested through the use of a short quiz given perhaps before the next job is begun. The quiz might include objective questions requiring one-word or one-phrase answers, and one or two essay questions to be answered in two or three sentences if possible. Such quizzes have value in preparing students for final or midterm examinations. In most cases they can be marked by pupils who are provided with key answers.

Developmental Lesson an Aid

Two things should be noted concerning this lesson. First, this training in reading skills closely parallels the developmental lesson which is the stock-in-trade of every teacher. Second, this procedure follows the steps taken in learning a language. We begin with listening and go on to speaking, reading and writing. If it is argued that the difficult words and phrases can be explained through the use of a technical dictionary, it should be understood that mere definition too often means substituting one set of unknown words for another set. For example, the definition of a set-screw as given in the glossary of W. L. Shaaf's *The Practical Outline of Mechanical Trades* reads, "A screw, usually hardened, which is used to lock a machine part in position by pressure on the point." However, when a set-screw is actually shown to a class and its function observed, its definition can be derived by the pupils themselves. In fact, preparing a clear definition of a term may be a test of knowledge in shop subjects. Such facility with trade language may not mean the making of a good workman, but all things being equal, a worker who can handle the language of his trade in reading and writing will probably be the more efficient mechanic.

Authorities on the subject of reading list a number of skills which should receive attention in developing the ability to following directions. Thus, in the bulletin "Reading — Grades 7-8-9" previously mentioned, such achievements as these are listed:

(1)   Recognizing need for preliminary reading.
(2)   Care for complicated or confusing statements.
(3)   Recognizing need for understanding the purpose of each step.
(4)   Recognizing need for second reading.
(5)   Visualizing steps during re-reading.
(6)   Need for final review before applying directions.

Most of these excellent skills will be acquired during the process of learning to read the job sheets as outlined above.

After some success with the job sheet, the instructor might attempt to use the text or periodical for reading purposes. An arrangement might be made with the school librarian to borrow appropriate trade magazines from her files to be read, studied and discussed in class.

The writer attempted to stimulate an interest in trade periodicals through the procedure mentioned above when he taught English in a vocational high school. However, the report formulated below, one of many, to be used as a basis for oral discussion, lacked vitality because there was no authority present to evaluate the relevance of the facts or their significance to the trade.

ELECTRICAL CONSTRUCTION AND MAINTENANCE
Vol. 55 No. 5   May 1956

Questions on the Code - - - - - - - Page 295
by B. A. Mcdonald, G. Powell and B. Z. Segall

Wiring for a Service Station

If a device had to be 18 inches or more above the floor level in order to comply with the Code, is it OK to install sealing fittings as close to the floor as possible?

The Code answers this question by stating that it permits the sealing fitting to be located on either side of the boundary where the Conduit run passes from a more hazardous to a less hazardous location. The answer means that you can if the pipe or other material that you are using comes out from an ordinary run and has to pass through a room of high explosives. It must be completely sealed and as tight as the sealing fitting can go.

If we were installing lights at a baseball field, could we run No. 14 wire circuits for individual light outlets which will be lamped with 1500 watt light?

We can use No. 14 wire if we limit the load on a branch circuit to 80% at 12 amps. But if you don't want to limit the load you can use No. 12 wire, which is a safer investment.

The teacher of English never did get around to asking the electrical shop teacher whether that written report made by an eighth-term student was related to the work in the shop. However, it seems that this library lesson was profitable because many boys did testify that they learned something therefrom. The English teacher did not have time in his program to include many such periods.

What is accomplished by using the assistant to teaching afforded by a job sheet, text or trade periodical? A student who uses printed sheets or textbooks in school really has two teachers: the living instructor with his foibles and sympathies, and a silent teacher who has no psychological reactions to every-day student activities. The first implements the program of learning which the curriculum envisages for the years the student will remain in school. The second will ready our student the continue to learn long after he has left school. Neither teacher can be very effective without the other. The pupil who uses no printed matter in his shop is almost at the same disadvantage as the student who takes home study courses. If we wish to train our students to take their places in the social-economic world, we cannot deny them the reading skills and habits needed to progress with the movements in industrial development.

Summary

To sum up we have tried to sketch the following points in this paper.

(1) Vocational students need training in reading trade subjects.
(2) The English teacher is willing but unable to provide such reading instruction.
(3) The vocabulary, idioms and language of the trades demand special language arts instruction to be provided only by one who is familiar with that trade.

(4) Even where language is not a barrier, reading the trade subjects requires application and activity appropriate only to a shop room.

(5) The tendency to compel the English teacher to solve such problems will compel us to change our objectives in vocational education.

(6) The reading skills taught in the English classroom cannot be used profitably in the trade subjects.

(7) A trade text or series of job sheets accumulates a host of concepts which must be mastered to make further reading possible.

(8) There are solutions to this problem which are not entirely realistic.

(9) Shop teachers should attempt a sample reading lesson in their trade and make such changes in procedure as their experiences dictate.

(10) Such reading lessons will have educational prerequisites which will facilitate attainment of our vocational high school objectives.

James Joyce in his novel "Portrait of the Artist as a Young Man," illustrated one of the fundamental concepts of this essay in these words (Modern Library Edition — Page 221):

> The language in which we are speaking is his before it is mine. How different are the words "home," "Christ," "ale," "master," on his lips and on mine! I cannot speak or write these words without unrest of spirit. His language, so familiar and so foreign, will always be for me an acquired speech. I have not made or accepted its words. My voice holds them at bay. My soul frets in the shadow of his language.

As long as students regard their trade texts with the same feeling as the person speaking above views his teacher's language, we as instructors have failed to prepare our boys and girls for vocational competency after their school days are over.

Questions For Discussion

1.   Look at the checklist of practices that Olson used in his research study. How do you and your fellow teachers compare on the responses?

2.   To what extent do you agree with Simmons that short stories present more reading problems for junior high students than novels, particularly the so-called adolescent novels?

3.   If you are a content area teacher, look at the textbook you are now using. What reading problems does it present for your students? Select one chapter and develop a reading skills lesson around the material.

4.   Let's examine a content area not discussed directly in any of the articles in this section. What are the special reading skills that a home economics teacher should be attentive to because of her subject matter and the way it is organized?

Reading Interests

IX

Any reading program at the secondary school level which hopes to be successful must provide books and materials which are of interest to adolescents and which meet their needs. In addition one objective which is part of most programs is the development and refinement of students' interests and tastes in reading. The articles in this section, therefore, focus on discussions of what the adolescent likes to read and how his taste and interests can be further developed.

The first two articles report on research studies designed to find out more about the reading interests of adolescents and the variables which affect these interests. Soares and Simpson studied the variables of sex, grade level, and intelligence as they affect junior high school students' likes and dislikes in short story reading. The two investigators also looked at those short stories consistently rated high by the students to see if certain elements were present in the stories which were not found in stories rated lower by the students. Olson and Rosen analyzed the reading interests of 264 ninth grade students through use of a questionnaire and concentrated their attention on the variables of sex and race.

In the third article, Arthur Heilman sets out to discuss the problems involved in defining what is meant by *reading tastes* and points out that no piece of literature can be assigned a fixed and permanent place on any continuum of excellence. He then identifies certain common practices which he feels do very little to develop reading tastes and in fact undermine any such attempt.

Frances Beck presents a number of concrete suggestions drawn from discussions with students and teachers for fostering students' interests in reading. David Sohn gives an historical prospective to the so-called "paperback revolution" and presents a rationale for making extensive use of paperbacks in all classes.

In the final article of this section, Frederic Hartz addresses himself to the controversial topics of obscenity and censorship. Hartz presents his interpretation of obscenity and reacts quite strongly to the attempts of certain groups who are attempting to ban certain books from the secondary school curriculum.

Interest in Recreational Reading of Junior High School Students*

ANTHONY T. SOARES AND RAY H. SIMPSON

Despite the research already conducted, there are still myriad unexplored areas concerning reading interests. One is the subject of our study — the investigation of the existence of differences in the ratings of interest for short stories by 1,653 junior high school students of all socio-economic levels, when grouped according to intellectual ability (high, average, low), grade levels (seventh, eighth, ninth), or sex.

The problem may be clarified by the following questions:

(1)   Are there differences in rating of interest for short stories when students are compared on the basis of intelligence, grade, or sex?

(2)   Are there differences in ratings of interest when students are compared according to any combination of these factors: grade and ability, sex and ability, grade and sex, or ability, grade and sex?

(3)   What are the elements in the stories which have high interest for each of the intelligence, grade, and sex groups?

The existing anthologies for junior high school students are not based upon differences in intelligence, sex, and grade level. Furthermore, though these anthologies are compiled by experts, research has shown that there is a decided discrepancy between what experts consider to be interesting and what the students themselves profess to be interesting. (2, 47)† In this study, the students were requested to rate the stories so that a more accurate and realistic picture of their likes and dislikes might be the outcome.

Junior high school students were selected as subjects because research has indicated that this is the age bracket when the amount of reading done begins to decline. Hence, it seems imperative that some effort be made to discover what these students like to read so they may be exposed to interesting reading material.

*Reprinted from *Journal of Reading*, 11 (October, 1967), pp. 14-21, by permission of the authors and the International Reading Association.

†Numbers in parentheses refer to references at end of article.

As a basis for the present study, 862 short stories from junior or high school anthologies were rated on the basis of interest by junior high school students. From the 862 stories, four types were selected:

(1)   The 15 stories with the highest average interest rating by all students (Category A).
(2)   The 15 with the lowest interest ratings for all students (Category B).
(3)   The 15 with a higher interest rating by the high intelligence group than the low intelligence group (Category C).
(4)   The 15 with a higher interest rating by the low intelligence group than by the high intelligence group (Category D).

Further analysis was made into the top 15 stories (Category A) to discover what elements (the content and mechanical factors) were in the stories which had high appeal for each of the various subgroups. The most important ones are type of conflict, type of story, content of the story, theme, characteristics of the main character, and the factors of suspense and realism.

Results

The analysis of variance design was applied to the ratings for all the stories by the junior high school students when grouped according to the three intellectual ability levels, the three grade levels, the sexes, and the combinations of these. The results are given in Table I, which reveals that there were significant differences when pupils were grouped on the basis of intelligence and grade. None of the other groups based on sex or combinations of intelligence, grade, and sex, had differences which were significant.

An analysis of variance treatment was then given to the average ratings for the stories in the four categories, with the following results (Table II).

(1)   For Category A, the differences existing among the various groups on their ratings of the highest interest stories were not significant for any of the groups.
(2)   A significant F-ratio was found for the grade levels only when the ratings of the lowest interest stories were analyzed (Category B).

	F	$F_{.99}$	$F_{.95}$
Grade	8.043	4.64	3.01

(3)   When stories of Category C (higher interest by high intelligence group) were considered, the analysis of variance design revealed highly significant differences among the intelligence groups.

TABLE I

ANALYSIS OF VARIANCE OF THE AVERAGE RATINGS OF ALL THE STORIES
BY THE DIFFERENT INTELLIGENCE, GRADE, AND SEX GROUPS

Source of Variation	Degrees of Freedom	Mean Square	F	$F_{.99}$	$F_{.95}$
Grade	2	604.637	10.797**	4.60	2.99
Sex	1	111.481	1.990	6.64	3.84
Intelligence	2	197.644	3.529*	4.60	2.99
Grade and Sex	2	20.934	.373	4.60	2.99
Intelligence and Sex	2	39.119	.698	4.60	2.99
Intelligence and Grade	4	51.749	.924	3.32	2.38
Interaction	4	64.787	1.156	3.32	2.38
Within	3222	55.998			
Total	3239				

*p < .05
**p < .01

TABLE II

F-RATIOS OF THE AVERAGE RATINGS OF THE STORIES BY THE
GRADE, INTELLIGENCE, AND SEX GROUPS

	Intelligence	Sex	Grade
All Stories	3.529*	1.990	10.797**
Category A			
High interest stories	1.520	.745	2.822
Category B			
Low interest stories	2.208	.890	8.043**
Category C			
High interest, high group	32.755**	.041	2.680
Category D			
High interest, low group	10.096**	1.147	4.304*

*p < .05
**p < .01

	F	$F_{.99}$	$F_{.95}$
Intelligence	32.755	4.64	3.01

(4)   The ratings for the stories in Category D (higher interest by low intelligence group) indicated significant differences among the three intelligence and the three grade levels.

	F	$F_{.99}$	$F_{.95}$
Grade	4.304	4.64	3.01
Intelligence	10.096	4.64	3.01

The most significant elements were:

(1)   Realism and suspense as against sentiment, satire, and humor.
(2)   Type of conflict — internal, external, and a combination of the two.
(3)   Type of story — essay, narrative, descriptive, and a combination of narrative and descriptive.
(4)   Content — animals, science, sports, adventure, vocations and careers, teen-age problems, fantasy, non-fiction.
(5)   Theme — success and failure, bravery and cowardice, generosity and cruelty, love and courtship, nature and living.
(6)   Main character — very attractive; adult, teen-ager, or child; male or female.

Intelligence

The three ability groups were composed as follows: 525 high students, 627 of average intelligence, 501 in the low group. The difference in interests in short stories was greatest between the high group and the low group. When compared, the high group and the low group did not include as many identical stories in the top 15 or the bottom 15 stories as did the high group and the average group or the average group and the low group. The high group probably has a wider range of activities and interests and also a higher developmental reading level than the average group and especially the low group.

The high intelligence group appeared to appreciate short stories more than the low group, and the average group also more than the low group. This was evidenced by the generally higher ratings of the stories by the high intelligence group. It may be because they read more, and they may read more because they are more interested in reading. It also may be that the stories in anthologies are more selected to meet the needs of the high rather than the low students. Also, the high group appeared to be more homogeneous with respect to reading interests, since it never had the largest dispersion of its average ratings for any of the four categories of stories nor for the stories taken as a whole. Perhaps the high group is more definitive about its interests for short stories than the low group or the average group.

Junior high school students, when grouped on the intellectual basis, appeared to have greater agreement in what they dislike than in what they like in short stories, and indicated by the smaller scatter of the average ratings for all three intelligence groups of stories of low interest than those of high interest. Then, too, the three intelligence groups had more stories in common in the bottom 15 stories than in the top 15 stories. The lack of commonality (that is, stories which all the three intelligence groups included in their top and bottom 15 stories) indicates that significant differences in reading interests do exist when students are grouped according to intellectual ability.

In regard to the elements of the stories, all three groups showed a preference for realism and suspense. The high and average groups liked external conflict rather than internal conflict, but the low group preferred a combination of the two. All groups selected the narrative type of story over the essay, the descriptive, and the combination of narrative and descriptive, although the high group did allow for the other types in their selection.

All three groups liked animal stories best. The high group indicated some liking for adventure stories, in contrast to the other two groups, but did not choose non-fiction at all. The average group was alone in its choice of stories with fantasy, as was the low group in its wanting to read some stories based on science. The theme of vocations and careers was not popular with any of the groups. Bravery and cowardice was the favorite of all groups and especially high for the high group. The high group's low second choice was love and courtship; for the average and low groups, success and failure. In addition, only the low group showed any liking for generosity and cruelty or nature and living.

The main character was preferably a very attractive male and overwhelmingly a teenager. There was no identification with a child as the main character, male or female, except a slight indication by the low group for a male child.

Grade

There were 612 seventh-grade students, 536 eighth-graders, and 505 ninth-graders. The eighth and ninth grades indicated more similarity in their short story interests than either one with the seventh grade. Besides the smaller difference in the means for the eighth and ninth grades, they had more identical stories in the top 15 stories and also had more similarity in their highest and lowest ratings and in their ranges for all the stories. It may be that since the eighth and ninth grades have shared more junior high school experiences and also possibly more experiences outside of school, they have more interests in common.

On the other hand, the seventh grade indicated a higher appreciation for short stories than the eighth and particularly the ninth. The seventh grade had the largest median for the average ratings for all the categories of stories while the ninth grade had the smallest median. Also, the seventh grade rated 46 of the 60 stories higher than the ninth and 43 higher than the eighth. There is also the implication that the seventh-graders may do more reading than the eighth or the ninth. This seems to be in agreement with the conclusion that the amount of reading students do begins to decrease approximately at the end of the seventh grade.

The seventh grade appeared to enjoy most of the stories which the eighth and ninth grades liked, but the converse was not as true for the eighth and ninth graders. It may be that the seventh grade is exhibiting the influence of the elementary school from which it graduated a few months ago, while the eighth and ninth grades have already had junior high school experiences. Thus, those factors which are interesting to the seventh grade are no longer interesting to the eighth and ninth. The eighth and ninth grades may have more mature and more definitive reading interests due to experiences in and out of school.

When viewed on the basis of grade levels, junior high school students appear to be more in accord as to which short stories they dislike then they are about which short stories they like. This tendency is not borne out in the story elements. In these, the grade levels are fairly close together. All preferred realism and suspense, a very attractive main character who is a male teenager, any type of conflict, and the narrative type of story about animals, with the most popular theme of bravery and cowardice. It was the seventh grade again which showed a wider range of interest by indicating some liking for a combination of the narrative and descriptive type of story and for the theme of nature and living. The seventh-graders also showed a greater intensity of interest for animal stories (usually associated with younger readers) and for the theme of bravery and cowardice. It is interesting to note that the seventh grade chose stories about teenage problems after animal stories, whereas the eighth chose sports and teenage problems, and the ninth, non-fiction and teenage problems for second place.

Sex

There were 824 males and 829 females. Pronounced sex differences were not revealed. Girls and boys may not, in fact, differ significantly at the junior high school level — not until physical maturity has been reached, perhaps.

Although Shores (3) did not find sex differences in his study, some research has indicated that sex may be important in influencing the reading interests of students.(2,5,8) Thorndike (6) stated that sex may be more influential than age or intelligence in affecting the pupils' choice of reading materials. Norvell (1) also concluded that sex was the most significant single factor affecting the reading choice of adolescents. But it should be noted that Norvell included students of high school age who are sharply differentiated for various reasons (among them, pubescence); and that, within his comprehensive study of various reading materials, short stories are liked almost equally well by both sexes.

In the story elements, the sexes were also closer together. The boys liked realism best, then suspense; the girls, realism, then sentiment. The main character was a very attractive male teenager for both, though the boys did allow for a male adult as a low second and the girls for a female teenager. The boys preferred external conflict, the girls internal conflict. Both sexes especially liked the narrative type of story and animal stories, with sports second for boys and teenage problems second for girls. Bravery and cowardice was the favorite theme of both, but it was particularly stressed by the boys. The theme next in popularity for the boys was success and failure, and for the girls, love and courtship.

Hence, the differences in interests for short stories between the sexes appeared to be much less than those for the three intelligence and the three grade levels. It appears that the reading interests in short stories at the junior high school level are influenced more by individual ability and maturity than by sex.

Summary

This study was undertaken to determine whether differences in liking for the short stories existed for junior high school students, when they were grouped according to intelligence (high, average, low), grade (7th, 8th, 9th), or sex.

Students were requested to rate, on the basis of liking, 60 short stories, which were taken from anthologies in use throughout the country. These stories were selected on the basis of four categories — high interest for all students, low interest for all students, higher interest for the high intelligence group as compared to the low intelligence group, and higher interest for the low intelligence group than for the high intelligence group.

Analysis of various results indicated that significant differences in reading interest for short stories did exist when students were grouped according to intellectual ability or grade level. The greatest differences appeared between the high intelligence group and the low intelligence group, and between the seventh grade and the ninth grade.

Further analysis made into the top 15 stories revealed these elements as most significant: realism, suspense, conflict, the narrative type of story, the animal story, the theme of bravery and cowardice, and the main character as a very attractive teenage boy.

References

1.   Norvell, G. W. *The Reading Interests of Young People* (Boston: Heath, 1950).
2.   —— *What Boys and Girls Like to Read* (Morristown, N. J.: Silver Burdett, 1958)
3.   Shores, J. H. "Reading Interests and Informational Needs of Children in Grades Four to Eight," *Elementary English,* 31 (1954), 493-500.
4.   Simpson, R. H. *Improving Teaching-Learning Processes* (New York: Longmans, Green, 1953).
5.   Taylor, Marion W. and Mary Schneider. "What Books Are Our Children Reading?" *Chicago Schools Journal,* 38 (1957), 155-160.
6.   Thorndike, R. L. *A Comparative Study of Children's Reading Interests, Based on a Fictitious Annotated Titles Questionnaire* (New York: Teachers College, 1941).
7.   Witty, P. "Reading in the High School and College," in *National Society for the Study of Education, Forty-Seventh Yearbook,* Part II (Chicago: University of Chicago Press, 1948).
8.   —— and D Kopel. "Motivating Remedial Reading: the Interest Factor," *Educational Administration and Supervision,* 22 (1936), 1-19.

A Comparison of Reading Interests of Two Populations of Ninth Grade Students*

ARTHUR V. OLSON AND CARL L. ROSEN

Explorations into the reading interests of students have been conducted by several authorities. (1, 2, 3)† However, in certain sections of the United States where various populations of students have for the first time been integrated, it becomes a matter of necessity to investigate these areas. If there are wide differences in reading interests among recently integrated students, then some instructional planning and adjustment should be considered to meet these differences. Rowland and Hill (4) reported in a recent study that interests of pupils, as measured by their voluntary selections in reading and the choice of topics in creative writing were influenced both by the racial content of the materials and the race of the child. Because of the potential impact of this information both on curriculum development and on the selection of materials, it appeared that further exploratory study in this area was necessary. The purpose of this study therefore, was to investigate similarities and differences, by race and sex, in specific reading interests and choices of types of reading materials. Ninth grade students enrolled in two recently integrated high schools in the southeastern part of the United States were selected for the study.

Subjects

The population used in this study consisted of the total ninth grade enrollment of two recently integrated high schools in a middle-sized southeastern city of the United States. The population numbered 264-ninth grade students, the Negro group consisting of 60 male and 80 female students. The Caucasian group contained 64 male and 60 female students.

Instruments

To measure reading interest and choice of materials a questionnaire was constructed consisting of forty items. Of the forty items, choice of the source of

---

*Reprinted from *Adolescence*, (Winter 1966-67), pp. 321-326, by permission of the authors and the publishers.
†Numbers in parentheses refer to references at end of article.

reading involved six items: reading newspapers, books, picture books, comics, poetry, and magazines. Thirty-four items in the questionnaire measured reading interests which included such areas as: sports, world events, local interests, biography, humor, adventure, hobbies, topics relating to one's own sex, family life, personal problems, personal appearance, teen-age problems, jobs, romance, religion, occupations, animal stories, violence, social problems, clothing, styles in clothing, music, and others. Responses for each of the forty items were made by students based upon one choice out of six possible choices which they felt best described their feeling about the reading materials. The six choices were: (1) like very very much, (2) like quite a lot, (3) like a little, (4) dislike a lot, (5) dislike quite a lot, (6) dislike very very much.

All of the students in the sample were given the *California Short Form Test of Mental Maturity,* Level 4, (5) and the California Reading Tests, Advanced, Form W. (6) Significant differences were found between the two groups in verbal IQ and reading vocabulary with the difference in favor of the Caucasian males and females.

Analysis of the Data

Chi-square analysis of the responses to the questionnaire was employed to determine the significance of differences, if any, in choices of the various groups to the forty-four items. The responses to the various items of the questionnaire were tabulated by rank order-response among the groups by sex and race concerning (choice 1) the most liked (choice 6) least liked. Tables 1-3 describe the findings of the study.

It can be noted from Table 1 that of the 18 significant chi-square values differentiating the two groups, two "choice" and sixteen "interest" items were found to be significantly different. The eighteen items significantly differentiating the two groups can be noted in the table. Inspection of the distributions of responses for the eighteen items, between the two groups, indicated that in each of the eighteen comparisons the responses of Negro students appeared to be heavily weighted in the positive choice categories. The white students' choices in each case were characterized by a significantly wider distribution among the choice categories for each of the eighteen items. No significant differences between the groups were noted for the remaining twenty-two items in the questionnaire. Negro students appear to have stronger choices for reading current materials such as newspapers and magazines, and stronger reading interests in such topics as social relations, romance, teen-age problems, humor, and occupational areas than whites.

Tables 2 and 3 summarize the rank-order of choices of materials and interests categories selected by sex and race in terms of most and least liked categories respectively. In general, it can be noted from the two tables that for

TABLE NO. 1

ITEMS SHOWING A SIGNIFICANT DIFFERENCE (.01 LEVEL) BETWEEN

RESPONSES OF THE CAUCASIAN AND NEGRO STUDENTS

Items	X^2
a. Reading newspaper	41.46
b. Reading the comics in the newspaper	37.47
c. Reading about things of local interest in the newspaper	20.54
d. Reading books that are funny	21.98
e. Reading books about women	39.28
f. Reading mystery stories	42.21
g. Reading books about family life	38.33
h. Reading books with some romance in them	56.66
i. Reading about sports	20.33
j. Reading books about teen-age problems	40.65
k. Reading books about jobs	34.48
l. Reading animal stories	57.11
m. Reading books about social problems	42.17
n. Reading magazines	38.03
o. Reading romance magazines	37.35
p. Reading magazines about clothing and styles	27.23
q. Reading magazines about women	32.31
r. Reading detective magazines	25.31

TABLE NO. 2

MOST LIKED

Negro (Female)	*Caucasian (Female)*
1. Magazines: clothing, styles	Magazines: clothing styles
2. Books: teen-age problems	Books: adventure
3. Books: personal problems	Mystery Stories
4. Magazines: music	Books: general
5. Books: real people	Books: teen-age problems

Negro (Male)	*Caucasian (Male)*
1. Books: sports	Books: adventure
2. Newspapers: sports	Books: sports
3. Books: adventure	Magazines: sports
4. Magazines: sports	Newspapers: sports
5. Books: personal problems	Newspapers: comics
6. Magazines: jokes	Mystery Stories

TABLE NO. 3

LEAST LIKED

Negro (Female)	*Caucasian (Female)*
1. Books: violence	Magazines: detective
2. Magazines: women	Books: hobbies
3. Animal Stories	Newspapers: sports
4. Magazines: detective	Animal Stories
5. Books: men	Books: violence

Negro (Male)	*Caucasian (Male)*
1. Magazines: clothing, styles	Poetry
2. Books: love	Magazines: music
3. Magazines: romance	Books: love
4. Magazines: men	Books: romance
5. Books: romance	Animal Stories

this population with some exceptions sex appears to be more expressive of differences in choices of materials and interests than racial differences.

Exceptions noted in Tables 2 and 3 include choice of books concerned with personal problems that appeared in "most liked" categories for both male and female Negro students but did not so appear for Caucasians. It was also noted in Table 3 that Negro students, both male and female, appear to rank magazines about men and women in the least liked category while Caucasians do not. Caucasian females rank as least liked books related to hobbies, and newspaper sports, while these are not so ranked by Negro females. Caucasian males include poetry and music in least liked categories while Negro males do not.

Conclusions

Differences noted in descriptive variables between racial groups resulting from such factors as environmental and educational differences are frequently considered to be related to interests and types of reading materials chosen. Differences between the two racial groups in reading interests and choices of materials in this population of students have been noted in this study. In general, differences in reading interests between racial groups as well as sex differences were apparent in the findings of this investigation. Further study in this area, especially interest inventories of integrated groups from other geographic and socio-economic areas, should be undertaken. On the basis of the results of this study those concerned with curriculum planning should consider the desirability of making provisions for the differences in interests and reading ability between the racial groups, as well as the sex differences in reading interests within the two groups.

References

1. Witty, P., "Study of Pupil's Interests, Grades 9, 10, 11, 12," *Education,* 1961, 82, 100-10
2. Strong, R., "Scope Adolescent Interests," *Education,* 1963, 83, 463-7.
3. Vaughan, J., "Reading Interests of 8th Grade Students," J. *Develop Read,* 1963, 6, 149-155.
4. Rowland, M., & Hill, P., "Current Trends in Negro Education and Shorter Papers-Race, Illustrations, and Interest in Materials for Reading and Creative Writing," J. *Negro Ed.,* 1965, 34, 84-87.
5. Clark, W., & Tiegs, E., *California Short Form Test of Mental Maturity, S-form, Level 4.* Monterey, California: California Test Bureau, 1963.
6. Tiegs, E. & Clark, W., *California Reading Test, Advanced, Form W.* Monterey, California: California Test Bureau, 1957.

Developing Reading Tastes in
The Secondary School*

ARTHUR W. HEILMAN

Taste in reading is usually thought of as the ability to recognize, understand and enjoy literature that is beautiful and moving. Taste is more than the ability to label excellent writing. It includes being moved by such writing. One connotation of taste is "to experience, feel or perceive – to grasp the flavor of a substance." Reading taste involves the ability to grasp and perceive the substance of a piece of writing. In addition, one may taste without savoring. But one cannot develop a taste for good literature without savoring. Mere contact with good literature without understanding is not a way to develop taste in reading.

Positing the existence of taste in reading literature implies a standard of aesthetic qualities which can be applied to all writing. Starting from such a premise a person may be said to have good taste for literature if he reads and appreciates writing and authors which lie above a given cut off point on the good-literature-continuum. The difficulty lies in the fact that both the standards and the continuum are of necessity arbitrary. From the standpoint of the nature of the reading act and of literature as a creative endeavor, teachers and critics should not expect to be able to assign each piece of literature to a fixed niche on any ascending scale of excellence.

Perhaps we should inquire for a moment as to why teachers should be concerned with the problem of helping students develop taste in literature. All legitimate answers will be found to focus on personal growth. First, the reading of good literature should be a source of pleasure which holds up for a lifetime. This factor alone is enough of a justification for teachers' concern with taste and appreciation.

Second, reading and understanding of literature must inevitably make a significant contribution to personal growth and insight into self. Good literature deals with a wide range of human problems. Literature acts as both mirror and beacon for the lonely, handicapped, or misunderstood individual. Literature is a form of potential therapy for the alienated, those in flight from involvement,

*Reprinted from *High School Journal,* 49 (April, 1966), pp.320-326, by permission of the author and the editor.

and those who fear freedom. There are few human problems, fears, or aspirations which are not treated in literature. Taste leads one to such sources and critical reading results in assimilation and reconstruction of vicarious experiences.

Chase states that two kinds of illiteracy threaten civilization. The first of these involves the inability to decipher printed words. The second he calls the "higher illiteracy" found in individuals who read but cannot understand. These persons can absorb and repeat ideas but cannot relate them to life or to their own personal experience.[1] Thus, the higher illiterate can decipher words but is incapable of thinking and feeling as he reads. Apparently the educational experiences provided by the school are no guarantee against the higher illiteracy.

Basic to any logical approach to developing reading tastes is recognition of the fact that appreciation comes only from active participation. Reading is in essence a dialogue between reader and writer. Appreciation is personal; it cannot be standardized. Thus, one does not develop taste by such tactics as:

(1) Exhorting students to develop it.
(2) Providing a list of acceptable authors or established literary classics.
(3) Prescribing an inflexible agenda of reading materials for groups of students.
(4) Assigning the same reading to all students in a given class.
(5) Assuming that all students in a given class or school year have the readiness for and the skills needed to mine a traditional "reading list."
(6) Relying on evaluative methods which imply that all students should arrive at a concensus as to the worth of a play or novel; or uniform character analyses and insights into an author's purpose.

Unfortunately the above procedures, in modified and sometimes disguised form, are often followed in actual teaching situations. These practices, of course, negate what we know about reading, readers, the learning process, and finally, the development of taste in reading. There is a consensus that the high schools' approach to teaching literature fails a great number of students who partake of the experiences provided.

The above list of non-recommended procedures will serve as an introduction to and background for a brief discussion of some of the major issues in developing literary taste among high school students. First, let us explore the logic of and the alternatives to a rigidly prescribed literary diet for high school students.

---

[1] Francis S. Chase. "In The Next Decade," *Controversial Issues in Reading and Promising Solutions.* Supplementary Educational Monographs, No. 91, University of Chicago Press, 1961.

Acquiring Taste Is a Developmental Process

Acquiring taste in reading is not a function of chronological age, grade placement or even intellectual level, but it is a long term process. Taste is not a threshold that one crosses but once. Each teacher at every grade level seeks to induct the reader into the world of good books or great literature. Each success conditions the reader so that he will cross the threshold again, with less reluctance and with more appreciation.

Implicit in the concept that acquiring taste is developmental, is the fact that students in a given classroom are found at different points on a continuum representing ability to appreciate literature. Although Shakespeare or Milton may be in the curriculum, many students about to be exposed to these curricular materials are in no way ready for this experience.

The school assumes a highly unrealistic posture when instruction implies the existence of literary readiness of students – particularly in the face of overwhelming evidence to the contrary. The student's presence in a classroom or a teacher's predilection to follow a particular course of study will not change the student's readiness for a given set of literary experiences. The issue here is not the merits of the classics, but rather that prescribing them for students whose instructional needs are far below these works constitutes an indefensible educational practice.

The fact that some students are not ready for certain literary works and authors, does not mean they are incapable of developing an appreciation for literature. It should not be inferred that a curriculum devoid of literature should be devised for them. On the contrary, these students *particularly* need to be exposed to good literature but this must be material they are capable of understanding and appreciating. The key to this problem lies in differentiation both of material and of teaching procedures.

Required Reading

One view of the ideal high school graduate sees him as: "A habitual, voluntary reader who recognizes the power of literature to further his understanding of himself and of human problems; he considers reading a pleasurable pastime, not a schoolroom activity; he has developed standards of excellency by which to measure literary worth of what he reads . . . ."[2] It is undoubtedly a concensus that few high school graduates actually attain this ideal.

How might one account for the fact that great numbers of students finish

[2] Eunice H. Helmkamp, "Appraising Reading Interests and Attitudes," *Evaluation of Reading,* Supplementary Educational Monograph, No. 88, University of Chicago Press, 1956, 93-97.

high school without having developed a love for good literature? Without being avid readers? These results must be traceable to the experiences these students have had with reading and with literature. Many teachers feel that a rigid prescription of reading material is more likely to inhibit than to enhance growth. Students who are vastly different as to interests, background and reading skills will not be equally motivated to read a particular book or list of required books.

In this regard Cooper notes, "In many literature courses the materials which children must read in order to satisfy the requirements for the course are so rigidly prescribed that little or no deviation from the designated list is permitted."[3] Weiss raises the question as to whether justification exists for asking all students in a class to read the same material at the same time. He suggests choosing a theme, such as, "Man's Search for Justice," and have students read in different books to find out how authors of all times in all countries of the world have treated this theme.[4]

Providing for Student Interaction and Feedback

There are in our schools several barriers to effective teaching of appreciation of literature. A few of these are: (1) the wide range of individual differences among students; (2) large classes; (3) the practice of attempting to cover relatively large amounts of material in a given course, and (4) the fact that most of the literary compositions covered are in themselves relatively large blocks of material. Each of these and other factors militate against structuring a learning environment in which students develop their own interpretations and test them in open discussion with peers and teachers.

In developing appreciation and taste in literature it is essential that students have the opportunity to work intensively with smaller literary units and that these be analyzed thoroughly. This does not mean memorizing interpretations or character analyses handed down from teacher to teacher but rather real discussion and feedback among students. As one English teacher expresses this concept, ". . . it seems to me imperative to preserve – or is it regain? – discussion as the basic method for English classes if we are not to lose the creativity which arises from the interaction of young minds and ideas."[5]

[3] J. Louis Cooper, "The Basic Aim of the Literature Program," *Improvement of Reading Through Classroom Practice,* Proceedings, International Reading Association, Vol. 9, 1964, 188.

[4] M. Jerry Weiss, "The Role of the Library in Junior High School Reading Programs." *Improvement of Reading Through Classroom Practice,* Proceedings, International Reading Association, Vol. 9, 1964, 200-201.

[5] Cleveland A. Thomas, "Fostering Creativity in High School English," *The English Journal,* LI, December, 1962, 625-27.

Provocative Questions

While it is true that a number of factors are responsible for the gradual erosion of "give and take discussions" in the classroom, teachers' failure to provide stimulation through the use of incisive thought producing questions is also a factor. When one becomes dominated by the necessity of covering a given amount of reading rather than by the magnificent obsession of guiding students' growth in understanding, reliance on factual and mundane questions is likely to become habitual.

What constitutes a good or poor question is in the final analysis relative. That is, one cannot make a list of questions which are a priori good or bad. For instance, the question, "What is the climax of this story?" might be bad if one insists that a specific preordained answer be given. But if one is prepared to accept the student's own reasoning and let his answer provide the basis for other inquiries, the question meets the chief criterion of open-endedness.

The effectiveness of questions must be judged by the impact they have on the reader – not by how they are phrased. Some questions by their nature inhibit contemplation and encourage factual nit picking. Good questions by definition arouse and sustain intellectual curiousity, lead one to entertain new hypotheses; in short – lead the reader to think and experience.

Use of Films and Recordings to Develop taste in Literature

There are critics who tend to overgeneralize that movies based on literary works are poor substitutes for reading these works. On the other hand, some teachers report the use of films as having great potential for developing appreciation of good literature. Manchel states, "both modern work and classics come alive in motion pictures." As examples he cites eleven movies of plays and novels which were used as part of an English course. His list included, *Lost Horizon, Gentleman's Agreement, Mister Roberts, Arsenic and Old Lace, The Bad Seed, Dr. Jekyll and Mr. Hyde,* and *The Ox-bow Incident.*

A recent publication dealing with motion pictures as a means of sharpening literary perceptions has been sponsored by the *National Council of Teachers of English.*[6] The point is made that films have unparalleled power to illuminate and augment the study and understanding of literature. The fact that films are primarily a visual media rather than verbal is of course stressed. The advantages of camera-art in achieving meaning are illustrated by detailed analysis of selected scenes as well as entire classics such as *Citizen Kane* and *The Grapes of Wrath.*

[6]Marion C. Sheridan, et. al., *The Motion Picture and The Teaching of English,* Appleton-Century-Crofts, New York, 1965.

Teachers as Readers

Teachers are undoubtedly the key factor in the student's development of taste and appreciation. The teacher's classroom behavior inhibits or enhances such development. While taste can never be forced upon a reader, teachers do wield great influence. Studies have found that students tend to prefer material which teachers have praised or recommended. Thus, it is important that all teachers be reading-teachers as well as reading teacher.

The teacher who is an avid reader will naturally wish to share with students those literary passages he loves. He will read to students – and the grade level he teaches will never be a deterrent to this practice. His reading to students will always have as its purpose *Communication,* and as he reads he will provide students with worthy models for their own interpretive reading.

Teachers who do not love literature will find little they wish to share with others. Such teachers cannot instill a love of reading in those they teach. To attempt to teach literature without this love is not to teach, and day to day activities become an educational ritual for both teacher and student.

Conclusion

The development of taste in literature is not an inevitable outcome of formal educational experiences with literature. In fact, some current instructional practices may inhibit growth of appreciation. We must question certain traditional methods and devise new approaches if we wish to help students develop literary taste.

Often the school functions as though it is believed that taste and literary appreciation can be mass produced. This, despite the fact that every teacher knows that students in a given classroom must inevitably react differently to the same literary stimulus. And second, that students in a given classroom or age group must, because of their differing backgrounds, develop at different rates. When high school students are expected to move systematically through an anthology or to read a limited prescribed number of literary works, we are not applying the best available knowledge relative to motivation, interests and human growth.

Bibliography

Broening, Angela M. "Development of Taste in Literature in the Senior High School, *English Journal* LII, April, 1963, 273-287.

Early, Margaret J. "Stages of Growth in Literary Appreciation," *English Journal*, XLIX, March, 1960, 161-167.

Joll, Leonard W. "Developing Taste in Literature in the Junior High School," *Elementary English*, XXXX, February, 1963, 183-88.
Parkins, William L., Jr. "Motion Pictures and Written Composition," *English Journal*, LII, January, 1962, 31-35.
Squire, James R. "Literacy and Literature," *English Journal*, XLIX, March, 1960, 154-60.

Fostering Interest in Reading in Grades Nine Through Fourteen*

FRANCES M. BECK

All good teachers feel they know their students. But some probably know them only narrowly – as personalities, already unalterably shaped, to be coped with. Others have observed each developing characteristic carefully and have turned to the professional literature to help them enrich their teaching with more knowledge of their students' particular age group. Reports of recent surveys and inventories are also invaluable to teachers who want to learn more about their students.

If you haven't yet read it, I'm sure that you will be interested in the article "The Teen-Agers" in the March 21, 1966, issue of *Newsweek*. I learned from this article that *Seventeen* was the favorite magazine of adolescent girls and *Hot Rod* the favorite of adolescent boys; that *16* magazine had some eight hundred thousand readers; that some adolescents read five to six books a month; that, although some were serious scholars, librarians found that the tastes of most were heavily influenced by movies and television; that sex was one of students' primary interests; and that there was so much pressure on "grades" that even the good student did very little reading on his own.

In my research for this paper, I asked students if they remembered the ways in which their teachers had intrigued, coaxed, led, or forced them into reading. There were various kinds of responses, but generally they took the following forms: "He asked us to make suggestions to each other about what we should read." "She asked us to choose readers for the roles in the class play." "She listened to our ideas." "He made the book he was reading so important and so interesting that we all wanted to share it."

Suggestions from Teachers

I also asked a number of teachers what they did to cultivate better reading habits and enrich interest in reading. One, Mrs. Helen Smith of Bradford

*Reprinted from *Reading: Seventy-Five Years of Progress*, Supplementary Educational Monographs, No. 96, edited by H. Alan Robinson (1966), pp. 115-119, by permission of the University of Chicago Press.

(Pennsylvania) High School, a teacher of "reluctants" this year, told me of many ingenious ways of catching and sustaining interest. They included the following:

(1) Sharing my thumbnail sketches. Every two weeks I select about five books, display them on my desk, and after briefly commenting about each (by describing a character, reading aloud an amusing incident or crazy predicament, or asking, "What would you do if . . . ?"), I pass the books around the class.

(2) Inviting our librarian to roll her book cart into our room and talk about some of the books we have selected together.

(3) Arranging book jackets on the bulletin board. Sometimes these are on special themes — careers, foreign countries in the news, hobbies, teen-age problems. I try to enlist the aid of students interested in art or design. The Wilson Library Bulletin contains some good suggestions.

(4) Making available membership information about TAB or Campus Book Club. I take class time to read the monthly news aloud with my classes and often display some of the listed books on my desk or window sill. I'm amazed at the number of students who avail themselves of this opportunity to purchase books.

(5) Encouraging students to share something they have enjoyed reading — an idea expressed simply, a description, words that create a mood. Some times we form a circle. I start the sharing but never insist that everyone should contribute, but I'm pleased when they all do. Before the end of the period, we vote on the books with the greatest appeal.

(6) Helping students to design book covers and murals or to write a skit based on the books.

(7) Providing a guided free-reading period once a week for those students scheduled five days a week. I move about the room and discuss the books with individual students. If I find someone not too happy with his book, we try to find a new one together. I never require a student to complete a book he doesn't like, but I ask him to be fair and read a few chapters. I call it "tasting."

(8) Providing browsing days in the library. A few students use the card catalogue to find books on their hobbies or careers. Some have excellent lists which other students may use.

(9) Widening their horizons by discussing the "quote-of-the-week" written on the board or by introducing "round-the-world teen-agers" with their problems. So often the reluctant reader lacks self-confidence and this seems to help.

(10) Suggesting that three or four students read the same book and give a panel report.

Other teachers suggested several sources of ideas to promote interest in reading:

the publications of the National Council of the Teachers of English and the International Reading Association and the proceedings of the annual reading conferences at the University of Chicago.

Useful Classroom Activities

Every good librarian sometimes uses a "book talk" to catch the interest of a group of potential readers; and, as we can observe from Mrs. Smith's ten suggestions, good teachers do, too. As an illustration of some of the characteristics of this device, let me share with you a most engrossing book I've recently read. It is one I chose for myself in a local bookstore. This element of personal choice is supposed to be extremely important and to indicate immediate self-involvement; but note what happened next. My work, my family, my other reading – all of these combined to make time unavailable, and three months passed without an opportunity to read this particular book. Finally, the time came to write this paper. I *thought* myself still very busy; but in my reluctance to begin writing – for what new ideas could I present to experienced teachers in the field–I wrote long overdue letters to my family and friends; I put up hems in all my summer dresses; and I turned to this book.

In a sense, then, this book might be called an "escape" book, but it is more than that. It is really a collection of lectures by the artist, Ben Shahn,[1] who is also a truly gifted writer and teacher.

Although I've read most parts of this book at least twice, I feel that in the future I'll return to it often. Some parts of it I feel I have fully comprehended, but other parts – since I am really not very knowledgeable about the history of art, the artist and his craft, and the like – I have only half-understood. It is the kind of understanding one has when, with no ill intent, one happens to hear a whole conversation between two persons who are strangers to one's self on an unfamiliar but immediately intriguing topic.

You will want to read Shahn's lecture "The Biography of a Painting." Shahn wanted to try to assess, for his own enlightenment, "what sort of things go to make up a painting . . . to what extent I could trace the deeper origins, the less conscious motivations."[2] Since the particular painting, "Allegory," was based upon a report of a Chicago fire, it had great interest for me as a Chicagoan and as a city-dweller.

In "The Education of an Artist"[3] Shahn revealed some provocative ideas about the artist and the student artist, which also have a general application to the profession of education and to the teaching of reading:

[1] Ben Shahn, *The Shape of Content* (Cambridge, Mass.: Harvard University Press, 1957).

[2] *Ibid.*, p. 31.

[3] *Ibid.*, pp. 128-51.

Attend a university if you possibly can. There is no content of knowledge that is not pertinent to the work you will want to do. But before you attend a university work at something for a while. Do anything. Get a job in a potato field; or work as a grease-monkey in an auto repair shop. But if you do work in a field do not fail to observe the look and the feel of earth and of all things that you handle — yes, even potatoes! Or, in the auto shop, the smell of oil and grease and burning rubber. Paint of course, but if you have to lay aside painting for a time, continue to draw. Listen well to all conversations and be instructed by them and take all seriousness seriously. Never look down upon anything or anyone as not worthy of notice. In college or out of college, read. And form opinions! Read Sophocles and Euripides and Dante and Proust. Read everything that you can find about art except the reviews. Read the Bible; read Hume; read Pogo. Read all kinds of poetry and know many poets and many artists. Go to an art school, or two, or three, or take art courses at night if necessary. And paint and paint and draw and draw. Know all that you can, both curricular and non-curricular — mathematics and physics and economics, logic, and particularly history. Know at least two languages besides your own, but anyway, know French. Look at pictures and more pictures. Look at every kind of visual symbol, every kind of emblem; do not spurn sign-boards or furniture drawings or this style of art or that style of art. Do not be afraid to like paintings honestly or to dislike them honestly, but if you do dislike them retain an open mind. Do not dismiss any school of art, not the Pre-Raphaelites nor the Hudson River School nor the German Genre painters. Talk and talk and sit at cafes, and listen to everything, to Brahms, to Brubeck, to the Italian hour on the radio. Listen to preachers in small town churches and in big city churches. Listen to politicians in New England town meetings and to rabble-rousers in Alabama. Even draw them. And remember that you are trying to learn to think what you want to think, that you are trying to coordinate mind and hand and eye. Go to all sorts of museums and galleries and to the studios of artists. Go to Paris and Madrid and Rome and Ravenna and Padua. Stand alone in Sainte Chapelle, in the Sistine Chapel, in the Church of the Carmine in Florence. Draw and draw and paint and learn to work in many media; try lithography and aquatint and silk-screen. Know all that you can about art, and by all means have opinions. Never be afraid to become embroiled in art or life or politics; never be afraid to learn to draw or paint better than you already do; and never be afraid to undertake any kind of art at all, however exalted or however common, but do it with distinction.[4]

As you may well surmise, I regret that Ben Shahn was unknown to me before I read his book; but let me tell you of the "bonuses" I've reaped since learning of him. Recently I went into the home of some friends. There on the wall was a reproduction of a Ben Shahn poster. I spoke at length with the owner,

[4]*Ibid.*, pp. 130-31.

Francis Lloyd, who told me that his interest in Shahn had been sparked by a student of his who derived considerable inspiration from Shahn.

I discovered another bonus in the acknowledgments of permission to reproduce the pictures used in the book; there I learned that a local alderman, Leon Despres, was the owner of three of the drawings. The pleasure I derived from this knowledge was as important as the pleasure I later felt when I received an invitation, in response to my letter to the alderman, to visit his office to see the drawings.

Next, I spoke of reading this book to the most literate, articulate (at least on literature and art) family that I know. The wife immediately handed me a current issue of *Ramparts* the cover of which displayed a Ben Shahn sketch of Senator Fulbright.

Now you see the broadening directions in which the reading of one new book can lead — deeper friendship, more social and political awareness, and even a new magazine to become acquainted with, to say nothing of the new learning from the content of the book itself.

Another useful device that many good teachers use is the comparison or contrast of two or more books. Since Ben Shahn represents the professional creative artists and can serve as a prototype for male students, we might wish to contrast his book with a book by Phyllis McGinley.[5] Here is a lady, a professional writer of charm and wit, who is proud she is a woman. One may want to talk back to her as one reads, but one cannot deny that she has a gift for writing and living.

Although their styles vary greatly and their intentions in writing are not identical, we can compare selections from each of these authors — McGinley's "The Consolation of Illiteracy" with Shahn's already mentioned "The Education of an Artist." McGinley's is just loaded with the books you all have read; but her special delight in them is the delight of self-discovery by a literate (despite everything she says to the contrary), mature reader. Two other selections may usefully be compared:

Shahn's "Biography of a Painting" and McGinley's "The Other Side of the Shield: A Note to the Reader";[6] both have addressed themselves to the same question. "Why do you devote your skill, your creative talent to a particular production which is later available to the scrutiny and contemplation of others?"

And if you will turn to the 1964 Proceedings of the Annual Conference on Reading, you will find a number of other suggestions of book pairs[7] which may

---

[5]For example, see *The Province of the Heart* (New York: Dell Publishing Co., Inc., 1959).

[6]*Ibid.,* pp. 7-10.

[7]Frances M. Beck, "Motivating Students To Read: In Grades Nine through Fourteen," in *Meeting Individual Differences in Reading,* compiled and edited by H. Alan Robinson ("Supplementary Educational Monographs," No. 94; Chicago: University of Chicago Press, 1964), pp. 68-69.

encourage a wider range of interest and contribute to the development of taste and discrimination.

The Congressional Record

Another useful source of material to interest the too-busy-for-much-reading adolescent is the *Congressional Record,* which, among other qualities, is a serious contender for the "best buy" in terms of words-per-penny. It is published every day that the House of Representatives and/or the Senate meet. Many days it must publish three hundred thousand words. The range of materials, when one considers the boundless appendix, is wide – a tiny poem, sections of novels, and speeches, in addition to the daily proceedings – and may, indeed, meet the interests of many students. If your school does not receive a complimentary copy, the subscription fee is $1.50 a month.

One successful technique for using the *Record* is to distribute a copy to each student with a sheet of general questions that could apply to any issue. Each student then skims quickly to secure answers to questions about present church-state relationships, proposed bills and their content, and other legislative concerns. Although my students generally skim quickly and find answers to these questions, they usually reward me further by reading many other items (possibly noted in peripheral vision while looking for a small detail I may have asked for) and sharing them with their neighbors.

The Promise of Paperbacks*

DAVID A. SOHN

Publishers' Weekly recently re-printed an item from the TEE-PEE, bulletin of the Toledo Public Library system. Librarian Mary Wheat received a request for help from a woman who wanted either *Lord of the Flies* or *The Babe Ruth Story* for her son, saying also, "They're both baseball stories, aren't they?" Miss Wheat commented that perhaps she should have suggested *The Catcher in the Rye*. Through humorous at first glance, it is significant to notice that the woman, ill-informed as she was, at least wanted books for her son. She had heard of the books she mentioned. It is interesting to wonder whether she would have noticed them if there had not been a paperback revolution that began in our country in about 1939.

Five years ago, in 1959, *Paperbound Books in Print* listed but 6500 titles. The October issue of the same publication this year list 29,500 titles, an increase of over 450%. Two hundred and seventy seven publishers sold 300 million paperbacks in 1963. A random sample of four issues of *The Month Ahead* reveals 630 new titles for September, 500 titles for April, 400 titles for July, and 345 titles for December of this year. It is safe to say that there are now over 30,000 titles in paperback form at this time, and over one million paperbacks are sold during each business day.

When Karl Tauchnitz of Leipzig published the first paperbacks as we think of them in 1809, his wildest nightmare would not have envisioned what he started, in all probability. The nineteenth century saw the dime novels that were so popular with Civil War soldiers, ruthless literary piracy of the type that helped to starve Poe and other authors due to a lack of an international copyright agreement, and the sudden end to professional publishers' thievery when the agreement, was signed in 1891. Though comic books were popular with soldiers in the first World War, much more interest was shown in cheap hard cover reprints in the first third of the twentieth century. The paperback revolution as we know it began with the formation of the Pocket Books Company in 1939.

*Reprinted from *The Philosophical and Sociological Bases of Reading*, Fourteenth Yearbook of the National Reading Conference, Erie L. Thurston, editor, 1965, pp. 57-63, by permission of the author and the editor.

Pocket Books sold more copies in its first ten years of existence than all the best-sellers combined since 1880, including book club selections, according to John Tebbel. Today, its sales have passed the billion copy mark.

It is natural that teachers of reading and educational institutions should become interested in this phenomenon, especially in its potential for stimulating and encouraging the reading habit at all stages of the educational process. The New York City Public School System recently conducted a study through its Bureau of Educational Research called *A Study of Certain Factors Relevant to the Use of Mass Market Paperbacks in High School Literature Classes*. Two thousand five hundred students, 2000 parents, 85 department chairmen, and 45 teachers examined the paperback as an educational tool. Factors studied were students' attitudes toward such books, teachers' and department chairmen's opinions on the educational merits of such books, parents' reactions toward the issuance and use of such books in English classes, and durability under regular conditions of use. The books were examined, compared and contrasted with hardcover textbooks.

Seventy-five percent of the student respondents favored paperbacks over hard-cover texts. Seventy-five percent of the English department chairmen also favored paperbacks over hardcover texts. Sixty percent of the parents were favorable to the use of paperbacks, and when all facets of teacher opinion were examined, there was more approval than disapproval about the use of paperbacks in English classes. In regard to durability, after one semester of use, 2% of the "quality paperbacks" were rated unfit for further use, while 34.4% of the mass-market paperbacks were rated as unfit for further use. Individual titles differed greatly in specific types of wear, in average ratings, and in suitability for further use. Among the recommendations of the committee of investigators were the following: (1) that literary works in paperback form be purchased with Board of Education funds at the discretion of the principal and the department head; (2) that the problem of paperback textbooks be approached from the viewpoint of educational merit rather than that of economy.

Other research studies are being conducted. An extensive study will soon be released by the New Jersey Department of Education, and I understand that another study is being conducted in Washington, D. C. There is obviously a need for much more research in this area.

In an informal study two years ago, I made available to my students a 350 volume classroom paperback library containing a wide variety of titles. I neither compelled nor motivated them to check books out of it. I mentioned that the books were available to them if they wished to check them out. One hundred seventeen students read an average of 3+ books during the school year. Seventy-five percent to eighty percent of them had a book from this library at any given time, and the range of ability encompassed poor, average, and superior readers. The students reacted enthusiastically to the availability of paperback books. The factors which influenced their feelings toward the library were the ease with which they could check out books, the absence of a rigid time limit, the probability of a popular book being accessible, the opportunity to discuss books with other classmates from day to day, an increasingly familiarity with the library's contents as they browsed through it frequently, and the appeal of books with attractive covers, lightness of weight and apparent brevity in comparison with hard-cover books. Last year, a similar pattern emerged, though I did direct students to the library at various times. One hundred and twenty four students read an average of 3.5+ books from the class library. Other competing sources were also available to them. They included a school paperback bookstore, a book fair (where 700 students bought 1,406 books), the school library, class book clubs, class libraries in other subject area classes, and normal community outlets such as drugstores, book stores, the town library, and home libraries. This year, students continue to check out books from the library eagerly. I am sure that a more formal, rigorously controlled study would yield pertinent data, but I discovered for myself the answer to the major question that was in my mind: Does a classroom library of paperbacks serve to stimulate reading? Yes, I submit that it does, if it includes a wide range of books that appeal to the students who use it.

Teachers were also stimulated. Requests from English teachers for similar classroom libraries were so numerous that the administration decided to allow each English teacher in the Middlesex and Mather Junior High Schools in Darien to form a paperback library. This year, science and social studies classes also have such libraries.

Students find the paperback appealing. If they did not, the Scholastic Book Clubs would not have a total of 8 million members in 200,000 individual club groups, ordering books for their personal libraries every month. One should note that 12% of the 300 million books sold in 1963 were sold to high schools.

Many teachers also find the paperback a flexible, attractive tool for their purposes. Literature anthologies always have had a tendency to impose themselves on course outlines and to shape curricula. Public domain titles, such as *Silas Marner, Invanhoe,* and *The Last of the Mohicans* have been rammed down students' throats mainly because of publishing economy. Some students come away from these literary experiences thinking that *Middlemarch* is eight pages long, *Wuthering Heights* a six-page short story, and *War and Peace* a twelve-page diversion by a Russian with a funny name. Viewed in their proper light, anthologies can be marvelous literary samplers, excellent springboards to the reading of whole works, but one wonders how often the unimaginative teacher trots from page to page, snippet to snippet, extolling the hapless Evangeline and her agonized meanderings that are described in what must be the sorriest poetry ever concocted by a prosaic poet, then moving backward to the turgid prose of Cooper, or forward to a brief, unsatisfying glimpse of Mark Twain. Whole works to be read in depth are what paperbacks offer to the teacher. A new world of flexibility and selectivity is now within the teacher's economic grasp. A trend toward units of paperbacks that serve as large anthologies of whole works is apparent, and several publishers are making packaged units built around themes, genres, or forms of literature available.

In secondary schools, thousands of students are never taught the important skills of underlining and marginal note-making because schools own books and they must be used by students over a period of years. If students own the paperbacks they study, they can learn these skills and practice them. The economics of paperbacks makes such a scheme possible.

Where classroom libraries exist, the ideal of individualizing reading can be realized. A wide range of books can be purchased for a relatively small amount of money. Multiple copies of popular books can be provided.

Lack of long-range durability might be considered an asset as well as a defect where paperbacks are concerned. Curricula change rapidly these days, it seems. When schools are saddled with expensive texts, there is a noticeable reluctance to burn them as better materials are developed. If more frequent evaluation of curricular materials is possible and even necessary due to a need to replace books, improved education can result.

The paperback movement has overcome, for the most part, the unfortunate image it projected in the early days of the lurid "best-seller". The BIPAD Committee (composed of members of the NEA and the American Association of School Librarians) annually selects nearly 3600 titles suitable for secondary school use. The emerging education market has forced publishers to eliminate sensational covers and blurbs on many volumes and an aura of respectability has grown around the educational paperbacks.

Because of the cost structure and favorable publishing methods, paperback publishing offers education a medium whereby new techniques can be tested. Such experimentation often has an influence on curriculum reform. I have already mentioned the impact of paperbacks on anthology. In Project English centers such as Euclid Junior High School, the staff has developed thematic and genre units which undergo continual evaluation and revision. Examples of genre units are *Symbolism, Satire,* and *Allegory.* Thematic units include *Men and Nature, Justice, Man and Culture and Survival.* Paperbacks play a major role in this unit approach. The unit on *Survival* includes study of *The Bridge Over The River Kwai, The Nun's Story, Men Against the Sea,* and various short stories and plays for the ninth grade. *Coming of Age,* an eighth grade unit, includes *Johnny Tremain, The Member of the Wedding, Bread* (a play) and *Inside a Kid's Head* (a play). *Symbolism,* a ninth grade genre unit, has *The Pearl,* "The Butterfly", poetry and fables, and Biblical parables. Because of the low cost of class sizes of paperbacks, such units are feasible where they would be prohibitive if secured in hard-cover editions.

Curriculum reforms in mathematics and science have been aided by the paperback. The Science Study Series in physics and in the New Mathematics Library, sponsored by the School Mathematics Study Group are examples of paperback publishing presenting reform. When Scholastic Magazines publishes paperbacks for elementary schools printed in the Initial Teaching Alphabet (ITA) in the near future, it will be interesting to observe the impact of this availability on the acceptance of the technique. Programmed instruction has previously appeared in quality paperback format. One of the drawbacks that the acceptance of this selfinstructional technique has faced is the high cost of purchase. Few programers and fewer paperback publishers have realized the potential of publishing programs in mass-market paperbacks. Recently, however, some programs have begun to appear in books selling for under a dollar. We will probably see an increase in the publication of programs in mass-market paperbacks.

Because of the increased interest in the educational area, the major paperback publishers have formed educational divisions to serve the schools. This trend has resulted in special series for leisure reading, a growing emphasis on original textbook materials, and better service for the schools. Competition is intense and consequently healthy. Obscure titles that have been out of print for decades are now available in paperbacks. Great effort goes into making a better product for the reader.

One example of this effort is the recent Shakespeare competition. As reading teachers, it is interesting to compare and contrast the various editions. Emphasizing the merit of the various editions may demonstrate the thinking that has gone into wooing the reader and teacher. The Bantam editions offer a marginal notation device that allows the reader's eye to dart to the side of the page when he encounters an obscure word in the text instead of wondering all over the page looking for the note. This device interferes less with the continuity of thought than the traditional footnote. As a sidelight, it is amusing to note that a major textbook publisher imitated this device in its Shakespeare series in hardcover. Washington Square's Folger Library Shakespeare has the text on the right-hand side of the page and the notes on the facing page, which is also an advantage for the reader. Another recommendation for the student here is the ample space for student notes. Dell's Laurel Shakespeares have the largest typeface for readability. Avon's Shakespeares have rounded corners to discourage dog-earing the books.

Every subject in the curriculum has felt the influence of the paperback, from history to home economics, from chemistry to physical education, where the new isometrics technique is gaining popularity.

It is not always easy to keep up with the pace of paperback publication when 300 to 600 titles per month are being published. Consider, for example, the case of the Michigan teacher who wanted to order supplementary reading material for a social studies unit on the Civil War and Reconstruction. He was gratified to see his class, and indeed, almost the entire school, show such an interest in his subject, for almost everywhere he went throughout the building, a student was avidly reading a book the teacher has assigned but had neglected to preview – *The Carpetbaggers*. *Caveat emptor* is still good advice.

What is the significance of this medium? In a society geared to obsolescence, where architects omit bookshelves from their plans, the nature of the paperback appears to be in tune with the hum of frenetic living. Reading teachers observing students buying books for personal libraries at school book fairs must feel good about the trend. The attractive covers of many editions flooding the market place invite the reluctant reader and the sophisticate alike to share the pleasure of print for a while. If we are to encourage the lifetime reading habit with out teaching, reading must be rewarding, the book must suit the reader, and the environment, to borrow from Omar Moore, must be responsive. One way to surround our students with good reading without going bankrupt is to consider the paperback and what it can do for our cause. Its promise is powerful if we learn to use its potential to build the love of reading.

Obscenity, Censorship, & Youth*

FREDERIC R. HARTZ

> If all mankind minus one were of one opinion, and only one person were of the contrary opinion, mankind would be no more justified in silencing that one person than he, if he had the power, would be justified in silencing mankind. — John Stuart Mill, "On Liberty" (1859).

Through the United States, private organizations concerned with the morality of literature are increasingly going beyond their legitimate function of offering to their members, and calling to public attention, opinion or instruction about books, and are in effect imposing censorship upon the general public. And since any kind of censorship infringes the principle of that constitutionally guaranteed freedom of the press which protects the free exchange of ideas in our country, it is imperative that the American people become informed of the issues.

Freedom of speech and freedom of the press, with certain exceptions defined by law, are a part of our national heritage and are accepted and defended by our courts. Official censorship and restriction of news in peacetime are considered typical of totalitarian rather than of democratic states.

There can be no quarrel with the right of a sectarian group to recommend to its own members that they abstain from the reading of books of which such group may disapprove for any reason whatsoever. However, some decent literature committees, citizens committees, and decency crusades present a plan of action which goes beyond mere recommendations. The activity of such groups becomes vicious, at the point where they seek to impose upon members of the general public, who are not members of the special group, private standards of their own which differ substantially from the standards established and enforced by law. The fact that these groups may act from the best of motives cannot alter the fact that their attempt to impose such extralegal standards is a clear infringement of the right of the reading public to select for itself what it will read. In a pluralist society, no minority group has the right to

*Reprinted from *Clearing House,* 36 (October, 1961), pp. 99-101, by permission of the author and the editor.

impose its own religious or moral views on other groups, through methods of force, coercion, or violence.

Material is obscene if it makes a certain appeal to the viewer or reader. It is not sufficient that the material be merely coarse, vulgar, or indecent in the popular sense of those terms. Its appeal must be to prurient interest (i.e., inclined to lascivious thoughts and desires). The test is whether a work as a whole, judged by contemporary standards, would appeal to the average man's prurient interest. This test rejects the older, more inclusive view that a book was obscene if any part of it would corrupt not the average man but those most susceptible, such as youth. And herein is the problem.

The censors, and especially the precensors, seem totally to lack faith in the role of parents, the school, the church, and the library; they would deny certain books to adults because they may possibly be read by the young also. The effect is to reduce the adult population to reading only what is fit for children. The essential point of this matter is that most books are not basically designed for children or aimed at the juvenile. A child old enough to understand or to be interested in these books – or the newspapers, for that matter – cannot be harmed by them.

This view was most effectively stated by Judge Curtis G. Bok of Pennsylvania who, in a decision rendered on March 18, 1949, cleared a group of books of the charge of obscenity.

Judge Bok said in part "... It will be asked whether one would care to have one's young daughter read these books. I suppose that by the time she is old enough to wish to read them she will have learned the biologic facts of life and the words that go with them. There is something seriously wrong at home if those facts have not been met and faced and sorted by then; it is not children so much as parents that should receive our concern about this. I should prefer that my own three daughters meet the facts of life and the literature of the world in my library than behind a neighbor's barn, for I can face the adversary there directly. If the young ladies are appalled by what they read, they can close the book at the bottom of page one; if they read further, they will learn what is in the world and in its people, and no parents who have been discerning with their children need fear the outcome. Nor can they hold it back, for life is a series of little battles and minor issues, and the burden of choice is on us all, every day, young and old. Our daughters must live in the world and decide what sort of women they are to be, and we should be willing to prefer their deliberate and informed choice of decency rather than an innocence that continues to spring from ignorance. If that choice be made in the open sunlight, it is more apt than when made in shadow to fall on the side of honorable behavior. . . ."

In one best-selling novel after another, frank descriptions of sex with complete candor and realism appear with frequency. These trends appear in all media of public expression, in the kind of language used and in the subjects discussed by polite society, in pictures, advertisements, and dress, and in other ways familiar to all. Much of what is now acceptable would have shocked the community a generation ago. Today such things are generally tolerated whether we approve or not.

Fortunately the situation has continued to improve with the years, and we seldom read currently, at any rate, of the Brooklyn superintendent of schools, or member of the board of education, who was stirred to the depths of his soul by the recitation in our public schools of such an immoral poem as Longfellow's "The Building of the Ship." His objection was based upon the fact that the ship was pictured as leaping "into the ocean's arms," and that Longfellow went on to say:

How beautiful she is! How fair
She lies within those arms, that press
Her form with many a soft caress
Of tenderness and watchful care!

That there are many excellent books published that are undesirable for youth is undeniable. But as a general thing the young people are not attracted to these because they are usually of the "heavy nature." If, however, such a book is chosen, to take it away is only to whet curiosity and possibly emphasize the very thing that one wishes to soft-pedal. It all comes down to the fact that you can't keep children in cotton wool. They come up against life in hundreds of ways and in many guises often worse than what they may read in books. There is greater danger in a false picture of life than in the admissions of certain true but disagreeable facts.

What is good literature, what has educational value, what is refined information, what is good art, vary with individuals as they do from one generation to another. But a requirement that literature of art conform to some norm prescribed by an official or group smacks of an ideology foreign to our system. From the multitude of competing offerings, the public will pick and choose. What seems trash to one may have for others fleeting or even enduring values.

The main test of a book is the personal one: how does it affect me?

Questions for Discussion

1. Do your students' reading interests coincide with the research findings presented in the articles in this section? Look at the findings of Soares and Simpson regarding the elements present in the most popular short stories. Why is it that those elements seem to be significant?
2. What does the expression *great literature* mean to you? What are your

standards or criteria for determining the greatness of a literary work? What are your students' standards?

3. What is your reaction to Frederic Hartz's definition of obscenity and his opinions concerning various citizens committees attempting to control what is read by students? What can a school or teacher do to prevent such controversy from arising?

The Teaching of Reading to Special Groups

X

Although the primary purpose of this textbook is to clarify what is involved in the teaching of developmental reading at the secondary school level, certainly some attention must be given to those programs designed to help students not reading up to expectations. There are unfortunately large numbers of secondary school students who for a variety of reasons are severely deficient in reading skill development and who need special remedial and corrective programs.

One such group of students have recently come to be known as *disadvantaged* and a great deal of thought and effort is now being directed toward them at all levels of our school systems. In the first article of this section, Dominic Thomas reviews the research findings regarding the characteristics of those older students suffering from social and cultural deprivation. Thomas then presents a plan for the establishment of experimental remedial reading centers in Detroit, Michigan as a means of helping such students.

Lillie Pope explains in considerable detail the JOIN project in New York City which was designed to help the type of student that Thomas described. Of considerable practical value are Pope's observations on the problem faced in the JOIN program such as recruitment of students, instructional sites, retention of students, use of volunteer tutors, and selecting appropriate instructional materials.

Robert Harris describes a combination reading-vocational training program in a Youth Training School in California. Too often perhaps, remedial reading instruction and vocational training are separated, but in Harris' program there is a definite melding of the two pursuits.

In the final article, Nancy Vick does not present so much a description of an organized program but rather describes approaches and techniques an English teacher can use to help the severely retarded reader in the secondary school. She sees benefits from her ideas not only in terms of reading skills acquisition but also in terms of the personal and social adjustments of such students.

Our Disadvantaged Older Children*

DOMINIC THOMAS

While there can be little doubt that the effects of social deprivation are cumulative, the characteristics of older disadvantaged children are quite similar to those of their younger counterparts. In this paper the research findings on such children, as summarized in the *Review of Educational Research,* December, 1965, form the basis for discussing their home environments, language developments, patterns of intellectual functions, and motivations and aspirations.

Home Environment

Listed among the research on the family and neighborhood environment of socially disadvantaged children were the following features:

(1) About one sixth of the breadwinners were unemployed.
(2) Few children regularly ate a meal with their parents.
(3) Parents were usually satisfied with their children's progress in school, so long as they were not in trouble.
(4) Homes had few books; children were read to less frequently and spoke less with their parents.
(5) Children exhibited a fear of parental authority and a dependence on siblings and peers.
(6) Parents were inaccessible to children's communication.
(7) Girls were overprotected; discipline of boys was inadequate.
(8) Strong mother-dominated environments were more prevalent.
(9) Lack of systematic stimulation plus the presence of much noise fostered inattention and poor concentration.
(10) Parents reacted to children's misbehavior in terms of immediate

*Reprinted from *Vistes in Reading,* Proceedings of the 11th Annual Convention of the International Reading Association, J. Allen Figuerel, editor, 1966, pp. 349-352, by permission of the author and the International Reading Association.

consequences of action, not on an interpretation of their intent.
(11) Mothers expected husbands to impose restraints upon the children rather than to be supportive.
(12) Fathers felt that child-rearing was the responsibility of the wife.
(13) Familes tended not to frequently participate in group activities.

Gordon summarized the home and family environment as being ". . . noisy, disorganized, overcrowded and austere, . . . lacking many of the cultural artifacts often associated with the development of school readiness, such as books, art work, variety of toys and self-instructional equipment. Adult models. . . have been seen as being incongruous with the demands of the school, . . . and the parents of these children often have been reported as failing to support their children's academic pursuits"(1).†

Language Development

Jane Raph summarizes the characteristics of disadvantaged children's language developments with the following statement: "Research to date indicates that the process of language acquisition for socially disadvantaged children, in contrast to that of middle-class children, is more subject (a) to a lack of vocal stimulation during infancy, (b) to a paucity of experiences in conversation with more verbally mature adults in the first three or four years of life, (c) to severe limitations in the opportunities to develop mature cognitive behavior, and (d) to the types of emotional encounters which result in the restricting of the child's conceptual and verbal skills. Distinctive qualities of their language and speech include (a) a deficit in the auditory-vocal modality greater than in the visual-motor areas; (b) a meagerness of quantity and quality of verbal expression which serves to depress intellectual functioning as they grow older; and (c) slower rate and lower level of articulatory maturation" (2).

Perceptual Styles and Patterns of Intellectual Function

Gordon noted that disadvantaged children have perceptual styles and habits which are inadequate or irrelevant to academic efficiency. He listed the following characteristics from the research:

(1) The absence of any high degree of dependence on verbal and written language for cognitive clues was prevalent.
(2) Traditional receptive and expressive modes have not been adopted.
(3) Concentration and persistence needed on learning tasks were lacking.
(4) Auditory discrimination and recognition of perceptual similarities were relatively poor.

†Numbers in parentheses refer to references at end of article.

(5)   Slowness appeared as a feature of cognitive function.

(6)   A "so what" attitude toward difficult problems resulted in a proportionate decrease in learning overtime.

(7)   Feelings of inadequacy were displayed in school.

(8)   Dependence was more on external as opposed to internal control.

(9)   Low self-esteem, high incidence of behavioral disturbance, and distorted interpersonal relationships characterized ego development.

Motivation and Aspiration

The research on motivation and aspiration revealed that motivation in socially disadvantaged children was frequently inconsistent with the demands and goals of formal education. The nature of their aspirations was usually consistent with their perceptions of the availability of opportunity and reward. Symbolic rewards and postponements of gratification appeared to be ineffective as a means for motivation. Drive was present; but its direction may not be complementary to academic achievement. Socially disadvantaged children tended to be less highly motivated and had lower aspiration for academic and vocational achievement than did their middle- and upper-class school peers. High levels of aspiration and positive attitudes toward school were only infrequently encountered in lower socioeconomic groups.

Remedial Programs

Characteristics of socially disadvantaged children should be used as information for designing meaningful curricula. While there is agreement on the general characteristics of such children, it must be pointed out that individually they demonstrate widely differing characteristics.

John I. Lee indicated that, "Teachers and schools must, at an early age, discover and identify each child, and must comprehend his development, his individual capacities, and his needs." School services, ". . . must be provided promptly to remove or minimize each child's disability and to educate him 'over' or 'around' or 'in spite of his limitations. . . " (3).

Reading Centers

For example, the failure of a considerable number of culturally disadvantaged children to achieve reading proficiency suggests that a need exists for diagnostic, evaluative, and remedial services for these children. Currently Detroit is in the process of establishing experimental remedial-reading centers. The purposes of the centers are (1) to reduce the extent of reading retardation of socially disadvantaged children from low-income families in grades 4 through 12, and (2) To gain further knowledge and skill for the remediation of reading deficiencies for large numbers of disadvantaged children and youth.

In order to accomplish the objectives as outlined above, five reading centers have been established to give intensive remedial services to disadvantaged pupils who are seriously below their potential in reading achievement. A request for Federal funds to establish the centers was approved under the Elementary and Secondary School Act. Sixty-four public schools and forty-nine non-public schools in three (of nine) administrative regions in Detroit were included. These region areas are characterized by older and often substandard multiple-dwelling housing and populations below the city mean in family income, occupational status, and adult-education level. School data reveal a higher dropout rate, higher degree of overageness for grade placement, and a greater reading retardation for pupils in these regions than for the city as a whole.

Each of the three administrative regions has two centers: one to accommodate elementary-junior high students and, the other, a senior-high unit. On the senior-high level, the centers are housed in highschool buildings where space permits. Elementary-junior high classes are held in mobile units, 20 feet wide by 40 feet long. These have been placed on selected sites adjacent to public school. At the present time, four such mobile units adjoin each of three elementary schools and one senior-high school. Each elementary-junior high unit serves approximately 18 to 25 public and non-public schools. The transportable buildings provide office and classroom facilities, and air conditioning makes it possible for them to operate during the summer months. Small classrooms are equipped with a wide variety of multi-level books and SRA reading laboratories. Controlled readers, tape recorders, filmstrip projectors, and other visual equipment are provided in each room.

Staff

The staff of the reading centers is unique. Each center is made up of experienced Detroit public-school personnel, especially choosen for this assignment, and includes an administrator, a reading diagnostician, a social therapist, a psychologist, and six reading teachers. If there is evidence of need, more specialized professional help (such as, services of an audiologist, neurologist, ophtalmologist, or psychiatrist) is available. In this way, the centers provide thorough diagnosis of a child's reading disability and correction of physical, emotional, or neurological defects suspected of being contributing causes of this reading retardation.

Selection of Pupils

The students are selected from certain public and non-public schools in the project regions. A principal or teacher from a participating school may refer a student from grade 4 through 12 who is reading at a level which is significantly below his measured or estimated-learning capacity. In general, the criteria for selection are as follows: the student must be reading one or more years below his grade level; he must possess an I.Q. of 80 or above; and he may not be a candidate for a special-education program. After his referral, comprehensive diagnostic tests are administered by the reading diagnostician. The diagnostician may, or may not, enlist the services of the social therapist or psychologist, depending upon the analysis of the testing data. Referring schools are then notified of test results and the names of the students to be admitted to the center. After parental permission has been obtained, the student is assigned to a class and is provided with bus transportation from the participating school to the center.

Schedule of Classes

Students who attend elementary-junior high centers spend one hour, two days per week in class; students who attend senior-high centers spend one class period, four days per week. Small class size of eight to ten students enables the reading diagnostician to design a remedial program individually tailored to meet the specific needs of each student. Adequate time for planning and evaluating is provided since the teacher has only four classes per day on the elementary-junior high level and five classes on the senior-high level. No classes are scheduled on Wednesdays, this day being set aside for in-service training, staff appraisals of student progress, conferences with parents, and conferences with teachers of children from the participating schools. It is not possible to estimate the length of time that a child receives instruction at the center because kinds and degree of reading retardation will vary with the individual student. However, before a student is released from the center, all concerned personnel must concur that he is ready to operate without further instruction from the center.

Evaluation

In order to measure the value of such services, a tentative-evaluation design has been formulated by the Research Department of the Detroit schools. This design includes measurement in terms of the project's expected outcome (product evaluation) and in terms of the services provided and the methods used (process evaluation). The product evaluation will be based on a random sampling of experimental- and control-group pupils. The experimental group will consist of pupils who have had remedial instruction at the project centers; the control group will consist of eligible pupils who have not had remedial instruction at the project centers. The process evaluation will include a continuing examination of the specific objectives of the project and of methods, materials, facilities, services, and staff effectiveness. The main purpose of the process evaluation is to identify changes that should be introduced to increase the effectiveness of the project in attaining the general objectives.

It is the hope of the project staff that as the result of their efforts pupils' attitudes toward themselves and reading will improve, reading-achievement levels will be raised, and the centers will prove beneficial to instructional personnel of participating schools.

References

1. Gordon, Edmund W. "Characteristics of Socially Disadvantaged Children," *Review of Educational Research*, 35 (December 1965), 377-78.
2. Lee, John J. "We Consider the Children: Their Needs Shape our Efforts,'" *Graduate Comment*, 4 (April 1961), 17.
3. Raph, Jane Beasley, "Language Development in Socially Disadvantaged Children," *Review of Educational Research*, 35, No. 5 (December 1965), 396-97.

A Reading Program for School Dropouts*

LILLIE POPE

President Johnson's program for the Great Society is now properly focused on education as a major weapon to break the poverty cycle. Anti-poverty programs throughout the country are concentrating on eradicating adult illiteracy, and at the same time are providing marketable skills to hundreds of thousands of adults and young adults who are now unemployable, employable solely in marginal jobs, or because of the expected impact of automation, will soon be unemployable. Youth over the age of 16 who are out of school and out of work are an important segment of the adult group that must be educated — or re-educated.

In New York City alone there are an estimated 77,000 young people between the ages of 16 and 21 who are out of school and out of work. Of this number, approximately one-half are functionally illiterate, reading at or below the fifth-grade level — a level that is vocationally disabling. The reading level of the whole group ranges from complete illiteracy (some knowing no words, and unable to recognize all letters of the alphabet) to ability to read at the twelfth-grade level. Academic upgrading must be made available to all of them, for they all are capable of learning beyond their present levels of achievement and deserve the opportunity to compete in the Great Society with the most important tool man has developed for learning, reading skill.

One organization set up to attack the problem of the school dropout in New Your City is JOIN (Job Orientation in Neighborhoods). This agency was originally designed to rehabilitate school dropouts in economically disadvantaged areas by counseling and job placement. It was hoped that many of the approximately 77,000 school dropouts, ages 16 to 21, in New York City would seek and receive vocational rehabilitation through JOIN's neighborhood centers located in the disadvantaged areas of the city. It quickly became apparent that the degree of academic disability of many of these young people was so great as to be vocationally disabling. Thus they could have only menial or

*Reprinted from *Journal of Reading*, 9 (May, 1966), pp. 367-378, by permission of the author and the International Reading Association.

"dead-end" jobs, they could not fill many openings currently available, and they had no chance for present or future upgrading. A program of remedial instruction emphasizing reading skill was therefore essential for them.

In August, 1964, eight months after the start of the counseling and job placement programs, remedial education was incorporated into the total JOIN program. This remedial program will be discussed in detail here. It is important that workers in this new field know the procedures that are or have been followed and their rationale. They should also be aware of which procedures show promise of success, even though there has been insufficient time to evaluate the results in a rigorous statistical fashion.

The Bureau of Instruction of JOIN was given the responsibility to make available remedial education to New York City school dropouts who were clients of JOIN. These clients are youngsters who may walk in from the street because they see the word "job" on the sign in the window of the neighborhood center, who are referred by other agencies, or who have come because of word-of-mouth recommendation. A large proportion of these youths are Negro or Puerto Rican, and more young men then young women apply. Although counseling, remedial education, training, and job placement are offered in neighborhood centers, they are centrally administered.

Before describing the instructional program, it is important to note that the teachers in this agency were surrounded by non-instructional staff, laymen and professional, who were naive about the problems of teaching and learning. Even though the non-instructional staff — counselors, center directors, and policy-making staff — identified with the youngsters and understood how disabling their academic deficiencies were, their expectations were unrealistic. It was not uncommon to have a request to prepare a second-grade reader for the high school equivalency examination. It was a daily struggle to educate this group, particularly on the policy-making level, so that they could comprehend that the day of "instant" instruction had not yet arrived. They had to comprehend that learning requires constant effort by the student and cooperation of all those working with him, that a quality program requires an investment of time, materials, and personnel, and that a compromise with quality may be more harmful to the youths served than no program at all.

Student Body

Since New York City requires compulsory school attendance through the age of 16 and JOIN's clients are products of an era of automatic promotion, most had reached the ninth or tenth grade before dropping out of school, but some had completed the eleventh grade. There was little correlation, however, between reading level and grade completed.

At the outset it was decided that no youngster interested in admission to this remedial program would be excluded for any reason. It was the goal of the Bureau of Instruction of JOIN to offer remedial and educational services to *every* client with whom it could make contact, since this might be the "last chance" for many. Every school dropout eligible for JOIN services was presumed to have an untapped learning potential. Since the causes of failure are so complex, intelligence testing was ruled out as a criterion for admission to the program. Testing was available *only* for analyzing puzzling cases of persistent lack of success. There was a firm rule, however, that no test of intelligence could be given initially, in order that the youngster would be judged by performance and effort, not by test scores. In addition, the JOIN program would be open to all, including the non-reader. In contrast, some other anti-poverty programs offered basic education only to those youngsters with reading and mathematics levels of grade five and above. As it developed, the non-reader was a rewarding challenge.

Our clients had sat through at least 10 years of schooling before coming to JOIN. Their reading levels, as noted earlier, ranged from non-reader (not recognizing the letters of the alphabet) through twelfth grade. Of 500 students tested in May, 1965 with the Wide Range Achievement Test, fully half were functionally illiterate, reading at the fifth-grade level or below. Nine percent tested at 2.0 grade level or below. However, in an area serving of predominantly Puerto Rican extraction, 18% tested at 2.0 grade level or below. On the other hand, 24% tested at Grade Nine and above, making the High School Equivalency Certificate a realistic goal for many of them. In this group, many had dropped out during the eleventh and twelfth grades for economic reasons or because of unusual personal situations.

Scheduling

Another basic guideline was that, except in special cases, no less than two contact per week were required of each student in remedial instruction and academic skill upgrading. Each session lasted a minimum of one hour, but could last as long as three hours. Many students attended three, four, and five times per week; rarely did a student attend fewer than two sessions weekly. (The few who attended less than twice a week came not for remedial instruction, but for supportive tutoring, which will be explained later.)

Another key aspect of the instructional program was the formation of person-to-person teacher-student relationships. Instruction was therefore planned for groups no larger than 15. Often, groups were far smaller, and sometimes instruction was individual. In all cases it was hoped that instruction would be individualized to meet the special needs of each student and give him confidence in his ability to learn, despite a history of unremitting and disheartening academic failure.

Instructional Program

Increased skill in basic tool subjects is essential for vocational upgrading; whenever possible, the equivalent of a high school diploma is desirable. With *primary emphasis on reading,* and with arithmetic as the auxiliary basic subject on which the instruction would concentrate, the bureau set up the following courses of study immediately:

(1)   Academic skill upgrading (including high school equivalency examination preparation) for clients who were receiving counseling as preparation for employability.

(2)   Academic skill upgrading as an integral part of all training programs for those whom JOIN was providing vocational skills as preparation for employability.

(3)   Academic skill upgrading for those clients already working, but requiring further upgrading.

(4)   English for Spanish-speaking youngsters whose limited English was vocationally disabling or restrictive.

(5)   Supportive tutoring of those clients who had been persuaded to return to school. In these cases, one contact per week was permitted.

The plan was for each youngster to enter the program at whatever level he was at the moment, as determined by a careful diagnostic evaluation of his reading and arithmetic skills. He would also be given realistic goals to work toward and a chance to perceive successes, no matter how minute, at frequent intervals. To accomplish this task, teachers required patience, confidence, and a capable grasp of the skills being taught.

Incentives

The Bureau of Instruction of JOIN was faced with two major problems: how to reach the students, and how to teach them. As a rule, the experience of the dropout with the traditional school has been a history of repeated failure, which to him is proof of his inability to learn. The result is an almost irreparable damage to his self-esteem. Although he may have some desire to learn, he is suspicious of anything resembling the traditional school situation and uneasy about risking failure once more. He prefers to modify his goals because, convinced he cannot upgrade his academic skills appreciably, he does not want to exert himself. Furthermore, he may not realistically appreciate the vocational limitations of his present level of skills. The implication of all this is common to the teacher: those most in need of remedial instruction are frequently most reluctant to accept it. Realizing that we would have to make this experience as easy as possible for him, we reached out to the dropout by making the teaching center readily accessible geographically (minimizing travel) and by offering him a stipend or allowance when we could. Above all, through the support of the counselor, center director, or a work supervisor who encouraged the youngster to continue to study, we achieved our greatest "reachability."

One type of monetary assistance offered to the dropout was a $1.25 stipend per session. When a client was placed on a job, he was urged to continue attending counseling and remedial education sessions for further upgrading; these were then conducted at night, after work. For such post-placement sessions, no monetary allowances were available.

At the same time that remedial academic services were incorporated in the total JOIN program, specific skill training programs were also established. These provided training for positions such as auto mechanic's assistant, clerical helper, and building maintenance helper. Skill training was conducted for approximately 15 hours weekly, plus 10 hours of remedial education and counseling. A training allowance of $20 weekly was paid to each trainee, contingent upon attendance.

On March 1, 1965, JOIN became responsible for making remedial education available to JOIN clients who were employed by the Neighborhood Youth Corps under the Economic Opportunities Act. The Act recommends that the youngsters be offered, in addition, 10 hours of academic instruction and counseling per week, for which they receive no stipend.

Thus there was a variety of arrangements tied in with the opportunity for remedial education: academic instruction parallel to counseling alone, reimbursement at $1.25 per session; post-placement academic instruction on a completely voluntary basis; academic instruction as an integral part of training programs, with an incentive allowance for academic instruction; and academic instruction as a supplement to a work program (Neighborhood Youth Corps), with no incentive allowance. Before comparing the results of each arrangement, the instructional sites should be discussed.

Instructional Sites

As mentioned earlier, the first group of teachers assigned to this mission was no larger than the staff of a small elementary school in this city. For greatest efficiency of administration and supervision, as well as in-service training, it would have been best to centralize instruction in one building and have students travel from all parts of the city to learn from us what they had failed to learn before. This we did not do. It was clear from the beginning that with youngsters most difficult to motivate, it was essential to go to them and minimize the distance they would have to travel to us. Thus the teachers were initially assigned to the Join neighborhood centers so that they could reach the dropouts at the same place they were being counseled and where the placement officer also was stationed. When training programs were set up, teachers were assigned to training centers so that, whenever possible, the youngsters could receive remedial instruction directly at the training site.

After Join became responsible for teaching youngsters working for the Neighborhood Youth Corps at several hundred sites in the city, teachers were, whenever possible, assigned to the actual work sites so that as little travel time as possible would be imposed upon the dropouts in their efforts to receive instruction. For example, when almost 100 Neighborhood Youth Corps workers were assigned to the Methodist Hospital in Brooklyn for an excellent work program, the hospital cooperated by providing space for the workers to receive academic upgrading there.

The teaching staff was quite dispersed and often had to travel from one site to another during the day or be assigned to one site for two days a week and to another for three days a week. Thus supervision, coordination, and holding of staff conferences were difficult. But the impact on the youngsters was far better than if all instruction had been centralized. In addition, since the instruction was community- and work-centered, we could enlist the cooperation of JOIN center directors and interested work supervisors. Their dedication to the youngsters and appreciation of the importance and difficulty of academic instruction were reflected in the improved attendance of the youth with whom they dealt.

Attendance

As expected, $1.25 per session was an incentive for many to "try" once more, or to see what we had to offer; but when not backed up by effective instruction, the stipend did not hold them. Our greatest rate of dropout was prior to the first contact with the teacher, after referral from the counselor; those who remained beyond the first week of instruction were more ready to believe that they could learn, and were willing to try. When no incentive allowance was offered, as in the case of post-placement evening academic instruction for dropouts who were working on full time jobs, a gratifying number chose to continue their academic upgrading. Two-thirds, however, did forego further study while working, even though it was apparent to the youngster that the job was only a stopgap and genuinely useful only as further training for upgrading. The resolve to study was tenuous, even with many of the motivated dropouts; study, in addition to holding a job, was too demanding for many, despite all good resolutions.

When the allowance for training programs was contingent upon attendance in remedial instruction, attendance was excellent. In both an Office Practice training program and a Carpenter's Helper training program, youngsters initially resisted the academic instruction and attended only because they would lose their training allowances if they did not attend. After the first few sessions, their interest was awakened. They became involved, progressed well academically, and appreciated the training so much that at the end of their training program they formally requested a continuation of their academic instruction, even though they were no longer eligible for the stipend.

Individualized Instruction

Of course, teaching problems were complex because of the nature of the students. These economically and socially disadvantaged youths had low morale and a record of repeated failure. In most cases, dropping out of school represented for them a final statement — "throwing in the sponge"; for many it was a release from "captivity." Teaching was further complicated by a lack of suitable materials for remedial work with young adults, particularly those from a disadvantaged urban background. In addition, the problem of "how to teach" was aggravated by the administrative complexities of our organization. Since our primary requirement was to teach clients near where they lived or worked and in a center that was an agency or office center, traditional teaching conditions were not the best. Noise and traffic frequently simulated a small active railroad terminal. Though attempted, homogeneous grouping was dependent on the number of students available at a given time at a given teaching site, because academic scheduling depended on work and training schedules and on student availability.

The diagnostic evaluation of the client's basic reading and arithmetic skills formed the basis for the instructional plan. The teacher had to set short-range goals capable of achievement within a two-week period. The teacher shared these goals with the student and then shared with him his successes, no matter how small. They were required to report these bi-weekly on the checksheet, on which the original diagnostic evaluation was recorded. Needless to say, biweekly successes were not measured in terms of grade level, but in terms of specific learnings in reading, such as improvement in blending or fluency, or in a diminishing tendency to reverse.

When the schedule permitted individual instruction, or even groups of two or three, this plan was followed without difficulty and progress was excellent. However, when groups were larger, individualized instruction was limited in many cases by the shortage of materials and equipment.

Materials and Equipment

When the program was established, major purchases were generally subject to a six-month delay because of complex purchasing procedures. During this time the only equipment available were tape recorders in several JOIN centers, duplicating machines, and, of course, blackboards, tables, and chairs.

Lack of materials was our major handicap. Teachers were hired and students appeared at the same time that materials were ordered. Fortunately, some materials were rushed within three months. Thus, ingenuity and industry were demanded of the teachers, and they didn't fail. They made flash cards, reading charts, experience charts, and exercise material. When JOIN's machines frequently didn't work, the teachers borrowed machines and enlisted the help of friends, husbands, and former employers. Each teacher developed material to fill her needs and borrowed from other teachers when necessary. And the needs of the students were met.

Programmed instruction was investigated with the hope it would allow the greatest latitude for individualized instruction. Each student could enter the program at his level and progress at his own rate, motivated by repeated successes. At no time did we believe that "antiseptic" programmed instruction (in which contact with the reader is excluded or minimized) could be effective with our students, who had to be coaxed to learn and for whom education held little lure. But no effective and comprehensive programmed reading instruction was available for our group when the program began. Many good programs were being developed simultaneously with our work. Hopefully, good material will appear soon.

Semi-programmed material available in reading laboratories was of greatest help to us. With this material, individuals in groups could proceed at their own rate, with teacher intervention and interaction with the students that is so necessary for motivating and rebuilding self-confidence in these youngsters. We discovered to our dismay, however, that the semi-programmed material became a helpful crutch to some teachers, who settled down to being monitors of the groups they should have been teaching. They supervised the students' selection of materials and maintained order, but neglected the main task of working with each student or with the group directly. To rectify the situation, the answer booklets (with which the students checked their own responses) were withdrawn. The teachers thus had to check all answers personally, face to face with each student. Although this was difficult for the teacher with a large group, instruction became more effective.

Non-programmed material in reading and mathematics which is of interest to the young adult – and particularly to the disadvantaged urban young adult – was also of limited availability, but is now being developed and published. A wide variety of traditional materials was ordered of the highest interest level available, with some care to avoid material that was culturally remote from or offensive to our youngsters. We had great difficulty providing materials (and motivation) for the middle range of readers, those from the fourth-to the seventh-grade levels. Well-motivated beginning readers were satisfied with most materials that were properly presented because success was more important to them than content. Relatively high interest material was available for the more advanced readers. Newspapers could be used, as well as library and reading material already on the market. But for the middle range, little material was available that combined appropriate reading level with interest level. This group was the greatest challenge.

In those groups in which academic instruction was related to trade skill training – and vocabulary and reading material were applicable to the trade – the academic teachers worked closely with the trade teachers to coordinate instruction. Trade teachers, in turn, helped motivate the trainees for academic instruction by pointing out that basic academic skills were needed by an automobile repairman's assistant, for example, or a garage attendant, or an electrician's helper, and that academic skills were required for each student to take advantage of further training or promotional opportunities. The fact that job placement was available at the end of every training program was a powerful incentive to learn all the skills needed for the job, academic skills included.

Many students were from Puerto Rico, and their spoken English was vocationally limiting or disabling. The language competence of this group varied. Some were literate only in Spanish; some were totally illiterate. Some did not understand English; some had a fair command of spoken English – though it was heavily accented – but were too shy and self-conscious to speak in vocationally or academically critical situations. For this group we planned to develop modified programmed instruction. This program would use tape instruction correlated with written material, all presented with the active participation of the teacher. Its aim was to improve the communication skills of this group so that these youths could express themselves in spoken English and also increase their level of literacy.

Volunteer Tutors

When the remedial program was first announced, the agency was besieged by volunteers eager to help dropouts. Offers came from high school students, college students, graduate students, office workers, professionals, and retired women. Glad to accept any useful assistance, the agency required that volunteers assist at JOIN instructional centers for no less than two sessions weekly, each session to be a minimum of one hour. Though eager to be helpful, many of the volunteers were reluctant to travel to the neighborhoods in which the work had to be done; and many were glad to contribute one evening or afternoon weekly, but not two. Since a single weekly contact was considered too casual for the students, these offers were declined. For those remaining who were of college age or above, a manual was prepared to assist them in teaching the dropout.

Every volunteer tutor was oriented and supervised very closely by the Area Remedial Supervisor. Several of the most talented and sensitive volunteers produced excellent results in closely supervised work with individual students. Generally, they were most helpful in assisting a teacher with groups, where they were able to work closely with individuals in the group who needed special assistance.

Student Assistants

Outstanding students in the groups helpfully assisted the teacher with weaker students, and were thus rewarded and encouraged. They communicated well with their peers and gave substantial aid to the overworked teachers. When the Neighborhood Youth Corps was formed, some of these more capable students were assigned as Teacher Aids, to assist the teachers with clerical work, mimeographing, and in some cases again, with closely supervised instruction. As a result, the more capable students were additionally motivated to continue their studies.

Effectiveness of Program

Our greatest holding power was with those youths for whom there was some financial incentive in accepting academic instruction, and in whom, as stated earlier, a counselor or work supervisor took a personal interest. Our greatest success was with beginning readers and with advanced readers. The beginning readers were eager when shown that they really could learn something. The patient, conscientious teacher did well with them. The advanced readers, who were close to and eager for the high school equivalency certificate, made good progress. The middle readers – fourth to sixth grade – presented the great challenge. They failed to grasp that they could aspire to jobs requiring greater reading and arithmetic skills than they had. Good teaching materials of high interest level were hard to obtain, and it was most important with this group that reading and mathematics be directly related to the trade skill training. Only in direct relation to the trade he was learning was the youngster at this level motivated.

Conclusion

Now that the nature of the problem population is clear and the parent agency has clearer form and direction, gaps and unavoidable weaknesses in the program are being filled in. The teaching staff has been greatly increased. For the first time we can allocate personnel for a Materials Development Unit, which is vitally important since an agency such as JOIN must develop new materials appropriate and effective for their clients. This unit will develop trade-related materials. Additional supervisory staff will be assigned to each area to maintain and upgrade the quality of instruction by regular staff members and to assist in the supervision of volunteers. Because the dialects of many of the disadvantaged (Southern and Spanish) compound the reading problem, it is hoped to add a speech specialist to provide a fresh approach to the communication problems of these youngsters. Now that the program is stabilized, JOIN must establish a program of research into the most effective methods and techniques of teaching school dropouts.

Programs like JOIN must coax back into the "classroom" youngsters for whom education has no lure. Now that they have had a taste of the outside world and a smell of the "job hunt," they are ready to be shown that reading and arithmetic are really tools – just like a hammer or a typewriter – tools which they must and can acquire.

Salvaging Failures Through Improved Reading: Reading in Vocational Classes*

ROBERT L. HARRIS

I represent a school of failures. We have over 1200 youths, ages 17 to 22, who are with us because they have broken the law. Their commitment to us as law breakers is a sympton reflecting their character defects, of failures in families, communities and schools.

With a group such as this, it is amazing to see a majority of them functioning effectively in their classes, interested and involved in their assignments and work, showing enthusiasm and pride of accomplishment.

Before I explain the part reading plays in salvaging failures, let me describe our school and its students.

The School

The Youth Training School is located approximately 40 miles east of Los Angeles. It is one of 5 schools for boys, 2 schools for girls and 4 conservation camps operated by the Department of the Youth Authority in California as part of its legislative responsibility for the treatment of delinquency. (The Department also has responsibilites in the prevention of delinquency). Each school has a different program designed for wards of specific age levels and needs. The Youth Training School is designed for the older group of boys.

The overall goal of all Youth Authority treatment is to train its wards for lives as useful law abiding citizens. The primary program of our school is intensive industrial education to equip students with skills, work habits and attitudes so they can secure gainful employment on their release.

Our basic plan is to integrate in the instruction the application of work experience in the maintenance and operation of the school. The students perform almost the entire maintenance and operational functions of the institution under the supervision of their instructors. The only exceptions are

*Reprinted from 29th Yearbook of the Claremont Reading Conference, 1965, pp. 160-167, by permission of the author and the Claremont University Graduate School.

the operation of the boiler plant, the telephone and security sound system and the repair and installation of the locks.

Performing the work experience under the supervision of the vocational instructors is the unique aspect of the plan. The vocational instructors possess valid credentials for teaching vocational subjects. They are experienced journeymen in their trades. During the first years of employment as instructors they take courses in professional education which is comparable to professional education courses taken by academic teachers.

Student Characteristics

One-third of our students are from adult criminal courts throughout California; two-thirds are from juvenile courts. Approximately 10 per cent are up to or within one year of grade level based on their age as measured by the California Achievement Test. The remaining 90 per cent are from 2 to 4 years below grade level. We find their functional level is from 1 to 2 years below the test score. In other words, most of our students function from 3 to 6 years below grade level in their classes.

We estimate that the intelligence of our students is close to average. This is not according to the several group intelligence tests; these tests probably would shown a mean score in the low 90's. However, the different tests vary greatly, so much so that we hesitate to rely on them. A great deal has been written recently concerning the poor application of these tests for the culturally different (or deprived) students. We generally agree with these critics.

The General Aptitude Test Battery is quite helpful in making assignments to the vocational classes. This test, administered by the State Employment service, provides us with information which shows both intelligence and performance factors. This enables us to identify students who score high in performance although they are low in verbal and abstract areas. It provides specific scores which guide us in selecting students for classes.

Student Attitudes

The attitudes of entering students are generally well established, and for the most part follow three patterns: rebellion, passive resistance and surface compliance. Almost all tend to be fearful, anxious, suspicious and distrustful of adults and hostile toward authority. They generally lack real depth of feelings; they want immediate satisfactions. Many resist or refuse class assignments for fear of failure or ridicule; it is easier and safer to say "I can't" or "I won't" rather than try.

The Youth Training School started 5 years ago in January, 1960. We were aware that assigning all students immediately into vocational classes is radical in terms of good industrial education practice. Almost always some minimum prerequisites in mathematics and reading are required.

We met this problem, in part, by assigning students on the basis of interest, aptitude and how close they came to reasonable standards in reading and mathematics. Many are assigned with skills below the reasonable minimums.

Teaching Reading

We also recognized that each instructor would need to teach some basic skills. It was hoped that the interest they created would motivate students and help them to learn the necessary skills. However, while the instructors have competence in their trades, they have no training or background for teaching reading or mathematics.

Looking now at the instructors' problems in teaching these skills, I recognize the value of the definition of reading of this conference. This broad view encompassing both objects and symbols as part of reading is most meaningful and useful in our program. It confirms that all of our teachers, both vocational and academic, are reading teachers.

Here we have students in a situation which involves manipulative instruction, the how, and the related technical, the why. The students see and use the tools and equipment in action oriented learning. At the same time they study why. Somehow most of the students learn to read the material used in the why study. The instructors do a remarkably good job of teaching reading as they teach their subjects. They work with the immediate means, and apply the methods and techniques developed for industrial education. They make frequent use of demonstration and examples. In explaining a process or procedure, not only do they make diagrams or drawings on the board, but they write or print the names of the things they are talking about. In most classes the students are making notes. They explain, then give the students an opportunity to make an application, either as a group or as individuals, or both. And lastly, they test for results. They patiently repeat and review instructional material, both in class and with individual students.

For each class an individual course of study is developed by the instructor. The learning is sequential, and taken one step at a time. Textbooks and references of all types are used. Often the references are materials secured from industry. The instructor develops instruction material which includes job sheet, procedure sheets, operation sheets, assignment sheets and information sheets. Students in all classes use these. They are essential where students are working in all phases of the course at the same time. It enables some to advance more rapidly while others, who do not learn as fast, take longer. In all instances, a student finishes one job or assignment in a satisfactory manner before going on to the next. There are many instances where instructors arrange so that more advanced students help the newer students in studying their lessons.

Student Involvement

The instructors find some way to get the student interested and personally involved in some phase of the instruction. Once the student is involved, he then becomes willing to work at his technical instruction, mathematics, reading, or whatever he needs, not only in his vocational class; many times students become interested in also enrolling in an academic class.

How do instructors do this? Here are some of the ways.

1. They are enthused about the subject they are teaching. This is a genuine enthusiasm developed out of their own experiences in their trade; out of confidence that the students, too, can make a living and a good life if they will apply themselves.

The instructors make the work important and alive. A recent example is that which took place in the beginning Nursery and Gardening class, one in which the education level is quite low, and where motivation is particularly difficult. In preparation for a meeting of our Trade Advisory Council, 3 students learned to identify 50 plants by their Latin names, and almost all of the other 17 students were able to identify at least 5. Some of these were students with a reading ability of 3rd, 4th or 5th grade.

2. The instructors accept the students at the level at which they are functioning. It is true that even they, like other teachers, prefer students who have aptitude and capability, but they accept *every* student and work with him. In many instances the point at which they must start working is on a purely emotional level establishing some kind of effective relationship.

3. The work experience program provides an opportunity for the students to carry on responsible functions, to demonstrate initiative; sometimes to fail and then to re-do correctly. For the beginning student this becomes a goal to work toward. The same enthusiasm is seen in the student whose assignment is mopping and waxing a floor in the Building Maintenance class as a student in the Electricity class who is checking an electric motor or making an installation. The work which is done is useful and necessary. Because it is necessary, the student doing the assignment becomes important.

4. In many instances students undertake work projects and are able to carry them through. Some of these are completely on their own; others are group projects. Many are rather complex, detailed projects. To be able to start something and actually complete it is for many of our students a new experience.

A good example of a project is the model house which we are building during this year. Already all of our Building Trades classes have spent many fruitful hours of study on making lay-outs for their particular trade. Then they estimated the amount and type of materials required and figured the costs. Bear in mind, each student, or in some cases, pairs of students, did the actual work. Soon we will start actual construction. When finished the house will be sold, by bid, and moved to a home site for use.

The most rewarding aspect of this is that the students not only learn; they recognize that they have learned something of value. We see them become self-reliant and confident individuals with goals and purposes. The record of their successes in the community after they are released, which is not surpassed by any other institution in the country, confirms this.

High School Reading for the Severely Retarded Reader*

NANCY O'NEILL VICK

"That there is the best book written! And you know what else? It's the first book I ever read from start to stop!"

These were the words of thirteen-year-old Butch. These were amazing words for him to say, for three short semesters before Butch had been identified as a potential dropout. He had reached – agewise and promotion wise – junior high school with problems bigger than he was. His attendance for the past two years had been very irregular. He had bragged that men didn't need "book-learning" – and then he had become one of the silent ones in the classroom, offering no problem but just an indifferent "I don't know" to any question or just one of those who stoically sit and wait until enough birthdays have passed so that they can legally be released from the confines of the classroom. What else could he do? He couldn't even read!

When he walked into the special English class, he made a bargain with the teacher. "I won't bother you none if you won't try to make me read."

What can be done for these young adolescents? They are caught in a school where 80 per cent of the learning is based on reading. They are faced with a world where job interviews are often dependent upon a high school diploma. They are confronted with technological changes in jobs, requiring three or more retraining periods during a man's productive years. Yet failure with books and with the usual procedures in reading have resulted in complete withdrawal from reading. What can be done for these young people?

Try a New Attack

Only one thing is possible – try a new attack. And that is what Butch's teacher did. In fact, this approach is the big thing we have learned in three

*Reprinted from *Vistas in Reading*. Proceedings of the 11th Annual Convention of the International Reading Association, J. Allan Figurel, editor, 1966, pp. 227-230, by permission of the author and the International Reading Association.

years of special classes which have been formed to study this problem.

First, the teacher reads aloud a little each day. It may be a humorous poem, a tear-jerking short feature story from the newspaper, a joke, or riddle — anything interesting enough to capture the pupil's attention, short enough to hold interest, and different enough that the students would respond to it.

Next, she planned work which these pupils could do — and do well. Success was a new and exciting experience for these pupils. So, success was built into these programs. Nothing was finally presented as an assignment to the pupils until enough background had been provided that the pupils could complete the assignment satisfactorily, meaning perhaps that several experiences would be provided in order to build the necessary conceptual informational background which could insure understanding. Frequently this planning included a field trip, a motion picture, some film strips, slides, bulletin board pictures, and newspaper or magazine articles. Always, much work was done on vocabulary, for without an understanding of the concept represented by both the spoken and the written word, the culminating lesson and assignment would result in confusion and frustration for the learner. We learned that these special pupils must be so immersed in the necessary vocabulary and the needed experiences that these become a part of the learner's very being.

Include Reading Skills

But what about reading instruction *per se?* Until the resentment toward books had been overcome, few books were used by pupils. Reading in other formats was substituted: experience stories, kit-type materials which were brief and interesting, newspapers, directions for their hobbies, film strips on a controlled reader, and paragraphs or exercises on a transparency. Frequently, the tape recorder was used to develop listening skills and to assist the severely retarded, stumbling reader to acquire correct phrasing and help with difficult words.

Memory work, particularly of good poetry, did much toward increasing vocabulary and improving phrasing and intonation. This progress in turn built reading comprehension and led to more fluent oral and written language. Here, the erasure technique for teaching poetry was used, making this activity a most pleasurable one. Again, the tape recorder was used to record the choral reading of selections. Pupils became quite involved as they listened to themselves, discussed their performance, and made suggestions for improvement. Here, records were frequently used to show pupils how a professional interpreted the same selection. It was most gratifying to hear the lively discussion which frequently followed such a comparison!

Finally, the teacher had to be most flexible. When the students came into class complaining that they could not remember their science book, the teacher put aside her own plans, for the moment. This hour was the right one to teach these pupils how to read and study another book. This day was the time that she could show them that the many days they had spent in "guessing what this new word meant by reading the sentence" was to show them how to gain meaning from context in other subject areas. This day was the one to show pupils how to apply in another context what they knew about main ideas and supporting details. So this was the day the teacher had long awaited: the day her pupils realized that they were making real and substantial gains in their reading ability and that they really could read some books!

Are these suggestions "unorthodox" according to the established techniques for teaching reading? Perhaps. But no one can build a lasting superstructure without a good foundation. The teacher must first understand that all pupils who have failed to learn to read up to their own expectancy level (mental age -5 will yield the grade-level expectancy) have a learning problem. For many, this deficit will be an experiential-conceptual-information one which must be removed before even the brightest pupil can function up to his innate potential. To overcome this deficiency the teacher must literally saturate the pupils with meaningful experiences and mediate so effectively that permanent, well-understood concepts will evolve. Next she must use for all, a multi-sensory approach which will involve the pupils through sight and sound, using as many of the audiovisual aids as are available or as can be devised. She will involve pupils through the tactile and kinetic senses. This practice will involve much speaking and much writing. Finally, she will involve listening – listening to class discussions, to tape recordings, to records, or to the sound track on a film. She will use listening exercises to develop the pupils' abilities to differentiate between sounds and to reproduce sounds correctly. She will, at last, involve critical listening skills to develop listening-thinking power.

Finally, everything the teacher plans must strengthen the relationship between reality, the spoken word, and the written word. For only as these become integrated within the pupil's mind can true reading occur.

Materials Necessary

What must the school provide? First of all, it must provide a teacher with interest, empathy, and insight; next, audio-visual equipment and materials which will enable the teacher to use many approaches to develop a single, wanted concept; third, an abundance of reading materials: books, magazines, and kits appropriate to the ability and interest-level of the pupils; and finally a counselor who can assist in testing and in conferring with the pupils.

Mental Health Aspect

How does this program of reading carried on in the English classroom assist the counselor?

1. Success, built into the program in small, manageable steps, helps to destroy the defeatist attitudes of the pupils. The teacher, using praise and encouragement in a carefully structured environment, must balance adequate challenge with success and recognition. To get pupils who are inured to failure to believe in success is a difficult task.

2. As the defeatism diminishes, a sense of personal worth increases. Since a good self-image is necessary to achievement and to general life adjustment, this rise in ego usually results from enjoying small successes. Butch, who had never read a book, first wanted the teacher to bargain with him – he would cause no trouble if she would not ask him to read. Then one day in the library, backed with months of intensive work designed to increase reading ability and faced with a stack of gaily-jacketed books, he wanted to know – "Can I read one of these now, maybe?"

"This is one I have been wanting you to read. It is about a man – independent like you are – who was shipwrecked. You'll really like this book," the teacher said as she handed him a rewritten version of *Robinson Crusoe.* How many months had she waited for this question! Now Butch tells other boys casually, "I read this here book last week. It's real neat. You oughta read it, too." So he is gaining status with his peers as he develops his own self-image through success in reading.

3. Goal-setting which is at once challenging and realistic is almost nonexistent for these pupils. Yet going through life without a goal is like setting out on a journey without a destination. A harsh environment coupled with continuous failure in school-oriented work usually results in the pupils' feeling powerless to exercise any control over their futures. Therefore, they live for today only. The teacher must assist pupils in developing realistic, clear, definite, shortterm goals. Then, as these goals are achieved, new ones must be set up. Only in this way can pupils learn that goals achieved, are stepping stones to success. Only in this way can their level of aspiration be raised. But this gain can happen only if the pupils are taught in such a way that they *are* learning and achieving, encouraged at points of failure, and praised at points of success. But a conscious effort to widen their horizons must be made.

4. Our society holds tenaciously to certain values that are not likely to have been assimilated by disadvantaged pupils. Without these values, pupils frequently encounter ridicule or rejection. More seriously, they may run into problems with our laws which reflect these values. Respect for personal and property rights of others, respect for law and authority, love of country, and understanding of citizenship responsibilities can be structured in many of the activities for these pupils. Skillfully-led classroom discussions, carefully-planned

classroom experiences, and well-selected reading are effective ways for building these values with pupils. Society expects the schools to inculcate these values into today's pupils so that tomorrow's citizens will perpetuate and improve our heritage.

Summary

So, to teach the severely retarded reader in the classroom situation, try a new approach. Get really acquainted with each pupil so that you can know his potential and his needs. Recognize the voids in his educational background and plan for the reteaching of these skills or concepts.

Plan a variety of ways to teach any single item. This method is necessary for many reasons. These pupils have an extremely short span of attention; therefore, several approaches must be available to provide an adequate amount of drill. Also, different pupils learn in different ways. Johnny learns only through the kinesthetic sense; Judy learns only by seeing; Billy learns only by hearing. All people learn by doing so all must be involved in the way they learn best.

Appropriate materials must be available. The sixteen-year-old pupil who struggles with a fifth-grade reader cannot cope with a tenth-grade world history book. Adaptations must be made of the materials; backgrounds must be developed in pupils. Many high-interest books must be readily available to encourage much independent reading.

Teachers must try a new attack. If the phonic approach to reading fails, they must try the sight-word method. If both have failed, then they must try the kinesthetic. An eclectic approach will be the appropriate one probably, and must be tried along with periodicals, kits, and experience stories. Then, teachers may let pupils return to books when success is assured.

Special, small classes must be provided so that the slow learner is not dominated and confused by brighter pupils who travel at the fast pace. Also, he must not serve as a drag to hold back and bore his more advanced peers.

Finally, the English program provided for him must be a broad-based language arts course. Although the course must be in writing and in speaking, it must build needed background, acceptable attitudes, and needed skills.

We have the money. Many materials are currently available, and more are in the offing. We have the pupils who have great needs. We have the researchers and the experimenters. But the teacher is the key to learning. If we meet the challenge of these high school retarded readers, we will do so because of teachers who have insight, inspiration, and imagination; who have empathy and understanding; who can bring together in a classroom research, pupils, and material, and produce the desired end product: responsible citizens for tomorrow.

References

1.   Board of Education, City of New York, *Teaching English for Higher Horizons,* 1965.
2.   Cervantes, Lucius F. *The Dropout.* Ann Arbor, Michigan: University of Michigan, 1965.
3.   Corbin, Richard and Crosby, Muriel. *Language Programs for the Disadvantaged.* Champaign, Ill., 61822: National Council of Teachers of English, 1965.
4.   Figurel, J. Allen, editor, *New Frontiers in Reading,* New York: Scholastic Magazines, IRA Conference Proceedings, Volume 5, 1960.
5.   Figurel, J. Allen, editor, *Reading and Inquiry,* Newark, Delaware, 19711: International Reading Association, 1965.
6.   Jewett, Arno, editor, *Improving English Skills of Culturally Different Youth in Large Cities.* Superintendent of Documents, 1964, Washington, D. C.
7.   Simmons, John S. and Rosenblum, Helen. *The Reading Improvement Handbook.* Washington: Pullman, 1965.
8.   Smith, Henry P. and Dechant, Emerald V. *Psychology in Teaching Reading.* Englewood Cliffs, New Jersey: Prentice-Hall.

Questions for Discussion

1.   For the most part, Dominic Thomas discussed characteristics of disadvantaged students in terms of weaknesses. From your reading and experience, what strengths do such students have which can be capitalized upon in remedial and corrective programs?

2.   What is your opinion of the use of programmed instructional materials with severely disabled readers?

3.   How would you answer the criticism of some writers who say that remedial reading programs are of little value on the secondary level and available staff, money and resources should be directed toward developmental reading instruction?

Materials and Resources

XI

It is hoped that those interested in implementing some type of reading program at the secondary school level have profited from the ideas presented in the preceding articles of this text. It is assumed that some readers of this text will want to pursue certain topics further and will want to have available lists of instructional materials that are appropriate for use at the secondary school level. For these reasons, three annotated bibliographies have been included in this final section.

Edward Summers reviewed six volumes of the annual conferences of the International Reading Association and identified all papers which pertained to reading at the junior and senior high levels. Summers located 145 such papers and his bibliography is divided into eleven different sections.

Edward Brown's bibliography deals with programmed reading materials suitable for use beyond the elementary school level and contains twelve items. Edwin Smith's annotated list is concerned with instructional materials primarily for use with adult illiterates; it is included here as a great deal of such material could be used with remedial readers at the junior and senior high levels.

An Important Resource for Secondary Reading *

EDWARD G. SUMMERS

Planning and organizing developmental reading programs at the secondary level can be a formidable task. Such programs should include provision for the successful reader, the student in need of corrective experiences, and the student who is severely retarded in reading. The school staff or individual teacher desiring to initiate a reading program to meet student needs has a wealth of information to draw upon for aid. A variety of resources exist which can provide valuable information and guidance on secondary reading, but the problem is to make such resources readily available to interested users.

One resource which contains excellent information on a wide array of topics is the report of the annual conference on reading of the International Reading Association. This bibliography lists pertinent papers relative to junior and senior high school reading which have appeared in the proceedings of the last six conferences. Sources are as follows:

1. *New Frontiers in Reading,* International Reading Association Conference Proceedings, Vol. 5, 1960.
2. *Changing Concepts of Reading Instruction,* International Reading Association Conference Proceedings, Vol. 6, 1961.
3. *Challenge and Experiment in Reading,* International Reading Association Conference Proceedings, Vol 7, 1964.
4. *Reading as an Intellectual Activity,* International Reading Association Conference Proceedings, Vol. 8, 1963.
5. *Improvement of Reading Through Classroom Practice,* International Reading Association Conference Proceedings, Vol. 9, 1964.
6. *Reading and Inquiry,* International Reading Association Conference Proceedings, Vol. 10, 1965.

In this six-year span there has been a marked increase in the number of papers dealing with the secondary level. The conference proceedings have been and will continue to be a valuable resource for pertinent research and information on reading at both junior and senior high school levels.

*Reprinted from *Journal of Reading,* 10 (November, 1966), pp.88-102, by permission of the author and the International Reading Association.

Reading in the Senior High School

I.   *Reading Programs*
   1. Bamman, Henry A., "Changing Concepts in Reading in Secondary Schools," *Changing Concepts of Reading Instruction,* 6 (1961), 41-45.
        Traces the progress and development of reading instruction and presents a plan of action for making reading instruction the responsibility of each teacher.
   2. Bond, Guy L., "Unsolved Problems in Secondary Reading." *Changing Concepts of Reading Instruction,* 6 (1961), 200-203.
        Discusses problems related to instructional outcomes and problems related to adjusting to ability differences.
   3. Fay, Leo, "Implications of Classroom Organization for Reading Instruction," *Improvement of Reading Through Classroom Practice,* 9 (1964), 59-60.
        Presents characteristics of new organizational approaches.
   4. Karlin, Robert, "Nature and Scope of Developmental Reading in Secondary Schools," *Reading as an Intellectual Activity,* 8 (1963), 52-56.
        Explores the different elements of developmental reading programs, and provides guidelines for consideration in planning a program.
   5. Wilson, Rosemary Green, "Changing Concepts of Reading Instruction in the Development of Basic Skills," *Changing Concepts of Reading Instruction,* 6 (1961), 45-48.
        Presents a brief background of the development of reading instruction and discusses the organization, approaches, and materials of the reading program.
   6. Simpson, Elizabeth A., "Responsibility for Secondary Level Reading Programs," *Changing Concepts of Reading Instruction,* 6 (1961), 203-206.
        Discusses the components of a balanced program, and the responsibilities and roles of the different members of the reading program.
   7. O'Donnell, C. Michael, "Teaching Reading via Television," *Improvement of Reading Through Classroom Practice,* 9 (1964), 139-140.
        Describes "High School Reading," a 10-week basic remedial course consisting of 20 30-minute television lessons.
   8. Green, Margaret G., "Solving Vocational and Personal Problems Through Reading." *Improvement of Reading Through Classroom Practice,* 9 (1964), 205-206.
        Outlines a summer reading course offered by Daytona Beach Junior College.
   9. Sparks, J. E., "Experience Needs of Capable Students," *Reading and Inquiry,* 10 (1965), 57-59.
        Discusses the criteria, curriculum, procedures, and evaluation of the seminars for the academically-talented at Beverly Hills High School.
   10. Johnson, Gwen F., "A Plan for Low Achievers in Reading on the Secondary Level," *Improvement of Reading Through Classroom Practice,* 9 (1964), 62-64.
        Decribes in detail the reading program of the Beaufort County Reading Project.

II. *Reading Personnel*
   11. Artley, Sterl A., "Educating Teachers for Secondary Reading Instruction," *Improvement of Reading Through Classroom Practice,* 9 (1964), 19-20.
        Expresses need for adequate pre-service preparation for teacher trainees and in- service programs for those now teaching.
   12. Jan-Tausch, James, "Qualifications of Reading Clinicians," *Reading and Inquiry,* 10 (1965), 229-230.
        Discusses the functions and responsibilities inherent in the clinician's position and describes the necessary experience and training.

13. Haven, Julia M., "Opportunities for the High School Reading Specialist," *Reading and Inquiry,* 10 (1965), 230-232.

Discusses the role of the specialist in regards to federally-funded programs, teacher responsibility, and life-time reading goals.

III. *Methods and Grouping*

14. Melnik, Amelia, "The Formulation of Questions as an Instructional-Diagnostic Tool," *Reading and Inquiry,* 10 (1965), 36-39.

Advocates the use of questions for revealing individual differences and for focusing on the process rather than the content of reading.

15. Nason, H. M., "Using the Multi-Media in Building Reading Power," *Improvement of Reading Through Classroom Practice,* 9 (1964), 134-135.

Discusses different facets of multi-media and offers suggestions for making the approach more successful.

16. Clark, Bernice T., "Organization Based on Appraisal," *Reading and Inquiry,* 10 (1965), 139-141.

Discusses various ways to assess student's abilities and several means for utilizing grouping.

17. DeBoer, John J., "Through Organizational Practices," *New Frontiers in Reading,* 5 (1960), 36-40.

Discusses the problems and criteria of grouping, makes provision for individualization in regular classes, and offers proposals for a reading program.

18. Karlin, Robert, "Methods of Differentiating Instruction at the Senior High School Level," *Improvement of Reading Through Classroom Practice,* 9 (1964), 60-62.

Discusses different features of both individualization and grouping in reading instruction.

19. Weber, Martha Gesling, "Means Versus Ends," *Improvement of Reading Through Classroom Practice,* 9 (1964), 101-102.

Discusses four general approaches to individualized instruction in reading.

20. Carlson, Eleanor G., "Sound Principles for Individualizing a High School Reading Class," *Reading and Inquiry,* 10 (1965), 160-163.

Illustrates ways in which various approaches to individualizing can be weighed in terms of factors influencing instruction.

21. Gold, Lawrence, "A Comparative Study of Individualized and Group Reading Instruction with Tenth Grade Underachievers in Reading," *Improvement of Reading Through Classroom Practice,* 9 (1964), 102-104.

Applies elementary-type reading instruction to secondary underachievers.

22. Skeen, Bearnice, "Individualizing Instruction Through Pupil-Team," *Improvement of Reading Through Classroom Practice,* 9 (1964), 104-105.

Considers several guidelines for procedure and evaluation on pupil-team learning.

IV. *Developing Reading Skills*

23. Schick, George, "Developing Vocabulary and Comprehension Skills at the Secondary Level with Particular Attention to Motivational Factors," *Reading as an Intellectual Activity,* 8 (1963), 60-63.

Discusses the analytical and contextual approaches in vocabulary growth and considers both general factors and analytical exercises in regard to comprehension.

24. Smith, Helen K., "Research in Reading for Different Purposes," *Changing Concepts of Reading Instruction,* 6 (1961), 119-122.

Investigates the abilities of and the methods used by 15 good and 15 poor readers when reading for two divergent purposes, details and general impressions.

25. Shafer, Robert E., "Using New Media to Promote Effective Critical Reading," *Improvement of Reading Through Classroom Practice,* 9 (1964), 137-139.

    Defines critical reading and discusses the environmental element; discusses current methodological and technological developments.

26. Wolf, Willavene, "The Logical Dimension of Critical Reading." *Reading and Inquiry,* 10 (1965), 121-124.

    Presents two aspects of logic in critical reading: validity and reliability of materials and validity of teaching.

27. Levin, Beatrice Jackson, "Developing Flexibility in Reading," *Improvement of Reading Through Classroom Practice,* 9 (1964), 82-84.

    Describes program of defining and developing flexibility of reading rate according to reader's purpose and difficulty of material.

28. Moore, Walter J., "Improving Reading Rates," *Improvement of Reading Through Classroom Practice,* 9 (1964), 135-136.

    Discusses several reasons for failure of rate development and offers overall suggestions for the reading programs.

29. Ives, Sumner, "Recognizing Grammatical Clues," *Improvement of Reading Through Classroom Practice,* 9 (1964), 233-234.

    Explains clues which are all examples of interaction between grammatical forms and lexical meanings.

30. Rankin, Earl F., Jr., "A New Method of Measuring Reading Improvement," *Reading and Inquiry,* 10 (1965), 207-210.

    Presents evidence showing that current methods are faulty and discusses a new technique for measurement.

V.   *Materials*

31. Kopel, David, "The Rationale for Reading Textbooks," *Improvement of Reading Through Classroom Practice,* 9 (1964), 82.

    Describes briefly reading materials beginning with the middle thirties through the present and discusses the objectives underlying their construction.

32. Joll, Leonard, "Evaluating Materials for Reading Instruction at the Secondary Level," *Challenge and Experiment in Reading,* 7 (1962), 198-200.

    Evaluates materials according to the following categories: vocabulary, organization, critical thinking, appreciation, speed, comprehension, and word attack.

33. Early, Margaret J., "Through Methods, and Materials," *New Frontiers in Reading,* 5 (1960), 40-44.

    Discusses lecture-demonstration methods in team teaching and materials, beginning with the single textbook and progressing to differentiated instruction.

VI.   *Reading in Content Areas*

34. Hahn, Harry T., "Who Teaches Reading in the Secondary School?" *Challenge and Experiment in Reading,* 7 (1962), 45-47.

    Emphasizes that direct teaching of reading and study skills is not enough. Content area teachers must be involved. In addition, teaching instruction and materials must be integrated into the entire curriculum.

35. Vinagro, John V., "Rate of Comprehension in the Content Subject," *Improvement of Reading Through Classroom Practice,* 9 (1964), 42-44.

    Discusses the needs, problems, advantages, and principles connected with flexibility of reading.

36. Niles, Olive S., "How Much Does a Content Teacher Need to Know About Methods of Teaching Reading?" *Improvement of Reading Through Classroom Practice,* 9 (1964), 41-42.

    Describes six lessons which provide a foundation from which a teacher can develop as a content teacher of reading.

37. Horsman, Gwen, "Some Useful Classroom Practices and Procedures in Reading in the Content Fields," *Improvement of Reading Through Classroom Practice,* 9 (1964), 44-45.

     Reviews some practices which have helped eliminate reading difficulties in the different fields of instruction.

38. Durr, William K., "Improving Secondary Reading Through Content Subjects," *Reading as an Intellectual Activity,* 8 (1963), 66-69.

     Emphasizes adequate evaluation of abilities, direct teaching in vocabulary, and purposeful reading.

39. Niles, Olive S., "Developing Essential Reading Skills in the English Program," *Reading and Inquiry,* 10 (1965), 34-36.

     Offers criteria for appraising the success of the English teacher: his understanding of the reading process, seeing relationships, choosing functional material, and setting a defensible goal.

40. Jewett. Arno, "Learning to Write Through Reading Literature," *Improvement of Reading Through Classroom Practice,* 9 (1964), 123-125.

     Presents three arguments for using literature as a medium for teaching writing and describes the University of Nebraska program in composition.

41. Fay, Leo, "Reading Instruction in the High School Literature Class," *Challenge and Experiment in Reading,* 7 (1962), 49-52.

     Discusses the reading skills that relate directly to successful reading of literature.

42. Berg, Paul C., "Reading in Literature – A Lively Art," *Reading and Inquiry,* 10 (1965), 103-106.

     Discusses world culture, teacher attitudes, and mass media in regards to the teaching of literature.

43. Moore, William, II, "The Creative Approach," *Reading and Inquiry,* 10 (1965), 81-83.

     Suggests that literature is concerned with all the language arts and lists some literary skills and activities involved in the literature lesson.

44. McDonald, Arthur, "Reading in History: Concept Development or Myth Making," *Reading and Inquiry,* 10 (1965), 102-103.

     Defines history as research for investigation of relevant data, and describes student's task as one of achieving a conceptual framework in regards to history.

45. Herber, Harold L., "An Experiment in Teaching Reading Through Social Studies Content," *Changing Concepts of Reading Instruction,* 6 (1961), 122-124.

     Discusses the basis and structure of an experiment now in progress and gives a mid-way evaluation of the study.

46. _____, "Teaching Reading and Physics Simultaneously," *Improvement of Reading Through Classroom Practice,* 9 (1964), 84-85.

     Cites an experiment which shows reading instruction as a part of course content.

VII. *Developing Interests and Tastes*

47. Russell, David H., "Impact of Reading on the Personal Development of Young People," *New Frontiers in Reading,* 5 (1960), 77-82.

     Discusses the five levels of reading and the effects each of these levels has on personal development.

48. Strang, Ruth, "The Influence of Personal Factors on the Reading Development of Young People," *New Frontiers in Reading,* 5 (1960), 82-87.

     Reviews literature on personal factors influencing reading development and notes that while much attention has been given to negative characteristics, little has been given to positive factors.

49. George, Marie G., "Stimulating Reading in the Senior High School,"

Improvement of Reading Through Classroom Practice, 9 (1964), 105-107.
    Considers methods for stimulating interest and developing reading skills.

50. Witty, Paul, "Some Interests of High School Boys and Girls," *Improvement of Reading Through Classroom Practice,* 9 (1964), 186-187.
    Reports results of a series of studies of the interests of children and youth.

51. Torrant, Katherine E., "Survey of Factors Involved in Building the Lifelong Reading Habit and Practices Which Promote It," *Improvement of Reading Through Classroom Practice,* 9 (1964), 187-188.
    Considers several ingredients which promote a life-long reading habit.

52. Gunn, M. Agnella, "A Different Drummer," *Reading as an Intellectual Activity,* 8 (1963), 160-163.
    Stresses need for building reading tastes as soon as reading begins along five levels of instruction.

53. Weiss, M. Jerry, "Promoting Independent Reading in the Secondary School," *Reading as an Intellectual Activity,* 8 (1963), 63-66.
    Stresses planning thematic units based upon a thorough knowledge of the interests and abilities of the class.

54. Sohn, David A., "Stimulating Student Reading: The Paperback as a Cool Medium Afloat in a Sea of Hot and Cold Media," *Reading and Inquiry,* 10 (1965), 163-166.
    Concentrates on the many and varied opportunities the paperback offers the reading teacher.

55. Llewellyn, Evelyn, "Developing Lifetime Reading Habits and Attitudes Through Literature," *Reading and Inquiry,* 10 (1965), 79-81.
    Identifies some of the habits and attitudes to be developed and stresses wide knowledge and careful guidance on the part of the teacher.

56. Cooper, J. Louis, "The Basic Aim of the Literature Program," *Improvement of Reading Through Classroom Practice,* 9 (1964), 188-189.
    Lists three types of illiterates and emphasizes aspects of promoting lifetime reading habits.

VIII. *Linguistics and the Teaching of Reading*

57. Kegler, Stanley B., "Language, Linguistics, and the Teaching of Reading," *Improvement of Reading Through Classroom Practice,* 9 (1964), 231-233.
    Suggests developments in language studies which are important in the instruction of reading.

58. Lefevre, Carl A., "Contributions of Linguistics to English Composition," *Reading and Inquiry,* 10 (1965), 250-252.
    Presents the rationale of a basic composition program designed for students in Grades Eleven through Fourteen.

59. Malmstrom, Jean, "Linguistics and the Teacher of English," *Reading and Inquiry,* 10 (1965), 248-250.
    Presents some fundamental principles of linguistics and looks at linguistically-oriented textbooks.

IX. *The Library and the Reading Program*

60. Duggins, Lydia A., "Teacher-Librarian Teamwork in the High School Reading Program," *Improvement of Reading Through Classroom Practice,* 9 (1964), 203-204.
    Stesses importance of shared experiences, mutual goals, and general enlistment of the children and the community in the library program.

61. Canale, Orlando J., "Establishing a Working Relationship Between the Librarian and the Consultant," *Improvement of Reading Through Classroom Practice,* 9 (1964), 204-205.

Presents a three-fold teamwork approach for more effective use of library resources.
62. Strang, Ruth, "How the Library Contributes to Students of Different Abilities and Backgrounds," *Improvement of Reading Through Classroom Practice,* 9 (1964) 202-203.
Shows how libraries function for individualized instruction, retarded readers, and independent learners.

X. *Reading and the Bilingual Student*
63. Smith, Edgar Warren, "A High School Program for the Bilingual," *Reading and Inquiry,* 10 (1965), 280-282.
Gives a detailed discussion of materials, methods, and pupil growth in a program for bilinguals.
64. Robinett, Ralph F., "Skills or Concepts in Second Language Reading," *Improvement of Reading Through Classroom Practice,* 9 (1964), 169-171.
Analyzes a narrow but fundamental range of problems related to bilingualism and the conflict of languages and alphabet systems.
65. Zintz, Miles V., "Reading Success of High School Students Who Are Speakers of Other Languages," *Reading and Inquiry,* 10 (1965), 277-280.
Reports the historical background of achievement problems, the cultural conflicts, and the problems of learning English as a second language for the Spanish-American Indian students of New Mexico.
66. Sizemore, Mamie, "Teaching Reading to the Linguistically Disadvantaged at Senior High Level," *Improvement of Reading Through Classroom Practice,* 9 (1964), 171.
Discusses the cultural-meaning problems of the bilingual student in the high school classroom.

XI. *Reading and the Disadvantaged*
67. Grant, Eugene B., "Building Rapport with the Disadvantaged," *Improvement of Reading Through Classroom Practice,* 9 (1964), 173-174.
Stresses development of mutual respect through understanding, recognition of limitations, classroom atmosphere, and appropriate materials.
68. Spiegler, Charles G., "As the Bee Goes to the Flower for its Nectar," *Reading as an Intellectual Activity,* 8 (1963), 155-159.
Attempts to bridge the gap between the advantaged and the disadvantaged through the power of positive reading, using all possible motivational forces.
69. Watson, Richard L., "Early Identification of High School Dropouts," *Reading and Inquiry,* 10 (1965), 265-267.
Reviews the problem, procedure, results and recommendations of a dropout study conducted in Evansville, Indiana.
70. Dorney, William P., "Effect of Reading Instruction on Modification of Certain Attitudes," *Improvement of Reading Through Classroom Practice,* 9 (1964), 171-173.
Suggests that the treatment of delinquents retarded in reading should stress reading instruction as a therapeutic instrument for rehabilitation.

XII. *Diagnosis and Treatment of Reading Difficulties*
71. Fox, Esther, "What Can We Do For the Disabled Reader in the Senior High School?" *Improvement of Reading Through Classroom Practice,* 9 (1964), 154-155.
Discusses both unique and common factors to be considered in setting up a secondary reading program.
72. Karlin, Robert, "Characteristics of Sound Remedial Reading Instruction," *Reading and Inquiry,* 10 (1965), 184-186.

Presents methods of instruction based upon well-known principles of learning.

73. Mills, Donna M., "Corrective and Remedial Reading Instruction in the Secondary School," *Reading as an Intellectual Activity,* 8 (1963), 56-59.

Discusses different types of programs, guidelines, and activities for both teachers and students, as well as reviews of some specific projects.

74. Ross, Joan B., "Remedial Reading Techniques a High School Teacher Can Use," *Reading and Inquiry,* 10 (1965), 182-184.

Summarizes some of the ways a classroom teacher can help students develop study skills in order to conquer course materials.

75. Smith, Helen K., "Remedial Instruction in Comprehension," *Improvement of Reading Through Classroom Practice,* 9 (1964), 152-153.

Lists six steps in remediation of comprehension, planned in harmony with the needs of the students.

76. Van Guilder, Lester L., "Improving the Comprehension of the Emotionally Disturbed," *Reading and Inquiry,* 10 (1965), 205-207.

Discusses causal factors and psychological functions underlying reading disabilities.

77. Abrams, Jules C., "The Rule of Personality Defenses in Reading," *Improvement of Reading Through Classroom Practice,* 9 (1964), 153-154.

Examines emotional factors and ego defenses which may impede the process of learning.

Reading in the Junior High School

I. *Reading Programs*

78. Cooke, Dorothy E., "Techniques of Organization," *Reading and Inquiry,* 10 (1965), 133-136.

Discusses three different programs of reading, including an approach for retarded readers, a creative approach, and a general developmental approach.

79. McInnes, John, "Can Organization Patterns Enable Us to Improve Reading Skills?" *Improvement of Reading Through Classroom Practice,* 9 (1964), 58.

Stresses importance of constant testing of organizational patterns for instructional possibilities or limitations.

80. Paulo, William E., "Improving Reading in Junior High School," *Challenge and Experiment in Reading,* 7 (1962), 164-166.

Identifies the primary considerations for organizing or evaluating a reading program.

81. Natchez, Gladys, "Pupil Behavior: A Clue to Teaching Reading," *Improvement of Reading Through Classroom Practice,* 9 (1964), 150-152.

Cites an example of a complete and successful restructuring of a reading program as a result of understanding meanings behind behavior.

82. Wilson, Robert M., "New Perspectives on the Multi-Media and the Junior High Reading Program," *Improvement of Reading Through Classroom Practice,* 9 (1964), 132-133.

Looks at two different programs each of which emphasizes flexibility, individual difference, student interests, and periodic evaluation.

83. Torrant, Katherine E., "Reading Centers and New Developments in The Teaching of Reading in the Junior High School," *Changing Concepts of Reading Instruction,* 6 (1961), 124-127;

Presents a detailed picture of the reading program at Newton, Massachusetts, including research endeavors, roles of the specialists, available materials, and reactions to the program.

84. Janes, Edith C., "Reading Essentials in the Junior High School Program,"

Improvement of Reading Through Classroom Practice, 9 (1964), 76-78.
Gives a detailed plan for instruction in the complex skills of mature
reading.

85. Andresen, Oliver S., "An Experiment in Class Organization for High School
Freshmen," *Improvement of Reading Through Classroom Practice,* 9 (1964),
57-58.
Discusses the merits of scheduling three required class days per week
and two optional days in which the students engage in independent study.

86. Vickery, Verna, "Practical Problems and Programs," *Reading and Inquiry,* 10
(1965), 274-276.
Analyzes different programs in teaching reading to speakers of another
language.

87. Field, Carolyn W., "Stemming the Pressure on the 'So-Called' Advanced
Reader," *Improvement of Reading Through Classroom Practice,* 9 (1964),
198-199.
Emphasizes the responsibility of both parents and teachers of personal
guidance and realistic expectations of junior high students.

II. *Reading Personnel*
88. Stanchfield, Jo M., "The Role of the Reading Specialist in the Junior High
School," *Improvement of Reading Through Classroom Practice,* 9 (1964),
51-52.
Discusses the organizational patterns, functions, and future role of the
reading specialist.

89. Early, Margaret J., "The Interrelatedness of Language Skills," *Reading and
Inquiry,* 10 (1965), 32-34.
Stresses that every teacher be a teacher of not just reading, but of
language skills.

III. *Methods and Grouping*
90. Durrell, Donald D., "Evaluating Pupil Team Learning in Intermediate Grades,"
New Frontiers in Reading, 5 (1960), 112,115.
Reports pupil team learning as a method of providing for individual
differences.

91. Carline, Donald E., "Applying Clinical Practices to Individualizing the Junior
High School Reading Program," *Reading and Inquiry,* 10 (1965), 154-156.
Analyzes and conceptualizes reading difficulties from a clinical
approach, but with terms and procedures suitable for the classroom teacher.

92. Underwood, William J., "Effective Grouping in Junior High School," *Reading
and Inquiry,* 10 (1965), 136-139.
Traces the various trends in grouping and reviews a current plan.

93. Briggs, Daniel A., "Grouping Guidelines," *Improvement of Reading Through
Classroom Practice,* 9 (1964), 50-51.
Suggests basic principles to be considered in establishing a grouping
program.

94. Sartain, Harry W., "Evaluating Research on Individualized Reading,"
Improvement of Reading Through Classroom Practice, 9 (1964), 96-98.
Raises questions to consider in evaluation of research reports.

95. Putnam, Lillian R., "Controversial Aspects of Individualized Reading,"
Improvement of Reading Through Classroom Practice, 9 (1964), 99-100.
Criticizes, on the basis of observations, certain practices in
individualized reading programs and gives some suggestions for improvement.

96. Lauck, Mary Ruth, "Practical Individualization with Basal Materials,"
Improvement of Reading Through Classroom Practice, 9 (1964), 80-82.
Outlines methods, procedures, and activities which have been tested in
a classroom situation.

IV.   *Developing Reading Skills*

97.   Smith, Nila Banton, "Reading for Depth," *Reading and Inquiry,* 10 (1965), 117-119.

Categorizes and discusses the different meaning-getting processes of reading.

98.   James, Sister Mary, "Helping Junior High School Students Get to the Heart of Their Reading Matter," *Improvement of Reading Through Classroom Practice,* 9 (1964), 79-80.

Lists and explains four general factors to help students gain a total and purposeful command of reading matter.

99.   Gordon, Lillian G., "Promoting Critical Thinking," *Reading and Inquiry,* 10 (1965), 119-121.

Stresses the importance of a language-oriented reading program and total school involvement in the process of critical thinking.

100.   Cleland, Donald L., "A Construct of Comprehension," *Reading and Inquiry,* 10 (1965), 59-64.

Reviews other writers' ideas of comprehension and proposes a model to explain the intellectual processes involved in comprehension.

101.   Devine, Thomas G., "Listening: The Neglected Dimension of the Reading Program," *Improvement of Reading Through Classroom Practice,* 9 (1964), 119-120.

Shows that instruction in listening skills reinforces instruction in reading skills.

102.   Caroline, Sister M. IHM, "Word Recognition and Vocabulary Development," *Reading and Inquiry,* 10 (1965), 227-229.

Explains the various implications and operations of word recognition.

103.   Deighton, Lee C., "Experience and Vocabulary Development," *Reading and Inquiry,* 10 (1965), 56-57.

Emphasizes increasing word power through direct experience or contextual setting.

104.   Spache, George D., "Clinical Assessment of Reading Skills," *Reading and Inquiry,* 10 (1965), 202-205.

Examines clinical evaluation of oral reading, silent reading, applied or study-type skills, and word analysis abilities.

105.   Kinder, Robert Farrar, "Teaching Reference Study Skills," *Reading and Inquiry,* 10 (1965), 96-98.

Discusses skills of location, evaluation, organization, and usage.

106.   Courtney, Brother Leonard, F.S.C., "Study Skills Needed in the English Classroom," *Reading and Inquiry,* 10 (1965), 98-102.

Lists basic principles of common study skills, and discusses practical points for the teacher in emphasizing skill areas.

107.   Robinson, Helen M., "Perceptual and Conceptual Style Related to Reading," *Improvement of Reading Through Classroom Practice,* 9 (1964), 26-28.

Considers a number of studies investigating visual perception on primary level through college level.

V.   *Materials*

108.   Carrillo, Lawrence W., "Methods of Teaching Reading in the Junior High School," *Challenge and Experiment in Reading,*7 (1962), 47-49.

Emphasizes the importance of using a combination of both basal readers and multi-level materials.

109.   Bliesmer, Emery P., "Analysis of High School 'Basal Reading Materials,' Preliminary Efforts," *Improvement of Reading Through Classroom Practice,* 9 (1964), 85-86.

Describes types of material presently available and expresses some tentative conclusions and comments.

110.   Culliton, Thomas E., Jr., "Effective Utilization of Basal Materials at the Junior

High School Level," *Improvement of Reading Through Classroom Practice,* 9 (1964), 78-79.

Stresses thorough and continued diagnosis, careful evaluation, and a wide variety of materials in addition to the basal reader.

111. Groff, Patrick, "Materials Needed for Individualization," *Reading and Inquiry,* 10 (1965), 156-59.

Advocates the teaching of reading, using children's literature, rather than programmed or basal materials.

VI. *Reading in Content Areas*

112. Coulter, Myron L., "Changing Concepts of Reading Instruction in the Content Areas," *Changing Concepts of Reading Instruction,* 6, (1961), 35-38.

Argues that since reading a general reading text does not ensure reading adequately the specialized texts in content areas, reading instruction must take place in the content area.

113. Robinson, H. Alan, "Teaching Reading in the Content Fields: Some Basic Principles of Instruction," *Improvement of Reading Through Classroom Practice,* 9 (1964), 36.

Advocates teaching of reading and study skills for general improvement of learning in content areas.

114. Summers, Edward G., "Review of Recent Research in Reading in Content Subjects at the Junior High School Level," *Improvement of Reading Through Classroom Practice,* 9 (1964), 38-41.

Gives a summary of recent research and provides a reference list and brief description of pertinent studies.

115. Buechler, Rose Burgess, "Vocabulary Development in the Content Fields," *Improvement of Reading Through Classroom Practice,* 9, (1964), 37-38.

Values the use of cultural tools and visual aids in placing vocabulary words in a contextual setting.

116. Brown, Charles M., "Reading Among the Language Arts," *Improvement of Reading Through Classroom Practice,* 9 (1964), 118-119.

Gives examples of approaches used in the study of how children learn.

117. Hillocks, George, Jr., "Language Studies and the Teaching of Literature," *Improvement of Reading Through Classroom Practice,* 9, (1964), 229-230.

Applies language theory and literary theory to teaching the reading of literature.

118. Woestehoff, Ellsworth S., "Teaching Reading Skills Through Literature," *Improvement of Reading Through Classroom Practice,* 9 (1964), 36-37.

Applies a six-step reading skill approach to a chapter from a Mark Twain novel.

119. Sipay, Edward R., "Selecting Suitable Material for the Literature Program," *Improvement of Reading Through Classroom Practice,* 9 (1964), 120-121.

Gives criteria for teacher selection and teacher-guided student selection of material.

120. Stewart, David K., "From the Complexity of Reading to the Clarity of Simple English," *Improvement of Reading Through Classroom Practice,* 9 (1964), 121-122.

Advocates a four strand skill approach built into every lesson plan, providing a sequential learning pattern ranging from kindergarten through high school.

121. Evertts, Eldonna L, "The Nebraska Curriculum: Literature, Linguistics, and Composition." *Improvement of Reading Through Classroom Practice,* 9 (1964), 227-229.

Defines the importance of a three-fold approach in the English program, including emphasis on literature, linguistics, and composition.

122. Carlsen, G. Robert, "Adolescents and Literature in Three Dimensions." *Changing Concepts of Reading Instruction,* 6 (1961), 196-199.

Discusses three kinds of activities repeated with variation each year: individualized reading, reading in common, and thematic reading of literature.

123. Newton, J. Roy, "Desirable Experiences Through Language Arts," *Reading and Inquiry,* 10 (1965), 54-56.

Emphasizes a variety of in-school experiences to develop specific reading readiness and advocates a fusion of reading and writing instruction.

124. Carlson, Ruth Kearney, "The Vitality of Literature," *Reading and Inquiry,* 10 (1965), 74-76.

Discusses variety, reading procedure, and appreciation levels of poetry.

125. Bennett, E. Harold, "Multi-Level Reading of the Novel," *Reading and Inquiry,* 10 (1965), 76-79.

Discusses an experiment in developing inquiring minds through guided study of individually chosen novels. Plan includes interaction of both homogeneous and heterogeneous groups.

VII. *Developing Interests and Tastes*

126. Robinson, Margaret A., "Developing Lifetime Reading Habits – A Continuous Process," *Improvement of Reading Through Classroom Practice,* 9 (1964), 179-180.

Traces reading from initial interest to development of permanent interest and literary taste.

127. Boutwell, William D., "Can Book Reading be Made a Habit?" *Improvement of Reading Through Classroom Practice,* 9 (1964), 180-182.

Presents five factors that deter the enjoyment of reading and suggests nine programs of action to make reading a habit.

128. Clark, Marie, "What We Read – and Why," *Improvement of Reading Through Classroom Practice,* 9 (1964), 184-185.

Stresses building personal, historical, and literary concepts by letting students read for enjoyment.

129. Gable, Martha A., "T. V. Lessons to Stimulate Interest in Reading," *Improvement of Reading Through Classroom Practice,* 9 (1964), 133-134.

Gives examples of several TV lessons and describes the team teaching relationship of the TV teacher and the classroom teacher.

130. Gunderson, Doris V., "Research in Reading Habits and Interests at the Junior High School Level," *Improvement of Reading Through Classroom Practice,* 9 (1964), 182-184.

Reports findings of several research studies.

VIII. *Linguistics and the Teaching of Reading*

131. Shuy, Roger W., "Linguistic Principles Applied to the Teaching of Reading," *Reading and Inquiry,* 10 (1965), 242-244.

Discusses the principles of system, sounds, and society and their application to the junior high reading program.

132. Fries, Charles C., "Linguistics and Reading Problems at the Junior High School Level," *Reading and Inquiry,* 10 (1965), 244-247.

Contrasts the linguistic approach and the traditional approach in the teaching of reading.

IX. *The Library and the Reading Program*

133. Weiss, M. Jerry, "The Role of the Library in the Junior High School Reading Program," *Improvement of Reading Through Classroom Practice,* 9 (1964), 200-201.

Offers ideas to support use of the library as the core of the reading program.

134. Pitts, Anne W., "The Role of the Library in the Junior High School Reading Program," *Improvement of Reading Through Classroom Practice,* 9 (1964), 201-202.

Prefers that library skills relative to a specific subject be taught by teacher rather than in an organized course in library instruction.

X.   *Reading and the Disadvantaged*
   135.   Brown, Judith, "A Rationale for the Teaching of Reading to Disadvantaged Children," *Improvement of Reading Through Classroom Practice,* 9 (1964), 168-169.
   Discusses some positive factors of motivation for disadvantaged children and lists typical characteristics of their style of learning.
   136.   Downing, Gertrude L., "Compensatory Reading Instruction for Disadvantaged Adolescents," *Improvement of Reading Through Classroom Practice,* 9 (1964), 167-168.
   Describes the goals, procedures, and outcomes of the Queens College BRIDGE Project with disadvantaged students in New York City.
   137.   Gibbons, Marilyn, "Teaching Reading to the Disadvantaged-Junior High Mobilization for Youth Reading Program," *Improvement of Reading Through Classroom Practice,* 9 (1964), 165-166.
   Describes an experimental program designed to attack juvenile delinquency through re-motivation to learning.
   138.   Nason, Harold M., "The Developmental Program Meets the Challenge of Potential School Dropouts," *Reading and Inquiry,* 10 (1965), 263-265.
   Discusses the characteristics of disadvantaged children and lists some "musts" for their reading program.
   139.   Cohen, S. Alan, "Factors of Format Relative to Comprehension or Mediocrity on East Houston Street," *Reading and Inquiry,* 10 (1965), 267-269,
   Presents conclusions that have guided materials development at New York City's Mobilization for Youth Program.

XI.   *Diagnosis and Treatment of Reading Difficulties*
   140.   Roswell, Florence G., "Improved Diagnostic Procedures in Reading at the Junior High School Level," *Reading and Inquiry,* 10 (1965), 180-181.
   Discusses the three-fold purpose of diagnosis and cites case studies showing how schools might use existing diagnostic facilities.
   141.   Saine, Lynette, "General Principles Underlying Good Remedial Instruction," *Improvement of Reading Through Classroom Practice,* 9 (1964), 149-150.
   Summarizes principles basic to the functioning of a program, rather than its instructional procedures.
   142.   Smith, Helen K., "Identification of Factors that Inhibit Progress in Reading," *Reading and Inquiry,* 10 (1965), 200-202.
   Discusses methods of identifying specific factors related to reading retardation.
   143.   Jan-Tausch, James, "Classroom Application of Clinical Findings," *Improvement of Reading Through Classroom Practice,* 9 (1964), 148-149.
   Stresses the necessity of translating clinical discoveries into classroom practicality and terminology.
   144.   Cohn, Stella M., "Organizing and Administering Public School Reading Clinics," *Reading and Inquiry,* 10 (1965), 224-226.
   Describes in detail the clinical program of the Special Reading Services of New York City.
   145.   Feuers, Stelle, "Individualizing Instruction in the Reading Skills Class," *Improvement of Reading Through Classroom Practice,* 9 (1964), 98-99.
   Describes the approach, technique, and organizational patterns of the remedial reading program in a Beverly Hills school district.

Programmed Reading for the Secondary School*

EDWARD T. BROWN

The primary bibliography[1] of programmed materials and its supplements contain twenty-two entrees of items for school use beyond the elementary school grade level. Two initial entrees are relisted by individual items in a supplement, thus twenty are non-duplicating entrees. Twelve of these entrees, grouped into their series of course alignment, will be described in this article.

Junior High School Level

Building Reading Power. (Charles E. Merrill Books, Inc.) ($25.00). This is a kit containing five copies of fifteen different programmed booklets, a teacher's manual, masking cards, and a class supply of response sheets. The manual was developed as a project of the New York City Board of Education for remedial use in the Junior high schools of the city. It has a vocabulary and content level of upper fourth grade, and has undergone several revisions as a result of student feedback. On the average, a booklet has 41 frames and several application exercises of the skill taught; thus each booklet is a relatively short assignment. The answers to the exercises are only in the teacher's manual.

The series on Context Clues has eight booklets identifying clues that occur within sentences. The definition of context and the process of using context are presented by examples. Successive booklets cover the topics of clues from pictures; membership in a series; space; pronunciation; the words, phrases, and punctuation which identifies definitions synonyms; antonyms; and restriction of word meaning through selection of its correct definition.

The series on Structural Analysis has two booklets: the first defines base (root) word and prefixes; the second defines suffixes. Each booklet teaches

*Reprinted from *High School Journal,* 49 (April, 1966), pp. 327-333, by permission of the author and the editor.

[1]Carl H. Hendershot. Programmed Learning: A Bibliography of Programs and Presentation Devices; including 1964 supplements of April, July, and October, and 1965 supplement of April. Bay City, Michigan: The Author, 1964, 1965.

several common examples and provides exercises with other prefixes or suffixes as well.

The series on comprehension skills has five booklets. The first in the Basic Skills Series, and Content Analysis for the reading series. Each answer frame is illustrated by a face with a surprised, worried, pleasant, or disappointed expression.

The booklet "Following Directions" establishes the rules for following oral directions (learn all steps, know sequence, understand all words, ask if in doubt) and the rules for listening (listen carefully, take concurrent notes, ask for explanation if necessary, get confirmation). Then follows a series of practices in following directions which involve coin operated machines, secret messages, arithmetic calculations, capitalization instruction, and several others; each of these emphasizes accuracy both in reading and in the skills of following directions.

The booklets "Reading Interpretations I" and "Reading Interpretations II" parallel each other in content; they are not sequential, however. Each teaches the procedures for finding the meaning of what is read through the skills of finding of word, phrase or sentence, and paragraph meaning. Definition, instruction, and practice is given in the skills for finding the key idea of a paragraph, making inference from facts, using imagination to add interpretation, and identifying the author's purpose.

The fourth booklet "Reference Skills: The Dictionary" is not within the definition of reading as used for this article.

Steps to Better Reading. (Harcourt, Brace, and World) (3 books – $1.80 each). Books 1,2, and 3 are for the 7th, 8th, and 9th grade respectively. There is a teacher's manual for the series, and test booklets that contain both unit and final tests for each book. These programmed books are adjunct to the publisher's *Adventures in Literature Series;* only the final small non-programmed section on timed reading, however, could not be used entirely independent of it if the literary selections that are analyzed were otherwise made available.

Each book is similarly organized; the first two units teach getting the meaning of words from their structure and their context; the third and fourth units teach getting meaning from sentences and from paragraphs; the fifth unit analyzes two literary selections; and the sixth unit, non-programmed, describes and provides practice in the skills of previewing, scanning, and rapid reading. Each unit is divided into an appropriate number of chapters averaging about sixty frames each. Short exercises for skill practice occur at the end of each unit and frequently after chapters within the unit. A lengthy non-programmed exercise covering all of the skill instruction defines a paragraph as related sentences, set off by indentation, and containing a central thought. Then successive booklets emphasize correct identification of the topic of a paragraph by using all of the details, finding the single central thought, and seeing the relationship among the details. Almost all of the instructional paragraphs have the topic sentence as the first sentence, but some of the exercises are more complex.

How to Improve Your Reading. (Coronet Instructional films) ($1.50). This is a sixty page booklet with a specially designed soft cover which incorporates its own answer mask. It was developed and tested with 7th and 8th grade students. The material is presented in eight sections averaging thirty frames each. Several of the sections include a few review frames, the ninth section is review for integration; and the tenth section can be used as a review or as a test. Single sections would be a very short assignment; the entire program, however, would require several hours. There is some relationship between this program and Coronet's five film series, "Reading Improvement."

The Program first differentiates between recreational and study type reading improvement. The skill of each step is explained, practiced by example, and reviewed. In sequence, the six steps are: (1) enjoyment – comes from daily reading of books in areas of interest; (2) word recognition – develops from other words in the sentence, illustrations, and analysis of the word structure – root, prefix, and suffix; (3) vocabulary building – encourages keeping a vocabulary notebook, and deliberate use of new words; (4) comprehension – aids include identifying the key idea in a chapter; (5) speed – results from breaking the bad habits of pointing, head movement, and lip movement (remedies are suggested), and also from widening the eye span; (6) critical reading – develops by reading several articles on a subject and making comparisons and judgments. These are in eight sections; the ninth section provides a recall opportunity for each principle and provides a performance of each.

Reading Comprehension, Series E-F (California Test Bureau) ($4.00). This is a set of four booklets, three of which contain "reading" in the title or sub-title. Each is an intrinsic or branching type program written for use at seventh and eighth grade level with a Dale-Chall readability formula of not more than fifth grade. The series includes a student response sheet for each booklet (which must be used), a teacher's manual which is identical for all subjects follows Unit IV and is an opportunity to practice all of the skills on a single complete selection.

Book I has eleven chapters (593 frames) to teach general reading skills; five of them are in Unit I on word structure. Prefixes, suffixes, and word roots are defined; common forms of each are introduced, and practice in their use is provided. Unit II on context clues cites signal words and punctuation; both instruction and practice are provided in the comma, parentheses and dash, and several of the common signal words. Unit III on sentences defines key words and provides practice in their recognition; also the skill of generalizing from them is introduced. Unit IV concerns topic sentences within several types of paragraph organization. The two literary seclections analyzed through the programmed format are Jane's short story "The Surprise of His Life" (118 frames) and Lowell's poem "Sea Shell" (96 frames).

Book 2 (887 frames) parallels *Book I* but has more extensive and intensive instruction in each of the general skill areas. The number of frames in each unit is greater; the word parts, the instruction, and the practice presentations are at least a grade level more complex. Increased depth in skill instruction includes combining word forms, recognizing synonyms and contrasts, characterizing and differentiating key words, and linking paragraphs. The literary selections include Irving's short story "The Legend of Sleepy Hollow" (115 frames) and Whitman's poem "O Captain!" (86 frames).

Book 3 has almost as many frames (794) devoted to general skill instruction as *Book 2*; greater length occurs in Unit II on sentence context and in Unit IV on paragraphs. Additional prefixes, suffixes word roots and forms, signal words and punctuation, synonyms, key words, and pronoun clues are taught and practiced but with fewer frames than in the earlier texts. The new or advanced word recognition skill instruction includes recognizing and practicing the use of modifiers without signals as aids, recognizing parallel structure, and using longer total context. In the skills of getting meaning from sentences, the advanced skills include additional sentence patterns, pronouns in a pre-reference situation, literal and figurative comparisons, and narrative progression. Paragraph skill advances include examining paragraphs without topic sentences, and analyzing paragraphs of combined organization patterns.

Unit V has a special programmed section (93 frames) on "How To Read Short Stories" which identifies the basic elements and design of short stories with the intention of developing a pattern for analyzing short stories. The literary selections include Millay's poem "Winter Night" (129 frames) and Shakespeare's play "Romeo and Juliet" (197 frames).

Senior High School Level

Reading Comprehension I and Reading Comprehension II (National Institute of Education) ($2.95 each). These are units 15 and 17 of a twenty unit series titled "College Prep Course." Each Program has approximately 150 content frames contained in a small cardboard machine which rolls successive frames into a view window. The instructional pattern has three phases, presentation of the skill, practice exercise, and review.

The major skills included in the first unit are getting the main thought from a paragraph, including finding it through inference; getting the supporting details, including organizing them into an outline; summarizing the content through restatement, including paraphrase, conclusion, and inference.

The major skills included in the second unit are skimming for finding specific information; recognition of "bias" words; following directions, including some emphasis on how to take tests; adjusting reading rate to reading purpose; and noting punctuation clues.

Steps to Reading Literature: (Harcourt, Brace, and World, Inc.) (3 books – $1.80 each). Books 1, 2, and 3 are for the 10th, 11th, and 12th grade, respectively. There is a teacher's manual for the series; it discusses the use of the text; and for each literary selection, it presents try-out data, and over-view of the work and comments about the author, objective test questions, and essay test questions. These programmed books are adjunct to the publisher's *Adventures in Literature* series; they could be used independently of the series only if the literary selections were made available. Representative literary forms – novel, short story, poems, and plays of the grade level – are analyzed; each selection is followed by suggested questions for class discussion, suggested topics for compositions, and suggested key elements through which to analyze each literature form.

Book 1 analyzes Poe's short story "The Cast of Amontillado," (134 frames), Frost's poem "Birches" (108 frames), Gibson's play "The Miracle Workers" (243 frames), Shakespeare's play "Julius Caesar" (237 frames), and Eliot's novel "Silas Marner" (229 frames).

Book 2 analyzes Stegner's short story "The Wolfer" (200 frames) and Wilder's "Our Town" (332 frames). Two additional programs are more than an analysis; "A Program on Reading Poems" (237 frames) provides a guided reading through Frost's "Stopping by Woods on a Snowy Evening," then develops seven guides to poetry reading, and finally applies them to Eberharts's "On a Squirrel Crossing the Road in Autumn, in New England;" "A Program on Reading Plays" (106 frames) provides the classic play pattern and applies it to O'Neill's "In The Zone."

Book 3 analyzes Shakespeare's poem "sonnet 73" (157 frames), Shakespeare's tragedy "Macbeth" (292 frames), O'Connor's short story "The Man of the House" (176 frames), and Conrad's novel "Typhoon" (231 frames).

This series leads students into experiences with almost every analytical device – surface meaning, plot, theme, character, moral, rhythm, tone, rhyme, parallelism, contrast, irony, imagery symbolism, among many others.

The Residue

Programmed materials afford a new way of both organizing and presenting knowledges or skills. It requires presentation through a series of small steps called frames organized so that the learner adds, in sequence, a bit more to what he already knows. The learner establishes the acquisition of the new knowledge or skill by responding to the program and is immediately reinforced or retaught by the same or additional frames.

Learning from a program is measured by conventional testing but these tests are not a part of the program. The addition to conventional instruction of self-administered and corrected tests, workbook exercises with answers immediately available, or hardware which adds automation or auto-instructional capability does not convert it into programmed learning material. The following eight items pertinent to this level of reading are listed in the bibliography but do not conform to a reasonable definition of program. Elimination of them from this discussion does not have any reference to the quality of the items; only sufficient description is given to establish their non-programmed nature.

"Listen and Read" and *"Listen and Read – Advanced"* (Educational Developmental Laboratories) provides recorded lessons on tapes or discs. The lessons are followed by test or work activity in a workbook, and then the student is presented with answers or corrected responses. Similarly, the reading laboratories "IIIa," "IIIb" "IVa," and *Reading for Understanding, General"* (Science Research Associates) provides developmental reading selections on cards, requires completion of comprehension tests, and then presents answers for teacher or self correction.

"Automated Speed Reading Course" and *"Pre-High School Reading Motivation"* (National Institute of Education) each consists of eight rolls that must be presented through an accompanying plastic, spring-operated machine. The first course contains perception exercises, presentation of the reading skills, vocabulary exercises, eye-span exercises, and reading selections. The second course contains graduated perception exercises using letter groups, word groups, and phrase groups; also there are graduated reading selections which begin with vocabulary exercises and are followed by short comprehension tests. The machine speed for each activity in each exercise is specified; this provides a scheduled increase in speed.

Instructional Materials for Adult Basic Education and Literacy Training*

EDWIN H. SMITH

The National government's concern with literacy education for our native born adults has tended to follow a crisis pattern. World War I saw campaigns to eradicate illiteracy (a silly or naive aim). The Great Depression resulted in literacy training in the CCC camps. World War II saw the reluctant development of Armed Forces Literacy Classes. All of these efforts were dropped as the crisis passed. Now we are involved in the crisis of the revolt of the undereducated, many of whom are functionally illiterate.

The history of Literacy Education for the foreign born indicates that the training was primarily concerned with *preparation for citizenship.* The new approach to teaching the native born illiterate has as its primary goal the *development of better citizens.* The programs have as their aim the development of the skills that are fundamental to full participation in the Great Society. The goals thus set are far broader than merely learning to read and write at a minimal level. They include the attainment of the ability to read materials written for the general adult public, the mastery of the basic mathematics skills, and the learnings or the general knowledge needed for the utilization of the resources available for self and community development. We have moved from Literacy Education to Adult Basic Education.

To understand how greatly Adult Basic Education diverges from even recent literacy education we can look at one of the contemporary campaigns to teach people to read – Operation Alphabet, the TV series that has been so widely used. As with other such projects, emphasis is on learning to read. The method is (due to the medium used) a lock-step approach. By the time (projected by the developers) a person reached a grade three read-ability level he had not, in the program, been exposed to a systematic curriculum other than one designed to teach the reading skills. Operation Alphabet has value, but it does not adequately develop the curriculum content proposed for Adult Basic

*Reprinted from *Vistas in Reading,* Proceedings of the 11th Annual Convention of the International Reading Association, J. Allen Figurel, editor, 1966, pp. 385-390, by permission of the author and the International Reading Association.

Education. This is not meant to be a negative note. The demand for such a curriculum is new – as is the market. But if we are agreed that the General Knowledge Area should be systematically developed, it seems that materials such as packaged programs must be developed. To rely on a teacher, usually untrained in adult basic education, to select such materials is unrealistic in terms of his training, his materials budget, and so often his part time involvement in the program. At the time of this writing no single source provided reading materials that were flexible enough, complete enough, or well enough correlated to provide an even development of such curriculum content.

Adult Basic Education (or Fundamental Adult Education) is pretty well defined by the act that has provided the funds, and thus the stimuli, for its presently rapid growth. In essence it is education designed to bring the adult's reading and mathematical skills up to a junior high school level and to provide him with the general knowledge needed to effectively use the resources available to most Americans. As the law is written, and in the spirit with which monies are distributed, it is assumed that Adult Basic Education teachers will use reading to teach occupational orientation, consumer education, basic legal concepts, civic responsibilities, personal and community development, awareness and utilization of cultural sources, basic science concepts, and attitudes conducive to life in our democracy.

The expansion of the concept of Literacy Education to the concept of Adult Basic Education has brought with it a need for new materials. These are needed to teach the General Knowledge Area of the Curriculum as well as the skills of reading and writing. As in elementary school classes, most adult basic education classes contain students with reading levels of one through six. To meet the needs of all the students and to give them essential common learnings to be reenforced and expanded in discussion, the same areas of knowledge should be available on at least five or six reading levels. But readability levels comprise only one of the aspects that must be considered.

The social composition of the classes, differences in learning modality strengths and modes of perceiving should be considered. The students differ greatly within the classes and the classes differ in make-up from class to class. Classes include the unemployed, high school dropouts, foreign born, rural underprivileged, urban underprivileged, persons with brain injury and specific learning disabilities. Ideally the teacher should have access to materials which promote emphasis of the kinesthetic and auditory modalities according to their strength. He should, particularly with those pupils at level one, have materials that allow him to use a part-to-whole or whole-to-part word learning method with equal facility. Method should be selected in terms of the adult's strengths, weaknesses, and needs. Materials should be available to implement the method so selected.

To take care of the range in classes and between classes a broad range of interests and readability must be allowed for. For most effective teaching, materials should be organized in meaningful segments so that they can be used as needed. All persons should not be expected to move through the same materials at the same rate. Materials appropriate for developing the reading and computational skills are available and are at least adequate. More and more emphasis is being given to what should be a sequential developmental program for teaching the concepts of the General Knowledge Area of Adult Basic Education while developing reading. Such sequential and integrated programs should emerge in the future. The Mott Foundation, as one example, appears to be moving in this direction. At present, materials for the General Knowledge Area must be gathered from widely scattered sources, and often rewritten, in order to even come close to the state curricular objectives. This is too much to expect of part-time teachers.

Perhaps the best way to teach the teacher the content area of adult basic education is to provide him with packaged programs which may be used as a core in his teaching. As he works with the students he will move from the concept of literacy education to the broader one of Adult Basic Education.

Despite the fundamental curricular materials needs that exist, there are many sources of good materials for teaching reading to adults. These sources do cover many of the concepts we wish to develop. There are so many, and in my opinion they vary so widely in quality, that I will review a few for each stage that we considered among the most useful and most flexible. Some have not been developed specifically for adults. But there is little in them that is offensive to adults, and experience indicates that adults react well to them and find them acceptable learning tools. The materials designed for retarded readers in the upper elementary and junior high schools are often far superior to some materials designed specifically for adults. Many of the so-called adult books have been written by persons obviously ill trained in the teaching of reading. The bibliography that follows is made up of those materials that our staff prefers. No one book or kit is sufficient for a total program at any level or any stage. Our center personnel shows no great preference for any one book or kit at the intermediate stage.

ANNOTATED BIBLIOGRAPHY:

Materials for the Introductory Stage

Level 1

I Want to Read and Write. Revised Edition. Steck Company, 1964, 128pp.
 Interest level is fair and exercises in basic writing skills are good. The vocabulary control is not good and the rate of introduction of new words is too fast for many students. The exercises meet immediately felt needs of adults. This text should be supplemented with other texts on Level 1.

My Country. Revised Edition. Steck Company, 1964, 96 pp.
 The content is social studies, the interest level is fair, and the legibility is excellent. Vocabulary control and the rate of introduction of new words are adequate when supplemented with other materials. The comprehension exercises and phonic program are adequate. The 1964 revision differs little from the earlier edition.

Operation Alphabet. National Association for Public School Adult Education 1962, 11 pp.
 This text is designed to accompany the Operation Alphabet television course but it may be used independently of the course. Each lesson is self contained and the vocabulary and the rate of introduction of new words are controlled. Writing exercises are included but no provision is made for a phonics program. It should be used as supplementary material or be supplemented by other texts.

Programmed Reading. A Sullivan Associates Program, 1964.
 A series in four parts. *Prereading* acquaints students with written symbols, their relationship to the sounds of words and builds a small reading vocabulary. Materials include teacher's guide, programmed primer, reading readiness tests, and alphabet and sound symbol cards.
 Series I is a basic text for first grade and remedial students. It offers a rapid and pleasant way for children and adults to learn to read and spell English. Materials include seven programmed texts, seven storybooks, test booklets, teacher's guide, 29 sound symbol cards, a set of seven filmstrips and a special diagnostic placement test. Vocabulary includes 400 words.
 Series II is a basic text for the second grade. It can also be used by advanced first graders and by remedial students. Materials include seven programmed texts, seven storybooks, a test booklet, teacher's guide, answer key and a special diagnostic placement test. Vocabulary included 1,379 words.
 Series III is a basic text for third level. Materials include seven programmed texts, seven storybooks, a test booklet, teacher's guide, answer key, and a special diagnostic test. Information on vocabulary not available.
 Programmed Reading as a method of teaching reading has been proven valuable. Series would be better off without filmstrips.

The Mott Basic Language Skills Program, Series 300. Allied Education Council, 1965.
 The "total language program" covers readability levels 1 through 12. It is designed for adults but could be used with retarded readers in both junior and senior high school.

Reading 300 deals with materials designed for levels 1 through 3. The word attack approach used stresses phonics. The series provides for the systematic development of word attack, spelling, writing, composition and listening, and understanding skills.

Basic Language 300A. This book provides for initial instruction in reading, writing, and spelling. Initial consonants, vowels, blends, and final endings are included. Many written exercises for the student are included.

Basic Language 300B. Additional instruction on vowel combinations and irregular spellings is presented in this book. Reading selections are included as well as numerous exercises on vowels, reading and writing. Assignments are done by the students in sequence.

Word Bank 300. The book is divided into 12 units. Each unit presents photo vocabulary with the word written in manuscript and cursive. Space is provided for copying sentences using the new words. At the end of each unit is a reading selection using the words previously introduced. Comprehension exercises are included.

Basic Numbers and Money 300. The purpose of this book is to help the students use numbers, handle money, and use newspaper advertisements. There are worksheets for practice examples. Skills introduced in this book are addition, subtraction, simple multiplication, and division examples. Simple word problems provide another type of exercise. At this same level, supplementary reading is provided for by the *Fair Chance Series 300*. The occupational and vocational reading is found under the *Apprentice Series 300*. Titles include: *The Auto Mechanic, The Filling Station Attendant, The Meat Cutter, Polly Looks for a Job, The Road Workers, The Carpenter, Needlecraft 300,* and *Homecraft 300*.

Reading for a Purpose. Educational Opportunities Project, Follett Publishing Co.

A sight-word approach to teaching reading to adults. It is a fairly comprehensive developmental approach beginning with readiness skills and progressing through dictionary skills. The lessons usually follow along the same general format. The style of the elementary basal series approach is generally used. A detailed teacher's guide is included.

Reader's Digest Adult Series. Reader's Digest, 1964-65, 32 pp. each.

A series of twelve books extending from Level 1 to Level 4. The first four books are for Level 1. This series was especially designed for adults and adolescents. The books have a high interest level, appearance is similar to the regular *Reader's Digest,* legibility is excellent, and the subject matter is articles from the *Reader's Digest.* Exercises for the development of comprehension and vocabulary are included and the teacher's manual for the series contains helpful suggestions. The series should be supplemented with other books in the *Digest* series.

Reader's Digest Skill Builder, Grade 1, Parts I and II. Reader's Digest, 1963, 64 pp.

Part of a series which extends through Level 8. The content is articles from the Reader's Digest. Legibility is good, interest level is high, and the vocabulary and comprehension program is good. The teacher's manual offers practical suggestions for use of the series.

SRA Reading Laboratories, Science Research Associates.

The SRA reading laboratories suitable for the introductory stage of reading include Reading Laboratory I, Ia, Ib, and Ic and the older, but not out-moded, Elementary Edition (1958). The laboratories contain many articles as separate items which are grouped according to readability level. They are suitable for adults and are a great boon to the teacher who is teaching students at various levels of reading. Teacher's manuals are complete in every detail and lessons are designed so that much of the learning is self-instruction. The laboratories should be supplemented with vocabulary development materials.

Level 2

News for You, The Adult Newsletter. New Reader Press, Edition A.

This four page newspaper for literacy classes comes with a teacher's guide. It contains photographs, feature articles and news items. Edition A is written at readability level 2-3.

Level 3

The Job Ahead: New Rochester Occupational Reading Series, Level I. Science Research Associates, 1963, 169 pp.

This series, written on three different readability levels (Levels 3, 4, and 5), does not use the same story content as the original Rochester Occupational Reading Series. Each book contains the same stories written on different readability levels. Thus, three different groups can deal with the same material. The materials are highly interesting to adolescents and adults. The accompanying workbooks can be used to build both vocabulary and comprehension skills. They should be supplemented.

Reader's Digest Adult Education Readers. Books A and B. Reader's Digest, 1954, 128 pp. each.

Adult appearance and adult interest level. Exercises for developing vocabulary and comprehension skills are excellent. These books may be used as basic texts at this level or as supplementary aids. The books were designed by adult educators for adult use.

Reader's Digest Readings: English as a Second Language, Books 1 and 2. New York: Reader's Digest Educational Division, 1964, 144 pp.

This is a new series of six books designed for teaching the foreign born to read the English language. The articles are from the Reader's Digest and are of high interest to adults. The books contain exercises for building vocabulary and comprehension skills. They will prove useful with both foreign and native born students.

Reader's Digest Science Reader, Grade 3. Reader's Digest, 1963, 128 pp.

This is one of a series of four books which are designed for reading Levels 3, 4, 5, and 6. Appearance, interest level, and legibility are high, an excellent supplementary book for each of the levels for which it was designed. It will prove of value both in developing reading skills and building the general knowledge area of adult fundamental education.

Materials for the Elementary Stage
Level 4

Achieving Reading Skills. Glove Book Company, Inc., 1958, 245 pp.

The various reading skills are handled on several levels of readability. The materials are arranged in order of difficulty extending from the third grade readability level to about the sixth grade level. It has been used extensively with adults and adolescents.

EDL Study Skills-Library for Reference. Educational Development Laboratories, 1962.

Organized like the other EDL packaged programs, this program teaches the use of reference skills and places great stress on critical reading.

EDL Study Skills-Library for Science. Educational Development Laboratories, 1962.

This packaged program contains individual lessons in science for reading Levels 4 through 9. These self-correcting lessons develop the principal comprehension skills and also contribute to vocabulary growth. They are of proven worth in teaching reading to adolescents and adults and are a great aid in individualizing reading instruction.

EDL Study Skills-Library for Social Studies. Educational Development Laboratories, 1962.

This packaged program is similar to the *EDL Study Skills-Library for Science,* except that the content is social studies.

Gates-Peardon Reading Exercises: 1963 Edition, Elementary and Intermediate. Bureau of Publications, Teachers College, Columbia University Press, 1963, 62 pp.

Although not designed for adults, the books in this series are acceptable to them for the interest level is high. There are six books suitable for use at the elementary stage. Three have a readability of about grade four and three have a readability of about grade five. The books separately treat reading for the main idea (Type SA), reading for details (Type RD), and reading to follow directions (Type FD). This series should be used for corrective work in specific comprehension weaknesses.

New Practice Readers. Webster Publishing Company, 1960, 144 pp.

A series of workbook type exercises which present lessons in three parts. There are questions to prepare for the reading and a comprehension check. Some work in vocabulary is offered. While not designed for adults the series should be acceptable to them. Books A, B, and C are for readability levels of grades four, five, and six.

Reading for Meaning. J. B. Lippincott Company, 1962, 72 pp.

An excellent series to use for developing comprehension techniques. While not designed for adults, the format and content are acceptable to them. Vocabulary development is worked into the selections in an interesting way. This series has proven to have great value in teaching both adolescents and adults. There are books for readability Levels 4, 5, 6, 7, and 8.

Standard Test Lessons in Reading, Book D. Bureau of Publications, Teachers College, Columbia University Press, 1961, 78 pp.

This is one of a series of high interest comprehension-building books that are designed to build reading power and speed. Books in this series may be used as self-teaching devices.

Turner-Livingston Reading Series. Follett Publishing Co., 1964, 48 pp.

This well-constructed series deals with such topics as citizenship, economics, and the general social studies. It is designed for adolescents and adults and will prove valuable in adult basic education classes, both in developing reading skills and reenforcing subject matter learnings. It should be supplemented or perhaps be best used as a supplement to other books for developing reading skills. Some of the books in the series are *The Person You Are, The Money You Spend,* and *The Town You Live In.*

Using the Context, Barnell Loft, 1962, 52 pp.

A series of three books for Levels 4, 5, and 6. This series develops skill in developing vocabulary and comprehension skills through the use of the context clue. Acceptable to adults and an excellent supplementary drill book.

Level 5

Building Reading Confidence. C. S. Hammond Company, 1964, 220 pp.

Can be used as a basal text as it covers most of the reading skills needed at this level. Joseph Gainsberry is well known for his corrective reading books for adolescents. A fairly complete text.

Effective Reading. Globe Book Company, 1953, 214 pp.

This text is designed to teach the various reading skills. The exercises are good and the interest level is fair to good. It offers specific help in developing study type reading skills.

Successful Reading. Globe Book Co. 1953, 210 pp.

This book, developed for corrective work in junior and senior high schools, is still one of the better books for teaching adults specific vocabulary and comprehension skills. The exercises are well constructed and the readings are acceptable to adults.

Spelling Word Power Laboratory, IIB (Revised), Science Research Associates.

This kit includes many exercises for studying sounds and how words are put together. Vowels, consonants, abbreviations, contractions, plurals, homonyms, and difficult words are presented in the form of learning wheels. The students may find questions by turning a wheel and answers by another turn of the wheel, hence immediate reinforcement. A variety of check tests, spelling key cards, a student record book, and a teacher's handbook are included.

Level 6

Better Reading. Globe Book Company, 1962, 447 pp.

This is an excellent book for both adolescents and adults. The exercises in comprehension and vocabulary are well constructed and the content is acceptable to adults. Very little supplementary instructional material will be needed when this book is used as the basic text.

Teen-Age Tales. D. C. Heath and Company, 1954-59.

Six books of high interest for adolescents. Each book contains a collection of short stories concerned with teen-age sub-culture. Not recommended for older adults or disadvantaged persons.

Materials for the Intermediate Stage
Level 7

Be a Better Reader, Book 1. Prentice-Hall, 1963, 128 pp.

A relatively complete text for teaching comprehension and vocabulary skills on the seventh grade level. While developed for adolescents, it has proven effective with adults. Interest level is high and study type reading is stressed. This series extends through the high school levels.

Help Yourself to Improve Your Reading, Part I. Reader's Digest, 1962, 160 pp.

As with other Digest offerings the material is adult in nature and of high interest level. The source of readings is Reader's Digest. Vocabulary and comprehension exercises are sound and the book is designed so that it may be used as a self-help book by students whose reading is sixth or seventh grade level.

Lessons for Self-Instruction in Basic Skills: Reading Interpretations I, Series E-F. 160 frames, California Test Bureau.

This programmed self-instruction book may be of some value in developing comprehension skills but it suffers from many drawbacks. Recommend for supplementary use only.

Level 8

Test Lessons in Reading-Reasoning. Bureau of Publication, Teachers College, Columbia University Press, 1964, 78 pp.

This text was devised to improve the critical reading and thinking ability of adolescents and adults. It consists of seventy-eight lessons which teach ways of uncovering fallacies in reasoning and give practice in detecting such fallacies. Adults enjoy the exercises and the book makes an excellent supplement to other more general texts.

Words, SRA, 1962, 224 pp.

A programmed text of 2,200 frames in 14 chapters. This text has a real place in adult literacy training. It teaches the student that he can learn on his own and prepares him for self-learning and the use of a type of material that will be best used in the future for on-the-job training. Excellent supplementary material.